Old-Age Security
in Comparative Perspective

Old-Age Security in Comparative Perspective

JOHN B. WILLIAMSON
Boston College

FRED C. PAMPEL
University of Colorado

New York   Oxford
OXFORD UNIVERSITY PRESS
1993

Oxford University Press

Oxford   New York   Toronto
Delhi   Bombay   Calcutta   Madras   Karachi
Kuala Lumpur   Singapore   Hong Kong   Tokyo
Nairobi   Dar es Salaam   Cape Town
Melbourne   Auckland   Madrid

and associated companies in
Berlin   Ibadan

Published by Oxford University Press, Inc.,
200 Madison Avenue, New York, New York 10016

Oxford is a registered trademark of Oxford University Press

Library of Congress Cataloging-in-Publication Data
Williamson, John B.
Old-age security in comparative perspective
John B. Williamson, Fred C. Pampel
p.   cm.   Includes bibliographical references and index.
ISBN 0-19-506859-9
1. Old age pensions.   2. Social security.
I. Pampel, Fred C.
II. Title.
HD7105.3.W55   1993   368.4—dc20   92-17455

TP

2 4 6 8 9 7 5 3 1

Printed in the United States of America
on acid-free paper

For my brothers, Bradford, Bruce, Burgess,
Craig, Glen, Scott, Todd
and the memory of my sister, Rosanne
J. B. W.

For my parents, Fred Sr. and Joanne,
and my brother Bill
F. C. P.

Preface

This book presents an analysis of cross-national differences in old-age security policy. While old-age security programs in the industrial nations have received a great deal of attention in recent years, a number of interesting developments in Third World nations have received much less attention than they deserve. This is one reason that our study is based on three Third World nations (Brazil, Nigeria, and India) as well as four industrial nations (Germany, United Kingdom, Sweden, and the United States). Due to the inclusion of case studies in both categories, we are able to make comparisons among the four industrial nations and among the three Third World nations as well as some comparisons between the industrial and Third World nations. As one illustration, we discuss why Brazil has been so much more successful than India and Nigeria in extending coverage to the rural population. In our chapters on Brazil, Nigeria, and India comparisons are also made with other countries in the region. For example, we contrast Brazil's public pension system with a largely privatized alternative recently introduced in Chile, a model that so far has proven quite popular and is now being seriously considered in several other nations.

We began quantitative research on issues closely related to this book 10 years ago. At the outset we expected to extend and build upon prior studies in the social democratic tradition. The social democratic thesis embodies a widely held belief about the relationship between working-class strength and post-World War II pension (and welfare state) policy developments in the Western industrial nations. Central to this thesis is the view that the expansion of spending on public pensions and the many structural reforms that took place in these countries up through the late 1970s represented victories for organized labor and leftist political parties in their efforts to obtain a larger share of society's resources for the working class and the poor.

Our early work on the social democratic thesis was in large part based on quantitative analysis of public pension spending for a sample of 18 industrial nations. Our findings raised doubts about the thesis, particularly the simple version of the thesis that was current at the time. They also raised doubts about much of the quantitative evidence that had been amassed in support of the thesis. We found that with the introduction of a few key statistical controls that had not been used in prior studies, due in part to their dependence on small cross-sectional samples, the case for the social democratic thesis (and class theory interpretations more generally) became at best very weak. What emerged from our analysis was evidence suggesting that the postwar increase in public pension spending was more a reflection of an increase in pressure from the middle class and of the elderly, than an increase in pressure from the working class and the poor.

By the mid-1980s, the literature espousing and offering support for the social democratic thesis was extensive. While studies we published between the mid and late 1980s raised doubts about most of the quantitative evidence in this tradition, important questions remained because much of the support for the social democratic thesis was based on qualitative historical evidence. Given the theoretical importance of the issue as well as the profound implications for politics and public policy, we decided to undertake the present study. Our focus on the comparative historical method has allowed us to consider arguments and explanations that do not lend themselves to quantitative analysis. It has also allowed us to consider a much broader time span making it possible to expand the scope of our analysis to include developments in connection with the original old-age pension legislation.

At the outset our goal was to assess the relative influence of organized labor, leftist political parties, and the working class more generally in shaping key developments in old-age security policy over the years. As the study progressed, our focus shifted from an analysis of the evidence pertaining to the social democratic thesis to a more general effort to look at the relative utility of explanations drawn from several different theories of welfare state development. The goal changed from demonstrating that this or that theory was right or wrong to explicating those contexts in which one or another tended to be most useful. What has emerged is a set of conclusions that strongly emphasize context. We emphasize, but do not limit ourselves to explanations that can be linked to each of five general theoretical perspectives: (1) the industrialism perspective, (2) the social democratic perspective, (3) the neo-Marxist perspective, (4) the neo-pluralist perspective, and (5) the state-centered perspective. We find each of these perspectives useful in accounting for some developments, but we have not found that any one of them is by itself sufficiently powerful to account for all or even most of the important developments. We are generally able to provide much more adequate interpretations when we combine explanations drawn from several of these perspectives.

Our historical case study evidence suggests that, with the notable exception of Sweden, support for the social democratic thesis is weak. In our quantitative analysis we qualify this conclusion; it suggests that the social democratic thesis and class theory more generally tend to be useful in accounting for developments in nations with well developed corporatist structures, an interpretation that combines explanations linked to both the state-centered perspective and the social democratic perspective. We find the neo-Marxist perspective most useful in connection with our analysis of developments surrounding the origins of old-age pension policy, particularly in Germany and Brazil. The industrialism perspective, in contrast, tends to be most useful in connection with developments since the end of World War II. The neo-pluralist perspective proves to be particularly useful in the analysis of developments in nations with well developed democratic structures, but with appropriate qualification it is also useful for the analysis of developments in countries such as Nigeria and Brazil that lacked well developed democratic structures during much of the period being considered.

While our analysis of the importance of context takes many forms, we give particular attention to the relevance of aspects of state structure. In our analysis of developments in the industrial nations we emphasize the role of democratic corporatism. We find that in nations such as Sweden which have well developed corporatist structures, class-based factors are more important and demographic factors less important in determining public pension policy than is the case in nations such as the United States that lack democratic corporatist structures for societal mediation between class groups.

We find historical evidence that another variant of corporatism, authoritarian corporatism, has had an impact on pension policy in some Third World nations. Due to the lack of appropriate quantitative indicators, however, we were unable to test hypotheses involving this variable in our pooled time series analysis of pension spending in Third World nations. Nevertheless, we do find evidence that another aspect of state structure (level of democracy) functions as an important contextual variable for Third World countries. In the more democratic Third World nations percent aged tends to be a relatively strong predictor of spending on public pensions, but in less democratic Third World nations the impact is much weaker. Our interpretation of this evidence is that interest groups such as the aged are able to exert a greater influence on public spending levels when more democratic political structures are in place.

While there have been many quantitative studies and many comparative historical studies of cross-national differences in public pension and welfare state policy, the present book represents an effort to contribute to the much smaller literature made up of studies that combine these two very different approaches. While the decision to combine the two approaches may seem quite reasonable in the abstract, it has not been an easy task. Scholars in these two traditions tend to ask very different questions and having just completed this study, we have come to better appreciate why.

The nature of the data to be analyzed has profound implications not only for the methodology used, but also for the questions the researcher is likely to consider worth asking. Our quantitative data made it easy to ask detailed questions about the strength of various interaction effects and allowed us to measure these interaction effects with much greater precision than was possible based on our comparative historical data. Our historical case study data, in contrast, allowed a much richer and more finely textured analysis. It allowed much greater freedom with respect to what questions were asked and what factors were taken into consideration when answering those questions. In the context of our comparative historical analysis we found that the questions we were asking and the explanations we were giving often defied specification in terms of concepts that lent themselves to operationalization as quantitative measures appropriate for comparisons across 32 or even 18 nations. This immersion in both types of data and both types of analysis has been a humbling experience. Simultaneously considering the evidence and conclusions based on two very different methodologies has forced us to starkly confront the reality that each has its very real limitations as well as its strengths.

We have accumulated many debts over the seven years it has taken us to write this book. This includes debts to those who have helped us locate resources and data, those who have commented on preliminary drafts of chapters, those who have served as expert informants, and those who have in other ways made important contributions to our thinking about the issues considered in this book. Of particular note in this context are the contributions of: Peter Baldwin, Robert Bédard, John Blackwell, Clair Brown, Ricardo Campbell, Francis G. Castles, Manoel Costa, Richard Coughlin, Charles Derber, Allen Fairfax, Lisa Fuentes, Fred Groskind, Shari Grove, Leif Haanes-Olsen, Elizabeth Johnson, Martin Kohli, Celso Barroso Leite, Concepcion McNeace, Mike Miller, Ujubuonu Okwologu, Joakim Palme, Gösta Rehn, Martin Rein, Vladimir Rys, Rolf Stadié, Ann-Charlotte Stålberg, George Steinmetz, Barbara Boyle Torrey, Evaldo Amaro Vieira, Jill Quadagno, Joseph Quinn, Gretchen Walsh, and William White. While many have helped us in a variety of ways there are a few who we owe special thanks to for feedback on chapters and suggestions for revision that went far beyond what we might reasonably have expected. In this context we mention contributions by Karl Hinrichs to Chapter 2, by James Cronin to Chapter 3, by Sven Olsson and Lars Andersson to Chapter 4, by Andrew Achenbaum and Eric Kingson to Chapter 5, by Thomas LeGrand, James Malloy, and Eliza Willis to Chapter 6, by Kishore Mandhyan to Chapter 7, and by Olatunji Oyeneye and Margaret Peil to Chapter 8. Robin Stryker co-authored a paper with us that formed the basis for Chapter 9, and her influence on our ideas in that chapter remains strong. We want to express our thanks to Henry Pratt, Christine Day, and Richard Tomasson who served as Oxford's outside reviewers for this project. Their efforts were very much appreciated and their insights have made this a much stronger book than it would otherwise have been. We wish also to express our appreciation to all of those at Oxford who have been of assistance with particular thanks to David Roll, Stanley George, Mary Garrison, Sharon Lahaye, and Wendy Driscoll. While we want to share the credit for this book with all of those who have in one way or another facilitated our work, we take full responsibility for any and all errors that remain.

Parts of Chapter 8 have appeared in: John B. Williamson and Fred C. Pampel. 1991. "Ethnic Politics, Colonial Legacy, and Old Age Security Policy: The Nigerian Case in Historical and Comparative Perspective." *Journal of Aging Studies* 5:19–44 copyright © 1991 by JAI Press. Parts of Chapter 9 have appeared in: Fred C. Pampel, John B. Williamson, and Robin Stryker. 1990. "Class Context and Pension Response to Demographic Structure in Advanced Industrial Democracies." *Social Problems* 37:535–50 copyright © 1990 by the Society for the Study of Social Problems. This research was funded in part by the National Institute on Aging, Grant No. AG01580 and Grant No. AG07683. It was also supported in part by research expense grants from Boston College and the University of Colorado, Boulder.

Chestnut Hill, Mass.   J.B.W
Boulder, Colo.   F.C.P.
June 1992

Contents

Old-Age Security
in Comparative Perspective

1

Introduction

The arguments and evidence presented in this book challenge what many consider the current orthodoxy with respect to the causes of old-age security policy development. We call into question the conventional view that policy developments in this sphere inevitably reflect the outcome of conflict between labor and capital.[1] Various class theorists differ in their views as to the relative influence of labor and capital, and they disagree in their assessments of the redistributive impact of various old-age security programs, but they generally share the assumption that capital and labor are the major actors driving these policy developments. We do not deny the relevance of class actors, rather we specify the contexts in which these actors are important, and we introduce evidence that a number of other actors defined by such ascriptive attributes as age, ethnicity, language, religion, and region are also very important.

One of the most widely held perspectives on old-age security policy is embodied in the social democratic thesis that social security policy as it has evolved in the industrial nations, particularly since the end of World War II, reflects the outcome of a struggle between organizations and political parties representing the interests of capital and those representing the interests of labor (Castles 1982; Esping-Andersen 1985; Hewitt 1977; Korpi 1983; Myles 1984; Shalev 1983; Stevens 1979). Much of the evidence presented in this book challenges the conventional social democratic perspective on old-age security policy developments. One of our central arguments is that the social democratic thesis does not adequately take into consideration the influence of a number of nonclass factors that have had a major influence on the historical evolution of old-age security policy. It does not give adequate attention to the influence of a number of nonclass interest groups, and it does not give sufficient attention to the role played by characteristics of the state such as the presence or absence of democratic corporatist structures for mediation between labor and capital.

Our previous work presents quantitative evidence that calls into question conventional class theory views with respect to the determinants of public pension spending and of social security spending more generally (Pampel and Williamson 1985; 1988; 1989; Williamson and Pampel 1986). As much of the class theory evidence in the literature is based on historical case studies, we wanted to test some of our most important findings using historical evidence, and we designed the present study with that goal in mind.

While many historical case studies have been done that deal with pension policy or welfare state policy more generally, the analysis presented in this book is distinctive in its effort to include both industrial and Third World nations. Four industrial nations (Germany, United Kingdom, Sweden, United States) were selected, one for each of four different types of welfare state regimes identified by previous scholars as providing distinct differences in contexts for welfare state development (Esping-Andersen 1990; Castles and Mitchell 1990). In addition, we include case studies for three Third World nations (Brazil, India, Nigeria) selected so as to represent diversity with respect to level of development and democratic institutionalization. With this selection of countries it is possible to make comparisons among our industrial nations, among our Third World nations, and between our Third World and our industrial nations.

The focus of this book is on assessing the utility of explanations derived from class theories. To this end we find it useful to make comparisons with explanations derived from other theoretical perspectives. As a result the book provides an assessment of how each of five general theoretical perspectives can be used to shed light on the historical evolution of old-age security policy in the nations considered. The growth of explanations of the welfare state in general and of pension policy in particular has led to a huge and contentious literature. There has been a tendency in this literature to pit competing theories or variables against one another, implying that the success of one view implies the failure of the other. The goal of our analysis is not so much to show that this or that perspective offers valid or invalid explanations as it is to specify the conditions under which the various perspectives offer the most insight. The diversity of our case studies provides a great deal of variation with respect to level of democracy and level of development as well as with respect to state structure, ethnic homogeneity, and cultural context. The broad time spans considered also allow for a great deal of contextual variation within individual countries. This diversity helps us specify those contexts in which each of the several theoretical perspectives considered is most useful.

Although this book will be read by some as a Weberian critique of the neo-Marxist and social democratic class theories of old-age social security policy development, it is important to keep in mind that we do find the class theories useful in accounting for some developments in some countries. In our case studies we find support for a version of class theory that takes into consideration national and historical context. Furthermore, in our quantitative analysis we find evidence that supports a variant of class theory that takes into consideration contextual factors such as the presence of democratic or corporatist state structures. While our quantitative evidence does not support the conventional version of class theory, it does support a qualified version that takes into consideration the role of corporatist state structures.

The present analysis represents a marriage of quantitative and qualitative analysis in two important respects. While we have not limited ourselves to hypotheses and explanations derived from our prior quantitative research, the comparative historical analysis presented here was motivated by the desire to cross-validate some of the more controversial conclusions of that research.[2] Given the vast number of prior studies that claimed to offer empirical support for the social democratic thesis and given our dramatic findings to the contrary, we wanted to determine which findings could be replicated using comparative historical data. A second respect in which the present study integrates the two modes of analysis is the inclusion of a quantitative analysis (Chapter 9) that builds upon, extends, and in important respects qualifies the findings of the historical case studies presented earlier in the book.

There have been many previous studies of social security policy development based on historical case studies and many based on the multivariate analysis of national level aggregate data, but there have been very few studies to date that have attempted to integrate the two approaches. We believe that this is unfortunate as there are insights to be gained from such an integration. In the present volume we explore issues in our historical case studies that were impossible to consider in the context of our multivariate statistical analysis.[3] Similarly, we deal with issues in our quantitative analysis that we were unable to deal with in our historical case studies.[4] Consideration of evidence from both approaches makes this a much more comprehensive study than it might otherwise have been.

In summary, the goals of this book are several. First, it attempts to provide a more integrative view of the validity of competing explanations of old-age security policy by considering the national and historical context of program development. Second, it studies both advanced industrial and Third World nations. Although the processes differ greatly across groups, comparisons of the processes provide a broader frame-work for understanding old-age security policy. Third, it relies on both qualitative and quantitative analysis. To capture contextual influences, the emphasis is on the qualitative studies, but quantitative models that confirm, extend, or qualify various findings from the historical case studies are presented as well.

Theories of Old-Age Security Policy Development

In this section we review five general theoretical perspectives that we will be making extensive use of in the chapters that follow. These theories of old-age security policy are derived from closely related theories of welfare state development. This is possible because old-age security policy is generally a major component of social welfare policy. While many of the interpretations and arguments offered in the following chapters can be linked to one or another of these theoretical perspectives, we will not be limiting ourselves to explanations that can be derived from them. Some arguments will emphasize factors that are unique to a particular country at a specific point in time and explanations that do not derive from these or any other general theories of welfare state development.

The Industrialism Perspective

The industrialism perspective [5] can be traced back to the late nineteenth century. For example, Wagner's ([1883] 1983) law of increasing state activity asserts that the size of the public sector relative to the private sector increases as real per capita income increases. In short, public sector spending, including spending on pension programs and other old-age security programs, grows because the demand for services as well as the willingness to pay for such services increase with economic development. The need for public pensions and other social welfare programs occurs simultaneously with the increased economic resources which make it possible to fund such programs.

While the industrialism perspective can be traced back to the nineteenth century, it is most strongly associated with the work of Kerr et al. (1964), Wilensky (1975), and a number of other theorists who were interested in the causes and consequences of economic development in the industrial nations during the post-World War II era. Theorists in this tradition have been particularly interested in evidence of convergence in a number of institutional spheres among all industrial nations, socialist as well as capitalist, due to the imperatives of the industrialization process (Inkeles 1981; Form 1979; Williamson and Fleming 1977; Pryor 1968). One aspect of this convergence has been the introduction of a similar set of social insurance programs across nations. Another has been the dramatic increase in spending on public pensions and other social insurance programs in all industrial nations, socialist as well as capitalist.

The industrialism perspective explains the introduction of public pensions and other social welfare programs as a necessary result of technological development. These programs are viewed as helping to maintain social equilibrium, as meeting the functional necessities (or requirements) of modern economies, and as responding to the technological imperatives of the industrialization process. State spending on public pensions is viewed as a more or less automatic response to the needs generated by industrialization. The functionalist origins of the perspective are quite explicit, particularly in the early formulations of the perspective (Kerr et al. 1964; Wilensky and Lebeaux 1965).

According to this perspective the root cause of spending on public pensions and other social programs is economic development (Wilensky 1976, p. 13); however, much of the impact of economic development on pension spending is indirect. For this reason indicators measuring some of the consequences of industrialization are considered as well. For example, industrialization is viewed as producing an older age structure, as leading to the establishment of public bureaucracies devoted to social insurance needs, and as producing other such changes which in turn are often the more proximate causes of increases in spending on public pensions and other forms of pension policy development (Wilensky 1975).

Industrialization transforms the labor force. Workers are drawn away from the agricultural sector into the industrial and service sectors. Self-employment is replaced by wage labor making an increasing proportion of the labor force vulnerable to swings in the business cycle. There are sharp increases in urbanization as well as much geographical and social mobility. Fertility rates drop contributing to a graying of the age structure. Industry increasingly wants young recently educated workers. As families become smaller and the number of siblings fewer, the burden on adult children of providing for dependent elderly parents becomes greater. These changes undercut the traditional forms of social support, the extended family and the local community. They create a need that the government must respond to so as to promote social harmony and economic growth (Kerr et al. 1964, p. 152). The introduction of pension programs is one such response as is increased spending on existing pension programs.[6]

Industrialism theorists tend to de-emphasize the independent role of political factors in shaping the major institutions and policies in industrial nations. Many studies just ignore political factors. Others explicitly consider political factors and then present evidence that they are not useful in accounting for the dependent variable of interest, such as social security effort (Wilensky 1975). Among the political factors that have been considered and rejected as adding little if anything to the variance accounted for by various industrialism related indicators are: political structure,[7] elite ideology,[8] degree of political democracy, socialist party strength, and union strength.[9]

As is the case with most of the perspectives we will consider, in most research applications industrialism theory is simplified, some would say oversimplified. In its most simplified form it reduces to what is sometimes referred to as the *developmental hypothesis* that the dependent variable of interest (e.g., pension quality or pension effort) is in large measure determined by the level or rate of development. Some studies use a richer more complex version of industrialism theory in which an effort is made to include other aspects of social structure and social change typically associated with the industrialization process, such as urbanization, literacy rate, birthrate, and percent aged. A few studies also check the prediction that political factors will have little if any independent impact (Pampel and Williamson 1988; 1989; Williamson and Weiss 1979).

The industrialism perspective has most typically been used in the analysis of trends in the industrial nations. But the emphasis on the importance of industrialization and economic growth makes it appropriate to test hypotheses derived from this theory in studies that include developing nations as well (Mishra 1977). A number of studies have used the theory in the analysis of samples that have included developing nations or focused on developing nations (Williamson 1987; Pampel and Williamson 1985; Jackman 1975; Wilensky 1975).

The Social Democratic Perspective

The social democratic perspective (also referred to as the working-class strength or working-class mobilization perspective) can be traced to the work of Karl Marx and some scholars classify this perspective as neo-Marxist (Hicks 1991, p. 211; Myles 1984, p. 82). However, it is common to make a distinction between the social democratic perspective as reflected in the work of Esping-Andersen (1985), Myles (1984), Shalev (1983), Korpi (1983), Stephens (1979), and Hewitt (1977) and the neo-Marxist perspective as reflected in the work of Gough (1979), Poulantzas (1973), O'Connor (1973), Offe (1972), and Miliband (1969). Both perspectives emphasize class structure and class conflict, but they offer fundamentally different interpretations of the welfare state.

Although the social democratic perspective can be traced back to Marx himself, in its contemporary form it emerged during the 1970s in response to the neo-Marxist ambivalence about the welfare state, which ranged from an attitude of skepticism about how much progress had been made and about how much more was likely given the imperatives of capitalist economies, to an attitude of hostility toward such programs due to their social control aspects.[10] The social democratic perspective, in contrast, views the introduction of various social welfare programs and increases in spending, particularly redistributive spending, on such programs as real gains for the working class.

Marx had relatively little to say about social welfare legislation, but what he did say on related issues suggests that he was ambivalent. This ambivalence has characterized the Marxist perspective on the topic ever since. Marx was skeptical about how far social legislation could advance in a capitalist society; however, he did view the English factory legislation enacted between 1833 and 1853 as a major victory for the working class that did improve their welfare (Marx [1867] 1967, pp. 381–382). This acknowledgment of the possibility of meaningful social policy reform in response to working-class pressure is consistent with the social democratic perspective.[11] However, his more general and frequent expression of skepticism about the prospects for meaningful long-term reforms based on social legislation enacted in capitalist states is consistent with the neo-Marxist perspective which we will return to in the next section.

Advocates of the social democratic perspective tend to be optimistic about the potential long-term outcome of social welfare legislation enacted by social democratic governments. Many see such legislation as a possible route by which at least some capitalist democracies will eventually make the transition to democratic socialism (Stephens 1979, p. 200). Sweden is often mentioned in this context as a country that may be among the first to make such a transition.

According to the social democratic perspective, government spending on public pension programs and other social welfare programs is an outcome of class conflict. Evidence that more of a nation's gross national product (GNP) is being spent on such programs is interpreted as support for the claim that labor has been successful in its class struggle with capital (Shalev 1983, p. 319). The welfare state is viewed as very much a class issue. The relative level of expenditure on such programs tells us something about the balance of power between capital and labor.

The social democratic perspective emphasizes the role of organized labor and leftist political parties as determinants of how much influence the working class is likely to have. A strong labor movement helps elect leftist governments, and leftist governments are more likely to enact progressive social welfare legislation including progressive pension legislation (Myles 1984, pp. 83–89; Shalev 1983, p. 323; Stephens 1979, pp. 99–103). This in turn improves the lot of the working class and reduces the extent of economic inequality. Level of spending on public pensions and other welfare state programs is viewed as an outcome of a democratic class struggle in which parties representing the interests of the working class compete with those representing the interests of capital.

Explanations for why labor is stronger in some countries than in others often emphasize unique historical circumstances. However, there is agreement that labor tends to be stronger when a high proportion of the labor force is unionized, when there are a relatively small number of unions, and when the unions are centralized (Myles 1984; Stephens 1979). In contrast, labor tends to be weak when a relatively small proportion of the labor force is unionized, when there are a very large number of small unions, and when the unions are highly competitive with one another (Korpi 1983). If union power is decentralized and there is very little coordination at the national level, labor tends to be weak and unable to exert much control over the state.

Social democratic theorists view the state as much more subject to the independent influence of political power than do neo-Marxists.[12] While it is assumed that capital controls the state in the absence of a strong working class, it is also assumed that it is possible for labor to wrest substantial control of the state from capital through democratic class struggle. Labor can come to control the state apparatus if a large well organized working class is successful in electing leftist governments and keeping them in office.

Theorists in this tradition point out that in capitalist democracies workers are under the control of the owners of capital in the economic sphere, but labor can obtain power in the political sphere that can be used to counteract the harmful effects of markets through spending on public pensions and other welfare state programs (Esping-Andersen 1985). In the economic sphere labor's lack of capital ownership is a disadvantage, but in the political sphere labor's relatively large numbers are an advantage.

The social democratic perspective was formulated to explain developments in the industrial democracies. The perspective is most appropriately applied to nations in which there is sufficient political democracy that it is possible for labor to compete with capital in the electoral arena for control over state resources. Another precondition is that there be sufficient state economic resources available to support the introduction of welfare state programs. Due to these preconditions we should not expect the perspective to be of much utility for the analysis of policy developments in Third World nations.

The Neo-Marxist Perspective

The neo-Marxist (or monopoly capitalism) perspective can be traced to the work of Marx and Engels, but it is more typically associated with the extensive literature in the Marxist tradition that emerged during the 1960s and 1970s.[13] The neo-Marxist perspective shares with the traditional Marxist and the social democratic perspectives an emphasis on class structure, class conflict, and class determinants of social welfare policy.[14] Of the various theoretical perspectives we consider this one comes the closest to the traditional Marxist perspective, but it differs in some important respects, one of which is the degree of autonomy attributed to the state.

The traditional Marxist view of the capitalist state is presented in *The Communist Manifesto* where it is described as "but a committee for managing the common affairs of the whole bourgeoisie" (Marx and Engels [1848] 1955, pp. 11–12).[15] That is, in each Western industrial nation the government is viewed as being controlled by a ruling class. The traditional Marxist view is that the state recruits from and is controlled by the dominant (capitalist) class. From this perspective a major role of the state is to control labor and protect the economic interests of the capitalist class.

Neo-Marxists differ among themselves with respect to how much autonomy to accord the state, but all attribute more autonomy than is assumed by the traditional Marxist view. Miliband (1969) and O'Connor (1973), for example, allow for relatively little state autonomy. In contrast, Gough (1979), Offe (1972), and particularly Block (1977) allow for a greater degree of autonomy.[16]

The social democratic perspective views labor and capital as competing for control of the state and interprets spending on social welfare programs as a reflection of the relative strength of these two contending groups. In this sense the state may potentially be controlled by either capital or labor. From the neo-Marxist perspective while the state has some autonomy, it is viewed as an institution that does not come under the control of labor. While the state may from time to time make decisions that in the short-run favor labor, the long-run agenda is to foster the interests of capital (Przeworski 1985, p. 201). From the neo-Marxist perspective spending on public pensions and other social insurance programs is viewed more as a mechanism to control labor than as a victory for labor (Offe 1972).

From the neo-Marxist perspective spending on public pensions and other social welfare programs is viewed as having little impact on inequality (Miliband 1969, p. 22; Szmanski 1978). One argument is that pension spending represents transfers within classes rather than between classes; that is, pension spending involves transfers from one group of people to another within the same social class.[17] A related argument is that spending on various social welfare programs produces a modest amount of redistribution in the short-run so as to control labor unrest in the face of serious unemployment. It represents an effort to co-opt labor so as to reduce the pressure for a much more comprehensive redistribution of economic resources (Piven and Cloward 1971). This contrasts with the social democratic view that spending on public pensions and other social welfare programs tends to have an egalitarian impact.[18]

According to the neo-Marxist perspective it is not necessary to assume that the important positions in the government are filled by representatives of capital or that the state is directly manipulated by the dominant (ruling) class (Block 1977). Rather the state functions as a partner with capital in the effort to foster long-term economic growth and capital accumulation (O'Connor 1973). While the state is assumed to have some short-term independence, it is also assumed to function in the long run within certain constraints linked to the imperatives of capital accumulation (Przeworski 1985, p. 201).

The mounting evidence that Keynsian economic policy was not functioning as expected during the 1970s stimulated a great deal of theoretical debate (Mishra 1984, p. 69). Theorists in the neo-Marxist tradition began to refer with increasing frequency to the contradictions of modern capitalism and to the fiscal crisis of the state (Offe 1984; Frank 1980; O'Connor 1973). There are many differences among scholars concerning the exact nature of the contradictions. Basically the reference is to policies that are designed to promote social harmony (legitimation) while at the same time contributing to long-term economic growth (capital accumulation). According to O'Connor (1973), a fiscal crisis results in part because the state attempts to socialize the costs of production while privatizing profits. The state pays many of the costs associated with the promotion of economic growth and capital accumulation, but it does not appropriate a sufficiently large proportion of the surplus during the good times to pay for the infrastructure and social welfare expenses during the negative phase of the business cycle or during a decline in the world economy more generally.

Similarly, Offe (1984) argues that the state must preserve the commodification of labor in an effort to foster economic growth. But it must also decommodify labor to deal with the harmful effects of the market. Both of these processes are assumed to be necessary for the long-term functioning of a capitalist economy, but they are viewed as being inherently contradictory. This contradiction contributes to the recurrent fiscal crises of capitalist states. Gough (1979) points to the inherently contradictory nature of social welfare programs in capitalist states. They provide essential social welfare benefits and at the same time function as a mechanism of social control. Poulantzas (1978) argues that the state must neutralize the contradictions of the capitalist state in order to reproduce capitalist structures.

Neo-Marxists have in general been ambivalent about public pensions and the welfare state more generally. They have often criticized such programs as having little egalitarian impact and as serving to co-opt labor. They felt particularly free to criticize these programs during the late 1960s and early 1970s when there was a great deal of public support for them. It would be reasonable to conclude from much of the early 1970s literature that neo-Marxists would support policies aimed at eliminating or at least substantially cutting back many of these programs. But when efforts were made in this direction during the late 1970s and early 1980s by conservative governments in the United States, Britain, and in several other industrial nations in response to inflation, slow growth, and budget deficits, some neo-Marxists scholars strongly opposed efforts to cut back the same programs they had a few years earlier described as tools of social control (Gough 1979, p. 11).[19] One reflection of the ambivalence about welfare state programs is the general reluctance of neo-Marxists scholars to deal with this issue. Gough's ambivalence is implicit in his conclusion that such programs serve some positive social welfare functions while at the same time serving other undesirable social control functions.

The neo-Marxist perspective has been most extensively used in the analysis of developments in the industrial nations, but it has also been used in the analysis of Third World nations. Dependency theory and world system theory[20] can be viewed as variants of the neo-Marxist perspective that have emerged for the analysis of the impact of colonialism, foreign trade, foreign investment, and foreign aid on economic growth and inequality in Third World nations.

Theorists in the dependency theory tradition argue that relationships between the industrial nations and the Third World are structured in such a way as to favor the industrial nations. This was most obvious during the colonial era, but it also continues today through various forms of neocolonialism. While most of these countries are now formally independent, for many, internal affairs continue to be strongly influenced by a relatively small number of industrial nations in the "core" of the world economy by large multinational corporations and international financial institutions such as the World Bank.

Marx himself was not consistent on the issue of colonialism. In the case of Ireland, which he was most familiar with, he concluded that English domination had only adverse consequences with respect to the nation's economic development and standard of living. In the case of India, by contrast, he took the position that British colonial policy was a positive influence.[21] Marx was a Victorian and as such shared many notions of that era about non-Western backwardness (Carnoy 1984, p. 175). The traditional Marxist view of colonialism would be more accurately described as the Leninist perspective.[22] Lenin's ([1917] 1939) views on colonialism were consistent and unambiguous; the colonial nations were exploited by the advanced capitalist nations. He argued that imperialism was the logical extension and a necessary phase of capitalist development.

The major thesis of theorists in the dependency theory tradition is that colonialism in the past and various forms of neocolonialism today (based on foreign trade, foreign investment, and foreign aid) have created obstacles to development (Frank 1978). These various forms of dependency tend to drain much of a nation's economic surplus away as profits and interest are repatriated to industrial nations. The local economy becomes oriented around a highly specialized export industry which has adverse consequences for long-run economic development (Galtung 1971). A number of empirical studies suggest that dependency tends to have an adverse impact on economic growth and inequality (Nolan 1983; Bornschier 1981; Bornschier et al. 1978).

How can we link dependency theory to pension policy and social welfare policy more generally? To the extent that spending on pensions and other social programs represents an effort to control certain key sectors of the labor force, a neo-Marxist analysis would lead us to expect, all other things being equal, more spending in those nations in which there has been more foreign investment. Where there is more foreign involvement in the economy, there will be more need to control labor and this will be reflected in greater spending on pensions and other social programs. In many Third World nations public pension benefits go disproportionately to more affluent groups such as civil servants, military officers, and a few relatively well-paid workers in modern sector industries (Neysmith and Edwardh 1984, p. 35). To the extent that benefits go to a narrow segment of more affluent workers while being paid for directly or indirectly out of a surplus generated by low wages for other workers, these pension benefits may increase rather than decrease the nation's level of economic inequality.

The Neo-Pluralist Perspective

The pluralist perspective can be traced back to Alexis de Tocqueville's *Democracy in America* ([1840]1976). Tocqueville was impressed by the immense number of voluntary associations in America and concluded that the formation of and competition among these associations (a process we today refer to as interest group competition) was a key to the maintenance of democracy. Pluralism has been described as the official ideology of capitalist democracy (Carnoy 1984, p. 10). It is the average citizen's model of how government should and does work. Much of the most influential work in this tradition was done in the 1950s (Dahl 1956; Lipset 1959; Nisbet 1953; Galbraith 1952), but the tradition continues strong particularly among political scientists.

In pluralist theory social policy is assumed to be the outcome of competition among various groups that have an interest in influencing decision making on a particular issue. Which interest groups participate and how hard each pushes will vary from one issue to another. Central to pluralistic theory is the assumption that the way citizens can influence government policy is by joining with others to form an association or interest group. Of particular note in connection with the traditional version of the pluralist perspective is the assumption that a population category such an occupational, ethnic, or age group will have relatively little influence on social policy unless it is organized as an interest group.

Interest groups serve both representative and defense functions. They help the group pursue its goals by advocating policy changes the group favors and by resisting policy changes being proposed by other interest groups that are viewed as contrary to the group's interests. The typical structure of a democratic society that involves a large number of crosscutting interest groups helps reduce conflict, encourage compromise, and foster equilibrium. Traditionally pluralists have assumed that competition among a variety of interest groups keeps one group from taking exclusive control and provides a mechanism for the formulation of social policies that most adequately meet the needs of society as a whole.

At a time when many scholars accepted traditional pluralism uncritically, some began to question how accurately it described the actual policymaking in capitalist democracies, and others began to ask questions about possible negative consequences of the process of interest group pluralism. In *The Lonely Crowd* David Riesman (1950) argued that government policy in the United States was often stalemated due to the existence of numerous "veto groups" that were able to block the introduction of needed new programs and policies. During the 1960s and 1970s a less optimistic version of pluralism began to take shape, a version we refer to as neo-pluralism.[23] In the work of scholars such as Mancur Olson (1965) and Morris Janowitz (1976) questions were raised about the possible negative long-run consequences of interest group politics particularly with respect to welfare state development.

Commenting on the sharp rise in spending on welfare state programs in the United States during the post-World War II era Janowitz (1976, p. 75) argues that this growth reflects much more the pressure of a variety of nonclass-based interest groups than that of class-based interest groups. He views the expansion of political rights and the incorporation of formerly excluded groups into the political system in the industrial democracies as contributing to a proliferation of nonclass-based interest groups that are tending to replace class-based interest groups as the dominant political actors in shaping government social policy.

The emergence of the aged as a major political force in the industrial nations illustrates this trend (Wilensky 1976, pp. 3–13). The aged represent a nonclass-based group defined by an ascriptive characteristic. The group has emerged in part as a response to the demographic changes (particularly the decrease in fertility) that economic growth has produced.

Mancur Olson (1965) is one of the most important contributors to the neo-pluralism perspective.[24] He emphasizes the disproportionate influence that small well organized groups have in democratic societies (M. Olson 1982, pp. 29–34);

this observation will prove germane for the analysis of the small but influential organizations formed by the nineteenth century social reformers who were the early advocates of public pensions in Britain. He points to the accumulation of interest groups that takes place in democratic nations during prolonged periods without political upheaval. He argues that due to the free-rider problem[25] it is difficult to get an interest group organized, but once organized such groups tend to persist and to advocate policies in their own interest which may or may not be in the best interest of society more generally (M. Olson 1982, p. 37). Similarly, once a program benefiting an interest group is implemented such as a provident fund or pension program for retired workers, it too tends to persist.

Political democracy is seen as greatly facilitating interest group politics. Political parties are viewed as loose coalitions designed for the purpose of winning elections rather than formulating policies. The assumption from the neo-pluralism perspective is that in liberal democracies voting is often based on economic self-interest. Latent interest groups as well as formally organized interest groups may demand support for particular programs, such as an increase in social security benefits, in return for votes.[26] Thus government spending is viewed as an inherently political process. This form of collective political action is influenced by what various groups perceive to be their own self-interest.

This emphasis on voting links the perspective to public choice theory.[27] When applied to pension policy and welfare state policy more generally, public choice theory provides a set of assumptions about human behavior that imply a need to take into consideration the government response to voter demand for more spending on pensions and other social programs.

Discussions of interest groups and of interest group politics typically refer to organized groups that share certain goals and seek to influence public policy (Berry 1984, p. 5). However, Olson (1965, p. 8) refers more broadly to groups of individuals with common interests who stand to share the benefits of group action to influence government policy. He points out that such groups may advance their interests through the formation of formal organizations or through voting and other means. The term *latent interest group* is sometimes used when referring to those groups that function as interests groups even though they have not been formally organized.

The neo-pluralism perspective being outlined here uses the term *interest group* in a broad sense. It includes class as well as nonclass-based interest groups and it includes organized as well as latent interest groups. The neo-pluralism perspective differs from the industrialization perspective in its emphasis on the importance of political democracy and interest group politics. It differs from the social democratic perspective in its focus on nonclass as well as class-based interest groups and its emphasis on the growing importance of the nonclass-based interest groups.

Neo-pluralism differs from traditional pluralist theory in that no assumption is made that all groups are represented in the political process, that the competition among interest groups contributes to equilibrium, or that the process leads to policy decisions that are in the long-run in the best interest of society (M. Olson 1982, p. 37). There is an acknowledgment that interest group politics may yield policy decisions that in the long run have an adverse impact on economic growth and tend to increase inequality (Mishra 1985, p. 7). The interest group process may lead to policy decisions that would be more accurately described as catering to powerful special interests than as efficiently meeting the general social welfare needs of society.[28]

While the perspective has emerged primarily to describe trends in the industrial nations, with appropriate modifications it can be applied to the analysis of developments in Third World nations as well.[29] In this context the theory leads to an emphasis on the role of nonclass-based interest groups in the shaping of old-age social security policy and social welfare policy more generally. Again the perspective does not assume that policies that emerge from the interest group process are in the best interest of society as a whole. The policies that emerge may do little to reduce inequality or to foster economic growth, and they may do little to help the poorest segment of the population. As countries democratize, the assumption is that an increasing share of national resources will be allocated to various social welfare programs due to greater pressure from the larger number and the increased strength of the various interest groups.

To sum up, the neo-pluralist perspective offers two key insights which differentiate it from the others. First, it asserts that multiple groups—not only organized labor or monopoly capital—are central in the growth of the welfare state. The perspective is thus in part defined by its opposition to the class-reductionist views of the social democratic and neo-Marxist perspectives. It argues that diverse groups and multiple actors including, but not limited to, those defined by region, ethnicity, religion, occupation, age, voluntary organization, and gender are crucial to the expansion of the welfare state. Classes are important as well; yet, the neo-pluralist perspective gives special weight to middle-class groups that are less clearly defined by their relationship to the means of production than by their education, status, and income. The proliferation of such varied groups in modern societies must be considered along with the more commonly identified actors, union members and business owners, in understanding the emergence and growth of pension systems.

The second insight of the neo-pluralist perspective is that pension policy is inherently political. Democratic political competition, in particular, facilitates group interests. Groups have their most influence on policy when politicians and political parties compete for their votes in democratic elections. The neo-pluralist attention to politics contrasts with that of the more functionalist theories of the industrialist and neo-Marxist variety which see pensions as a more or less automatic response to industrial and demographic changes or changes in productive relations.

It is not possible to set forth a simple argument concerning the impact of group influence and democratic competition. Depending on the constellation of groups and their influence, they may hinder or facilitate expansion of the pension system. During the early stages of pension program development, democratic competition among interest groups may retard the introduction of centralized systems. The existence of widespread and specialized programs for diverse groups creates resistance to a more centralized public program that distributes benefits to a larger part of the population. Hence, national public pension systems have often been adopted earlier in less democratic nations. Once in place, however, a centralized pension system directs interest group activity in the opposite direction—toward expansion of public benefits. As political parties compete for support, interest group activity in democracies fuels spending for dominant programs. The proliferation of diverse groups with interests in higher spending drives pension policy in more mature welfare states.

Although the neo-pluralist perspective focuses primarily on demands from societal groups and the existence of means to express and realize those demands, it also recognizes that the organization of interests may depend on the state. Democratic procedures that influence the way interest group activity influences pension spending depend on state-based constitutional arrangements. Further, state-based corporatist structures, which formally recognize and legitimize monopolistic representatives of labor and employers, shape the nature of interest group activity.

The State-Centered Perspective

In this section we consider several arguments which emphasize the autonomous impact of the state on pension and social welfare policy more generally.[30] While it is possible to draw links between some of the different perspectives we consider here, the various arguments outlined cannot be combined into even a loosely structured overall theory of how state structures have influenced the development of pension policy. The various state-centered theories do share, however, the assumption that the influence of the state cannot be entirely accounted for in terms of pressure from societal groups such as a ruling class, a mobilized working class, or various interest groups. The state is viewed as more than a neutral structure mediating between various class or nonclass interest groups.

Some of the arguments considered emphasize the impact of certain structural characteristics of states such as the degree of democratization, the structure of the tax system,[31] or how centralized the government is. Some emphasize the role of history considering such factors as the influence of past social policies, how developed the civil service was at the time the nation became democratic, or the nation's colonial background (Williamson and Pampel 1991, p. 36). Other arguments emphasize the role of small groups of appointed or elected officials, for example, the role of the civil service, or even the role of a single leader. The reasoning here is that important pension policy decisions are sometimes strongly influenced by the personal agenda of a specific powerful individual or by the agenda of a small influential group of civil service technocrats.

Democracy[32] (or level of democracy) is an aspect of state structure that has received much attention over the years. One of the most frequently cited versions of the theory that democracy tends to affect the distribution of the social product is outlined by Lenski (1966, pp. 313–325). A number of empirical studies have presented evidence in support of the thesis that level of democracy has a positive effect on social security spending (e.g., Williamson and Pampel 1986; Richter and Parrish 1983; Cutright 1965; 1967). Other studies report evidence of interaction between level of democracy and other determinants of pension spending such as the proportion of the population over age 65 (Pampel and Williamson 1985).

A variant on this thesis is that the spending will be greater in nations in which political competition is more intense (Pampel and Williamson 1988). Another variant of this argument is that democratic nations tend to introduce social security programs earlier (Cutright 1965). The electoral business cycle thesis is another state-centered argument. The thesis is that spending on public pensions and other social welfare programs tends to increase just prior to elections (Tufte 1978). The legislation is aimed at enhancing the electoral prospects of incumbents due in part to good will from those who benefit directly and in part to the short-term benefits to the overall economy and the general population that such an economic stimulus often produces.

Another state-centered argument is that nations with more centralized government decision-making structures tend to enact more generous pension policies and social welfare policies more generally (DeViney 1983). Some countries such as Sweden and Britain have a unitary form of government with social welfare policy decisions being made by the central government. Other countries such as the United States, Canada, and Switzerland have a federal governmental structure in which responsibility for much social welfare legislation is split between the central government and a subnational unit of government such as the state, province, or canton. Nations with a unitary as opposed to a federalist structure tend to have more generous public pension programs and more generous social welfare programs more generally (Castles 1982). The existence of a second level of government decision making often means resistance to generous (expensive) social welfare legislation as it provides more opportunities to block proposals for policy liberalization.

Corporatist theory is one of the most developed and extensively used of the state-centered perspectives (Western 1991; Williamson 1989; Wilensky and Turner 1987; Malloy 1979; Schmitter 1974).[33] It is useful to distinguish between two quite different forms, democratic corporatism and authoritarian corporatism. Both forms call for an integration or coordination of social welfare policy and economic policy. Both point to the strong impact on economic and social welfare policy of committees made up of government officials, the leaders of highly centralized labor unions, and the leaders of highly centralized employers' associations. Central to corporatism is the idea that a very limited number of interest groups are allowed to participate in the formulation of national economic and social welfare policy. Basic to the corporatist model of decision making is the emphasis on cooperation and interdependence as opposed to conflict. Also central to corporatism is the state-based, legitimized monopoly of labor and business organizations over their members.

The democratic form of corporatism[34] is illustrated by countries such as Austria and Sweden. Democratic corporatism refers to formal or informal state-sanctioned structures that foster collaboration between labor and capital. In these countries labor has been organized at the national level into very powerful union centrals. Employers are also organized into highly centralized organizations representing their interests. When the leaders of labor, capital, and the government meet to discuss public pension policy as well as other economic and social policies, those representing labor are selected by labor and fully accountable to labor.[35] Labor's participation in democratic corporatism is voluntary, not imposed. Both labor and capital participate in the process because they view it to be in their mutual best interest to do so. The assumption is that a certain amount of give and take by both labor and capital is necessary to assure the best long-run outcome for both groups.[36] In this process the representatives of labor are assumed to have as much say as the representatives of capital.[37]

The authoritarian form of corporatism[38] emerged in several fascist European countries during the 1920s and 1930s. Of particular note was the corporatist influence in Italy and Portugal (Williamson 1989, p. 34). It also emerged at about the same time in many authoritarian Latin American countries, including Brazil and Argentina (Erickson 1977, p. 4; Malloy 1979).[39] In the context of authoritarian and totalitarian states, corporatist structures are typically imposed by the government as mechanisms of social control. Labor is represented in such structures, but those "representing" labor have typically been selected by the government (or from lists of candidates approved by the government). These fascist and authoritarian regimes saw in corporatist ideology a rationale for substantially increasing the power of the state while at the same time decreasing the influence of various interest groups, particularly organized labor (Schmitter 1974, p. 103). In contrast to democratic corporatism, in the context of authoritarian corporatism, labor representatives are in reality more accountable to the central government than to rank-and-file union members.

A case can be made that both the democratic and authoritarian forms of corporatism contribute to increases in spending on public pensions and to pension policy development more generally. In the case of authoritarian corporatism such policies are designed to co-opt workers. In the case of democratic corporatism the assumption is that such policies promote industrial peace and labor–management cooperation. This in turn tends to foster economic growth and thus in the long run generate more by way of resources that can be allocated to public pensions and other forms of social welfare. However, it is possible that in the short run corporatism will result in less pension spending (or less of an increase in spending) as part of an agreed upon effort to stimulate economic growth or reduce inflationary pressure.

Many of the state-centered arguments emphasize historical context and the impact of prior legislation and programs dealing with the same problem (Skocpol and Amenta 1986; Skocpol 1985). Heclo (1974) agues that policymaking is an inherently historical process. He emphasizes the impact of prior legislation pointing out that current legislation often builds upon or represents a reaction against prior policies. He discusses the role of timing with respect to when civil service bureaucracies emerged relative to when democracy emerged. In countries such as the United States in which democratization took place prior to the emergence of an impartial civil service, political parties promised supporters various forms of patronage including patronage jobs. In contrast, in countries such as Germany and Sweden in which democratization came much later and after a highly developed civil service bureaucracy had evolved, the option of offering patronage jobs was not available. An alternative strategy to attract electoral support in these countries was to promise liberalization of pension benefits and other social policies aimed at a wide segment of the electorate.

A number of scholars making state-centered arguments have emphasized the role of civil servants (Skocpol 1985; Heclo 1974). Civil service bureaucracies are sometimes described as interest groups that seek to maximize their budgets through increased government spending on old-age social security and other social welfare programs. Civil servants are important as links to their counterparts in other countries. They serve as facilitators for the diffusion of policy models from one country to another. These civil servants become the technocratic experts who have a substantial impact on program formulation and reform due to their specialized knowledge. A similar role is played by those elected officials who take a special interest in social welfare legislation.

In some instances one individual has an enormous impact as in the case of Bismarck's impact on the German public pension system. While he had in mind the interests of the traditional elite, the pension idea was basically his. It is is not as if there was strong pressure from the ruling elite to institute his various social insurance programs. They did, however, back the effort once they were convinced of the social control potential of old-age pensions and other social insurance programs. The more general point is that a national leader or a small number of civil service technocrats sometimes have their own agendas that cannot be reduced to the preferences of various class or nonclass interest groups. Government officials often initiate new policies well ahead of pressure from various interest groups. This is particularly true with respect to a new program; once a program is in place it tends to generate an associated interest group that does exert pressure for increased benefits and other policy reforms.

Structure of the Book

We started our study with the idea that the relative utility of the different theoretical perspectives outlined earlier might well vary depending on national and historical context. To test this idea we selected a sample of seven very diverse nations for our historical case studies. This sample of four industrial and three Third World nations gave us a great deal of contextual variation to work with and provided a way to test the generalizability of explanations derived from each of the general theoretical perspectives outlined.

In each of these case studies we begin with an historical narrative in which we review the evolution of old-age security policy developments from the introduction of the nation's first program up through the present. As part of this narrative we discuss a variety of factors that contributed to the way in which policy developed in that particular country. As we have found that the historical context from which the first program emerged has always had a substantial impact on subsequent developments, we typically start the narrative a number of years prior to the introduction of the nation's first old-age security program. We conclude each chapter with a theoretical analysis of old-age security policy developments in that particular country. One goal of this discussion is to explain why policy evolved as it did. Another is to assess the relative utility of explanations linked to the different theoretical perspectives.

Germany (Chapter 2) was selected in part because it is a particularly crucial case for assessing explanations derived from the state-centered perspective. During the era when Bismarck was chancellor the German state had a great deal of autonomy. It is also of great interest because it was the first industrial nation to introduce a public old-age pension scheme, a scheme that was to have a great deal of influence on pension policy developments in a number of other nations. The United Kingdom (Chapter 3) was selected because it is a particularly crucial case for assessing the utility of the industrialism perspective. At the turn of the century Britain was the world's leading industrial nation, but it did not enact its first pension scheme until almost 20 years after Germany. At that time Britain was also a bastion of laissez-faire liberalism making it a crucial case for an assessment of the neo-pluralist perspective as well. Sweden (Chapter 4) was selected because it is a crucial case for the assessment of explanations of pension policy development derived from the social democratic perspective. With almost continuous social democratic control of the government between 1932 and 1991 as well as a history of strong labor unions, it has the attributes that make it an ideal case for assessing explanations derived from this perspective. The United States (Chapter 5) was selected in part because at the time when its first public pension legislation was enacted it was one of the world's leading monopoly capitalist nations making it a particularly crucial case for assessment of the relevance of the neo-Marxist perspective. It was also a nation with very well developed democratic institutions that were strongly influenced by interest group politics making it an important case for assessing the utility of the neo-pluralist perspective as well.

Castles and Mitchell (1990) recently proposed that distinctions be made among four types of welfare state regimes. Their typology is an elaboration of a similar typology proposed by Esping-Andersen (1990, pp. 26–28).[40] An argument made by these authors with which we agree is that the dynamics of welfare state development (and thus of pension policy development) vary depending on the context, that is, from one type of welfare state regime to another. The four industrial nations selected for the present analysis illustrate each of the four types outlined by Castles and Mitchell. The German case illustrates what they refer to as a conservative welfare state regime.[41] The United Kingdom illustrates what they refer to as a "radical" welfare state regime.[42] Sweden illustrates the social democratic category.[43] And the United States is an example of a liberal welfare state regime (Castles and Mitchell 1990, pp. 13–14).[44]

In Chapters 6–8 we present historical case studies of old-age security systems based on the social insurance approach (Brazil), the provident fund approach (Nigeria), and a combination of the two (India). These countries were selected as representing diversity with respect to level of development[45] and degree of democratic institutionalization[46] as well as diversity with respect to geographical and cultural context. In the cases of Brazil, Nigeria, and, to a lesser extent, India, comparisons are made with schemes in other countries in the region. It would be risky to generalize from our three case studies to the Third World more generally, but our choice of countries provides enough variation to give us some idea of the sources of convergence and divergence in old-age security policy in the Third World. The inclusion of these Third World countries also allows us to make comparisons between industrial nations and Third World nations. While such comparisons must be made with care given the dramatic contextual differences, they can be used to highlight some important anomalies that contradict our taken-for-granted views about how and why policy has evolved differently in the Third World.[47]

In Chapter 9 we quantitatively test several hypotheses derived in part from our prior quantitative work and in part from the historical case studies presented in the preceding seven chapters. Here we substantially increase both the number of industrial nations (from 4 to 18) and the number of Third World nations (from 3 to 32). In this analysis we attempt to specify and measure more precisely the contextual sources of differences in the determinants of pension spending levels. For our sample of industrial nations we assess the interactive influences of corporatism, class structure, and age structure (percent aged). Among our sample of Third World nations, we find that age structure and social insurance program experience have a much greater impact on pension spending levels for the more democratic nations than for the less democratic nations. These interactions suggest ways to organize otherwise diverse findings.

In Chapter 10 we summarize the major conclusions of our study. We pull together the major findings of the case studies and discuss the extent to which these findings are confirmed or qualified on the basis of the quantitative analysis presented in Chapter 9. While many of those findings are confirmed, the quantitative analysis does lead to a qualification of some conclusions. The evidence presented in our historical case studies provides relatively little support for the social democratic thesis or for class theory more generally, but our quantitative analysis in Chapter 9 leads us to qualify this conclusion. Chapter 10 reviews both the case studies and the statistical results as they reflect on the utility of the five theoretical approaches.

2

Germany

In 1889 Germany became the first nation in the world to enact a national compulsory old-age and invalidity pension system. This scheme was one of several social insurance programs introduced in Germany during the 1880s, starting with enactment of sickness insurance in 1883 and industrial accident insurance in 1884. In view of its being the world's first national old-age pension scheme and in view of the impact this program has had on subsequent developments in other nations, we will want to take a close look at the structure of the original program and the factors contributing to its enactment.

The German contributions to old-age pension policy are not all in the distant past. During the post-World War II era Germany[1] introduced a number of policy innovations that have served as models for other nations. Of particular note in this context are the reforms of 1957, 1972, and 1989. German public pension policy, while noteworthy for the high degree of continuity over the past 100 years, has also proven to be important for its innovations.

The German case is also important for theoretical reasons. In recent years the state-centered perspective has emerged as one of the most promising alternatives to the neo-Marxist and social democratic perspectives on welfare state development. As the German state, particularly during the era of the German Empire (1871–1918), comes as close as any nation has to the structural characteristics of what Skocpol (1979, p. 106) and others describe as the autonomous state, the case will provide a crucial test case for the efficacy of the state-centered perspective. Of the four welfare state types described in the typology proposed by Castles and Mitchell (1990), Germany illustrates the conservative category. In view of this we will want to trace the policy consequences of this conservative welfare state tradition.

In this chapter we focus on the following set of interrelated questions about the evolution of old-age pension policy in Germany: (1) Why was the original program introduced when it was? (2) Is the evidence concerning early pension policy developments more consistent with explanations derived from the state-centered perspective, the neo-Marxist perspective, or with those derived from some other theoretical perspective? (3) How do we account for pension policy developments since the end of World War II? Are they more consistent with the state-centered perspective, the social democratic perspective, or some other perspective?

We begin with an analysis of the events leading up to the introduction of the original German pension scheme. We then consider developments since the turn of the century with an emphasis on the period since the end of World War II. In this context we emphasize recent changes that went into effect in 1992. We conclude with a theoretical assessment of the factors that have shaped old-age pension policy developments paying particular attention to the role that organized labor, leftist parties, big business, and the state have played.

Developments Before 1900

Unlike other major European powers such as Britain and France, in the 1880s Germany was still dealing with many of the issues of national unity that confront new nations. Between the tenth century and 1806 the German states were part of the Holy Roman Empire.[2] From 1815 to 1866 they were part of the German Confederation. In 1866 modern Germany started to emerge with the formation of the North German Confederation which united with a number of South German states in 1871 to become the German Empire.[3]

The Holy Roman Empire was not a territorial state in the modern sense of the term. One indication of this was the independent foreign policies that the constituent states were allowed to follow.[4] The creation in 1815 of the German Confederation, made up of 39 monarchical states, was also a very loose confederation of states, the most powerful of which were Prussia and Austria (Pachter 1978, p. 4). As with the Holy Roman Empire, the major states continued to follow their independent political, economic, and foreign policies (Carr 1979, p. 4). During the period of the Confederation people were much more likely to consider themselves Austrians, Prussians, or Bavarians than citizens of Germany (Passant 1959, p. 15).

The Prussian constitution of 1850 established a dualistic state with the power divided between the king and the Parliament. The Parliament consisted of a hereditary House of Lords and an elected Chamber of Deputies. There was near universal male suffrage for the Chamber of Deputies, but the votes of those who paid higher taxes (the affluent) were weighted a great deal more heavily than those who paid very little in taxes (Pachter 1978, p. 9). This assured Junker (squire) control of the Chamber of Deputies for the first several years. By the 1860s, however, a strong industrial bourgeoisie emerged shifting control of the Chamber of Deputies to the liberals. Basically the same voting system was used in Prussia during the era of the North German Confederation and subsequently during the era of the German Empire.

In 1866 Prussia, by far the largest and most powerful of the North German states, after a brief war against Austria, annexed several states in northern and central Germany to form the North German Confederation. Otto von Bismarck, at the time the minister-president (prime minister) of Prussia, was appointed chancellor of this confederation.[5] In 1871 in the wake of the Franco-Prussian war, a number of South German states, most notably Bavaria, were added to form the Prussian-dominated German Empire with Bismarck appointed chancellor (Passant 1959, p. 57).

The civil servants in Prussia and the subsequent German Empire were noted for their discipline and professionalism. This highly efficient administrative bureaucracy concentrated power in the hands of the central government reducing the influence of the traditional landed nobility, despite the heavy recruitment of civil servants from Junker landowners (Skocpol 1979, p. 109).[6]

Representatives to the Reichstag (the lower house of the Parliament) were elected on the basis of near universal suffrage.[7] However, the influence of the Reichstag was checked by Bundesrat (upper house) which was made up of appointed delegates (ambassadors) for the various monarchical states in the empire and by the chancellor who was appointed by the kaiser. Any legislation had to be approved both by the Reichstag and the Bundesrat.

By the end of the 1870s six major political parties had emerged, one of which was the Social Democratic Party founded in 1875 by the union of two earlier groups, the Social Democratic Labor Party (formed in 1869) and the General German Workers' Association (formed in 1863).[8] Bismarck became very concerned about the evidence of growing support for the Social Democratic Party and in response he successfully pushed for enactment of the Anti-Socialist Bill of 1878 (Katzenstein 1987, p. 168).[9] As a result Social Democratic meetings and newspapers were banned.[10] Nevertheless, the Social Democratic Party was able to continue its political activities underground. At first the socialist vote decreased, but within a few years it was again on the increase. The Social Democrats who were elected were allowed by a vote of the Reichstag to take office, much to Bismarck's displeasure (Hertz 1975, p. 355).

The organization of labor unions was legalized in the North German Confederation in 1869 (Katzenstein 1987, p. 128).[11] Prior to this workers' associations such as the General German Workers' Association and the Union of German Workers' Associations did exist, but they were not unions in the modern sense (Carr 1979, pp. 84–85).[12] When enforcing the Anti-Socialist Bill of 1878 the police not only suppressed the Social Democratic Party, but also the union movement, particularly the socialist trade unions (Zöllner 1982, p. 11), which technically were not covered by the law (Kosok 1933, p. 18). In addition to the trade unions organized by the Social Democrats there were a number of Christian, liberal, and independent unions organized by various nonsocialist groups. After the Anti-Socialist Law expired in 1890 the socialist trade unions were reorganized so as to be much more independent of the Social Democrats, but close ties did remain (Katzenstein 1987, p. 128). In 1885 only 137,000 Germans were union members, a small fraction of the industrial labor force, but the number had increased to 849,000 by 1900 and this rapid expansion continued up until the start of World War I (Hohorst et al. 1978, p. 135).

Signs of industrialization begin to appear in the 1830s (Zöllner 1982, p. 6). With this change came an increase in the proportion of the population that was wage dependent.[13] The late nineteenth century was a period of rapid industrialization (Passant 1959, p. 57). By 1900 Germany was the foremost industrial power on the continent (Mann 1968, p. 201). In 1882 Germany had a labor force of 19 million. Of these 4 million (21 percent) were industrial workers. By 1895 the labor force had increased to 22 million and of these 6 million (27 percent) were industrial workers (Hohorst et al. 1978, pp. 66–67; Alber 1988, p. 5). Thus at the time when Germany's original social insurance legislation was enacted, industrial workers still constituted a minority of the labor force, but this segment was expanding rapidly.

The growth in the number of industrial workers contributed to the rise of an industrial working class and a Social Democratic Party that was viewed as representing the interests of workers. The rise of the industrial working class and particularly its support for the Social Democratic Party was perceived by Bismarck as a threat to both the traditional Junker elite and the new industrial elite (Dawson 1912).

Where did Bismarck get the idea of old-age pensions? While Germany was the first nation to enact an old-age pension system, the idea was being discussed during the 1880s in several other nations including England and Sweden; yet, it seems that the most important single source was Bismarck's exposure to the French system of demogrants for industrial workers (introduced in the 1850s) during visits in the 1850s and as Prussian ambassador to France in 1861 (Tomasson 1984, p. 220). He was impressed with the social control value of Napolean III's limited social protection efforts (Rimlinger 1971, p. 106).

The introduction of old-age pensions must be viewed as one aspect of the more general decision to introduce compulsory social insurance legislation. By the 1870s a number of prominent academics and industrialists were calling for enactment of some form of compulsory social insurance. One reason industrialists were supporting the proposal is that they viewed it as a way to reduce the number of liability suits being brought against employers in connection with the Liability Act of 1871 (Zöllner 1982, pp. 23–24). Support was strongest among industrialists representing heavy industries with high accident rates and recruitment problems (Steinmetz 1990, p. 266). For some industrialists these were as great a concern as the growing influence of organized labor and the socialists.[14]

From the Middle Ages on miners had been free and had experienced living conditions that were similar to nineteenth century industrial workers.[15] Very early on they had established voluntary provident funds to cover various risks (illness, disability, death) that miners faced (Steinmeyer 1991, pp. 75–76). Eventually, contributions to many of these funds became compulsory. These miners' provident funds served as another important model for Bismarck's original social insurance legislation (Zöllner 1982, pp. 21–24).

The ideas behind Bismarck's social insurance legislation had many other sources as well. The first compulsory pension program for Prussian civil servants was introduced in 1825 (Kohli 1987, p. 131).[16] Also relevant is the evidence with respect to much of the Prussian social legislation enacted during the preceding 40 years or so. Prussian factory legislation limiting child labor had been enacted in 1839. In the 1840s a new form of guilds for craftsmen and artisans was organized. These guilds also covered many factory workers. In connection with this legislation many employers were required to establish funds designed to provide pensions to sick and disabled workers and to those no longer able to work due to old age (Tampke 1981, pp. 72–73). In the 1850s and 1860s nearly half of Prussia's miners and industrial workers were covered by government mandated programs providing some form of economic protection (Katzenstein 1987, p. 171).

In addition to the government mandated schemes there were a number of corporate old-age pension schemes that had not been mandated by government legislation. These schemes responded to a very real need among industrial workers for social protection, but they were designed so as to maximize labor control objectives. Workers who moved from one employer to another typically lost all pension credits; this provided an incentive to remain loyal to one's employer. In addition, those who participated in questionable labor actions or political activities were often denied pension benefits (Tampke 1981, p. 75). Big business support for Bismarck's social insurance programs was due in part to the desire to broaden the coverage of an approach to social provision that had been demonstrated to work by these corporate schemes; they had worked with respect to both the social control and modest social welfare goals.

Concern about the rising political influence of the Social Democratic Party led Bismarck to push for enactment of the antisocialist legislation mentioned earlier. However, it was clear that this repressive measure by itself was not going to be an adequate long-term solution to the "labor question" (Alber 1988, p. 5). He very openly called for a number of the measures that the socialists (Social Democrats) had been advocating, as a means to undercut their working-class support and to shift the allegiance of the workers to the state (Schulz et al. 1974, p. 109). As early as 1864 some labor leaders were calling for old-age pensions. The scheme they wanted was to be voluntary and administered by the unions. The Social Democrats supported the idea of social protection for workers including old-age pensions, but the leadership vigorously opposed the idea of a state-administered scheme. They did not want the elite-dominated state to control the workers' insurance funds (Zöllner 1982, p. 12).[17]

In 1871 Bismarck wrote: "The only means of stopping the socialist movement . . . is to put into effect those socialist demands which seem justified and which can be realized within the framework of the present order of state and society" (quoted in Zöllner 1982, p. 13).[18] It is generally agreed that social insurance was enacted with the backing of industrial interests despite opposition from the Social Democrats and small business (Ullman 1981, p. 133). There is no evidence that the workers themselves were pushing for state-based social insurance programs.

The introduction of various social insurance programs including old-age pensions was viewed as necessary in part to meet social welfare needs that were the result of industrialization, but it is unlikely that these programs would have been introduced as soon as they were in the absence of Bismarck's concern about the need to strengthen the nation-state by making low-income workers economically dependent on the state.[19] These programs gave those who might otherwise feel they had little to lose from social upheaval a vested interest in maintaining the status quo (Rimlinger 1971, p. 121).

Bismarck originally wanted an old-age pension system that was noncontributory. As his goal was to create the image of a beneficent paternalistic state, he did not want to ask for contributions from workers lest they view their benefits as earned rather than a generous gift from the state (Myles 1984, p. 34). It is a tribute to the increasing political influence of the middle class (the Liberal Party) that Bismarck was unable to get a noncontributory pension plan through the Reichstag. He had to make compromises with representatives of the middle class who were strongly influenced by the ideology of nineteenth century liberalism.[20] This legislation passed because it had the backing of the Conservatives and the Liberals, but it was vigorously opposed to the end by the Social Democrats.

Liberals were concerned that a noncontributory pension would undercut the workings of the free market. They wanted pensions to be market conforming; that is, they wanted the size of the old-age pension to reflect the worker's wages prior to old age. They highly valued self-sufficiency and favored workers providing for their own old age. Thus the pension system eventually enacted called for contributions from workers that were linked to wages (Kaim-Caudle 1973, p. 134). Benefits in turn were to reflect these differences in contributions.[21] However, Bismarck was successful in getting a modest 50 mark contribution from the state for all eligible workers independent of their prior contributions (Tomasson 1984, p. 221). But even with this state contribution, the scheme had very little redistributive impact (Baldwin 1989, p. 23).

The German old-age pension system was compulsory for covered categories of workers. At the outset it covered approximately 40 percent of employed workers, primarily blue-collar workers, but also low-wage white-collar employees. By 1895 approximately 54 percent of the economically active population was covered by the program (Esping-Andersen, Rainwater, and Rein 1988, p. 342).[22] The program was administered by a decentralized set of committees composed of both employers and employees; these committees were required to work within a set of strict government guidelines (Kaim-Caudle 1973, p. 134). While there was a 50 mark per year contribution from the state, benefits were for the most part paid for by a small payroll tax divided equally between the employer and the employee.[23] Contributions were earnings related with different contributions for each of four wage levels (Tomasson 1984, p. 221).

There was no adjustment of benefits based on the number of dependents and no survivor benefits. Benefits were very modest and designed to supplement the generally lower earnings of old workers. The benefit if unsupplemented protected the worker against total destitution, but it did not replace a significant portion of the worker's income. There was no requirement that the worker retire or that earnings fall below a specified level as a precondition for the receipt of benefits which were so low as to constitute little by way of economic incentive to retire.[24] Some critics have argued that the original German old-age pension program was no more than a modest liberalization of prior poor law statutes (Myles 1984, p. 33). The program did provide benefits without the stigma and loss of civil rights associated with poor relief, but pension benefits were below, not above poor relief benefits.

The first pensions were paid in 1891 to 122,000 workers, but none of these were old-age pensions; they were all invalidity pensions. The first old-age pensions were paid in 1899. In that year just under 600,000 pensions were paid (Hohorst et al. 1978, p. 156). Soon after its introduction the old-age and invalidity pension program became popular with workers.[25] Prior to enactment, however, the proposed legislation did not get much attention or support from industrial workers. It has been described as the least popular of the social insurance schemes that Bismarck introduced during the 1880s (Tampke 1981, p. 76). The old-age pension benefit would not be available until the worker was age 70. Given that only 20 percent of German workers survived to age 70 in the 1880s (Kohli 1987, p. 136), it is not surprising that many workers had doubts as to whether they would live long enough to receive benefits based on the contributions (taxes) they would be making throughout their working lives.

Developments Since 1900

Between 1890 and World War I membership in German trade unions grew from 6 to 32 percent of nonagricultural workers (Zöllner 1982, p. 34). This was in spite of the harassment of the unions by the government which continued up until the start of World War I (Markovitz 1986, p. 32). During this period the socialist unions became increasingly similar to the nonsocialist unions. Membership in the Social Democratic Party also increased, and by 1914 it had the support of approximately one-third of the electorate (Kosok 1933, pp. 18–22).[26]

During this period the Social Democratic Party and the labor unions supported efforts to liberalize pension policy (Baldwin 1990a, p. 2). The legislation of 1911 adding survivors' benefits for widows and orphans[27] in part reflected the increasing influence of organized labor and the Social Democratic Party, but as the Social Democrats did not control the government, this reform can also be interpreted as yet another effort by the state to contain the increasing popularity of the Social Democrats.

Another major development in 1911 was the decision to introduce a new and entirely separate pension system for white-collar salaried employees. This decision set a pattern that was to influence subsequent policy developments, separate programs for different categories of workers. It reflected the conservative (authoritarian corporatist) German desire to maintain status differentials between different categories of workers. This new program called for larger contributions from white-collar workers, but it also provided more generous benefits (Alber 1988, p. 6). The decision to introduce a new scheme rather than expand the coverage of the original scheme was in part motivated by the desire to divide the labor movement. The separate system was designed to contribute to a separate identity for this emerging class of workers who would then be less likely to join socialist unions or the Social Democratic Party (Esping-Andersen et al. 1988, p. 342; Kohli 1987, p. 134).

No major changes were made in pension policy during World War I,[28] nor during the era of the Weimar Republic (1919–1933) (Tomasson 1984, p. 222).[29] During the Nazi era pension benefits were extended to cover self-employed artisans (in 1938), but for the most part the old-age pension system was left unchanged.[30] There was, however, evidence of social security policy being implemented in biased ways with respect to Jews, the physically unfit, and other so-called undesirables (Zöllner 1982, pp. 52–56; Tomasson 1984, p. 222).

The Nazi's suppressed the existing independent labor movement and created a state-controlled organization called the German Labor Front that many workers were required to join (Alber 1988, p. 10).[31] Its goal was to control workers and help minimize conflicts between management and labor (Katzenstein 1987, p. 130). While the German Labor Front was disbanded at the end of the war, it did have some long-term effects on the German labor movement. For example, it contributed to the trend toward industrial unionism. Soon after the end of the war a labor federation, the Deutscher Gewerkschaftsbund (DGB), was formed based on 16 national industrial unions.[32] There was a great deal of overlap between these 16 industrial unions and the National Factory Groups organization in connection with the German Labor Front. During the early postwar years the preference of the leaders of the West German labor movement was to form one large national union, but that idea was opposed by the Allied powers that controlled the Western Zones of Germany at the time. The fear was that such a union would give labor too much power and in addition it might fall under the influence of the Communists. The DGB with its federated structure was much more acceptable to the Allied powers (Markovitz 1986, p. 65).

Instead of being organized as socialist, liberal, and Christian unions as during the Weimar era, they were reconstituted as nonsectarian unions. They were to be independent of political parties and not to overtly support or enter into agreements with any party. While the relationship between the DGB and Social Democrats (SPD) has been much closer than that between the DGB and the Christian Democrats (CDU), the inability to form overt political alliances with a party has been a factor limiting the power of the unions (Markovitz 1986, pp. 417–418). Also limiting the influence of organized labor has been the "juridification" of the labor movement; that is, the power of organized labor has been limited by an elaborate corpus of labor legislation assuring labor a part in decision making while circumscribing labor's flexibility and autonomy. There is, for example, a ban on the closed-shop. In addition German trade unions are bound to insure that their members fulfill their contractual obligations. In Sweden, the Landsorganisation (LO) and the other major labor confederations can participate in the collective bargaining of member unions, but this is not the case in Germany; the DGB cannot get directly involved in collective bargaining between its constituent unions and their corresponding employers' associations (Katzenstein 1987, p. 126).

The influence of labor is substantially limited by the nation's dual system of industrial relations. The unions are responsible for collective bargaining on issues such as wages on an industry-wide basis. The unions are also major actors in Germany's policy of *co-determination* (Katzenstein 1989, p. 334). Co-determination refers to the institutionalization of formal structures at the company level specifying that representatives of both owners and labor are to be represented on the board of directors (Markovitz 1986, p. 31). It involves the participation of representatives of labor in the actual running of German industries. Legislation first enacted in the early 1950s and amended several times since then assures the unions one-third membership on these supervisory boards.[33]

There is also a system of *works councils* (or workers' councils) made up of representatives of labor and management at the factory level.[34] While those selected to represent labor on these councils tend also to be union members, formally these works councils are entirely independent of the unions. The works councils are typically used to resolve factory specific disputes.[35] The trend seems to be in the direction of greater and greater decentralization in decision making, driven in large measure by changing technology, much of it linked to the microchip revolution (Katzenstein 1989, p. 334; Markovitz 1986, p. 421). As a result, the works councils are gaining strength at the cost of the unions, a trend that management is encouraging.

After the end of World War II membership in the new free trade unions grew rapidly to about 30 percent of the labor force by 1950 (Stephens 1979, p. 115). In the mid-1980s approximately 30 percent of blue-collar employees were union members (Katzenstein 1987, p. 130).[36] When comparisons are made among the industrial nations with respect to the level of unionization, Germany tends to fall somewhere in the middle between the highly unionized nations such as Sweden and Austria on the one hand and the weakly unionized nations such as the United States and France on the other (Markovitz 1986, p. 121).

The Pension Reform Act of 1957 was the single most important reform in pension policy between the end of World War II and 1989. It has been described as the most important piece of German social legislation during the 1950s and as the first major reform of the German public pension system since the turn of the century (Katzenstein 1987, p. 180). This legislation modified the formula for the computation of pension benefits in such as way as to substantially increase the size of pension benefits.[37] Prior to this point the goal of old-age pensions had been to assure a subsistence standard of living to pensioners who had little by way of alternative means of support. In 1957 the goal shifted to maintenance of the worker's pre-retirement relative standard of living during the retirement years (Greza 1989, p. 1; Hockerts 1981, pp. 328–329).[38] The value of the pension at retirement was to be based on the number of years of insured coverage and on the wage of the worker relative to the average wage in the year in which that wage was earned.[39] To the extent that the overall German standard of living continued to improve over the years, pensioners were expected to share in these improvements. To this end this legislation called for the annual indexation of future pension benefits. The legislation did not explicitly specify how this indexation was to be done, but in practice it has been based on changes in (gross) wage levels.

In 1972 several important pension policy reforms were introduced. Provisions were added making it possible for those with 35 or more years of coverage to retire early (at age 63) with full pension benefits (Steinmeyer 1991, p. 76).[40] Voluntary coverage was extended to the self-employed. This added many in the middle class who had not previously been covered. They were allowed into the program on very desirable terms; for example, they were able to purchase entitlements retrospectively at very attractive rates (Baldwin 1990a, p. 10).[41] Another important aspect of this legislation was that housewives were allowed to participate in the program (Eska 1980, p. 111). This innovation was important as it was the first time there was a departure from the principle that entitlement is to be based on participation in the paid labor force (Esping-Andersen et al. 1988, p. 342). Yet another important innovation introduced in 1972 was a change in the way that pensions were calculated for low-wage workers who had been covered for 25 or more years. If the pension benefit fell below a specified level, such workers were allowed to substitute a wage figure of 75 percent of the average wage during this period. This created something like a minimum wage benefit (Alber 1988, p. 23).[42] It also represented a major step away from the principle that benefits should as far as possible be market conforming.

During the postwar years we find the Social Democrats (SPD) typically positioning themselves to the left of the Christian Democrats (CDU/CDS) in connection with various pension reform proposals. This was very much the case with the Pension Reform Act of 1957. The CDU pushed for pension benefits in the range of 50 percent of pre-retirement income as opposed to the 75 percent range being advocated by the SPD; but support for this legislation was strong among the CDU, particularly the labor wing of the CDU, as well as the SPD (Tomasson 1984, p. 224).

The support for increasing old-age pension levels has been so pervasive during the postwar era that it would be very difficult to make the case that these increases represent victories for labor unions or the SPD. While these groups did support increases, the support was much broader with much of the increase and many important liberalizing reforms coming during periods when the CDU were in power and thus in a particularly strong position to influence policy.

The pension reforms of 1957 and 1972, as with all major public pension legislation during the postwar period, were the products of *grand coalitions*. There is a recognition that frequent shifts in pension policy due to changes in administrations would be undesirable. To assure continuity between administrations a compromise is worked out by the partners to the grand coalition that is acceptable to all. This means that opposition parties have more influence than would otherwise be the case, but they in turn are expected to support the policy if they find themselves in power within a few years. All parties share in the credit when the reforms are popular and share in the blame when choices must be made that may be unpopular.

Since the end of World War II there has been a substantial increase in the proportion of the population covered and in the proportion of the national income spent on public pensions.[43] In 1949 only 66 percent of the work force was covered; by the mid 1980s virtually all private sector employees were covered. Most employees not covered by one of the two major programs are covered by one of the separate programs for miners, public officials, and farmers. Many of the self-employed remain uncovered, but some are covered by compulsory privately financed pension programs administered by their professional associations (International Benefits Information Service 1989a). Between 1949 and 1978 the size of the average benefit as a percent of the wage of an average worker increased from 27 to 72 percent, and the combined employer and employee contribution to finance the scheme increased from 10 to 19 percent of wages (Katzenstein 1987, p. 188). The proportion of the German gross domestic product (GDP) spent on public pensions increased to 9.7 percent by 1960 and to 11.8 percent by 1985 (OECD 1988a, pp. 138–140).[44]

While there have been a number of important changes in German pension legislation since 1889, there has been a remarkable degree of continuity between the original scheme and current policy: (1) Today, as in the original legislation, there is no retirement test or means test for persons who have reached the normal age of retirement, although the normal retirement age has decreased from 70 to 65.[45] (2) Both contributions and benefits continue to be strongly earnings related, although the contributions are much higher and the benefits much greater today.

The combined contribution has increased from 1.7 percent in the original legislation to 18.7 percent in 1989 (*International Benefit Guidelines* 1989, p. 95). (3) Both employers and employees continue to contribute equal amounts. (4) Program administration continues to be decentralized and carried out by committees made up of both employers and employees (Alber 1988, p. 6). (5) The program is still financed on a pay as you go basis with the implicit contract between generations inherent in such financing mechanisms. (6) There continue to be subsidies from general revenues. Today the government provides a 14 percent annual subsidy to the pension program (Federal Minister of Labour and Social Affairs 1989, p. 57). (7) Today as in the past the pension scheme involves very little income redistribution between classes (Kaim-Caudle 1973, p. 138).

While there has been a great deal of continuity in German old-age pension legislation during the past 100 years, there have also been a number of important reforms; for example, those relating to benefits for women:[46] (1) In 1977 legislation was enacted specifying that in the event of divorce pension credits earned by both husband and wife during the marriage are to be split evenly. (2) In 1972 participation in the wage earner's public pension program was extended to homemakers on a voluntary basis with the size of the eventual benefit being a function of the contributions made over the years (Eska 1980, p. 111). (3) Women are now eligible to retire at age 60 if they have been covered for at least 15 years. (4) In 1984 the qualifying period for old-age pensions at age 65 was reduced to five years. This was another provision designed primarily for women with little or no experience in the paid labor force. (5) In addition, mothers were given one year of pension credit for each child.[47] Those who had raised fewer than five children could make up the difference by making voluntary contributions into the program for a few years.[48] While the German pension program has a number of provisions designed to respond to the special needs of women, it is of note that there is no special spouse or couples benefit (as in the United States) and no universal pension (as in Sweden). The lack of such provisions has negative implications for single-earner households.

The German pension system is set up in such a way that benefits are computed on the basis of an adjusted average wage and the length of time contributions have been made. Depending on the category of pensioner (e.g., age, gender), different amounts of time are required to qualify for these benefits. A distinctive aspect of the German program is the use of *substitute periods* that can be counted toward the time needed to qualify.[49] This includes time in the military service, time as a student at the university or in an apprenticeship, periods of illness, pregnancy, or rehabilitation, and periods of unemployment (Eska 1980, p. 112).

In late 1989 the most important reform in West German pension legislation since 1957 was enacted.[50] Like the 1957 legislation it was the product of a grand pension coalition. The changes outlined below began to be implemented in 1992.

The most important change is the shift in the way in which pensions will be indexed. The new procedure will be less generous and will result in lower pensions than would have resulted were the old procedure continued. It is not that pensions will actually be reduced, rather the size of the annual adjustments will be reduced. As German wages increase in the years ahead, only a portion of the increase in gross wages will be reflected in the annual pension adjustments. Rather than being based on gross wages they will be based on net wages (after taxes and social insurance contributions) (Greza 1989, p. 3).

The rational for this shift is that the present practice of using gross rather than net wages in the annual indexation has allowed pensioners to more than keep pace with increases in the German standard of living (Bundesministerium für Arbeit und Sozialordung 1988, Table 7.11). It has actually led to a more rapid increase in disposable income for the retired than for those still in the labor force.[51]

There is a great fear of the long-term consequences of this trend as the German population continues to age in the years ahead (Roland 1989, p. 3).[52] It has been estimated that today there are two people in the labor force for each pensioner and that if present trends were to continue there would be approximately one person in the labor force for each pensioner in the year 2030 (Greza 1989, p. 3; Juttemeier and Peterson 1982, p. 190).[53] According to German government projections between 1990 and 2030 the population age 20 to 60 (the active labor force) will decline in absolute size by 32 percent and the population age 60 and over will increase by 45 percent (Federal Minister of Labour and Social Affairs 1990, p. 5).

The shift to a less generous indexing procedure will help deal with this impending demographic burden. As the tax rate is increased to pay for these pension benefits, the worker's net (disposable) income will be reduced. By basing the annual indexation on net income, the size of the adjustment is reduced. This results in a sharing of the burden between the generations. Those in the labor force will be forced to pay a larger share of their income in old-age pension contributions, while pensioners will be faced with lower annual adjustments. At the same time that workers are paying higher social security taxes and pensioners are getting less generous adjustments, the federal government will be increasing its contribution to the cost of these pensions. Thus there will be a three-way sharing of the burden.

Another important reform in the 1989 legislation is that it increases the child-raising period from one to three years (Hinrichs 1991, p. 34). After the birth of a child one of the child's parents (usually the mother) will be able to leave the labor force for up to three years and be credited with the time and with having earned 75 percent of the average wage for the purposes of the eventual pension calculation. The legislation also specifies that care-providing periods can be taken off for other purposes such as providing care to an elderly parent. In this situation it is not assumed that the care-provider was earning 75 percent of the average wage for pension purposes, but the time does count toward the time required to become eligible for a pension.

The new legislation allows workers to retire up to three years prior to the normal age of 65, but with a reduction in the size of the pension benefit paid of 3.5 percent per year for each year early the pension is taken. At present men who have been contributing for 35 years can retire as early as age 63 without any penalty (Kohli and Rein 1991, p. 12). This lower limit will be gradually increased to age 65 starting in the year 2001 (Steinmeyer 1991, p. 83). Women are presently allowed to retire at age 60 with no penalty, and this lower limit will also be gradually increased to 65. Another important innovation is the introduction of partial pensions. Workers now have the option of withdrawing from the labor force gradually and getting a partial pension during this period.

Accounting for Developments in Germany

Any attempt to account for the emergence of old-age pensions at the end of the nineteenth century must emphasize a number of the same factors that would be used to account for the emergence of the German social insurance programs more generally. In this context one would mention a number of changes that were starting to undermine traditional family support mechanisms, in particular the process of industrialism, the trend toward wage dependency, and the concentration of the population in urban areas (Zöllner 1982, p. 80). Also important was the decline in mortality rates and the increase in the number of old people due to advances in public health and agricultural productivity (Pachter 1978, p. 20; Passant 1959, p. 80). By 1900, 4.9 percent of the population was age 65 or over (Laslett 1985, p. 217).[54]

Germany's severe depression of the 1870s was also a factor as it contributed to Bismarck's fear that liberal capitalism was leading to social disintegration (Kohli 1987, p. 132). He viewed his social insurance programs as a way to stabilize the situation and reintegrate workers who had been uprooted by the nation's very rapid pace of industrialization (Katzenstein 1987, p. 171). By the end of the century Germany was one of the major industrial nations of the world. It had the need and the resources for an old-age pension system. It is entirely consistent with the industrialism perspective that Germany introduced a pension program late in the nineteenth century.

The evidence that organized labor and leftist political parties were not influential in the formulation of the original pension legislation is also consistent with the industrialism perspective. But Bismarck did introduce old-age pensions and other social insurance programs as part of an effort to undercut the growing political influence of the socialists. Thus, contrary to the political tenets of the industrialism perspective, there is evidence that politics, at least in this sense, did play an important role in connection with enactment of the original old-age legislation. Furthermore, the theory as it is generally interpreted does not offer a good explanation for why Germany introduced its scheme prior to Britain, a nation that was substantially more industrialized than Germany at the time (Clark 1957, pp. 130–132, 138–141).[55] The example of Britain tends to undercut the case for explaining this early stage of pension policy development entirely in terms of industrialization and the correlates of industrialization.

How do we account for why Germany introduced its pension program prior to Britain? Germany had an etatist tradition of authoritarian intervention with respect to economic and social welfare policy. The bourgeoisie and laissez-faire ideology were less influential in Germany due in part to its more recent and less developed capitalist industrialization. In Germany the political-administrative elite (high level civil servants) had more influence. Also Germany had a greater need for policies that would promote national integration given its status as a new nation (Kohli 1987, p. 132; Schmidt 1989, pp. 57, 89).

One of the most important influences on pension policy during the post-World War II era has been Germany's economic growth (Esping-Andersen et al. 1988, p. 342). During this period Germany has had the most dynamic economy in Europe.[56] This growth has provided the economic resources needed to finance these structural reforms and spending increases. During the late 1970s and early 1980s, however, the German economy ran into problems. The oil crisis of the 1970s led to serious problems with inflation and near zero economic growth for several years (Alber 1988, p. 114). These economic problems put the nation's social insurance scheme in deficit. In response to these economic problems and their consequences for the pension funds, a number of changes were made in the way pensions were calculated and in the ways in which the annual pension adjustments were made. The annual adjustments were postponed for half a year in 1977 and again in 1982 (Zeiter 1983). Between 1977 and 1983 several changes were also made in the way in which the basic pension entitlement was computed (Alber 1988, p. 120). All these policy changes had the effect of reducing pension benefits below what they would have otherwise have been and thus amounted to benefit cuts.

A second factor has been the dramatic change in age structure. In the short period between 1950 and 1986 the proportion of the population age 65 and over increased from 9.4 to 15.1 percent (OECD 1988a, p. 33; 1988b, p. 11). This increased the number of people in need of benefits and contributed to political support for spending on these pensions. However, the cutbacks in future benefits enacted in the pension legislation of 1989 are also in large measure due to the impact of demographic change. While total spending on public pensions will continue to grow due to increasing numbers of pensioners, steps are being taken to reduce the size of these pensions in an effort to contain the magnitude of the spending increase. There is a great deal of concern about the adverse consequences of the trend with respect to the size of the pensioner population relative to the size of the active labor force.

Another factor that has had a major impact on spending trends has been the marked increase in the proportion of workers taking early retirement and electing to start benefits prior to the standard retirement age. Between 1962 and 1985 labor force participation rates for males aged 55 to 64 decreased from 83 to 58 percent (OECD 1988a, p. 144).[57] The proportion of pensions drawn at the regular retirement age of 65 decreased from 96 percent in 1960 to 62 percent in 1980 (Alber 1988, p. 45). These trends and their implications for the future old-age dependency burden are one reason that the 1989 legislation has a provision that will gradually increase the minimum age of retirement without penalty from age 63 to 65 for men and from 60 to 65 for women (Federal Minister of Labour and Social Affairs 1990, pp. 11–12). It is also one of the reasons for introducing the partial pension.

The social democratic perspective is of relatively little use in accounting for the decision to introduce a public pension program in 1889.[58] The program was not backed by organized labor or the Social Democratic Party. It was not a response to pressure for such legislation from the unions or parties representing the interests of the working class. While it did offer modest benefits to many German workers, the goal was to keep the socialists from obtaining sufficient working-class support to put them in a position to demand much more redistributive policies.

While much of the evidence concerning the introduction of the German pension program cannot be easily explained using the social democratic perspective, it does not necessarily contradict the theory. For example, based on this perspective we might have expected a nation with a strong social democratic party to have enacted a highly redistributive pension program and a nation with a weak social democratic party to enact a highly market-conforming program, which is what Germany did. Although Bismarck was not responding to direct pressure from labor or the Social Democrats to enact pension legislation, he was responding to the growing influence of the socialists and the urban working class. While his objective was social control, the approach did increase state spending on the social programs for the working class.

While organized labor and the Social Democrats advocated liberalization of public pension policies and benefits during the post-World War II era, such policies were supported by all political parties making it difficult to account for postwar developments on the basis of the social democratic perspective. Although both the Social Democrats and the Christian Democrats backed liberalizing reforms during this period, the Social Democrats tended to offer more generous reforms. In this sense their presence and influence probably resulted in more generous pension policies than would have been the case if the Christian Democrats did not have to be concerned about the Social Democrats.[59]

In its simplest form the social democratic thesis would attribute the increase in spending levels and progressive reforms to the influence of organized labor, the Social Democratic Party, and the working class. However, an alternative and more convincing interpretation is that these reforms in large measure reflect a change in the level of middle-class support for pension policy reform; that is, these reforms reflect a change of view by a large segment of the middle class that had come to view such reforms as in its own best interest (Baldwin 1990a, pp. 11–12).

While organized labor has not had as much influence on public pension policy in Germany as it has had in Sweden, it has had more influence on policy than in countries like the United States with very weak labor movements. Labor leaders are always consulted in connection with major pension reforms and have often been among the major actors in the formulation of policy, particularly during the Social Democratic Party administrations. Much of labor's influence has come from the inclusion of representatives of labor on the corporatist administrative boards that oversee the various pension programs. While labor has definitely had influence during the postwar era, it has not been a dominant actor as it has not had the power to impose its views and policy preferences on other key actors such as the powerful business interests.

In 1985 Germany was spending approximately 11.8 percent of its GDP on public pensions (OECD 1988a, p. 11). This was substantially above average for the industrial nations.[60] However, this high ranking with respect to spending would not have been predicted based on the strength of labor of leftist political parties.

In comparative studies that have been done among the industrial nations, Germany is generally ranked near the middle with respect to various measures of union strength and low with respect to measure of socialist control of the government during the postwar period (Myles 1984, p. 87; Stephens 1979, p. 118).

Spending level, however, is only one measure of pension adequacy. Another way to assess a nation's public pension system is by analyzing a variety of structural characteristics of the scheme. Myles (1984, p. 87) presents evidence that can be used to compare the German scheme with that in a number of other industrial nations using an index of what he refers to as *pension quality*. His measure is an index based on eight structural characteristics such as the size of the maximum pension paid to the lowest paid workers, the percent of the population covered by the pension scheme, and the degree of flexibility in retirement age. On the basis of these and other such structural characteristics, Germany is ranked toward the bottom of the distribution along with the United States and Britain. More recently Esping-Andersen (1990, p. 50) has ranked the industrial nations with respect to *de-commodification*, a measure of the extent to which a nation's pension program is based on universal rights of citizenship as opposed to being market conforming. With this measure we again find Germany ranked closer to Britain and the United States than to highly ranked Sweden.[61] These lower rankings are more consistent with the data on union and Social Democratic strength.[62]

Bismarck's reasons for introducing old-age pensions were in many respects consistent with a neo-Marxist perspective. The effort to undercut the political influence of the socialists and of organized labor, to give workers a greater stake in the political and economic status quo, to maintain social order and control, and to legitimize the state are all consistent with neo-Marxist analysis (O'Connor 1973). The reference to the social control function of public pensions makes the neo-Marxist perspective more useful than either the social democratic perspective or the industrialism perspective in accounting for why Germany introduced its old-age pensions system several years prior to Britain.

Over the years there has been a great deal of debate as to whose interests Bismarck's social insurance legislation was designed to serve. One theory is that his social policies were introduced to preserve the position of the traditional landed elite (Rimlinger 1971, p. 114; Bonham 1984, p. 210). The evidence of Junker opposition to Bismarck's social insurance legislation would seem to contradict this interpretation, however (Steinmetz 1990, p. 265). A second theory is that his primary concern was to increase the power of the state incumbents, that is, the influence of the monarchy and the civil service (Skocpol 1979, p. 106). A third theory is that such policies were designed to promote the interests of the nation's industrial elites (Blackbourn and Eley 1984).

Steinmetz (1990) outlines a theory and presents evidence that in effect combines the second and third of these theories. He argues that Bismarck pursued policies that favored the interests of the nation's industrialists because it seemed to be the best way to achieve his goals. This evidence supports a neo-Marxist "class correspondence" interpretation of Bismarck's social insurance legislation. Class correspondence theorists argue that the state while formally autonomous makes policy decisions that are in the interest of capital. There is a great deal of work in this tradition that traces how the dominant class controls the state indirectly. Some argue that at some earlier point in time the dominant class was able to structure state institutions in such a way that they tend to favor its interests. Another argument is that the state is dependent on the dominant class for the resources needed to carry out state activities. Unless the state acts in ways that favor big business, the economy will falter, reducing the flow of tax revenues the state depends on.

In the case of the German Empire Bismarck was concerned about social stability and maintaining a strong army. To these ends he needed the economic resources that rapid industrialization would provide. Social insurance programs were being called for by the leaders of heavy industry as a way to help pacify workers and to deal with the growing burden of industrial accident liability costs (Zöllner 1982, p. 23). These programs were viewed as central to the nation's industrialization effort. Industrialization was seen as a way to reduce unemployment and at the same time to build the infrastructure for a powerful military machine. This line of analysis adds up to the neo-Marxist class correspondence thesis, but with a twist that brings in the state-centered perspective. The state is seen as highly dependent on private industry and acting in the interest of the industrial bourgeoisie, but the reason for the state's action was in the last analysis to further its own interests (Steinmetz 1990, p. 270).

It is less obvious that progressive reforms in pension policy during the post-World War II era can be adequately accounted for using explanations derived from the neo-Marxist perspective.[63] Clearly, a number of other factors such as economic growth and the graying of the age structure have contributed to the increase in spending on public pensions during this period (Hockerts 1981, p. 332). While the increase in spending on old-age pensions has helped to legitimize the postwar government, the spending increases were greater than would have been needed for the purposes of regime legitimacy and social control alone (Esping-Andersen 1990, p. 14). The increase in spending during this period is consistent with a neo-Marxist perspective, but this perspective does not offer an explanation for why Germany came to spend so much more on public pensions than did Britain or the United States (OECD 1988a, p. 11).

Germany is a country in which class-based interest groups have played a much more important role than have nonclass-based interest groups, but we have found the neo-pluralist perspective of some use in our analysis. The original pension scheme was designed with the interests of Germany's elites in mind. Nonetheless, the middle class was another influential interest group, and Bismarck was forced to make modifications in his original proposal so as to get the support of this group. During the post-World War II era class-based interest groups have remained important, but in addition we also see evidence of a role for nonclass-based interest groups as well. The strong support for progressive reforms in pension policy coming from both of the major political parties, the CDU and the SPD, reflects an awareness of the ever increasing electoral importance of the elderly due to the graying of the age structure. By 1984 more than 32 percent of the voters in Germany were elderly (Statistisches Bundesamt, 1986). With the aged constituting such a large fraction of the electorate, it was not necessary that they be formally organized to have a great deal of political influence around the pensions issue.

But given the size of the interest group it is not surprising that organizations such as the Reichsbund and the VdK (Verband der Kriegs-und Wehrdienstopfer, Behinderten und Sozialrentner) have emerged to represent and lobby on behalf of the interests of the elderly. While organized groups representing the interests of the elderly are not as large or influential as those in the United States, their leaders are consulted when major pension policy reforms are being considered.

As Germany was an authoritarian nation that was just starting to develop democratic institutions at the time its old-age pension system was being introduced, it would be difficult to make a plausible case that democratic pressure played a major role in the enactment of this legislation. The lack of democratic competition to effectively represent interest groups made enactment of the pension program easier than it otherwise would have been. Democratic pressure, however, did play an indirect role in that Bismarck was concerned about the growing electoral support for the Social Democratic Party, and he did want to undercut that support. Germany's much more fully developed democratic institutions during the post-World War II era do seem to have contributed to the progressive reforms in pension policies; it is clear that party competition contributed to the postwar spending increases.

Pension policy development during the era of the German Empire can in part be accounted for using explanations derived from corporatist theory; the same is true with respect to developments during the post-World War II era. But we would not use the same variant of corporatist theory for the two periods. For the earlier period we would use authoritarian corporatism and for the more recent period we would use democratic corporatism.

The German Empire in many respects fits the description of an authoritarian corporatist nation. Bismarck's goal was to use his various social insurance programs to minimize class conflict and to stop the polarization of society that was taking place along the class axis. The goal was to promote a more organic view of society in which workers felt a strong sense of nationalism and loyalty to the monarchy (Esping-Andersen 1990, p. 24). Bismarck wanted to use these social insurance programs in part to promote antisocialist goals and to a lesser extent to promote antiliberal goals.

The original pension program covered primarily blue-collar wage workers. In 1911 an entirely separate and in some respects more generous program was introduced for white-collar salaried workers (Alber 1988, p. 6). Over the years a variety of other separate pension programs were introduced for other categories of workers such as miners and farmers. This pattern of separate programs for different categories of workers is very consistent with a corporatist model of society. Such a structure is designed to reinforce a hierarchical and highly segmented view of society. The German public pension systems seems to have been set up with more of an eye toward the preservation of status differentials than toward market efficiency (Esping-Andersen 1990, p. 27).

The Nazi years represented a return to corporatism, a much more repressive variant of authoritarian corporatism than had been in place during the era of the German Empire. The experiments with corporatism in such countries as Germany, Italy, and Portugal during the 1930s, for obvious reasons, ended up entirely discrediting the ideas of the early corporatist theorists such as Manoilesco (1934) and Murat (1944). It is now clear, however, that the admittedly conservative ideas embodied in their corporatist theories were cynically adapted in an effort to legitimize policies ruthless dictators found expedient.

After the end of the war a number of democratic corporatist structures were established in Germany. In connection with all major pension reforms labor leaders were consulted. The German commitment to co-determination that permeated industrial policy carried over into the formulation of social policy as well. The administrative boards overseeing the various pension programs all included labor representatives many of whom were consulted in connection with proposed reforms. The corporatist structure of public policymaking in Germany gave labor a place at the table, but labor was not a dominant voice.

The major labor federations and employers associations participate in the making of national social policy; but the influence of labor in these arrangements is less than it is in more highly corporatist nations such as Sweden and Austria. In Germany labor's autonomy is restricted by the juridification of the labor movement. German labor legislation sets strict limits regulating how and when organized labor can exercise its influence; yet it also assures that labor will have influence.

When comparisons are made among the industrial nations with respect to the degree of corporatism, Germany tends to rank in the middle between the highly corporatist nations such as Austria and Sweden on the one hand and those with little or no evidence of corporatist structures at the national level such as the United States and Britain on the other (Pampel et al. 1990). However, it is of note that Germany is the most corporatist of the large industrial nations (Katzenstein 1985, p. 31).[64]

While Germany has had democratic corporatist structures in place during the postwar period, it has been a form of democratic corporatism that restrains the autonomy of organized labor in many ways. It is possible that the nation's moderate degree of corporatism gives organized labor more influence than in a country such as the United States that lacks corporatist structures, but less influence than in Austria and Sweden, countries with more highly developed corporatist structures. This is an issue we will return to explore in more detail in Chapter 9. Consistent with this ranking Germany tends to rank in the middle with respect to Esping-Andersen's (1990, pp. 49–50) measure of de-commodification[65] and Myles's (1984) measure of pension quality. But Germany's relatively high ranking relative to other nations with respect to pension spending suggests that there may not be a strong relationship between democratic corporatism and spending level.

The corporatist explanations we have just considered illustrate the utility of a state-centered perspective. There are also a number of other quite different arguments that are also state-centered; for example, the German case supports the state-centered argument that it is easier to get old-age pension programs enacted in countries in which there are well developed civil service bureaucracies in place prior to full democratization. The nation's highly developed civil service bureaucracy played an important role with respect to the emergence of old-age pensions (Schmidt 1989, p. 34).[66] Bismarck had the backing of a number of high level civil servants some of whom were strong social insurance advocates (Tampke 1981, p. 74; Hertz 1975, p. 360). Bismarck himself was a product of the German civil service and depended on other high level civil servants to design and implement his pension legislation. By the middle of the nineteenth century Prussia had a large, influential, and well disciplined state bureaucracy (Myles 1984, p. 33).[67] The acceptance of bribes resulted in immediate dismissal. Examinations were required even for applicants with university degrees. High level officials were typically appointed to serve provinces other than those they were from so as to minimize opportunities for corruption.

During the nineteenth century the push for democracy in Germany was to some degree blunted by the size of the civil service bureaucracy.[68] Middle-class workers with civil service jobs were generally supportive of the monarchy and less interested in efforts to increase democracy. As those in the civil service were working for the monarch, any major political change might cost many of them their jobs or result in unwelcome changes in their jobs. While the civil service bureaucracy was in theory controlled by the monarch, in practice it was becoming increasingly independent and powerful as Bismarck's own influence with respect to the nation's early social insurance legislation so clearly illustrates.

Conclusion

Industrialization and a variety of social and economic changes linked to this process created the need for public pensions and created the economic surplus needed to finance such pensions. Explanations emphasizing factors associated with industrialization can be used to account for why many industrial nations introduced public pension programs at some point between the late 1800s and the early 1900s; however, the industrialism perspective does not by itself offer an adequate account as to why Germany was the first industrial nation to introduce such a program.

In the late nineteenth century Germany was still a very new nation that had recently emerged from the merger of a number of formerly independent and autonomous states. This historical context and legacy magnified the perceived threat of the socialist movement. Bismarck did not hesitate to use repression, but he felt that it was also necessary to take positive steps to win the loyalty of industrial workers. The old-age and invalidity pension program was one of several social insurance programs Bismarck introduced with this Bonapartist goal in mind. The introduction of Germany's public pension program cannot be accounted for in terms of these social control objectives alone; there were a number of other important factors as well. But Bismarck's desire to undercut working-class support for the socialists was certainly one of the most important reasons that Germany was the first of the industrial nations to get a public pension program.

The rapid reemergence of the trade union movement contributed to labor's influence on pension policy during the postwar years; however, that influence was tempered by the emergence of a variety of bureaucratic structures and a corpus of labor legislation that assured labor a role in the formulation of public policy while at the same time circumscribing labor's autonomy. The structures of co-determination and the juridification of the labor movement contributed to the unique form that democratic corporatism took in Germany.

When comparisons are made with other industrial nations Germany tends to rank above average, but not at the top with respect to spending level on public pensions. Among the major reasons that it ranks above average are the nation's large elderly population, the trend toward early retirement, and the availability of resources provided by the nation's rapid economic growth during the postwar years. Its not being ranked higher can be linked to the nation's unique corporatist structures and the influence that state and business interests are able to exercise relative to labor within those structures.

We make use of arguments and explanations derived from several general theoretical perspectives, but find that the utility of each varies with the historical context. Between the end of the nineteenth century and the end of World War II the change in context was particularly dramatic. We make extensive use of the state-centered perspective in our analysis of both of these periods, but with some important differences. During the turn of the century period authoritarian corporatism and a version of the class correspondence thesis that can also be viewed as support for the neo-Marxist perspective prove useful. In connection with developments during the postwar period we make extensive use of democratic corporatism. Arguments linked to the neo-Marxist perspective fit better during the turn of the century period than during the postwar period. The reverse is true with respect to arguments linked to the social democratic and the industrialism perspectives. Democratic procedures, party competition, and interest group demands certainly contributed to the growth of pension spending during the post-World War II period. During the late 1800s, the lack of strong interest groups and democratic procedures made implementation of a centralized system easier than it was in Britain or the United States.

In our analysis of events surrounding the introduction of the original public pension scheme, we find arguments derived from the state-centered perspective the most useful, but those linked to the neo-Marxist perspective are also quite useful. In our analysis of postwar developments, we again find the state-centered perspective the most useful. At the same time we find those linked to the industrialism perspective of greater utility than recent literature would suggest. Germany's conservative welfare state tradition has had a major impact on the evolution of public pension policy. Of particular note in this context is the way in which the German variant of corporatism has evolved and continued to influence pension policy over the years.

3

United Kingdom

While old-age pensions came to Britain relatively early (1908), such schemes had already been enacted in many other nations, several even before the turn of the century (e.g., Germany, 1889; Denmark, 1891; and New Zealand, 1898). This suggests that factors other than industrialization must be taken into consideration in any effort to account for differences between nations with respect to the timing of the introduction of these first pension systems.

The British case is of interest for a variety of theoretical reasons. At the end of the nineteenth century it was a bastion of laissez-faire liberalism and it had relatively well developed democratic structures. This makes it a particularly crucial case for assessing the utility of the neo-pluralist perspective. Due to its position as the world's leading industrial nation at the turn of the century, the case also provides an excellent context for assessing the industrialism perspective.

In the analysis of early developments in Britain our focus is on two questions: (1) Why were public pensions introduced in Britain after rather than before Germany? (2) Why did Britain adopt noncontributory flat-rate pensions as opposed to the contributory earnings-related approach adopted by Germany? In our analysis of developments during the postwar era we attempt to account for Britain's shift from an emphasis on solidaristic policies during the early postwar years to an increasing emphasis on market conforming policies in more recent years.

We begin by tracing developments up through the end of the nineteenth century. This sets the stage for our analysis of events during the Edwardian era including enactment of the original legislation in 1908. Following a brief discussion of reforms enacted between 1908 and the outbreak of World War II, we turn to an extended analysis of developments during the postwar era. We conclude with a theoretical assessment of British pension policy developments. Throughout the chapter an effort is made to assess the relative influence on pension policy of various political parties, organized labor, big business, the state, and other key actors.

Developments Before 1900

One of the earliest British efforts at state-aided social insurance was a program introduced in 1833 to encourage prudence by providing annuities that could be purchased at the post office in small denominations (Hannah 1986, p. 5). The program was not successful as very few people bought these annuities.[1] Many of those most in need were unable to set aside the monies needed to purchase them. The strong opposition of private insurance companies and of the friendly societies was another reason for the program's lack of success.

When the issue of public old-age pensions began to be seriously debated starting in the early 1880s, this opposition from the friendly societies continued. During the nineteenth century many European nations had friendly societies, but in no country were they as pervasive and powerful as in Britain. The British friendly society movement can be traced back to the eighteenth century, but the most dramatic growth took place during the nineteenth century (Gilbert 1966, p. 165). Members were typically skilled workers, members of the working class with incomes that were sufficiently large and steady to allow weekly or monthly payments to the society in return for insurance covering funeral expenses and sickness. These societies included the more affluent members of the working class who were also most likely to meet the suffrage qualifications that until 1885 had excluded most of those in the working class from electoral participation (Dunbabin 1988, pp. 104–111).[2] This is an important consideration as it helps account for the strong influence this interest group was to exercise.

By the early 1890s a quarter or more of the adult male population of England belonged to one of these organizations.[3] While these societies were not established to finance old-age pensions, the sickness benefits to those diagnosed as suffering from "infirmity" gradually evolved into de facto old-age pensions (Hannah 1986, p. 6). Up through the 1880s the friendly societies continued to expand, but gradually the proportion of younger workers participating started to decrease.[4] This, combined with increasing life expectancy, led to insolvency for an increasing number of the friendly societies (Hay 1975, p. 45).

Throughout the nineteenth century the friendly society movement opposed state involvement in old-age pensions.[5] Leaders of the movement viewed government involvement in sickness insurance or even old-age pensions as a threat to recruitment efforts that were essential for the continued fiscal solvency of these organizations.

By the 1880s these economic problems led some social reformers, such as the clergyman William Blackley, to question the adequacy of friendly societies as a mechanism to protect the respectable working class from the stigma of pauperization in old age. In 1882 Blackley organized a pressure group called the National Providence League and appointed Lord Shaftesbury, a Tory political leader, as its president.[6]

In 1885 this group was successful in getting the Salisbury government to establish a select committee of the House of Commons to look into the possibility of establishing a program of National Provident Insurance against pauperism. This investigation focused most of its efforts on evaluating Blackley's proposal. The Blackley proposal was that all working men between the ages of 17 and 21 be required to contribute a total of £14 to an annuity fund. This fund in turn would be used to provide sickness benefits of eight shillings per week to eligible workers of any age and old-age benefits of four shillings per week to those over age 70 (Treble 1970 pp. 266–267).[7]

The committee met over a period of three years and in the end recommended against the introduction of any public pension system. One reason given for rejection of the proposal was that it was not considered actuarially sound. Another was that the administrative infrastructure needed would be too costly. These were arguments made by government administrators. Outside the government, opposition came from the friendly societies and private insurance firms, groups that did not want competition from government programs. The proposal was also opposed by the Charity Organization Society and some of the older craft unions (Ashford 1986, p. 178).

One reason Britain did not enact old-age pension legislation until 1908 was the strength of liberal free-market laissez-faire ideology. There was a tendency among elites to minimize the extent of poverty among the aged and to minimize the need for government intervention. Furthermore, there was concern that intervention would undermine such fundamental values as thrift, independence, and self-reliance (Ogus 1982, p. 165). A series of empirical studies conducted at the end of the century began to undercut some of the assumptions elites had been making about the pervasiveness of poverty and its causes.

Great Britain is unique with respect to the role that social science played in the development of its old-age pension policies. During the late part of the century we begin to see the emergence of empirical social science. Particularly relevant in this context was a major survey undertaken by Charles Booth in 1887 dealing with living conditions among the working class in London.[8] His study demonstrated that the prevalence of poverty was much greater, some 30 percent of the population, than had previously been estimated on the basis of the number of persons receiving poor relief. Poverty was particularly pervasive among the aged. In 1891 he reported that 38 percent of those age 65 and over were paupers (Heclo 1974, p. 162). He found that old age was the single greatest cause of poverty, accounting for approximately 30 percent of cases (Gilbert 1966, p. 192).

Ten years later Rowntree conducted a similar study in York and again came up with a high estimate of the proportion of the population living in poverty (Brown 1982, p. 190; Lloyd 1970, p. 25). This empirical evidence on the prevalence of poverty in general population and among the aged served to undercut the assumption that poverty was due almost entirely to laziness and moral laxity; it became evident that destitution was often linked to external economic circumstances and the hazards of everyday life (e.g., old age, widowhood, disability) over which the individual had little control (Hay 1975, p. 47).

Charles Booth also played an important activist role in the development of public pension policy in Britain. In 1891 he presented his first old-age pension proposal which called for a universal noncontributory pension for all citizens over age 65.[9] While the proposal was little noticed at the time, it would eventually prove very influential in the formulation of the Old Age Pension Act of 1908.[10]

Scholars disagree with respect to the role that organized labor played in the early development of old-age pension policy. There is general agreement that labor did have an impact, but some argue that the impact was quite limited (Pelling 1968). The impact of the several socialist parties that existed in the late nineteenth and early twentieth century seems to have been very limited. The Labour Party, which sought to represent the interests of the working class, had more impact than did any of the socialist parties, but even it did not play a major role in the formulation of the legislation or in its eventual enactment in 1908.[11] Each of these three categories of actors (organized labor, the socialist parties, and the Labour Party) deserves further analysis.

Before 1815 very few British workers were involved in union activity (Hunt 1981, p. 192).[12] Between 1799 and 1824 most forms of union activity were illegal, but the legislation prohibiting such activity was generally not enforced.[13] During the first half of the century union membership grew rapidly, but also fluctuated dramatically with shifts in the economy. Many workers were willing to be members of a union as long as they were not forced to face the consequences of going on strike, particularly during periods of high unemployment.[14] By the late nineteenth century labor unions were stronger in Britain than in any other European country.[15] This continued even as late as 1913 when 10 percent of the British labor force was unionized in contrast to 5 percent in Germany and less than 3 percent in the United States (Hunt 1981, p. 296).

One reason that the working class did not have a greater impact on early developments in pension policy legislation was the number of deep cleavages in the labor movement. Of particular note was the so called *labor aristocracy*, a term used to describe the most affluent workers, particularly those in engineering (workers responsible for building and repairing the machinery on which the economy depended), in the building trades (e.g., carpenters and masons), and those in various craft unions (e.g., printers) (Hobsbawm 1964, p. 272).[16] This labor aristocracy tended to differ from other workers with respect to life-style, income, and values.[17] In addition to being better paid, their pay was much more stable and they were better treated by employers.

Social historians agree that there was a certain amount of stratification among British workers, but they do not all accept the labor aristocracy thesis. Some who question the utility of this concept point out that it tends to underemphasize a variety of other factors dividing the British working class such as religion, gender, and region (Wald 1983, p. 161; Gray 1981, p. 63). Also this concept does not take into consideration the reality that for many their privileged position tended to diminish in old age. In addition, those who were members of the labor aristocracy were linked by extensive kinship networks with others in the working class who were not part of the labor aristocracy.

Prior to the emergence of the "new unions" in the late 1880s the term labor aristocracy for all practical purposes referred to those who were trade union members (Hobsbawm 1964, p. 275). It included the most affluent 10 to 20 percent of the working class and represented a somewhat better-off segment of the working class than did the friendly societies. It was common to group those in the labor aristocracy with shopkeepers, small employers, and office workers as members of the lower middle class (Hunt 1981, p. 277).

The existence of this labor aristocracy is often mentioned in discussions of why British labor did not play a more active political role during the late nineteenth and early twentieth century. This segment of the working class tended to be politically moderate (Hobsbawm 1984, p. 216); however, there was little evidence of revolutionary potential or even support for government social reforms from other segments of the working class either. The failure of Chartism[18] and the steady rise in real wages seemed to have contributed to political moderation among many segments of the working class. In addition, labor was not unified either ideologically or socially prior to 1914 (Thane 1985, p. 183).

Most trade unionists had much more confidence in using strikes and other job actions to get desired goals than relying on social reform legislation; this was true even as late as World War I (Brown 1982, p. 206). Voting patterns between the 1880s and 1914 do not suggest that working-class voters were strongly influenced by social reform issues (Thane 1984, p. 878). Voting patterns were much more strongly influenced by such issues as religion and sectional advantage than by class-related social and economic policy considerations (Wald 1983, p. 250).

There is evidence that some in the labor movement supported proposals for a noncontributory old-age pension system (Ogus 1982, pp. 177–178). But there were also many who opposed or at least felt ambivalent about government sponsored social reforms (Hay 1978, p. 2). This opposition was due in part to distrust of the state and the assumption that government social programs were designed by and ultimately for the rich at the expense of the poor (Pelling 1968, pp. 2–5). Frederick Rogers, leader of the National Committee of Organized Labour on Old Age Pensions, mentioned that at the turn of the century he found it very difficult to generate interest in his organization's old-age pension scheme even among those in the working class (Thane 1984, p. 888).

Various proposals for a government sponsored old-age pension were discussed by members of the friendly societies. While not everyone agreed, the dominant view at the end of the century was that public pensions were a bad idea. This more affluent segment of the working class felt strongly that self-help was socially and morally preferable. They were concerned about the increasingly intrusive nature of the government as reflected in various social reform programs (Thane 1984, p. 878). Members of the friendly societies were on many occasions urged by their leaders to oppose government pensions as they would undermine labor's struggle for higher wages. The preferred alternative was to raise wages to the point that workers would be able to provide for themselves (Thane 1985, p. 194).

The social democratic movement was slow to emerge in Britain (Ogus 1982, p. 168). The unions were anxious to gain respectability and legal recognition. While Marx did much of his work in England, it did not receive much attention there during the nineteenth century. One reason the socialist parties did not become influential during the late nineteenth century was the lack of support from the trade unions (Brown 1982, pp. 191–192). It was common for union members to support Liberal Party candidates rather than the candidate of one of the socialist parties; this was particularly true in areas where labor traditionally had been strong in its support for Liberal Party candidates.

In 1881 the Democratic Federation was formed, and in 1884 the name of the organization was changed to the Social Democratic Federation. In 1893 another socialist party, the Independent Labour Party, was organized. In the 1895 general election both socialist parties ran candidates, but none were elected (Brown 1982, pp. 179–184).

In 1884 a group of socialists formed the Fabian Society (Ogus 1982, p. 169). The Fabians called for a variety of socialist reforms through parliamentary methods (Fraser 1973, p. 128). While the organization never included a sufficient number of followers to constitute a significant electoral force, it did include a number of influential intellectuals, such as Sidney Webb and George Bernard Shaw, who contributed to a shift in ideological climate, a shift away from the strict liberal individualism of the nineteenth century.

The Labour Party was organized in 1900, but until 1906 it was called the Labour Representation Committee (LRC). It was founded at a conference attended by representatives of the main socialist parties and representatives for unions making up about half of the one million workers who were in labor unions at that time (Brown 1982, p. 198). The twelve person executive committee included seven representatives of organized labor and five representatives of various socialist parties. In 1906 the party controlled 30 out of 670 (5 percent) seats in the House of Commons (Brown 1985, p. 2). Apathy, suspicion of socialism, and a reluctance to shift away from long-established party affiliations all contributed to keeping the party weak throughout the Edwardian era (Brown 1985, p. 12; Parkin 1967).

In 1885 suffrage was extended to include a substantial proportion of working-class males (Dunbabin 1988).[19] Based on democratic theory we might have expected this increase in the proportion of the working class eligible to vote to have translated into pressure for a variety of social programs such as old-age pensions, but this was not the case (Heclo 1974, p. 162). Among the elderly and the general public there was little discussion of the need for public pensions. The debate was confined for the most part to a relatively small group of middle-class social reformers, labor leaders, and members of Parliament.

Developments in Britain at the turn of the century were in part the outcome of conflict among a variety of different interest groups. In 1898 Booth joined with others to form the National Committee of Organized Labour on Old Age Pensions, also referred to as the National Pension Committee (NPC), and in 1899 he published a pamphlet calling for a universal old-age pension (Gilbert 1966, pp. 192–193).[20] Its leaders were largely drawn from the trade union movement, but its funding during the early years came in large measure from the middle class, that is, Charles Booth and a few other industrialists-philanthropists such as the Cadburys. This organization spent the next nine years pushing for noncontributory public old-age pensions similar to those already enacted in Denmark (1891) and New Zealand (1898) (Hay 1975, p. 46).

However, there were other much more influential groups that continued to oppose the idea, particularly the Charity Organization Society, the insurance companies, and the friendly societies (Ogus 1982, p. 177). The insurance companies opposed such legislation because they viewed public pensions as an economic threat to the industry. Insurers feared that if public pensions were available, there would be less demand for life insurance and private pension insurance. As noted earlier, the friendly societies were providing de facto old-age pensions to members and viewed proposals for public pensions as a threat to their interests (Treble 1970, p. 269). The Charity Organization Society (founded in 1869 to coordinate private charity efforts) strongly supported the poor law approach in dealing with poverty in old age (Lloyd 1970, p. 15). This group feared that public pensions would undermine the values of thrift and prudence.

In 1899 the NPC started a major effort to bring its case to the general public (Stead 1909). They were successful in getting the Trades Union Congress (TUC) to pass a resolution that year calling for pensions as a right for all citizens and to agree to make pensions an issue in the next general election. But in the election of 1900 the working class was much more interested in issues related to the Boer War than in old-age pensions (Gilbert 1966, p. 160). In the one district in which pension policy was the major issue, the candidate advocating old-age pensions lost overwhelmingly (Heclo 1974, p. 169). In 1900 public pension policy was not as yet an issue of major concern to the general electorate.

Movement Toward Enactment

By 1902 the political support for old-age pensions began to shift. An important early sign of the shifting political climate was that the National Conference of Friendly Societies passed a resolution in 1904 calling for noncontributory public pensions starting at age 65 and by 1908 nearly all of the friendly societies were supporting the views of the NPC.

Why was there a shift in policy shortly after the turn of the century? One theory is that there was a change in thinking among political and business elites with respect to the need for an efficient labor force. Industrialists came to believe that if the nation was to remain competitive with other nations it was important that the working class be healthy and relatively content (Ogus 1982, p. 160). The studies by Booth and Rowntree provided evidence that there were serious health problems and widespread poverty among the working class. Such squalid living conditions were not consistent with an efficient, productive, and content labor force.

While the activities of the NPC were important, the single most influential factor in turning the tide in favor of public pensions was the increasing support for the idea from the friendly societies. The friendly societies had very practical reasons for the reversal of their stand on the pensions issue; many were on the brink of insolvency. They were no longer able to pay for the de facto old-age pensions that so many were providing to their members. Some of these societies had already become insolvent and many more were facing imminent insolvency. Enactment of a noncontributory national old-age pension scheme would provide needed pension coverage for their members and would allow the societies to survive. Given the huge membership of the friendly societies, this shift in position carried with it major political implications.

The pension movement had come to be dominated by the NPC by 1902. In 1906 and 1907 the committee organized a series of rallies throughout England and was able to obtain the support of 150 members of Parliament representing all political parties to push for enactment of pension legislation.

As late as the 1906 general election the Liberal Party had not taken a stand in favor of old-age pensions (Russell 1973, p. 65), but in that election 69 percent of the Liberal Party candidates stated their support for enactment of an old-age pension scheme (Thane 1985, p. 185). Soon after the election the Liberal Party took a position in favor of old-age pensions. A major reason for the shift was concern about the rapidly growing working-class support for the new Labour Party, much of it coming from districts that had formerly been strongly behind the Liberal Party.[21] Asquith believed that this old-age pension scheme would be an asset for electoral purposes (Wilson 1991, p. 199; Ashford 1986, p. 179). A few key Liberal losses to Labour candidates in 1907 by-elections did not go unnoticed (Fraser 1973, p. 142; Pelling 1968, p. 12).[22]

By 1908 the interest groups in support of old-age pensions were stronger than those in opposition. While a majority of the Conservative Party members abstained from the final vote, there were very few negative votes even from them.[23]

The Old Age Pension Act of 1908 was very similar to Booth's original proposal. It called for a means-tested pension of five shillings a week (which was now an even more modest sum than when originally proposed by Booth in 1891) to citizens over age 70 who had been residents of the country for at least 20 years.[24] Eligibility was to be determined by local committees which were required to exclude those who had recently been in prison or on relief. Benefits were only to be paid to persons of "good moral character."[25] These criteria were designed to exclude the "undeserving" and reflected the poor law distinction between the "deserving" and the "undeserving" poor. One historian has aptly described this scheme as being "for the very old, the very poor, and the very respectable" (Thane 1978, p. 103). While these modest pensions did not have much impact on the overall distribution of income (Hay 1978, p. 10), government spending on those over age 70 increased from £2.5 million to £12 million per year (Ashford 1986, p. 179).[26]

Why did the British decide on a noncontributory flat-rate scheme? Very little serious attention was given to the alternative of a contributory wage-related scheme. One reason was that bureaucrats in the civil service were persuasive in arguing that the administrative structure needed for a contributory scheme did not exist and would be too costly to initiate. More importantly, however, the noncontributory flat-rate approach was viewed as less threatening to the interests of the politically influential friendly societies which had their own contributory scheme. At the turn of the century Britain had much more highly developed democratic institutions than Germany making it easier for powerful special interest groups such as the friendly societies to successfully oppose proposals calling for contributory wage-related pensions.

While the 1908 pension legislation was influenced by the scheme that the NPC had been advocating during the previous nine years, this group was not entirely satisfied with the final legislation. It included some important limitations on eligibility that the NPC viewed as undesirable, such as the exclusion of persons who had recently been on relief or in prison, the requirement that pensioners be age 70 or over, and a very restrictive means test (Thane 1985, pp. 193–194).[27] While the NPC viewed enactment of this pension legislation as at least a partial victory, as did the coalition of Labour and Liberal Party members which acted as the chief advocate in Parliament, it was not viewed by ordinary citizens as a major victory. Most workers did not expect to live to age 70 and thus did not anticipate receiving much by way of pension benefits. Nevertheless, within a couple of years after enactment the program had become very popular (Lloyd 1970, p. 14; Pelling 1968, p. 13).

The Old Age Pension Act of 1908 was similar to the German scheme in that benefits were to be paid at age 70 and were set sufficiently low as to constitute little if any work disincentive (Morris 1988, p. 70).[28] Benefits were designed to deal with extreme destitution, not to assure reasonable continuity with a worker's pre-retirement standard of living.

However, the British plan differed from the German pension scheme in a number of important respects. The British plan called for a flat-rate pension benefit; that is, all pensioners received the same benefit independent of previous wage differences.[29] A second difference was that it was a noncontributory scheme, so neither workers nor employers were required to make contributions earmarked for old-age pensions; rather the pensions were to be paid out of general tax revenues.[30] A third difference was that the British plan included a means test (Gilbert 1970, p. 236). Only elderly persons with incomes below £31 per year (£21 to be eligible for the full old-age pension) were eligible for benefits (Hannah 1986, p. 16). Despite the means test this was not a program for paupers. Pensions were paid through the national network of post offices and were entirely separate from the Poor Law bureaucracy (Fraser 1973, pp. 142–143). A fourth difference was that the British scheme was centrally administered.[31]

The NPC dissolved soon after enactment of the 1908 Pension Act as was common with most turn of the century ad hoc single issue pressure groups. During World War I inflation sharply reduced the purchasing power of old-age pensions (Hannah 1986, p. 16). There was agitation for adjustments, but it did not come from organizations of the aged themselves. The pressure came from a variety of other sources. For example, in 1916 a new pressure group similar to the earlier NPC was formed called the National Conference on Old Age Pensions. It was made up of trade unionists, members of Parliament representing all parties, the friendly societies, and representatives of the Free Church Council (Heclo 1974, pp. 196–202). After much agitation by this and related pressure groups, pensions were increased to compensate for the rise in the cost of living that had taken place. One adjustment was made in 1916 and another in 1919.[32]

In 1925 a number of important reforms were introduced. An allowance for the wife of an insured worker was added to the old-age pension scheme. In the same legislation benefits for widows and orphans were added (Lloyd 1970, p. 138).[33] Also important was the integration of the old-age pension scheme into the British social insurance program (called National Insurance).[34] One of the most important aspect of this legislation was the introduction of contributory pensions (Gilbert 1970, p. 235). All insured workers made the same flat-rate contributions independent of differences in wages. Contributions were made by employers as well as employees and the government continued to make a contribution financed out of general revenues. The 1925 legislation specified that male employees aged 65 to 70 would be eligible for a flat-rate contributory pension that would not be means tested, while those over age 70 would continue to be eligible for a noncontributory means-tested pension.[35] British civil servants played a major role in shaping the pension policy reforms introduced in 1925 (Ashford 1986, p. 179).[36]

Postwar Policy Developments

British pension policy during the first decade or so after World War II was strongly influenced by Sir William Beveridge, specifically a 1942 report which has come to be referred to as the *Beveridge Report*.[37] This report had a major impact on the entire British social insurance system (Shragge 1984, pp. 27–34). The Beveridge Committee was set up by the British government in 1941 due in part to pressure from the TUC (Hay 1978, p. 3).

The *Beveridge Report* called for a comprehensive universal contributory social insurance scheme that would provide flat-rate benefits to the aged, widowed, disabled, sick, and unemployed (Beveridge 1942). The goal was an integrated social insurance scheme that would assure an adequate minimum of economic security for all citizens (Lloyd 1970, p. 289). Entitlement would be based on having contributed to the scheme for a specified period of time. The means test, which had become very unpopular with organized labor, would be eliminated.

The National Insurance Act of 1946, which was implemented in 1948, embodied most of the policy proposals outlined in the *Beveridge Report*, but some significant changes were made. For example, the original report had proposed a transition period during which there would be less than full benefits for the newly included. During this period means-tested supplements would continue to be available. This part of the original proposal was changed due to influence from TUC, the Labour Party, as well as pressure from civil servants and other newly covered groups (Baldwin 1990b, pp. 129–130). The final legislation provided full benefits to the newly covered without a transition period and without means-tested supplements.

Within a few years it became clear that the flat-rate approach was not going to work. Inflation, the graying of the age structure, and the easy terms on which the transition generation was included all conspired to make it impossible to provide an adequate pension financed by flat-rate contributions (Baldwin 1990b, p. 232). The benefits provided were so low that many of the aged were forced to turn to means-tested social assistance (welfare) benefits to supplement their old-age pension benefits. The Beveridge-inspired insistence on a flat-rate structure for both contributions and benefits was a major reason that so many pensioners ended up with such low pensions (Heclo 1974, pp. 255–256). The benefit levels were set very low so as to minimize the risk of serious inflation in the aftermath of the war. The flat-rate financing made it very difficult for the government to raise benefit levels because the associated increase in contributions would fall so heavily on low-wage workers.

From the outset concern began to grow about the cost of providing adequate old-age pensions to all persons of pensionable age. As a cost containment measure, a retirement test was included; to be eligible for benefits the worker had to retire from full-time work.[38] In addition, a small increment was added to the eventual pension for those who delayed pension benefits for up to five years (from age 65 to 70 for men; 60 to 65 for women).

With respect to electoral strength the Conservative Party and the Labour Party were very evenly matched during much of the period from the early 1950s until the late 1970s. One consequence was intense electoral competition around the old-age pension issue. During the early 1950s the focus was on increasing the size of the pension, not on structural reforms. In 1951, for example, the Labour Party raised the pension benefit only three weeks prior to polling day. In the 1954 election both major parties tried to outbid the other in connection with the pension issue. Between 1948 and 1970 there were seven general elections. In each election except the 1950 election there was a pension increase enacted during the election year or the year prior to the election (Judge 1981, p. 518; Kincaid 1973, p. 201). By the 1950s both major parties were very much aware that the elderly were a large and growing segment of the electorate (Beer 1965, pp. 340–344).

During the 1950s the Labour and Conservative Parties moved much closer to one another than they had been on a variety of issues including old-age pensions. It was a period during which class divisions were less salient than they had been and a variety of new pressure groups emerged. Many of the new groups proved to be more permanent than the transient associations of reformers active during the Edwardian era.

One of these new pressure groups was the National Federation of Old Age Pensions Associations (Beer 1965, p. 342). The National Federation made regular appearances before the ministries administering old-age pensions as well as before all of Britain's national parties.[39] It persistently advocated for increases in the size of the basic pension as well as for increases in benefits for the elderly in connection with the National Assistance program (Pratt forthcoming, chapter 5).[40]

During the 1950s it became evident that unless an earnings-related component was added the nation was going to end up with a system of old-age provision based on occupational schemes for the more affluent and public assistance for the less affluent (Baldwin 1990b, pp. 235–236). A way was needed to get a more adequate pension to low-wage workers without increasing the extent to which pensions were subsidized from general government revenues. In addition, an earnings-related pension was needed for many urban blue-collar workers to provide the coverage enjoyed by most salaried workers based on their occupational pensions.

In 1959 some important changes were made in British old-age pension policy. Particularly influential in this context were a group of academics including Richard Titmuss. They were successful in convincing first the Labour Party and eventually the Conservative Party that the traditional flat-rate contribution system was no longer workable and that this structural characteristic was a major reason for the low level of British old-age pensions. Titmuss and his colleagues were largely responsible for an earnings-based pension proposal drafted for the Labour Party (Shragge 1984, p. 87). The proposal called for some redistribution to those with the lowest incomes, but in general those who contributed more would receive greater pension benefits. The TUC was reluctant to accept the proposal having long been committed to the flat-rate pensions.[41] The original proposal was subsequently modified to include a "contracting out" option designed to protect the interests of the middle class who already had substantial pension rights linked to existing union and occupational pension schemes.

The Labour Party proposal was strongly opposed by the British Chamber of Commerce and other business-related interest groups. The opposition was particularly strong from the insurance industry which viewed the proposal as a direct threat to its private pension business (Hannah 1986, p. 56). Critics argued that the Labour Party plan would result in serious inflation, would discourage savings, and quite possibly would lead to the nationalization of the insurance industry (Heclo 1974, pp. 266–267).

While the most important labor organization, TUC, gave its restrained endorsement of the proposal, the union movement as a whole was not strongly behind it. Lack of unity was one of the reasons that organized labor was not more influential in connection with the 1959 legislation. It is also one reason that labor was less influential in shaping pension policy during the postwar period than in Sweden.[42]

The Conservative government felt compelled to come up with an alternative to the Labour Party's proposal. Their proposal was much influenced by Labour's proposal and also called for an earnings-related pension. It differed from Labour's proposal in that the ceiling on earnings for contribution purposes was much lower. Earnings below a specified limit were also exempted and as a result the proposed earnings-related pension benefit was lower. It too had provisions for contracting out as long as the alternative private pension would be at least as generous as the state scheme. The Conservative's proposal involved much less threat to the interests of private insurance companies. For these reasons the Conservative alternative received the backing of a variety of interest groups that had campaigned strongly against the Labour proposal. It was the Conservative proposal, not the Labour proposal that was eventually passed in the 1959 National Insurance Act and implemented in 1961 (Hannah 1986, p. 58).

The British old-age pension system became a two-tiered system with a fixed basic pension that was the same for all workers and a second earnings-related component; however, much of the revenue generated by the earnings-related component was used to pay for flat-rate benefits. Relatively little was spent on the earnings-related component which at the outset provided minimal, some would say token, benefits (Baldwin 1990b, p. 240; Hannah 1986, p. 57).

The current British old-age pension scheme is in large measure based on the Social Security Pensions Act of 1975.[43] This legislation, which was implemented in 1978, called for a much more substantial earnings-related component than was provided for in the 1959 legislation. It is of note that this scheme was enacted at a time when a Labour Party was in control of the government.[44] In contrast, the minimalist scheme of 1959 was enacted during a Conservative government. The state earnings-related component, referred to as the Earnings-Related Pension Scheme (SERPS), called for an earnings-related pension equal to 25 percent of the worker's 20 best[45] year's revalued[46] covered earnings[47] (Morris 1988, p. 81).[48]

The SERPS scheme set forth in the Social Security Act of 1975 provides a strong incentive for employers to "contract out" of the state scheme.[49] As a result the proportion of employees covered by private (occupational) schemes has increased from about one-half to about two-thirds of the work force (Hannah 1986, p. 59). When an employer contracts out of SERPS, the alternative private scheme must include a guaranteed minimum pension (GMP) that is at least as generous as the SERPS scheme; that is, it must provide a pension equal to at least 25 percent of revalued average lifetime earnings. The government pays much of the cost of indexation for the GMP after the worker retires and thus indirectly subsidizes these private pension schemes (Morris 1988, p. 81).[50]

The Social Security Act of 1975 included inflation protection for both public and private occupational schemes. Protection with respect to change in wages was added for pension credits earned prior to retirement. In addition, pensions would be adjusted for subsequent changes in wages (standard of living) and prices (cost of living) (Shragge 1984, p. 143). In the state scheme a provision was added providing special dispensations for persons who spend part of their working years caring for elderly (or disabled) relatives or children and as a result are in and out of the labor force.

The Conservative victory in 1979 resulted in a distinct shift to the right in British social welfare policy. In an effort to control expansion of the welfare state a number of cuts were made. In 1980, for example, a shift was made to a less generous procedure for the indexing of pension benefits. The original formula had indexed benefits on the basis of either increases in prices or wages, whichever was greater. The change was to base indexing on prices increase alone. As a result there is no longer an automatic provision assuring that pension benefits will keep up with changes in wage levels (standard of living) as well (Parry 1988, p. 161).

The Social Security Act of 1986 included provision calling for future cuts in the SERPS benefits. Over a period of 10 years starting in the year 1998 the benefit will be reduced from 25 to 20 percent of the worker's revalued covered earnings (Wilson 1991, p. 204).[51] Another important change introduced in the Social Security Act of 1986 was a provision making all company pension plans voluntary. Workers now have the option of substituting personal pension schemes.

Given the trend toward the contracting out option for the British pension system, it is appropriate to ask how the picture changes if we take into consideration spending on private pension benefits. Considering spending on public pensions alone in 1980, Britain (at 6.4 percent of GDP) ranked below Germany (8.3 percent) and Sweden (9.7 percent), but above the United States (5.0 percent). When we add in spending on pensions for government employees (2.0 percent) and for private occupational pensions (1.0 percent), the total comes to 9.4 percent for Britain. Again this is below the total for Germany (11.0 percent) and Sweden (11.2 percent), but above that for the United States (7.9 percent). Thus, Britain's relative position does not change when we consider this more comprehensive spending measure (Esping-Andersen 1990, p. 84).[52] It is likely that this private component will increase substantially for Britain in the years ahead.

The British social security scheme includes a flat-rate widow's pension payable to widows over age 55.[53] At the death of a pensioner the surviving spouse continues to receive the basic pension at the single person's rate. A widow is also eligible for an additional pension based on the amount accrued in her husband's

SERPS account. Widowers must, however, be over age 65 to be eligible for this pension. There are no special pension benefits for divorced widows.

As an incentive to defer retirement, the size of the pension is increased by 7.5 percent per year for each year (up to 5) that it is deferred beyond age 65 for men and age 60 for women. To be eligible for a full pension a person must have paid or have been credited with National Insurance contributions for 90 percent of his or her working life; however, a person can be credited for years not in the labor force if the time was spent caring for a child or for an elderly or disabled relative. The pension is reduced if based on less than 90 percent of working life and a person becomes ineligible if the percentage falls below 25 percent.[54]

In Britain, as in all industrial nations, spending on public pensions as a proportion of GDP has increased substantially since the end of World War II. Spending increased from 2.3 percent in 1950 to 6.7 percent in 1985 (Morris 1988, pp. 70–71; OECD 1988a, pp. 140–141).[55] Despite this increase, in a comparative study of wage replacement rates Britain ranks at the bottom among the 12 industrial nations considered. It ranked 11th for single workers and 12th for couples when the average old-age pension was compared to the average wage in manufacturing (Inkeles and Usui 1988, p. 285).[56]

Accounting for Developments in Britain

The emergence of old-age pensions in Britain was linked to a number of the same factors that were important in other industrial nations such as Germany. The demographic and economic changes associated with the Industrial Revolution came sooner to Britain than to Germany. By the end of the nineteenth century Britain was more urbanized and more industrialized than Germany (Clark 1957, pp. 138–141). An even greater fraction of the population was made up of wage-dependent urban industrial workers.[57] This being so, why do we find a public old-age pension scheme emerging in Britain almost 20 years after such a scheme was introduced in Germany?

Industrialization and the concomitant demographic and economic changes contributed to the eventual introduction of old-age pensions in both countries, but this set of related factors is of little use in explaining why pensions were enacted in Germany so many years prior to enactment in Britain. Similarly, differences in working-class strength do not provide an adequate explanation.[58] In neither country were unions or leftist parties a major factor. In Germany the Social Democrats strongly opposed the introduction of compulsory public pensions as did the friendly societies in Britain, at least until 1904.

Socialist parties were much slower to develop in Britain than in Germany. This is one reason there was less perceived need on the part of ruling elites to attempt to undercut these parties through the introduction of various social insurance programs. There is little evidence to suggest that the British old-age pension scheme was introduced as an antisocialist measure (Hay 1975, p. 47).[59] By the turn of the century, unions were becoming stronger and starting to support the public pension movement, but most scholars agree that the British labor unions and Labour Party had little direct impact on the 1908 pension legislation.[60]

In the late nineteenth century Britain had more highly developed democratic institutions than did Germany. As a result the various interest groups that opposed the introduction of public pensions, groups such as the friendly societies and the Charity Organization Society, were able to delay enactment much longer than would have been possible in the more authoritarian German state. Once Bismarck decided he wanted an old-age pension system, he was able to get the necessary legislation on the books much sooner than would have been possible were he prime minister of Great Britain.

It is possible that the same combination of the Protestant ethic and laissez-faire individualism that contributed to the early emergence of industrialization in England also contributed to an ideological climate that tended to counteract the pressures for public pensions generated by the industrialization process. The value placed on self-reliance was also strong in other European countries during the late nineteenth century, but it was particularly strong in England.

In Britain private philanthropy was much more extensively developed than in Germany. For example, in the early 1860s private charities spent more in London than was disbursed by Poor Law authorities. One argument holds that much of this spending can be accounted for in terms of interdenominational struggles among various church groups and friendly societies. A case can also be made that the emphasis on private philanthropy rather than public relief was quite consistent with basic ideological values such as self-help and individualism. Private charities went a long way toward meeting the basic needs of at least the more affluent workers. This reduced the pressure for universal social insurance programs in Britain. Social insurance was viewed as consistent with the paternalism of Germany, but it was viewed as less compatible with the strong British commitment to self-help and individualism (Ogus 1982, pp. 163–165).

Another factor that has been suggested is the nature of the legal system in Britain at the time. In response to the development of industrialism and capitalism, private law was highly developed compared with public law. The greater emphasis on and development of property law served to uphold the free-market system and protect individuals against the abuses of government power, but it also tended to discourage state intervention with respect to social welfare legislation (Ogus 1982, pp. 158–159).

Between the turn of the century and the end of World War II there was a dramatic change in historical context which had implications for the factors driving public pension policy. During the Edwardian era Britain was at the height of its power and self-confidence, and few questioned the philosophy of minimal state involvement in economic and social policy. It was also a period during which class stratification was particularly salient.

In the aftermath of World War II the nation was more supportive of state involvement in economic and social policy and class cleavages had been muted to some extent by the mobilization for the war effort. During the immediate postwar period organized labor was much more influential than during the Edwardian era.

The elderly had become an important electoral constituency courted by all political parties. During the Edwardian era pressure groups including those advocating on behalf of pensions were small and transient; after the war they tended to be larger and more permanent. Demographic trends were to have a much greater impact after the war than during the Edwardian era.

One of the most important pension policy trends during the postwar period was the shift from the solidaristic orientation of the 1946 National Insurance Act toward an emphasis on increasingly market-conforming alternatives. This is reflected in the shift from a flat-rate pension in the 1946 legislation to the two-tiered approach in 1959 and 1975. It is reflected in the greater emphasis on the earnings-related component in the 1975 legislation than in the 1959 legislation. It is also reflected in the efforts to reduce the size of the state subsidy of expenditures by the shift to a less generous indexing procedure in 1980 and the call in the 1986 legislation for a less generous formula for computing SERPS benefits starting in 2000. In the 1986 legislation workers were also given the added option of contracting out of SERPS in favor of a personal pension scheme.

The 1946 legislation reflected the increase in the political strength of organized labor at the end of the war. This strength was due in part to the cooperation of labor that the government needed in connection with mobilization for the war effort. Full employment during the war years also contributed to an increase in influence for the working class (Shragge 1984, pp. 52–53). In addition, the war experience increased public support for state planning and public administration (Dunleavy 1989, p. 286).

Due to a variety of factors including risk sharing the war tended to blur and minimize class distinctions (Goodin and Le Grand 1987, pp. 47–56). The war required massive state intervention in the economy and as a result made the idea of state intervention more acceptable during the immediate postwar years. It also made it easier to raise the tax monies needed for a more generous public pension program (Baldwin 1988, p. 124).

During the immediate postwar years all major political parties supported solidaristic social policies. The basic idea of a welfare state was accepted by leaders of the Conservative Party as well as by those of the Labour Party (Parry 1988, p. 221). It was supported by organized labor (TUC) as well as by the organizations representing the interests of business such as the British Employers' Confederation (Shragge 1984, p. 36).

Between the late 1950s and the late 1980s Britain experienced a shift away from the solidaristic orientation of the immediate postwar years. Why did this take place? One reason was the recognition that the flat-rate system necessarily resulted in a very modest old-age pension.[61] If the lowest paid worker was to be making the same contribution as the highest paid worker, the size of both contributions and pension benefits had to be modest. While this was not a problem for the most affluent who could provide for retirement through private means, it left a large number of low and middle-income workers unable to set aside additional retirement monies during their working years.

As the standard of living increased, the gap between pre-retirement income and the old-age pension increased. Eventually, the gap became unacceptable to the low and middle-income aged as well as to elected officials who were dependent on their votes. The Labour Party tended to favor more generous pension reforms, but by the late 1950s it was clear to both the Labour and the Conservative Parties that supplementation of the existing flat-rate scheme was needed.

The election of the Conservatives in 1979 resulted in a dramatic shift away from the previous era of support for welfare state expansionism.[62] The influence of the Labour Party went into decline and with it the influence of organized labor. Class politics was after a long hiatus again ascendent. The pressure groups representing the interests of pensioners, while still influential, seemed to be less able to influence public policy than they had in the 1950s.

Many factors contributed to the privatization trend of the 1980s. Among them was the poor performance of the British economy during the 1970s. Many people were unwilling to support increases in social spending while their own standard of living was falling. Second, as the decades passed the solidarity created by the mobilization for World War II began to fade and to be replaced with the traditional class cleavages. The government's inability to keep the economy strong tended to undercut the early postwar confidence in state planning and public administration and to increase support for privatized alternatives. A third factor was the political influence of Margaret Thatcher with her emphasis on cost-containment (Pratt forthcoming, chapter 6).

As noted earlier, the policy context of the Edwardian era was very different from that of the postwar period. The differences have implications for the relative utility of the various general theoretical perspectives we have been using in our efforts to account for pension policy developments. We now turn to an assessment of the relative utility of these perspectives during each of these two periods.

Industrialization contributed to the proportion of British workers who were wage dependent and unable to be self-supporting. The concomitant increase in national income also made it possible to finance an old-age pension system. While there is general support for the conclusion that the process of industrialization was an important factor behind the eventual enactment of old-age pensions in Britain, it is of note that it was only one factor. The industrialism perspective is of use in explaining why public pensions were introduced in Britain, but as we have seen it is of less use in accounting for the actual timing of the introduction.

One tenet of the industrialism theory of pension policy development is that political structures, movements, and parties have little if any independent impact. In the British case, however, politics was relevant in that the Liberal Party did expect the introduction of an old-age pension scheme to help stem the growth of working-class support for the newly formed Labour Party. Similarly, political factors such as the opposition of the friendly societies and other interest groups are relevant in accounting for why the introduction of public pensions did not take place sooner.

Britain experienced a substantial increase in spending on old-age pensions during the post-World War II era (Parry 1988, p. 171). This increase was made possible by the nation's economic growth and increasingly necessary by the graying of the age structure.[63] Approximately 25 percent of the growth in expenditures on pensions between 1960 and 1981 can be accounted for by increases in the size of the elderly population (Ermisch 1989, p. 27). Also important was the decrease in labor force participation by elderly men.[64]

The economic crisis of the 1970s was a major factor leading to the nation's ideological shift to the right and to policies during the 1980s designed to reduce spending on pensions. This evidence of a reversal in the direction of pension policy in response to changes in the economy is consistent with the industrialism perspective. The support for explanations based on the industrialism thesis is even stronger for the postwar period than it is for the Edwardian period; however, contrary to the tenets of the industrialism perspective, during both periods partisan politics had a substantial impact on policy.

In the late nineteenth century organized labor was stronger in Britain than in any other country in Europe (Thane 1984, p. 878). In view of this it would have been more consistent with the social democratic perspective had Britain introduced its old-age pension scheme before rather than after Germany. One reason this did not occur is that during the late nineteenth century many British labor unions, particularly the craft unions, were ambivalent about or actively opposed to the idea of public pensions (Ashford 1986, p. 178). Another reason is that there were strong cleavages within the labor movement. The more affluent workers formed a labor aristocracy that tended to have different values and to be more conservative on political issues (Hobsbawm 1964, p. 272). In addition, the labor movement was also divided by cleavages based on religion and region.

Nevertheless, organized labor did have a substantial indirect impact on enactment of the original pension legislation (Gilbert 1966, p. 448).[65] Of particular note was its indirect impact through the activities of an influential pressure group, the NPC. During the early years this organization was largely supported by grants from Charles Booth and other industrialists such as the Cadburys. But after 1901 the organization's survival became increasingly dependent on support from trade unions. The leader of the NPC, Frederick Rogers, was a trade unionist as were the bulk of the board members.

The 1908 pension legislation would not have been enacted when it was were it not for an increasingly well organized labor movement. In addition, the leaders of the Liberal Party were much concerned about the threat posed by the recently formed Labour Party. While it was small and had very little clout in Parliament, support among the working class was increasing at a pace the Liberal Party found alarming.[66] Members of the Liberal Party and to a lesser extent those of the Conservative Party viewed support for the original pension legislation as a means to undercut the increasing working-class support for the Labour Party.

Organized labor and the Labour Party had relatively little direct influence on Britain's original pension legislation; however, they had more influence on developments during the postwar era, at least up through the late 1970s. They had their greatest influence during the immediate postwar years, but even then that influence must he qualified as there was so strong a convergence of views at the time among all segments of society in favor of solidaristic social insurance policies.

As noted in Chapter 1, Castles and Mitchell (1990, pp. 19–21) classify Britain as a "radical" welfare state regime. The term is used to refer to regimes with relatively strong labor movements that are generally excluded from control of the government due to the existence of plurality electoral systems. These authors use this set of characteristics to account for why Britain spends a relatively small share of its GDP on public pensions.

Consistent with the state-centered perspective is the evidence that members of the civil service have been influential in the formulation of pension policy (Ashford 1986, p. 179). During the late nineteenth century the judgment by a few key members of the civil service that an old-age pension proposal would not be economically or administratively feasible was often grounds enough for its rejection. Members of the civil service have always been active in the formulation of British pension policy, and this was even more true during the postwar era than it was at the turn of the century. Over time policymakers came increasingly to depend on technical specialists when deciding what was possible and when assessing the consequences of policy alternatives. The impact Beveridge had on social insurance legislation in 1946 is well documented, but civil servants also played important roles in connection with the pension legislation of 1959, 1975, and 1986 as well.[67]

In cross-national studies of democratic corporatism in the industrial nations, Britain generally ranks toward the bottom of the distribution for the industrial nations (Pampel et al. 1990; Schmitter 1981; Wilensky 1976). This was a particularly apt characterization for Britain under the Thatcher government. However, there have also been some periods during which corporatist decision-making structures have been in place and have impacted public policy. They have tended to be in place during Labour governments and have tended to increase organized labor's impact on pension policy.

The mobilization of the nation in connection with the war effort led to the creation of corporatist structures which were still in place when the National Insurance Act of 1946 was passed (Beer 1965, p. 320). These structures facilitated enactment of a solidaristic social insurance program which included a flat-rate pension. By the 1950s the class solidarity of the war years had begun to diminish. The decade is generally not characterized as a period of corporatist decision making in Britain; however, the creation of the National Economic Development Council in 1962 ushered in a new era of corporatism (Panitch 1976). In the 1960s and 1970s peak associations of labor and business periodically entered into temporary tripartite agreements with government during periods of crisis (Dunleavy 1989, p. 264).

During the mid-1970s the nation was faced with an economic crisis due to the dramatic increase in the price of oil. The Labour government dealt with the situation by using corporatist intermediation. Representatives of labor, business, and government all played major roles in the formulation of social policy during this period. This included the design of the Social Security Pension Act of 1975. Organized labor was willing to trade moderation with respect to wage demands in return for pension reform and the promise of more generous future pension benefits (Parry 1988, p. 224).

During the postwar period the British experience can be characterized as one of episodic corporatism (Dunleavy 1989, p. 264). While corporatist structures did from time to time facilitate labor's impact on pension policy, these structures were never as well institutionalized as in Germany and Sweden. The peak associations of both labor and business were severely restrained by internal divisions (Coates and Topham 1980, pp. 94–113).[68] With the election of a Tory government in 1979 tripartism came to an end and it has not emerged since.

A number of interest groups played direct and indirect roles in connection with enactment of Britain's original pension legislation. We have discussed labor's indirect role at some length. Also of note in this context was the role that the friendly societies, the Charity Organization Society, and the insurance industry played in delaying enactment of the original legislation and the positive role played by the NPC.[69] Democratic procedures and interest groups thus had an inhibiting effect during the early stages of pension development.

During the post-World War II era, particularly through the mid-1970s, organized labor had a much more direct influence on old-age pension policy; but other interest groups also played an important role in the shaping of the National Insurance Acts of 1946 and 1959 as well as the Social Security Acts of 1975 and 1986. There is evidence that much of the pressure for solidaristic universalistic social policy in the immediate postwar years came from those in the middle class. They had traditionally been excluded from social welfare programs and they wanted to be covered (Baldwin 1990b, p. 112). Similarly in 1959 and 1975 big business, salaried workers, and the private insurance industry were influential in getting contracting out provisions included.

Also influential during the postwar period were organizations representing the elderly such as the National Federation of Old Age Pensions Associations (NFOAPA) and, more recently, Age Concern. The NFOAPA was formed in 1940. Over the years its membership increased to several hundred thousand. During much of the postwar period this organization was very active as a pressure group on behalf of pensioners. Before automatic adjustments were introduced in 1974, the organization was active in efforts to get the pension increased every few years. There is much evidence that politicians in all major parties courted the senior vote (Beer 1965).[70] During the 1980s pension benefits were cut, but they were modest in comparison to those experienced by a number of other less powerful social welfare constituencies.[71] By the late 1980s there were more than 20 different age-advocacy interest groups active in Britain, and relative to other interest groups attempting to influence government old-age policy elites, their influence was strong (Pratt forthcoming, chapter 6).

Conclusion

There are a number of reasons why Britain did not introduce its old-age pension scheme until almost two decades after Germany did so. Britain was not a new nation and it did not view public pensions as a potential vehicle for the promotion of national integration. Similarly, there was less fear of socialism and of the industrial working class. Britain had more highly developed democratic structures which in this case were utilized by a variety of interest groups including the friendly societies and the insurance industry to oppose the introduction of public pensions.

The existence of these more developed democratic structures is also a major reason that Britain introduced a noncontributory flat-rate scheme rather than a contributory earnings-related scheme. The contributory earnings-related alternative was never seriously considered due to strong opposition from a variety of interest groups, most notably the friendly societies.

One of the most theoretically important developments during the postwar years has been the shift from de-commodified flat-rate pensions toward increasing dependence on two-tiered and more market-conforming alternatives. The mobilization associated with the war effort temporarily blunted class antagonisms making it possible to enact solidaristic social insurance reforms in the immediate postwar years. Over the years the traditional class cleavages reemerged contributing to a reduction in support for solidaristic policies and to an increase in support for more market-conforming alternatives.

While the nation's level of economic development at the turn of the century made Britain ripe for enactment of public pension legislation, the industrialism perspective cannot by itself account for the actual timing of the original British pension legislation relative to that for other industrial nations. The postwar economic expansion and the graying of the age structure were major factors driving spending increases during much of the postwar period. Similarly, the faltering of the economy during the 1970s is a major reason for restrictive legislation of the 1980s. But the industrialism perspective does not help us account for the role of interest groups and partisan politics, nor does it help us account for the the trend from a solidaristic program toward a more market-conforming program during this period.

In our efforts to account for developments at the turn of the century the social democratic perspective was of limited use; however, it was more useful in the context of the postwar era. During the latter period it helps account for the solidaristic National Insurance Act of 1946 (a period of union and Labour Party strength) as well as the policy changes that amounted to benefit cuts during the 1980s (a period of union and Labour Party weakness).

The neo-pluralist perspective is useful for the analysis of early developments as well as postwar developments, but the impact of interest group activity worked in different directions during the two periods. In our discussion of the original legislation we emphasize the influence of the friendly societies, the insurance industry, the Charity Organization Society, and the NPC as well as the effort by the Liberal Party to use its enactment of pension legislation as a means to undercut working-class electoral support for the Labour Party. In our analysis of postwar developments we mention that various middle-class groups had a major impact on the National Insurance Act of 1946 and that the NFOAPA had considerable influence in connection with regular pension increments between 1950 and 1974. In addition, groups representing the aged had a part in keeping pension cuts to a minimum during the 1980s.[72]

The state-centered perspective is useful in connection with developments during both the turn of the century and the postwar periods, but we generally do not emphasize the same arguments. During the early period we emphasize the role democratic structures played in facilitating the successful efforts for so many years by the friendly societies and a few other pressure groups attempting to block the introduction of public pensions. For the postwar period we point to the role that corporatist structures (when they were in place) played in facilitating the impact of labor on pension policy. However, we do find that high level civil servants played an influential role during both periods.

Each of the general theoretical perspectives considered has been useful in accounting for at least some aspects of pension policy development in Britain. Explanations linked to the social democratic and industrialism perspectives and those emphasizing democratic corporatism have been more useful in connection with efforts to account for developments during the postwar period. Those emphasizing the role of democratic structures have been more useful in connection with developments at the turn of the century. Neo-pluralism turns out to be a very useful perspective during both of these periods.

One of our theoretically most interesting findings is the evidence that certain aspects of state structure seem to play a role in facilitating the impact that factors suggested by other theories have had on pension policy. During the turn of the century period Britain's democratic political structures facilitated the efforts of the friendly societies and other interest groups that were opposed to the introduction of public pensions. In contrast, in the years immediately following World War II corporatist structures facilitated labor's efforts to get solidaristic pension legislation enacted.

4

Sweden

In 1913 Sweden became the first nation to enact a universalistic contributory public pension program. It was the first of many Swedish public pension policy innovations introduced over the years. Sweden's position as a leader with respect to welfare state development makes its public pension policies of particular interest. Today it has one of the world's most generous and highly developed pension programs.

The Swedish case is also of interest for a variety of theoretical reasons. The Swedish government was controlled almost continuously between 1932 and 1991 by the Social Democratic Party, longer control by a socialist party than in any other Western industrial nation. In addition, it is one of the leading nations in the world with respect to the strength of organized labor. These characteristics make the Swedish case particularly relevant for assessment of explanations of pension policy development derived from the social democratic perspective. Sweden is also an important case for assessing the utility of explanations derived from the corporatist perspective. It is a highly corporatist nation, more so than Germany and much more so than Britain or the United States (Pampel et al. 1990, p. 541).

In our analysis of policy developments in Sweden we focus on three interrelated questions: (1) Why did Sweden opt for a universalistic pension as opposed to limiting benefits to the most needy (as in Britain) or to the working class (as in Germany)? (2) How influential were organized labor and the Social Democratic Party in connection with the formulation of Sweden's original old-age pension program and in shaping policy developments during the postwar era? (3) What role have corporatist structures played in the evolution of Swedish pension policy?

We begin by tracing events leading up to the decision to introduce a public pension scheme in 1913. We then consider pension policy related developments between the wars and review developments during the postwar period. We conclude with a theoretical assessment of the evolution of Swedish pension policy. Throughout the chapter we attempt to assess those structural factors and political actors which have been most important in shaping the evolution of Swedish pension policy.

Early Developments: Sixteenth–Nineteenth Centuries

During the Middle Ages[1] and even prior to this time the majority of the Swedish population was made up of landowning peasants (Hallendorff and Schück 1929,

65

p. 44).[2] Unlike Germany and Britain the Swedish peasants were never forced into serfdom; there was no full-fledged feudal period in Sweden (Olsson 1990, p. 43; Andrén 1961, p. 9). In 1523 shortly after defeating the Danes, Gustav Vasa was elected king by an assembly dominated by representatives of the nobility and the clergy; however, it also included representatives of the peasantry.[3] From the sixteenth through the middle of the nineteenth century the peasantry had little power relative to the nobility,[4] but Sweden was one of the few nations in Europe in which the peasantry was at least represented in the National Assembly.[5] In the 1840s compulsory primary education was introduced (Olsson 1988, p. 4), which not only increased literacy rates, but also facilitated political mobilization among the agrarian population.

By the end of the nineteenth century politics was becoming more democratic and as a result the middle classes were able to exert greater influence; given the rural nature of the Swedish population, this meant more influence for independent farmers (Baldwin 1989, p. 21). By 1908 the proportion of the adult male population eligible to vote had increased to about 60 percent (Scott 1977, p. 402). Electoral reforms in 1909 further extended male suffrage.[6]

Soon after being elected king, Gustav Vasa set up a national centralized administrative apparatus.[7] This evolved into a highly efficient professional corps of civil servants by the middle of the seventeenth century. More than two centuries prior to the development of modern democratic structures Sweden had a highly developed civil service. The early emergence of a professional civil service made it possible for these administrators to dominate political and social policy. The civil service generally recruited its high level administrators from the nobility and many of these high level civil servants in turn served in the Riksdag where they had a great deal of influence given their familiarity with the workings of the government bureaucracy.[8] By 1900 the Riksdag was starting to exert control over the nation's civil service bureaucracy; prior to that the control was often in the other direction (Anton 1980, p. 5).

The industrialization of Sweden was distinctive in that it was late, rapid, and highly concentrated in two major industries. Today Sweden is one of the most affluent and highly industrialized nations in the world, but that was not true during the nineteenth century when it was one of the poorest and last of the Western European nations to industrialize (Clark 1957). It is generally agreed that the industrialization process was well underway by the 1870s.[9] Although industrialization came late to Sweden, once the industrial revolution began, it progressed rapidly.[10]

In 1870 some 72 percent of the Swedish population were farmers; this was higher than in Norway (56 percent) and Denmark (46 percent). Even as late as 1900, 55 percent of Sweden's economically active population worked in the agricultural sector (Scott 1977, p. 440).[11] In 1900 only 28 percent of Swedish workers as opposed to 46 percent of British workers were employed in the manufacturing sector. Urbanization began in the mid-nineteenth century.[12] The proportion of the population age 65 and over steadily increased during the last half of the century from 4.8 percent in 1850 to 8.4 percent in 1900 (Laslett 1985, p. 217). This trend was due in part to the sharp reduction in birthrates during this period (Metcalf 1987, p. 167).

The nineteenth century Swedish economy was dominated by two major industries, both of which were export oriented. One was timber and related products such as lumber, pulp, and paper. The other was mining including such export products as iron bars, pig iron, and iron ore (Scott 1977, pp. 446–452). Both of these industries were widely dispersed in rural areas. This had important consequences for the emergence of the nation's industrial working class. Unlike Germany and Britain, in Sweden during the nineteenth century the industrial working class was widely dispersed in rural areas rather than concentrated in large urban areas.

Because the nation's two major industries were so widely dispersed and because the nation was so late to industrialize, trade unionism was late in developing relative to Germany and Britain. Organizations calling themselves unions had existed since 1846,[13] but trade unions in the modern sense did not come into existence until the 1870s.[14] The first national trade union organization, the *Landsorganisation* (LO), was formed in 1898 (Olsson 1990, p. 75). Due to the late start a relatively small proportion of the industrial labor force were trade union members at the turn of the century. In 1905 approximately 5 percent of Swedish workers were labor union members, about the same as in Germany and the United States (6 percent), but much less than in Britain (11 percent) (Stephens 1979, p. 115). When analyzed as a fraction of the industrial labor force, however, the picture looks somewhat different. By 1900 about one-fourth of industrial workers were union members increasing to two-thirds by 1909 (Scase 1977, p. 27).

At the turn of the century trade unions were feared and resisted by the urban middle class. The nation's industrialists and the urban middle class more generally were aware of developments in Germany and were quite threatened by the reports of violence and militancy on the part of organized industrial workers.[15] Their concern about the threat to the economic status quo was, however, out of proportion to the actual strength of the labor movement. Their fear was based more on concern about the trend in labor mobilization than on labor's actual influence at the time.

In 1902 LO called a three-day national suffrage strike. This militant action was one reason employers formed the Swedish Employers' Confederation (SAF) (Scott 1977, p. 415).[16] The SAF was designed to deal with and if possible suppress the union movement. In 1909 after a series of small strikes, SAF called a national lockout that affected 100,000 workers (Scase 1977, p. 27). In response LO called a national strike that affected 300,000 workers. After several months LO had to give in. It was a major loss for organized labor and resulted in a very substantial drop in union membership. While SAF won this battle employers came away from the experience with a respect for the damage that LO was capable of inflicting.

Sweden was late with respect to the development of formal political parties. The first political party to be formally organized was the Social Democratic Party in 1889. Some 50 of the 70 organizations that participated in the formation of this party were unions (Korpi 1978, p. 61). After 1898 the party was very closely linked to LO. As one indication of this, LO's original constitution required that its member unions affiliate with the Social Democratic Party and the party was allowed to appoint a couple of members to LO's board of directors. While these provisions were eliminated in 1900 due to pressure from a number of member unions, the very close association between LO and the Social Democratic Party remains to this day.

Soon after the Social Democratic Party was formed, several other political parties were formed, the Liberal Party in 1900, the Conservative Party in 1904, the Agrarian Party in 1913, and the Communist Party in 1921 (Board 1970, p. 32).[17] While formal parties did not exist in the late nineteenth century (except for the Social Democratic Party after 1889), members of the Riksdag formed groupings that for the most part corresponded to the parties that eventually emerged. In 1896 the first Social Democratic representative to the Lower Chamber was elected. In 1902 the number of Social Democrats increased to four. From that point on the number of Social Democrats in the Lower Chamber grew rapidly to 64 in 1912 and by 1914 while still a minority it was the largest single party in that body (Metcalf 1987, p. 198).

During the nineteenth century Sweden, like most other European nations, had a network of organizations similar to the British friendly societies. Membership in these organizations was voluntary and the dues paid was used to provide modest sickness and funeral benefits to members. A number of these organizations were disbanded when the guild system was abolished in 1846, but many survived. In 1884 there were approximately 140,000 members of such organizations (Montgomery 1939, p. 215).[18]

The Original Pension Legislation

In 1884 Adolf Hedin, a member of the Riksdag and a social reformer, introduced a motion calling for the formation of a commission to study what measures might be taken to provide accident and old-age insurance for workers (Heclo 1974, p. 180). As political parties in the modern sense had not yet been organized, Hedin cannot be identified as a leader of a particular party, but he was a leading liberal intellectual of his day, an advocate of free trade, of religious freedom, and of universal suffrage. In making his case Hedin included among his reasons the contribution social insurance would make to social stability. Members of the Riksdag increasingly were becoming aware of the economic hardships for workers that were emerging in the wake of industrialization. They were also becoming concerned about strikes and socialist agitation. Hedin was widely read and very familiar with the recent (1883) enactment of social insurance legislation in Germany.[19] While there was some of the same concern about possible political instability linked to socialist agitation and propaganda, the fear was not as strong as it was among German elites. This difference would be expected given the relative size of the urban industrial proletariat in the two nations.

The commission Hedin requested was established and worked for five years preparing a report delivered in 1889 (Kuhnle 1981, p. 128). The report concluded that there was a clear need for something more than the poor law to provide for the elderly, but there was disagreement among commission members as to what that policy should be. The majority proposal called for a flat-rate universal compulsory old-age pension scheme (Baldwin 1989, p. 17). The final version of the

German old-age pension plan was not available in time to influence the delibera-
tions of this commission; however, the earlier German social insurance legislation
did help to legitimize the idea of social insurance. The majority proposal called
for compulsory contributions by all workers between the ages of 19 and 28. Contributions were to be the same for all workers independent of differences in
income. Similarly, all insured persons would be eligible for the same pension at
age 60 independent of differences in past earnings.

As was the custom, the proposal was submitted for review to the provincial
governors. A few supported the idea, but most opposed it. Given this strong opposition and the lack of consensus among members of the commission itself, the
proposal was allowed to die without even being debated in the Riksdag (Tomasson
1984, p. 230).

This commission was to be only the first of several. By the early 1890s there
was an increase in concern about the possible disruptive influence of the Socialists and organized labor. Such concerns led Conservatives in the Riksdag and the
executive branch of government to be favorably disposed toward the introduction
of social insurance in some form for its pacifying effect (Heclo 1974, p. 183).

In 1891 a second commission was established to study the issue. The final report
was returned in 1895. This commission closely studied and was strongly influenced by the German old-age insurance plan. The commission's proposal called
for compulsory coverage for all employed persons except for supervisory personnel and employees with high incomes. Thus it was limited primarily to the working class (Baldwin 1989, p. 17). Contributions were to be paid by employers, but
they in turn were to be able to deduct one-half of these contributions from
employees' wages. The pension would start at age 70 and its size would be a function of the amount contributed. This proposal was also rejected. It is of note that
the strongest opposition in this case came from the farm block representing the
largest group of employers and a significant presence in the Lower Chamber of
the Riksdag (Wilson 1979, p. 6). They were concerned that farmers would be unduly
burdened with pension contributions for their workers and as supervisory personnel
would not themselves be covered.[20]

In 1907 yet another commission was established, this time by a Conservative
government, but when it reported back in 1912 a Liberal government was in power
(Heclo 1974, pp. 190–192). This proposal was enacted in 1913.[21] As with previous
commissions representatives of all the major interest groups were included as
members (e.g., a representative of the farmers, a leader of the Social Democrats,
a representative of the insurance industry, an industrialist, etc.). Members of the
commission analyzed the pension schemes of other nations. The existing schemes
could be grouped into two broad categories: (1) those following the German model
of compulsory contributory coverage for wage earners and (2) those providing
noncontributory means-tested benefits as in Britain.

A problem with the German approach, in the opinion of the commission members, was that too many people would be excluded, particularly those who were
independently employed (e.g., small farmers) and those not in the labor force.
One problem with the British approach was that the benefits provided by a noncontributory scheme would necessarily be very low; a second was that the means

test would exclude many who did need pension coverage. In an effort to incorporate the best of both approaches, the final Swedish proposal called for a universal contributory scheme. Everyone (both men and women) between the ages of 16 and 66 was required to make contributions. There was some progressiveness in the contributions schedule; those in higher income categories did make somewhat larger payments. There was no payroll tax on employers and no government subsidy (Tomasson 1984, p. 231). The pension benefits were actuarially linked to contributions and paid from the assets in a reserve fund the government created from these contributions. At age 67 pensions were paid based on total prior contributions. There was no means test or retirement test as a precondition for the receipt of these benefits. Commission members realized that during the early years the benefits would be modest, but it was also clear that over the years these benefits would increase.

Due in part to the way in which this contributory scheme was to be phased in over time and in part to a need for special coverage for those who had very low incomes, the commission also proposed a supplementary pension program to be paid for out of government general tax revenues. This pension provided for the most needy and those presently near retirement, groups for whom the standard formula did not generate an adequate old-age pension due to low prior contributions (Schulz et al. 1974, p. 73). This supplementary pension provided means-tested benefits which were gradually reduced for those with incomes above the level at which a full supplementary pension was paid.

Prior to enactment there was considerable debate about the merits of the proposed pension legislation both inside and outside of the Riksdag.[22] Most of the Social Democrats believed that the benefits were too low and that the income test associated with the supplementary pension was too stringent (Schulz et al. 1974, p. 74). Many Social Democrats argued that it would be preferable to make the contributions more progressive. A number favored employer contributions and limiting benefits to those in greatest need (Baldwin 1990b, p. 91). Others pointed out that it did not provide adequate coverage for those who were already old. While many Social Democrats were critical of the proposal and would have preferred a program more focused on the needs of their primary constituency, industrial wage earners, they did vote for it. While they were critical of the specific proposal being offered, they were never opposed to the introduction of a public pension system.

There was some opposition to the proposed pension program from those responsible for administering the existing poor laws; they correctly perceived that the legislation was designed to reduce the number of persons dependent on poor law relief. These relief workers argued that the proposed legislation would undercut thrift and self-sufficiency.[23] Many in the Conservative Party also feared that the scheme would undercut the market and create an undesirable sense of entitlement to state support among workers. Despite reservations of this sort, most Conservative members of the Riksdag ended up voting in favor of the proposal. It had support across the political spectrum. With a few minor exceptions this legislation covered the entire population; Sweden was the first nation to enact so comprehensive a system (Kuhnle 1981, p. 129).

Any effort to account for why an old-age pension plan was introduced in Sweden necessarily involves consideration of a number of the same factors that led to such programs in other European countries at about the same time. In Sweden as in Germany and Britain a major reason was the set of changes associated with industrialization, more specifically, the increase in the number of wage dependent industrial workers, the increase in the proportion of the population living to old age, the increase in literacy among peasants and workers, the institutionalization of increasingly democratic procedures for the formulation of social policy, as well as the rise of unions and a socialist party.[24]

While the pension plan was supported by the left, its enactment cannot be viewed as reflecting the political influence of this group (Tomasson 1984, p. 231). Social Democratic support was important for final enactment, but so was Liberal, Agrarian, and Conservative support as well. As in Britain social reformers and the interest groups organized by these reformers played an important role. Hedin, a Liberal, was the first of these reformers. Subsequently, Gustav Raab was to play an important role. He organized the Committee for Public Pensions in 1897. Raab's agitation was in large measure responsible for getting the discussion of old-age pensions injected into the 1905 election (Heclo 1974, p. 189). The Old Age Pension Act of 1913 was passed when the Liberal Party controlled the government, and it contained many provisions, such as being contributory with benefits actuarially linked to contributions, that were dear to the Liberals. Thus the Liberal Party must be given a great deal of credit for this legislation.[25]

In the late nineteenth century Sweden was much less industrialized then either Britain or Germany (Esping-Andersen 1985, p. 48).[26] This is part of the explanation for the later date for the introduction of an old-age pension system in Sweden. But it is only part of the explanation as active consideration was being given to the introduction of such a pension system for a number of years prior to the introduction of the British system in 1908.

Another factor, and part of the explanation for why Sweden followed Britain, is that the farm block was much stronger in Sweden than it was in Britain or Germany. The farm block was able to reject the proposals of the first commissions that focused on the needs of industrial workers to the exclusion of independent farmers (Wilson 1979, p. 6). This factor is particularly relevant when analyzing the political unacceptability of the proposals that came out of the second (1895) and third (1898) Workers' Insurance Commissions; it is also relevant when addressing the question as to why Sweden introduced the first universal system.

In connection with the 1913 pension legislation the major dispute was between the civil servants and the Social Democrats who favored a pension program that focused on the industrial working class, and the increasingly powerful independent farmers who were pushing for universal coverage.[27] The final shape of this legislation reflected a victory for agrarian interests over those of the traditionally powerful civil service (Baldwin 1989, p. 22). The final legislation was generally supported, but not the idea of or a response to pressure from organized labor or the Social Democratic Party. Rather it was the idea of Liberal reformers, and its final form was very much a response to the demands of an agrarian middle class that did not want to be denied the benefits of a national pension system.[28]

Developments Between the Wars

Between 1913 and 1935 there were no major legislative changes in Swedish old-age pension policy; however, there were developments that had implications for pension policy. Originally it had been assumed that over time there would be a gradual shift toward greater emphasis on the contributory pension as the system matured and contributions built up over the years. This assumption proved to be incorrect; the trend was instead toward increasing dependence on means-tested pension supplements (Palme 1990a, p. 108). The original legislation had not adequately taken into consideration the long-term impact of inflation.[29]

The trend toward greater use of the noncontributory pension supplement tended to undercut the insurance aspect of the original legislation. Concern about the inadequacy of the pension system led to the establishment of a commission in 1928 which reported back six years later. The proposals of this commission were enacted in 1935. One change introduced by this legislation was to increase the size of both the supplementary and contributory pensions (Tomasson 1984, p. 231).[30]

A second change was the decision to shift away from strict insurance principles for the contributory portion of the pension. Prior to this point in time the contributory pension has been linked to workers' prior contributions by strict actuarial (insurance) principles. Now those who were eligible for a contributory pension would get a pension based on two components: (1) a basic yearly pension that would be the same for each worker and (2) a second component that would be equal to 10 percent of the worker's previous contributions.

A third change affected reserve fund policy. Prior to this point contributions has been set aside in a reserve fund; the new policy was to substantially reduce the size of the reserve fund. Most of the monies taken in would be immediately paid out to current recipients. Reflecting these modifications, the name was changed from pension insurance (emphasizing the insurance nature of the pension) to *folk-pension* (people's pension) (Carlson 1966).

The commission's proposals were strongly supported by the Social Democrats and by organized labor. But many Conservatives were critical of what was viewed as an abandonment of the insurance principle. They did not like the idea that workers with low incomes would now get a higher return on their contributions than would those with higher incomes. However, in the end even the Conservatives in the Riksdag did back the proposed reforms. They decided that the shift to a pay-as-you-go approach was preferable to the alternative of allowing a large government controlled reserve fund to build up over the years. They were convinced by the arguments of the insurance industry and banking industry that the reserve fund approach would eventually result in government control over a substantial portion of capital markets. The pay-as-you-go alternative would assure much greater private control over capital markets.

Even after the 1935 reforms were enacted, pension benefits remained very low, particularly in high cost of living areas such as the cities. A Social Democratic proposal calling for pension supplements for those living in high cost of living areas was defeated in the Riksdag. In response the Social Democrats called for new elections. The resulting 1936 election focused on the pension issue and resulted in substantial gains for the Social Democrats (Olsson 1988, p. 82).[31] Due in large measure to this increased influence, legislation granting pension supplements reflecting geographical cost of living differences was enacted in 1937. This legislation was enacted despite opposition from the rural population (Baldwin 1988, p. 132).

During the 1920s the Social Democrats had agitated on behalf of higher pensions. These efforts were not successful during the 1920s, but they do seem to have contributed to the electoral success of the party during the 1930s (Coughlin and Tomasson 1991, p. 150). During the 1930s the Social Democratic Party was the party of pension policy reform (Olsson 1990, p. 94).

Postwar Policy Developments

In 1938 a commission on social welfare provision was established. It found that a substantial fraction of those receiving supplementary pensions also needed public assistance to attain a subsistence standard of living. This commission came up with several alternative proposals for dealing with the problem that were presented for public debate shortly after the end of the war. One of these proposals called for a modest flat-rate pension combined with a means-tested supplement. This alternative was supported by the majority of the Social Democratic members of the commission and by the leadership of the Social Democratic Party. It was consistent with the traditional Social Democratic ideological commitment to redistributive social policies with its targeting of spending on those with low incomes.

Another of the commission's proposals backed by the Conservative and Agrarian members called for a much higher flat-rate pension, eliminating the need for means-tested supplementary benefits for most recipients. It was this more generous proposal that was eventually enacted in 1946 and implemented in 1948.[32] While the Social Democrats shifted their support to this proposal after a few months, the Conservative Party was strongly behind it from the outset. The early Conservative support for this legislation has been used to argue that the Conservative Party played a major role with respect to this legislation. Furthermore, since the shift away from means-testing toward universalism implicit in this legislation was to characterize much of Sweden's postwar social welfare legislation, the argument is made by some that the Conservative Party played a major role in setting the agenda for the evolution of the postwar Swedish welfare state (Baldwin 1990b, pp. 137–138).

One change made by the 1946 pension legislation was to substantially increase the size of the *folkpension* (Schulz et al. 1974, p. 75).[33] But even more importantly the *folkpension* was effectively transformed into a demogrant. All eligible persons were to get the same size *folkpension* starting at age 67.[34] Sweden had been the first nation to establish a universal contributory pension scheme and it now became the first to drop such a scheme in favor of a universal noncontributory scheme. The *folkpension* was now to be financed out of government general tax revenues.[35]

During the war the Conservative Party began to reconsider its traditional position of opposition to social policy legislation extending social welfare benefits.

After suffering a serious setback in the 1944 election, the Conservatives decided on a fundamental policy shift. They recognized that they could increase their support among the emerging class of white-collar salaried workers by supporting the extension of pension benefits to this group. Conservatives now argued that as their middle-class constituents were being taxed to pay for pension programs, they should be included as beneficiaries. They correctly perceived that the middle class stood to gain the most by a policy shift away from means-tested pensions to universalistic pensions.

Why were Conservatives suddenly against means-testing? Because this policy ended up excluding many in the middle class from pension benefits that, in the opinion of the Conservatives, they were entitled to and in many cases needed. Thus the Conservative Party shifted from its traditional position which had focused on minimizing increases in pension benefits to blue-collar workers to a position in support of restructuring programs so that middle-class white-collar employees would benefit as well (Baldwin 1990b, p. 137).

At first the Social Democratic leadership opposed the proposal calling for the elimination of means-testing. They favored targeting scarce resources on those who were the most needy. They did not look favorably on a sharp increase in spending on the affluent. But after a few months of debate the Social Democratic leadership shifted its position to support the proposal originally backed by the Conservatives and Agrarians (Baldwin 1988, p. 146). Why the change? One reason is that the leadership had to respond to pressure from the Social Democratic members of the Riksdag who supported the elimination of means-testing. There was strong popular support for a higher flat-rate pension without means-testing. Social Democrats did not want to face the electoral consequences of supporting a pension program based on means-testing while the Conservatives were backing a proposal based on universalism. The leadership found itself under pressure from pensioners and from organized labor (Olsson 1990, pp. 104–105).[36] The unions came to view universalistic pensions as a way to eliminate the stigma that had come to be associated with the means-tested supplementary pensions.[37]

The elimination of means-testing was part of a more general shift in Swedish policy on social welfare issues. It was a shift in the direction of universalism. While this orientation can be traced back to the pension legislation enacted in 1913, it seems to have been strongly influenced by the sense of interclass solidarity that evolved in response to the circumstances surrounding World War II (Baldwin 1988, p. 122).[38] In Britain a sense of class solidarity emerged in response to the common sacrifices made by all social classes and the need to mobilize the entire population on behalf of the war effort. A similar sense of solidarity emerged in Sweden even though the country remained neutral during the war.[39]

Sweden's rapidly changing occupational structure was another factor making universalistic social policies attractive to Conservatives and Social Democrats alike. It was becoming clear to all that during the postwar years the size of the blue-collar labor force would be contracting while the size of the white-collar labor force would be rapidly increasing (Baldwin 1988, p. 136).[40] Thus both Social Democrats and Conservatives came to recognize the need to advocate social policies that would appeal to this rapidly growing electoral constituency. To the extent that universalism meant the extension of benefits that had traditionally been targeted for blue-collar workers to more affluent white-collar workers, those advocating such universalism stood to benefit on election day.

Some scholars argue that the 1946 pension legislation was more a response to pressure from the middle class to be included in pension program benefits than it was a response to the position of power that organized labor and the Social Democrats found themselves in at the end of the war (Baldwin 1988, pp. 128–130). Others point out that the Social Democrats were not opposed to pension reform, they just had a preference for targeting benefits to those most in need. Such scholars generally accept the evidence that the Conservative Party did play a role in connection with the 1946 legislation, but they are hesitant to draw from this the conclusion that the Conservatives were in large measure responsible for the direction Swedish social policy was to take during the postwar years (Olsson 1990, p. 106).[41]

By the mid-1940s pensioners' organizations had become influential political actors with respect to Swedish pension policy. In 1944 they were able to get the government to reverse the recommendation of an important subcommittee dealing with pension policy. In connection with the 1946 legislation pensioners' organizations lobbied the trade unions, the Social Democratic Party, and the Social Democratic members of the Riksdag (Olsson 1990, p. 104).[42]

When the 1946 pension legislation was implemented in 1948, for the first time it was possible for most of the elderly to subsist on their pension benefits without other sources of support albeit at a modest standard of living (Cnaan et al. 1990, p. 94). Supplementation was still necessary for some, particularly very old women. Within a few years, however, the number needing means-tested supplementation started to increase as the pension benefits were eroded by the effects of inflation. In response legislation proposed by the Conservatives and Liberals was enacted in 1950 calling for the indexing of pension benefits.[43] Sweden became the first nation to index its old-age pensions. In addition to these regular[44] adjustments based on price increases, periodic adjustments were also made to reflect the increases in real wages (standard of living) that was taking place in Sweden (Coughlin and Tomasson 1991, p. 150).[45]

One of the most important of the postwar policy debates centered on the proposed introduction of an earnings-related pension (ATP). LO, the union representing blue-collar workers, had been calling for such a pension for wage earners throughout the 1940s and early 1950s. Blue-collar workers wanted earnings-related pension coverage similar to what many salaried employees had with their private occupational pension schemes; however, salaried workers were split on the issue. Those already covered by civil service or occupational pension schemes generally opposed the government's original proposal because it focused on the needs of blue-collar workers and unpensioned white-collar workers at their expense.[46] Yet, salaried workers who were not covered by an occupational pension scheme were supportive of the government's proposal (Baldwin 1990b, pp. 213–216).

In the mid-1950s a committee at the Ministry of Social Affairs prepared two alternative pension proposals. The majority proposal backed by LO and the Social Democrats called for compulsory supplementary earnings-related pensions to be paid for by employers and administered by the government. A minority proposal backed by the Conservatives, Liberals, and the SAF, called for a voluntary supplementary pension system administered by a nongovernmental agency. The Agrarian Party subsequently came up with a third alternative that called for a voluntary supplementary pension administered by the government (Coughlin and Tomasson 1991, p. 151).

LO and the Social Democrats wanted a pension scheme structured in such a way that the government would control the huge investment fund that would be created. In contrast, the Conservatives and big business wanted to maintain private control over these monies (Baldwin 1990b, p. 213).

In 1957 a highly unusual national referendum was held on the pension issue. None of the three alternatives received a majority of the votes. The proposal backed by the Social Democrats (calling for a compulsory scheme) won 46 percent of the votes, the highest of the three options; however, the two other alternatives, one backed by the Agrarian Party (with 15 percent of the votes) and one backed by the Conservatives and Liberals (with 35 percent of the votes), together came to 50 percent in favor of some sort of voluntary scheme. Thus the national referendum did not help to resolve the impasse (Esping-Andersen 1980, pp. 327–332).

Subsequently, the Social Democrats sent to the Riksdag the proposal it favored. It was defeated in the Lower Chamber and in response the government called for a new election which was held in 1958. In that election pension policy was the major issue. Both the Social Democrats and the Conservatives made gains at the expense of the Liberals (Olsson 1990, p. 221). The Social Democrats gained enough that they were able to reintroduce the pension legislation and this time it passed, but only with a one vote margin made possible by the help of a disgruntled Liberal who agreed to abstain from the final vote (Baldwin 1990b, pp. 220–221).

After a struggle that had lasted many years a compulsory earnings-related ATP pension covering all workers was enacted in 1959.[47] The scheme was structured so as to assure government, not employer, control, an outcome viewed by many as a major victory for labor. But concessions were also made by LO in that the final legislation was designed with white-collar salaried workers very much in mind.[48] While the Riksdag had been very evenly split for and against the ATP proposal for several years, soon after enactment public opinion was overwhelmingly in favor of this new second tier earnings-related pension (the first tier being the flat-rate universal *folkpension* or basic pension) (Coughlin 1980, pp. 73–74).

With enactment of the ATP a shift in goals was made from that of providing adequate subsistence to that of maintaining a worker's pre-retirement standard of living.[49] Unlike the earnings-related pensions in the United States, Germany, and Britain, no contributions are made by employees. The contributions are paid for entirely by a payroll tax on employers.[50]

In 1973 legislation was enacted that eliminated the employee contribution in connection with the basic pension. The entire cost of the basic pension is now paid for by a payroll tax on employers. This change was the result of negotiations between labor and management about wage increases (Esping-Andersen 1980, pp. 333–334). Labor agreed to a lower wage increase in return for shifting the entire cost of the basic pension to employers. While labor did pay a price in the form of a reduction in the wage increase that would otherwise have come out of those negotiations, this policy shift has been viewed by some as a victory for organized labor.

Another important policy change was the introduction of partial pensions in 1976 (Wilson 1979, p. 27).[51] The partial pension is paid to full-time workers who are age 60 and over who opt for partial retirement. They must substantially reduce the number of hours worked, but continue to work part-time. The partial pension makes up a substantial fraction of the loss of earnings due to the reduction in the number of hours worked. It is designed to ease workers into retirement.

In 1976 the Social Democratic Party lost its first election in 44 years. It was replaced by a bourgeois coalition government. In part this loss was linked to the heavy tax burden the nation was facing due to spending on pensions and other social welfare programs. But other factors were also at play. Many were questioning the position of the Social Democratic Party on the nuclear power issue (Milner 1989, p. 11). Also very important was the high inflation experienced in all industrial nations at that time due to the rapid increase in the price of oil. The Swedish economy did not perform well under the bourgeois coalition government during the late 1970s and early 1980s, and this contributed to a Social Democratic victory in the 1982 election (Korpi 1983, p. 3).

Since the late 1970s there has been little effort to expand the Swedish pension system. The changes that have been made reflect efforts to contain costs or to remove distinctions based on gender or marital status. In 1981, as an economy move introduced by the bourgeois coalition government, there was a reduction in the level of the partial pension from 65 to 50 percent of the worker's previous wage.[52] In 1988 as another economy move, this time under a Social Democratic government, legislation was enacted calling for a gradual phasing out of the widows' pension. It did, however, provide for an adjustment pension to be paid for one year after the death of an insured worker's spouse or cohabitant.

For the period between 1960 and 1985 the value of old-age pensions increased at a more rapid rate in Sweden than in Germany, the United States, or Britain.[53] In 1980 Swedish old-age pensions did a much better job of replacing pre-retirement wages than did those in the United States, Britain, or Germany. In this respect Sweden ranks first among all industrial nations.[54] Between the early 1950s and 1985 spending on pensions increased from 1.7 to 11.2 percent of GDP (OECD 1988a, p. 141).[55] During the postwar period the standard of living among the elderly has increased more rapidly than it has in the working population (Olsson 1988, pp. 41–42). During the economically troubled times of the late 1970s and early 1980s, pensioners were better able to preserve their standard of living than were those in the working population (Heclo and Madsen 1987, p. 160). Due to this increased standard of living, by the early 1980s the poverty rate among the elderly had fallen to 2.1 percent (Smeeding 1990, p. 12).[56] The decision to phase out the widows' pension was due in part to the evidence of increasing prosperity among the elderly and in part to concerns about the future costs of old-age pensions (Cnaan et al. 1990, p. 94).

In Sweden the occupational pensions form a third tier of the pension system. While these pensions are in a strict sense private pensions and not part of the nation's public pension system, the distinction between private and public is not as sharp as in countries such as the United States. Most Swedish workers are covered by occupational pensions because all employees covered by collective labor agreements are required to be covered by such schemes. Due to the very high percentage of workers who are union members, coverage by such schemes is near universal.[57] At present, however, the occupational pensions account for a relatively small proportion of pension expenditures and have relatively little impact on retirement income or on the degree of income inequality among pensioners (Esping-Andersen 1985, pp. 177–178).[58]

From the perspective of the Conservatives and particularly the business community, the major problem with the ATP was that it was to be run as a partially funded scheme rather than on a pay-as-you-go basis. As a result within a few years a substantial fraction of Sweden's capital markets were under government control.[59] This was considered problematic as the Social Democrats controlled the government and LO had a great deal of influence on the Social Democratic Party. For the first several years these assets were managed very passively, being invested primarily in municipal and housing bonds (Einhorn and Logue 1989, p. 177). Eventually, LO did start to insist that these monies be more actively managed in ways that reflected the social priorities of labor. One goal was to help Swedish industry adapt to rapidly changing international markets. Another was to create jobs in industries with a future. In 1973 the government began to manage a portion of these monies more actively with just such social priorities in mind.

For the first couple of decades the ATP took in more money than it paid out in benefits. This is no longer the case, but the Swedish National Pension Insurance Fund today has assets equal to approximately one-third of the Swedish GNP (Kollmann 1991, p. 27). One reason this reserve fund was created was to provide a buffer against short-term fluctuations in the relationship between receipts and expenditures. Another was to compensate for the decline in savings that was anticipated in response to the introduction of the ATP (Pension Commission 1991, p. 8). The National Pension Fund is presided over by a board made up of representatives of government, employers, and employees.

By the early 1990s many Swedes had come to believe that change was called for. One reflection of this new mood was the defeat of the Social Democrats in 1991 by a bourgeois coalition.[60] There was also by this time increasing concern about the tax burden associated with the nation's generous pension system and other costly welfare state programs. In 1990 a government commission issued a major report after a six-year review of the Swedish pension system (Pension Commission 1991). This commission did not explicitly endorse the proposals outlined below, rather it suggested that they were options for dealing with the impending burden should the economy fail to grow at a rate adequate to meet the anticipated pension burden (associated with the retirement of the baby boom generation starting in about the year 2015) without further tax increases.

One proposal calls for changes in the ATP benefit rules. The current policy of basing the ATP on the worker's best 15 years could be increased to the worker's best 20 years. The provision that calls for 30 years of coverage for full coverage could be increased to 40 years. These changes would make the ATP more market conforming and less redistributive. It would also bring Swedish pension policy more into line with policy in the countries in the European Community with obvious implications for Sweden's long-term competitiveness. These changes would create an incentive for workers to remain in the labor force longer and thus help alleviate the burden associated with the retirement of the baby boom generation.

This same report also discusses proposed revisions in the indexing formula (Pension Commission 1991, p. 27). Particular attention is given to a proposal for annual adjustments using an "economic-adjustment index" that would be based on the rate of real growth in the Swedish economy. The current policy of basing adjustments on price increases would be changed. In those years in which there was little or no economic growth adjustments would not necessarily keep up with price increases, but in those years in which there was substantial economic growth adjustments would more than compensate for price increases. This added adjustment during high growth periods would assure that pensioners share in any increase in the nation's overall standard of living. The argument is made that such an index would produce a more equitable allocation of resources between the active labor force and pensioners. It is proposed as a possible mechanism for intergenerational burden sharing should economic growth fail to produce the revenues needed to pay for the retirement of the baby boom generation.

Swedish policymakers recognize that it is very likely they will need to draw down the assets in the (partially funded) National Pension Fund to deal with the pension burden anticipated starting in about 2015. Consideration is also being given to an effort to add to the asset base in this fund during the next 15 years so as to provide a greater cushion to deal with that burden (Pension Commission 1991, p. 39). There is also some discussion of ways to increase the return on the funds in the National Pension Fund by allowing greater freedom with respect to investment alternatives; the choices could be modified to more closely approximate those enjoyed by insurance companies.

Accounting for Developments in Sweden

Britain's first old-age pension scheme was means-tested and thus limited to those with low incomes. Germany's first scheme was limited primarily to blue-collar wage earners. Sweden's universal pension, in contrast, covered the entire elderly population; it represented a far more radical alternative. How do we account for Sweden's early leadership in this respect?

Sweden's large agrarian population played an important role. At the turn of the century the rural population had far more political influence in Sweden than in either Germany or Britain. Those representing the farmers held up legislative efforts until a program was crafted that covered the entire farm population. It was not enough to cover just farm workers, it had also to cover the farm owners as well. Of the alternatives under consideration the universal contributory scheme best suited the needs and circumstances of Sweden's yeoman.

The influence of the peasants in the Riksdag can be traced back at least to the sixteenth century. Over a period of several hundred years Swedish peasants had much more political influence than either German or British peasants. During the nineteenth century this influence was further increased by the decisions to extend primary education to the entire population in the 1840s and to reconstitute the Riksdag as a bicameral body in 1866. The latter was done in such a way that the peasants were assured control over the Lower Chamber. Given this historical back-ground, the evidence that turn of the century Sweden was much more rural than Britain or Germany, and the preference of Swedish farmers for a contributory universalistic scheme, we can begin to understand why Sweden's first old-age pen-sion program was structured as it was.

While organized labor and the Social Democratic Party supported the intro-duction of old-age pensions, the legislation enacted in 1913 cannot be attributed to their efforts. It was enacted with their support, but it did not represent a victory for the left. Most Social Democrats wanted a scheme that was financed at least in part by employer contributions. They also wanted a scheme that would focus its benefits on the industrial working class. In the end they backed the proposal because it was all that was politically feasible. They lacked the influence to get their own alternative enacted.

By the mid-1930s the Social Democrats were in control of the government and in a position to exert their influence over pension policy.[61] In 1935 important reforms were made despite opposition from Conservatives and Liberals. The Con-servatives did not support the proposed restructuring. The flat-rate component called for in this legislation was redistributive and thus violated strict insurance principles. In 1937 the Social Democrats were able to get another reform through that granted pension supplements reflecting geographical differences in the cost of living. This legislation favored urban industrial workers and as a consequence was opposed by the rural population (Baldwin 1988, p. 132).

In 1946 a major reform calling for the elimination of means-testing in connec-tion with the supplementary pension and for a much higher flat-rate pension was enacted. This legislation was originally proposed by the Conservatives, not the Social Democrats. As in 1913 this was a major piece of legislation that passed with Social Democratic support, even though it did not represent a victory for organized labor or the Social Democrats. The most important aspect of this legis-lation was that it transformed the old-age pension into a demogrant paid for by the government. The reason for Social Democratic hesitation in connection with this legislation is that it substantially increased spending on the middle class; many Social Democrats would have preferred to target the low-income population.

After many years of political struggle a compulsory earnings-related pension was enacted in 1959. This legislation was strongly supported by the Social Demo-crats and by organized labor, but not by the Conservatives. However, the original proposal was modified so as to be less focused on the interests of blue-collar workers and more responsive to the interests of white-collar workers before being enacted.

While the Social Democrats have played a more important role in the formu-lation of pension policy since the 1930s than they did at the turn of the century, it is evident that other groups continue to be influential despite 60 years of nearly continuous Social Democratic rule. One of the most important observations about the postwar period is that the Social Democrats have maintained their influence by decreasing their focus on the interests of blue-collar workers while increasing their focus on the interests of white-collar workers. As a result the Social Democrats' constituency is not as working class today as it was 60 years ago. Although the Social Democratic influence has been only one of many factors driving Swedish pension policy during the postwar era, it has been a major factor and it has been a substantially greater factor than in Germany, Britain, or the United States.

Important to postwar pension policy reform and the growth of welfare state programs more generally have been the corporatist policymaking structures that have evolved particularly since the Saltsjöbaden Agreement in 1938.[62] In large part due to this agreement the nation has experienced unprecedented labor peace during the postwar period. Some scholars argue that this agreement and the resulting corporatist decision-making structures are a reflection of the strength of organized labor in Sweden (Stephens 1979, p. 135; Korpi 1983, p. 3); others point to the nation's long history of compromise and consultation (Anton 1980, p. 6; Tomasson 1970). Whatever the explanation it does seem that the "historic compromise" has resulted in an exchange of industrial peace and wage restraint for a comprehensive set of welfare state programs including one of the world's most generous public pension programs. In Sweden employers are willing to shoulder a much greater share of the pension burden than in the United States, a country without corporatist structures.

The Swedish version of corporatism has involved minimal government involvement in bargaining between the employers' organizations and the unions, but it has been the government that has enacted the social welfare program which have constituted a key component of the historical compromise.[63] There is, however, some evidence that during the 1970s and 1980s Sweden's corporatist structures began to show signs of breakdown (Olsson 1990, p. 212). In the early 1970s LO and SAF terminated the Saltsjöbaden Agreement (Korpi 1983, pp. 208–211). A major reason was that LO had turned to legislation when it was unable to get its way with management on the issue of greater influence for workers in the work place (Korpi 1982, p. 138). In the 1980s the most powerful union in LO, the Metalworkers' Union, and the most powerful employers' organization in SAF, the Metal Employers' Association, began to bargain outside the the centralized bargaining between LO and SAF (Lash 1985).[64] The 1980s has also been a period during which there has been some retrenchment in pension policy. While it is possible that the weakening of corporatist structures may have been a contributing factor, it is likely that both the pension policy retrenchment and signs of some weakening of Sweden's traditional corporatism are also linked to other factors, among them changes in the nation's economy (Pension Commission 1991, p. 12).

There is evidence suggesting that industrialization and economic development have affected the development of pension policy in Sweden. Industrialization and its correlates created both the need for old-age pensions and the economic resources to pay for such pensions.[65] The economic hardship facing an increasing number of old workers in the wake of the rapid industrialization during the late nineteenth and early twentieth centuries was a major reason late nineteenth century social reformers took up the cause of public pensions.

By 1900 Sweden had a higher proportion of the population over age 65 than either Germany or Britain (Laslett 1985, p. 217). Based on age structure one might have expected enactment of pensions in Sweden to have preceded that of Germany or Britain; however, based on level of industrialization at the turn of the century one would have expected public pensions to have come later than they did.

The marked increase in spending on pensions during the decades following World War II would not have been possible were it not for the extended period of economic growth that Sweden experienced (World Bank 1983a, p. 490). Similarly, in response to the stagflation of the late 1970s and early 1980s, in 1981 Sweden for the first time made changes in the way in which pensions were indexed with an eye toward cost containment (Zeiter 1983). It is entirely consistent with the industrialism perspective that in 1982 Sweden spent a larger share of its GDP on public pensions than did the United States or Britain given that it had a higher GNP per capita, a longer life expectancy, and a larger proportion of its population over age 65 (World Bank 1984, p. 219; OECD 1988a, pp. 140–141; 1988b, p. 11).[66]

While the industrialism perspective points to a number of factors that have influenced the evolution of Swedish pension policy, it does not account for the evidence that Sweden enacted its public pension system long before the United States, a much more industrially developed nation in the early twentieth century (Clark 1957). Similarly, during much of the postwar period spending on old-age pensions has increased at a faster rate than in Germany even though the German economy has been growing at a more rapid rate (World Bank 1991, p. 205; OECD 1988a, p. 49).

Central to the industrialism perspective is the argument that partisan political factors such as the strength of socialist parties and organized labor have little if any independent impact on pension policy development. The evidence from the Swedish case does not support this conclusion. Partisan politics played a role with respect to the enactment of the original legislation and it also played a role with respect to postwar developments.

Some aspects of Swedish pension policy development are best accounted for in terms of the social democratic perspective, but as we have noted earlier many aspects cannot be adequately accounted for on the basis of this perspective alone. No other industrial nation has had so large a proportion of its labor force unionized and no other capitalist democracy has had a socialist party in control of the government for so long. The close link between LO and the Social Democratic Party has increased labor's influence on pension spending and on various pension reforms, particularly since the mid-1930s.[67] A key to the Social Democrats being able to control the government for so long was the support from the farm block and the Agrarian Party until the late 1950s and increasing support from white-collar workers since then (Esping-Andersen 1985; 1990, p. 31).

How did labor become so influential in Sweden? The nation's late and rapid industrialization as well as the concentration of the economy in two major industries, iron mining and timber, contributed to the development of a highly centralized labor movement organized primarily on the industrial as opposed to the craft union model. The highly concentrated ownership of the mining and timber industries created an incentive for the labor movement to become highly centralized very early on. In 1950 Sweden had the highest union density of any industrial nation

(Stephens 1979, pp. 115–116). Over the postwar decades union density continued to increase. In 1950 some 62 percent of Swedish wage earners were members of LO, by 1980 the figure had increased to 92 percent (Esping-Andersen 1985, p. 64).[68]

Many commentators point to the marked increase in spending on pensions and the many structural reforms since World War II noting that the Social Democrats have controlled the government during most of this period. The implication is that the spending increase and reforms would not have taken place on the same scale were it not for the Social Democratic control of the government for more than four decades from 1932 to 1976. While the increase in spending may have been lower and the reforms fewer had a bourgeois party or coalition controlled the government during much of this period, it is worth noting that in many instances proposals to liberalize public pensions were initiated by one of the bourgeois parties. One reason is that proposals to spend more on public pensions were very popular across the political spectrum. Politics played an important role during the postwar period, but parties of all stripes attempted to use the popular issue of pension reform as a means to garner votes.

The evidence that all major parties attempted to win votes by backing pension reform is consistent with a neo-pluralist analysis. Pension policy was a cross-class issue that all parties used to broaden electoral support by drawing in voters from a variety of different classes. The role that the rural population played in connection with the original legislation as well as the role of white-collar workers in connection with postwar developments suggest the utility of a neo-pluralist analysis. The same is true with respect to the role of the broad middle strata that Baldwin (1988; 1990b) emphasizes in his analysis.

Also relevant in this context is the role that organized groups representing pensioners have played. The first such organizations were formed in 1940 (Heclo 1974, p. 228). Since then as part of the Swedish consultative process of decision making, such organizations have made their views known in connection with debates over all proposed pension policy reforms. Pensioners are split between two major organizations. By far the larger is the more Social Democratic *Pensionärernas riksorganisation* (PRO).[69] The other is the more nonsocialist *Sveriges folkpensionärers riksförbund* (SFRF).[70] While the pensioners are only one of several pressure groups that have been active and influential during the postwar period, they have been one of the most influential groups with respect to pension policy (Olsson 1990, p. 91; Wilson 1979, p. 9).[71] But this is not to say that they have been as influential as organized labor.

While pensioners and white-collar workers played an important role in connection with postwar pension policy developments, the farmers were one of the most important interest groups in connection with the formulation of the original pension legislation. A major reason that several early public pension proposals were turned down during the late nineteenth century was the opposition from the powerful farm block in the Lower Chamber (Wilson 1979, p. 6).

Another influential interest group in connection with the original legislation was the civil service. The Swedish civil service can be traced back to the sixteenth century. By the seventeenth century it was a highly professional bureaucracy with a strong influence in the Riksdag and a great deal of control over the day-to-day running of the government (Anton 1980, p. 5). Powerful figures in the civil service were in a position to make or break various social policy proposals including the early pension proposals. The civil service was a major factor behind the decision to enact a universal contributory scheme as opposed to a noncontributory scheme in 1913 (Olsson 1990, pp. 85–86). Over the years, major policy changes have been preceded by royal commissions responsible for carrying out detailed studies of the policy options. Typically high level civil servants play a major role on these commissions. They are the experts in a position to provide and evaluate much of the relevant data. They are often able to make the most accurate cost estimates and to work out the details of how programs will be implemented and administered.

A distinctive aspect of public policymaking in Sweden has been the effort made to include representatives from all relevant interest groups on the committees charged with evaluating alternative policy proposals prior to their consideration in the Riksdag. A common procedure has been to constitute a royal commission charged with carrying out an exhaustive analysis of the policy options. In connection with this analysis key experts on the topic are consulted as well as representatives of all relevant interest groups. Over the years the proposals prepared by such committees have had a great deal of influence.

The activities of these commissions can be interpreted as supporting a neopluralist model of decision making in that all major interest groups are given an opportunity to present their views. However, they are also consistent with a corporatist model in that a relatively small number of the country's major interest groups tend to have a disproportionate influence within these committees. It is a structure within which representatives of the state, organized labor, and representatives of employers often come to an agreement on proposed pension legislation, or at least greatly limit the number of policy options to be considered.

Sweden is often described as a corporatist state; in fact, it is generally considered more corporatist than Germany, Britain, or the United States (Pampel et al. 1990).[72] The reference is to the use of extensive negotiation between the leaders of government, industry, and labor prior to major changes in public policy that have significant implications for labor and industry (Schmitter 1974). This corporatist style of decision making on matters that deal with industrial labor relations, pension policy, and the like can be viewed as yet another instance of interest group politics at work. A particularly clear example of this was the agreement in 1973 between labor and industry in which employers agreed to pick up the entire cost of the earnings-related ATP pension in return for wage concessions from labor (Esping-Andersen 1980, p. 333).

Such examples of corporatist decision making can also be interpreted as illustrating the importance of state structure as a determinant of public pension policy. Much of the evidence we have considered in connection with the Swedish case during the postwar period is consistent with the findings of those scholars who report that nations with well developed corporatist decision-making structures often spend more on pension and other social security programs. It seems to be due in part to weaker taxpayer opposition to heavy social welfare spending in the more corporatist states (Wilensky 1976). Corporatist structures seem to give organized labor more influence than it would otherwise have with respect to pension policy and social policy more generally.

Conclusion

Based on the industrialism perspective we can argue that by the early part of the twentieth century there was a need for a public pension scheme in Sweden. But if we want to address the more specific question as to why Sweden introduced a universalistic contributory scheme, we must emphasize the influence of the agrarian population in the Lower Chamber of the Riksdag. This in turn leads us to a consideration of the influence of the peasantry in Swedish society since at least the sixteenth century, and particularly since the reforms of 1866 giving the farmers control of the Lower Chamber of the Riksdag.

Organized labor and the Social Democratic Party both voted in favor of the government's pension proposal in 1913 and supported the idea of public pensions, but enactment of this legislation cannot be viewed as a victory for labor or the Social Democrats. During the postwar era organized labor and the Social Democrats had a great deal more influence. The Social Democrats controlled the government continuously from 1932 until 1976 and this control contributed to the increasing share of the GNP spent on old-age pensions and to a number of liberalizing structural reforms made over the years. However, the bourgeois parties also played an important role. Some of the most important reforms, such as the legislation enacted in 1946, were backed by the Conservatives several months before the Social Democrats agreed to support them. It is evident that electoral competition between the parties was a major stimulus to pension policy reform during the postwar era. Those who argue that postwar pension policy developments can be accounted for almost entirely in terms of the influence of the Social Democrats overstate their case as do those who argue that postwar pension policy developments were driven primarily by the nonsocialist parties. A more appropriate conclusion is that both the Social Democrats and the nonsocialists were influential, but the Social Democrats were somewhat more influential.

If we are willing to grant the argument that the royal commissions constitute one component of Sweden's corporatism, then a case can be made that corporatist structures played an important role even in connection with the formulation of Sweden's original pension legislation. If we use a narrower definition referring to voluntary structures promoting national level centralized bargaining between the leadership of organizations representing employers and those representing labor, we would argue that corporatism did not emerge until the late 1930s and that it was not fully institutionalized until the 1950s. Between the 1930s and the present, corporatist structures have influenced pension policy. While they have served as a mechanism of wage restraint and industrial peace during much of this period, they have also given organized labor a great deal of influence with respect to various welfare state measures including many pension policy reforms during the postwar era. Increasingly these reforms have been crafted to meet the needs of an ever expanding class of white-collar workers. Thus it is easier to make the case that corporatist structures have increased the influence of organized labor (a category that includes most white-collar workers) in connection with pension policy developments than to make the case that these structures have increased the influence of the working class.

We have considered several theoretical perspectives and each has been useful in accounting for certain aspects of the Swedish case. However, pension policy developments in Sweden cannot be adequately accounted for in terms of any one of these perspectives alone. In comparison with the other industrial countries considered, we find the social democratic perspective particularly useful for explaining certain postwar policy developments. The same is also true with respect to the corporatist perspective. Both are more useful in connection with the postwar period than in connection with enactment of the original pension legislation. The reverse is true with respect to the neo-pluralist perspective. It is useful in connection with postwar developments, but even more useful in connection with turn of the century policy developments.

5

United States

The United States was the last major Western industrial nation to enact old-age social security legislation—the Social Security Act was passed in 1935, and the first old-age pensions provided for under this act were paid in 1940.[1] At the time when this legislation was enacted the United States was one of the world's leading monopoly capitalist nations and it had highly developed democratic institutions that were strongly influenced by interest group politics. For these reasons the United States is a particularly crucial case for assessing the utility of both the neo-pluralist and the neo-Marxist perspectives.

In addition, the United States was exceptional with respect to two aspects of public pension development: (1) the late date at which America's first public pension program was introduced and (2) the modest level of the nation's current commitment to public pensions. Throughout our discussion we seek to assess the relative influence of state structures and incumbents, political parties, and economic growth as well as that of big business, organized labor, and other interest groups, both with respect to the timing and the content of major pension legislation.

We begin with an analysis of developments prior to 1920. This includes a discussion of the Civil War pensions which served as de facto public pensions for many union soldiers and their widows during the late nineteenth and early twentieth centuries. We then turn to an analysis of events during the 1920s and 1930s leading up to enactment of the 1935 legislation and follow this with a review of the most important policy developments during the postwar period. The chapter concludes with a theoretical assessment of the relative utility of several alternative theories of pension policy development.

Early Developments: Military, Union, and Corporate Pensions

A number of scholars point to the Civil War pensions as the nation's first national public pension scheme (Fischer 1978, pp. 169–170; Tishler 1971, p. 89); however, a case can be made for tracing the origins of America's public pension system back even earlier.[2] By 1818 tariff revenues became the major source of monies to pay military pensions, and, as a result, sectional disagreement over these military pensions began to emerge. The northern states strongly supported efforts to liberalize the military pensions. This included proposals to increase the size of the pensions and extend pension benefits to all who had served during the Revolutionary War, not just those who had been disabled. But the southern states resisted such proposals because they opposed the use of tariffs to pay for these pensions. Southern senators pointed out that the northern states were pushing for liberalization of these military pension benefits so as to justify increases in protective tariffs on imports from Europe.

While these tariffs did stimulate manufacturing in the northern states, they had an adverse impact on the southern economy (Quadagno 1988a, pp. 32–36). The southern economy was based in large measure on the export of cotton and a few other agricultural products to Britain (Bensel 1984, p. 14). The net result of the American tariffs was a transfer of wealth from the southern to the northern states, a policy which understandably became increasingly unpopular in the antebellum South. And if the tariff issue were not enough, it became evident that most of the pension monies were being paid to those living in the northern rather than the southern states as there were many more Revolutionary War veterans living in the North.[3]

In 1862 legislation was enacted by Congress establishing a Civil War pension system. It very explicitly restricted benefits to instances of a service-related injury or death (Skocpol and Ikenberry 1983, p. 95). This legislation called for variation in pension benefits based on rank and degree of disability. These pensions were to be paid only to Union soldiers killed or injured in combat and to their dependents. By the late 1870s the number of these pensioners as well as spending on these pensions was starting to decline (Glasson 1918, p. 273).

During the Civil War the southern states were not represented in Congress and as a result it was easy to enact substantial increases in tariffs that were opposed by agricultural export interests in the South. These tariffs were used to pay pensions and to pay off the war debt. During the postwar years these tariffs were of sufficient magnitude to generate a substantial budget surplus. Given the desire on the part of northern manufacturing interests to continue these tariffs, this surplus created a source of pressure to liberalize the Civil War pensions. In 1866 military pensions were further politicized when Congress gave the president the power to appoint pension claims agents throughout the country (Oliver 1917, pp. 6–7; Quadagno 1988a, pp. 37–38). Thus the power of appointment could be used by the president to reward party loyalists with these patronage jobs.

In 1879 the Arears Act was passed. This legislation extended pension coverage to those who could show that they had war-related disabilities even if these disabilities were "discovered" years after the war's end. Not only were these veterans eligible for pensions, they were eligible for a lump sum payment for pension benefits due all the way back to the time of the original injury or disability (Orloff and Skocpol 1984, p. 728). The only votes against this act came from southern congressmen. After the Arears Act was passed, thousands of new claims for pensions were made. The Grand Army of the Republic (GAR), a lobbying organization made up of Civil War veterans, became very active in pushing veterans to sign up for pensions and pushing Congress to further liberalize military pension benefits (Dearing 1951).

In 1890 the Dependency Pension Act was passed. It extended coverage to any veteran who had served in the Union army at least 90 days even if he had never been injured and never seen combat. Pension coverage was further liberalized in

1912 by legislation specifying that being age 62 or over counted as a disability for pension purposes (U.S. Bureau of Pensions 1925, p. 43; Achenbaum 1978, p. 84).

The liberalization represented by these various acts led to a substantial increase in spending and in the number of Civil War pensioners. Lubove (1968, pp. 240–241) estimates that the number of pensioners peaked at just under one million in 1902 while spending peaked in 1912. Estimates vary with respect to the proportion of the elderly receiving Civil War pensions. Orloff and Skocpol (1984, p. 728) estimate that in 1901 some 30 percent of all men over age 65 in the entire United States were receiving Civil War pensions.[4] Between the 1880s and the 1910s expenditures on these pensions amounted to between 21 and 40 percent of the federal budget (Keller 1979, p. 311; Bensel 1984, p. 67; Glasson 1918, p. 273; Fischer 1978, pp. 169–170).[5]

While a substantial fraction of the population did benefit from the federal Civil War pensions, large segments of the population were systematically excluded. Most southerners were excluded as were most blacks and all postwar immigrants[6] (Orloff and Skocpol 1984, p. 729).[7] The benefits generally went to white native-born workers, who tended to be more affluent, and many of the lowest income workers were excluded (Rubinow 1913, pp. 408–409).

Concern about older workers began to emerge during the first decade of the twentieth century (Johnson and Williamson 1987, p. 10). After 1912 spending on Civil War pensions began to decline as did the proportion of the elderly eligible for benefits from this source (Glasson 1918, pp. 273–280). This trend was noted at the time and led some reformers to believe that the time was right for enactment of a federally administered old-age pension system similar to those found in many European nations.

There were three major groups of social reformers at the time, each with its own version of how best to respond to the plight of older workers (Pratt 1976, pp. 11–13). One group was made up primarily of charity organizers, settlement house managers, and social workers. Their proposals for dealing with the plight of the elderly tended to emphasize voluntary charity and changes in poor relief policy. Jane Addams and Paul Kellogg were among the more prominent spokespersons for this group (Williamson et al. 1982, p. 80). A second group was made up largely of economists working through the American Association for Labor Legislation (Fischer 1978, p. 159). Their proposals for dealing with the problem emphasized the need to create company pension systems. They argued that labor and management should work out the details of such schemes through collective bargaining. A third group of social reformers were more collectivist or socialist in their approach. This group included such people as Isaac Max Rubinow (1913) and subsequently Abraham Epstein (1922).[8] They were calling for enactment of a compulsory federal old-age insurance system.

In 1911 Representative Victor Berger, one of the few Socialist Party members of Congress at the time, introduced the first bill into Congress that called itself an old-age pension proposal.[9] Between 1910 and 1920 several old-age pension proposals were made by social reformers such as Rubinow and Epstein (Fischer 1978, p. 173).[10] These pension proposals generally reflected the influence of European socialists.

Despite the efforts of these social reformers, there was little immediate impact on public policy (Fischer 1979). Congress remained strongly opposed to the idea of a national old-age pension system. Most state legislators also remained opposed to the idea; only one state (Arizona in 1914) enacted legislation calling for the establishment of an old-age pension system and even that plan was declared unconstitutional by the state's supreme court the following year (Lubove 1968, p. 136).

In the United States as in Britain, Sweden, and many other industrial countries, craft unionism emerged prior to industrial unionism. In the United States there was relatively little organization of unskilled and semi-skilled workers prior to the mid-1930s. The Congress of Industrial Organizations (CIO) was not formed until 1935. During the first part of the century the American Federation of Labor (AFL), a federation of craft unions under the leadership of Samuel Gompers, was the strongest labor organization in the country. The only large industrial union for unskilled and semi-skilled labor during this period was the United Mine Workers (UMW).

Why was so little effort made to organize on an industry-wide basis until the 1930s? One reason is that by the 1890s a small number of large firms had come to dominate the economy and they vigorously contested unionization, particularly in those industries that were not yet unionized. By the early twentieth century when the mass-production industries were rapidly expanding, the large corporations had come to dominate the nation politically, economically, institutionally, and ideologically. Big business left little room for organized labor as an independent locus of power; the mass-production industries were determined to crush unionization efforts (Tomlins 1985, pp. 11–12).[11]

Another important factor was the impact of wave after wave of immigration during the late nineteenth and early twentieth centuries. Many were hired by mass-production industries as unskilled workers. They tended to differ from previously organized craft unionists not only in skill level, but also with respect to cultural background, language, and ethnicity (Mink 1986, pp. 41–42). The craft unionists wanted to distance themselves from these new unskilled immigrants who were culturally so different and often willing to act as scabs during labor disputes. This split within the labor movement is one reason that unionization did not expand as rapidly in the United States as it did in many European countries.[12]

The antagonism between these segments of the working class helps explain why an independent labor party never emerged in the United States. The AFL was dominated by craft unionists who preferred to form a coalition within the Democratic Party with farmers and segments of the entrepreneurial class, rather than joining with these new immigrants who they viewed as below them in the class hierarchy (Mink 1986, pp. 17–18).

At the national level the AFL was strongly opposed to the introduction of public pensions which were viewed as a threat to union autonomy. The fear was that they would be used as a mechanism of social control (Achenbaum 1986, p. 13). The union had reason to be suspicious of the government as both Congress and the courts had consistently sided with management in the often bitter industrial disputes of the late nineteenth century.

AFL president Samuel Gompers was also aware of how corporate pension schemes, some of which were introduced before the turn of the century, were being used by management in connection with strikebreaking efforts. One common provision was that pensioners could be called back to work (as strikebreakers) during labor disputes (L. Olson 1982, p. 35). If they refused, they risked losing their pension. Similarly, those who went out on strike risked losing pension eligibility.

Gompers was not opposed to the idea of pensions, rather he wanted workers to draw pensions based on union pension schemes rather than corporate, state, or federal pension schemes (Epstein 1922, p. 193). Efforts by unions to provide for the elderly can be traced to the late nineteenth century. In 1891 four railroad unions established old-age homes for their elderly members. In 1905 the Granite Cutters International Association became the first union to set up its own old-age pension scheme (Achenbaum 1986, p. 200). But after World War I craft unionism entered a period of decline. As union membership contracted it became increasingly difficult to provide pension benefits. Some unions discontinued these pensions, some substantially reduced the size of the benefits, and others added a number of restrictive criteria to keep down the number who would be eligible.

The early corporate pension plans were all noncontributory.[13] Many were entirely at the discretion of the employer. Others were based on a formula. For example, the employer might set aside 1 percent of the employee's wage with interest added each year. If the employee left in less than 10 years, there would be no pension benefit. If the employee retired or left after 25 or more years, he or she would be eligible for the full pension benefit. Those who left with between 10 and 25 years of service were often eligible for a fraction of the full pension benefit (Quadagno 1988a, p. 79). During the period between the turn of the century and World War I, most pension programs were noncontributory.[14]

Beginning in 1919 and continuing into the early 1920s big business initiated a major new effort to break union power and to stop union growth. This effort to break the unions was successful in many industries, but it did have its costs.[15] It resulted in a sharp increase in labor turnover and in a reduction in labor productivity. One response of big business to the new situation was the introduction of a number of corporate social welfare efforts constituting what came to be called welfare capitalism (Brody 1980, pp. 48–78). The corporate pension was one of the most important components of welfare capitalism. Management realized that such programs were needed to meet the health and welfare needs of employees, to help improve morale among workers, to improve productivity, and to help the company control workers (L. Olson 1982, pp. 34–35; Williamson et al. 1985, pp. 70–78). Changes in the federal tax code during the 1920s acted as a powerful incentive for the introduction of corporate pension schemes. Monies set aside in pension funds received favorable tax treatment (Achenbaum 1986, p. 15). Typically these pensions were graduated on the basis of prior earnings and available to those who retired after 20 or 30 years of service at age 65 or 70 (sometimes as early as age 60).

Starting in about 1925 there was a general shift from noncontributory to contributory corporate pensions. One reason for the shift was the realization that modern monopoly capitalism needed a mobile labor force. Consequently, a contributory pension system in which the worker would be able to move at least the portion he or she had contributed made more sense than the traditional noncontributory pensions that were not portable. These new pension schemes called for contributions from both employers and employees and the monies were often used to purchase annuities from insurance companies.

As for union pension schemes, by 1929 the problems funding them were of sufficient magnitude that the AFL leadership was urging caution to member unions considering the introduction of pension schemes. In 1930 only 11 out of more than 100 of the unions in the AFL were paying pensions (Quadagno 1988a, p. 55). With the deepening of the Depression the AFL shifted to a position of support for a federal public pension program. One reason for the shift was the evidence that most union pension programs were on the brink of bankruptcy (Rimlinger 1971, p. 209).

While the AFL at the national level consistently opposed the idea of compulsory contributory old-age pensions between 1903 and 1932 (Achenbaum 1986, p. 18),[16] it did support certain noncontributory pension proposals, for example, William Wilson's 1909 Old Home Guard plan. It also passed resolutions at various points between 1908 and 1913 in support of noncontributory old-age pensions. In contrast to this minimal effort at the national level, there was a much more active effort at the state level. Influence was exerted for old-age pensions by state AFL federations and state branches of the UMW (Quadagno 1988a, p. 66).

Movement Toward a National Pension System

Efforts in 1911, 1913, and 1918 by the UMW to promote the idea of state level old-age pensions in many states generally failed to have a significant impact on policy. In the early 1920s, however, there was renewed interest in the idea of state level old-age pension legislation (Fischer 1978, p. 174).[17] The Fraternal Order of the Eagles[18] under the leadership of Frank Hering played a major role in efforts to get state level old-age pension legislation enacted during the 1920s. In several states the Eagles formed an informal coalition with the local branch of the AFL and/or the UMW (Quadagno 1988a, pp. 68–70). Such a coalition was attractive to the Eagles in that it gave them access to a source of potential recruits to their fraternal order; it also provided help from groups that were already committed to the idea of old-age pensions and those who had skills with respect to how to organize around this issue. The collaboration was attractive to organized labor because it gave legitimacy to their call for old-age pensions;[19] it was more difficult for employers' organizations to form coalitions to oppose a program sponsored by the Eagles than to oppose a similar program sponsored by a labor union.[20]

The effort was successful; between 1923 and 1931, 18 states enacted old-age pension schemes (Achenbaum 1978, pp. 122–123).[21] The Eagles shared the AFL's distrust of compulsory contributory pensions. The schemes it advocated were voluntary and noncontributory. While the Eagles were actively engaged in promoting noncontributory old-age pensions, they were also actively opposing the idea of social insurance based contributory pensions (Quadagno 1988a, p. 67). One consequence of the voluntary aspect of these pension systems was that in many states very few people received pensions. In 1929 of the six states with operative pension programs only 53 out of 264 possible counties had made the decision to introduce old-age pensions (Commons 1935, p. 613).[22] This is one reason that by the late 1920s many in organized labor were withdrawing their support for the pension proposals being pushed by the Eagles. There was increasing concern that these pension plans did not go far enough and that they were undercutting labor's efforts to obtain more adequate pensions (Quadagno 1988a, p. 71).

In the late 1920s we begin to see renewed interest in federal old-age pension legislation that would provide more extensive coverage. In 1929 a group of railway employees formed the Railway Employees National Pension Association (RENPA) to push for a federal old-age pension program for railroad workers. A revised version of a bill initially submitted in 1932 was enacted in 1934, but it was soon declared unconstitutional by the Supreme Court. A modified version of this program, which was not rejected by the Supreme Court, was enacted in 1935 shortly after the Social Security Act was passed. One reason this legislation passed was that opposition from the railroad industry had softened. By the early 1930s the cost of the industry's own pension scheme for retired railroad employees was becoming a major burden given the impact of the Depression on profits.

By 1925 at least some of the leaders of the large manufacturing corporations that had introduced company pension plans were starting to openly question whether such schemes were going to be workable. In 1925 a study of industrial pensions by large manufacturers suggested the need for an alternative approach based on a central fund under the control of insurance companies or the government. The central fund idea was never implemented, but the fact that this group proposed it illustrates that by 1925 at least one segment of big business was starting to question the viability of individual company pension funds. Later calls for the establishment of a national old-age insurance program that would be compulsory and contributory stemmed from the need to provide coverage for those workers who frequently moved between states (Quadagno 1988a, p. 102).

By the late 1920s many corporations were starting to face severe financial problems related to the cost of their company pension programs. These problems were being discussed in the business press and in these same journals and magazines were an increasing number of articles calling for some sort of national pension legislation. A number of companies had by 1929 stopped paying pension benefits entirely, some had reduced the size of the pension benefits, or altered their eligibility criteria. The Great Depression thoroughly undercut a central tenet of welfare capitalism—that big business was able to adequately provide for the social welfare needs of most workers (Skocpol and Ikenberry 1983, p. 120). As the Depression wore on many more company pension plans were terminated.

Clearly the country was moving toward some sort of national old-age pension system. As this movement became evident, various interest groups attempted to position themselves so as to have as much say as possible in the formulation of the eventual legislation. Representatives of organizations such as the National Industrial Conference Board (NICB) and the National Civic Federation (NCF), which represented the interest of large manufacturing corporations, argued that if it should prove necessary to introduce a national old-age pension program, it should be a compulsory contributory scheme. In contrast, the representatives of small manufacturing interests, organizations such as the National Association of Manufacturers (NAM), remained strongly opposed to any national old-age pension scheme (Tomasson 1984, p. 249; Burch 1973, p. 99). By 1932 the AFL had also come to accept the idea of a national contributory scheme. But there were a number of Depression-related issues that were of more immediate concern to the AFL than Social Security legislation. The leadership tended to be preoccupied with issues such as the wages paid to workers on federally funded relief projects and conflict with management over union recognition (Skocpol and Ikenberry 1983, p. 122).

While at least some representatives of big business and some representatives of organized labor were supportive of the idea of a national old-age pension scheme by the early 1930s, neither of these interest groups were pushing hard for such pensions. But the old-age pension movement was now very active, particularly in California. The most influential of these grass-roots movements was organized by Francis Townsend (Skocpol and Amenta 1985, p. 573).[23] The Townsend movement became a national movement with several hundred thousand supporters (Pratt 1976, p. 23).[24] The Townsend Plan called for a federal government pension of $200 per month to each citizen over age 60 with the condition that the money be spent within 30 days (Altmeyer 1966).[25] The goal of this last provision was to help stimulate the economy. The plan was to help with two problems at once: it would reduce old-age poverty and it would stimulate the economy helping to bring the country out of the Depression.

While the Townsend movement put pressure on the Roosevelt administration to enact some sort of old-age pension legislation, the Townsend Plan was much too radical to be taken seriously by Roosevelt or his advisors. Representatives of both business and organized labor agreed that the proposal was not workable. Opinion is split about how much influence the Townsend movement had on the shape of the Social Security Act. Holtzman (1963, p. 87) argues that the inclusion of Old Age Insurance (OAI) was a response to pressure from the Townsend movement, but Altmeyer (1966, pp. 10–11), Witte (1963, pp. 95–96), and Pratt (1976, p. 23) do not believe that the Townsend movement hastened enactment or shaped its content. While policymakers in the Roosevelt administration did not seriously consider the highly redistributive flat-grant proposals being promulgated by groups such as the Townsendites, they recognized that something had to be done to deal with the concerns being expressed (Skocpol and Ikenberry 1983, p. 124).

The period leading up to enactment of the Social Security Act of 1935 involved a struggle between two competing schools of thought about social insurance (Lubove 1968). One group, referred to as the Ohio school and represented by such people as Abraham Epstein and Isaac Rubinow, sought programs that would involve substantial income redistribution between classes. The other group, referred to as the Wisconsin school and represented by such people as John Commons and John Andrews, advocated policies that would minimize cross-class income redistribution (Cates 1983, pp. 23–24). In the end the advocates of the Wisconsin school won out; the Social Security Act of 1935 came much closer to their vision of what a social insurance program should be like than to that of advocates of the Ohio school. However, the final legislation represented an effort to combine the goals of adequacy and equity (Light 1985). To this extent it was influenced by both schools.

During the late 1930s the Social Security Board (SSB) put a great deal of effort into discrediting the Townsend Plan and other such flat-grant proposals.[26] There is evidence that this effort even involved supplying Congress with deliberately inaccurate cost estimates designed to exaggerate the cost of the alternative proposals (Cates 1983, pp. 50–52).

The Social Security Act of 1935

The Committee on Economic Security (CES) was formed by Roosevelt in 1934 to draft the Social Security Act. He made sure that those selected supported the Wisconsin model of social insurance. Most had been affiliated at some point with the American Association for Labor Legislation (AALL), an organization that had become an advocate of the Wisconsin model during the 1920s (Pratt 1976, p. 13). The Wisconsin model opposed the idea of noncontributory pensions, particularly pensions which sought in some measure to redistribute income to those who were or had become poor. Instead, the goal was to require that workers set aside monies for old age in the form of compulsory contributions. This "preventive" approach was designed to be market conforming; that is, the eventual pensions would reflect differences in pre-retirement wages and have a minimal impact on the distribution of income (Cates 1983, pp. 23–24).

One of the most important aspects of OAI, Title II of the Social Security Act of 1935, was the provision that the old-age pensions were to be contributory and based on social insurance principles. The idea of contributory pensions based on social insurance principles was not new to Roosevelt. Many large corporations had been using such schemes for many years and more recently a number of states had introduced contributory schemes as well. As governor of New York Roosevelt himself had unsuccessfully attempted to get a contributory old-age pension scheme enacted.

The original Old Age Benefits proposal drawn up by the CES was supported by a number of business leaders which was not surprising given that experts who shared big business values had a strong hand in shaping it.[27] OAI did little to redistribute income, and it did not allow employers in certain regions of the country to avoid participation and in so doing gain a competitive advantage over those who did participate. No major labor leaders were asked to participate in the drafting of this legislation. Similarly, no effort was made to bring Townsend or any other leaders of the old-age pension movement into the process of preparing this legislation. Small business was also for the most part excluded. The representatives of small business, such as the NAM, did not have an alternative proposal; rather, their goal was negative, to defeat the legislation or to at least delay enactment as long as possible (Achenbaum 1978, p. 138).

In addition to big business, another interest group that had a major impact on the content of the Social Security Act was Southerners, particularly those with large agricultural holdings. Congressmen from the southern states were able to exclude agricultural workers and domestic servants from coverage under the OAI title. As a result, most black workers were excluded (Quadagno 1984, p. 643). The reason for wanting to exclude blacks was the fear that coverage would drive up wages, particularly in agriculture (Skocpol and Ikenberry 1983, pp. 131-132). Taken into consideration were not just the older workers who might decide to retire, but other younger workers who they might help support with their pensions. Southern congressmen and the interests they represented wanted to maintain control over tenant labor. As Roosevelt needed the support of southern congressmen to get his legislation passed, he had to compromise.

Another major compromise with southern congressmen was made in the formulation of Old Age Assistance (OAA), Title I of the Social Security Act. This was a noncontributory, locally administered, means-tested relief program for the elderly poor. It was a federal/state program in that it was financed in part at the state and local level and in part by the federal government out of general tax revenues, but states had control over the level at which benefits were set. The federal government was to match state expenditures up to a maximum of $15 per recipient. The result was a great deal of variation among states with respect to benefit levels (Achenbaum 1978, pp. 134–135). This allowed the southern states to set the benefit levels at a very low level so as to minimize any impact on the wages paid to poor blacks, particularly poor black agricultural workers. The states were also given control over eligibility criteria. In many states residency requirements were used to exclude black migrant farm workers from coverage.[28]

If the southern congressmen were successful in getting the OAA program structured so that each state was able to get its own benefit level and eligibility criteria, why didn't the OAI program end up with a similar structure? One explanation is that the actuaries who advised the CES were unanimous in their opposition to separate systems for each state. One of their major concerns was that due to the mobility of workers between states, state-by-state estimates of the size of the future working age population would be highly inaccurate. Due to the problem introduced by the geographical mobility of workers, the actuaries were able to convince the CES that a national OAI scheme made a lot more sense than alternatives that allowed state-by-state variation (Tomasson 1984, p. 249).

There was a marked discrepancy between what senior movement leaders had been requesting (e.g., $200 per person per month specified in the Townsend Plan) and the benefit levels called for in the final legislation (e.g., the first benefits were to be paid in 1942 with a minimum of $10 per month for those who met the eligibility criteria with the average benefit being just over $20 per month) (Achenbaum 1986, p. 203). The benefits paid to the first OAI (pension) recipients were actually lower than those being paid to OAA (public welfare) recipients in most states (Quadagno 1984, p. 634). This continued to be true even into the late 1940s. In 1949 the average OAA benefit was $42 per month while the average OAI pension was $25 per month (Myles 1988, p. 272). In view of the magnitude of the discrepancy and the lack of consultation with these advocacy groups in connection with the process of preparing this legislation, it is not surprising that most did not view the Social Security Act of 1935 as a major political victory (Achenbaum 1978,

p. 138).[29] There were virtually no senior movement leaders at the signing ceremony.[30]

Some analysts assumed that as Social Security pension benefit levels increased, the number of older people needing and eligible for OAA would decrease. But due to the slow rate at which old-age pensions were increased, the slow rate at which the program was expanded to include a greater share of the population, and the substantial proportion of the elderly who were already retired or too old to meet the requirement with respect to number of quarters of covered employment, as late as 1950 substantially more people were receiving OAA than Social Security pensions (Derthick 1979, p. 273).[31]

The old-age pensions enacted in the Social Security Act of 1935 were compulsory, contributory, and earnings-related, but not means-tested. The legislation specified that pensions would start in 1942 and be paid to eligible persons age 65 and over.[32] To make it politically more acceptable the pension program was to cover only employees in commerce and industry; as a result it excluded approximately 40 percent of the labor force, including domestic workers, farm labor, most of the self-employed, government workers, and several other categories of workers such as those employed by religious, educational, and charitable institutions (Schneider 1937, p. 82).

The pension component of the Social Security Act was much more influenced by (private) insurance than social welfare principles.[33] For example, there were to be no adjustments made for dependents, even for an elderly wife or young children. There was no provision for a widow or orphans in the event of the death of an insured worker. The pension was to be paid for by contributions of equal magnitude from both the employer and employee. Monies collected were to be put into what would become a very large reserve fund from which eventual benefits would be paid. Roosevelt supported the creation of a substantial trust fund as it would assure that the Social Security system would be self-supporting and not become dependent on general federal tax revenues (Schulz 1988, p. 124).[34] The benefits were to be market conforming in that those who contributed more to the system over the years would end up receiving larger pension benefits.

While the emphasis in the original legislation was on insurance principles, it did include some provisions based on social welfare principles.[35] Workers who contributed more would end up with larger pensions, but the formula used to compute pensions due did have a tilt in favor of those with low incomes.[36] That is, when the pension to be paid was actuarially analyzed in terms of contributions made, those with low earnings (lower contributions) would end up with a better return on contributions made.

Provision was also made to reduce the amount of time needed to become eligible for pension benefits during the early years (Schulz 1988, p. 121). This would provide at least some pension benefits for those who were close to retirement age; however, so as to reinforce the social insurance conception of Social Security, these early pension benefits were to vary as a function of the total amount of wages subject to taxation prior to retirement (Achenbaum 1986, p. 24). The relatively short contribution period during the early years made Social Security a very good "investment" for those who retired during the first few decades of the plan's existence. Nevertheless, it was clear to those who designed the scheme, if not to the public in general, that eventually the plan would "mature" and these windfall benefits would cease.

Almost as soon as the Social Security Act was passed, the process of liberalizing its benefits and extending its coverage began. While the original legislation was enacted in 1935, the payment of pension benefits was not to start until 1942. However, in 1939 before any benefits had been paid the first amendments were enacted modifying the program. It was already obvious that unless a shift were made to a pay-as-you-go approach, a huge reserve fund was going to accumulate (Schulz 1988, p. 124). This development was not looked upon with favor by big business which favored private control of capital markets. The argument was made by those who opposed this buildup that a large trust fund would put a fiscal drag on the economic recovery (Stein 1980, p. 51).[37] In their view spending was needed to stimulate production and create jobs. They argued that the creation of a large reserve fund would take money out of circulation that might otherwise be used in ways that would help spend the nation out of the Depression.

There was also pressure to liberalize the program by starting benefits sooner and by extending protection to widows and dependents. The 1939 amendments were important because they initiated the process of modifying the original Social Security legislation to give greater emphasis to social welfare as opposed to (private) insurance principles (Munnell 1977, p. 2). As one example of this, the benefit formula was modified so as to be more favorably tilted in favor of low-wage workers. The date for the distribution of the first pension benefits was rolled back from 1942 to 1940.

The 1939 amendments transformed Social Security from a worker protection program into a family protection program (Ball 1988a, p. 25). Benefits were added for the insured worker's wife and children. Coverage was also extended to widows and orphans of insured workers.[38] The decision to shift from a strict reserve fund system to a pay-as-you-go system provided the monies needed to pay for these changes in Social Security (Schulz 1988, p. 124). The shift was from a policy that would have been nearly fully funded and resulted in a very large trust fund to a trust fund that would best be described as a contingency reserve fund. The new goal was to limit the funds to approximately one year's obligations (Stein 1980, p. 51).

The 1939 amendments did represent a victory of sorts for organized labor. Most of the changes made were changes organized labor had been pushing for. It is unlikely that they would have been successful, however, had it not been the case that big business wanted to reduce the size of the Social Security trust fund and realized that support for labor's agenda was a means to this end (Quadagno 1988a, p. 121).

In the original Social Security legislation no mention was made of the term *social insurance*. Until the Supreme Court upheld the constitutionality of this legislation in 1937, explicit references to this term were avoided in official statements by members of the Social Security Board (SSB) that administered the program. The SSB feared that the Supreme Court would conclude that a social insurance program was unconstitutional (Meyer 1987, p. 11).[39] However, soon after the Supreme Court decision the SSB started emphasizing insurance terminology, and this terminology was used extensively in the 1939 amendments.[40] The effort to depict the Social Security program as a form of insurance was one way to deal with criticism from the left. During the first few years after enactment of the Social Security Act, critics from both the left and the right[41] sought to radically restructure or abolish the program.

Developments Since World War II

Between the mid-1930s and the mid-1940s there was a dramatic increase in the proportion of mass-production industrial workers who were unionized. By the mid-1940s most mass-production industries had been unionized. The major industrial union was the CIO formed in 1935 by several of the industrial unions which had been affiliated with the AFL. Given the dramatic increase in size and power, one might have expected to find the CIO pushing hard for Social Security reforms during the postwar era. But this did not happen. Rather, the CIO pushed for more and better company pension funds.[42]

One reason for this was the belief that it would be difficult, if not impossible, to get major reforms in Social Security enacted given the conservative composition of Congress.[43] As a result of the 1944 election a conservative coalition of Republicans and southern Democrats came to control Congress, and in the 1946 election the Democrats lost control of Congress. The election of a Republican president in 1952 further eroded any influence organized labor might have had on Social Security legislation. One consequence of this shift was enactment of antilabor legislation such as the Taft-Hartley Act in 1947 (Tomlins 1985, p. 25). Another was increased resistance to Social Security liberalization.

The CIO's response to the need for more adequate pension coverage in the face of evidence that Congress was unlikely to support significant increases was to focus instead on private company pensions. This effort was sufficiently successful that by 1960 more than 50 percent of industrial union members were covered by private pension schemes (Quadagno 1988a, p. 168). The downside was that this emphasis tended to divide the labor movement. Most nonunionized workers had only Social Security pensions to depend on in retirement, while many unionized workers were in a quite different situation economically as they had in addition a private pension. This division undercut class solidarity and is one reason that organized labor was not able to exert as much influence in the United States as in Sweden for increasing the share of the national income allocated to public pensions.

In 1955 the AFL and the CIO merged. The AFL had been working with technocrats in the Social Security administration ever since 1935 to find ways to improve coverage, provisions, and benefit levels. As we have noted, this is not the route that the CIO had been taking. But after this merger the AFL approach prevailed (Quadagno 1988a, p. 172). The AFL-CIO also moved closer to the Democratic Party. During the Kennedy and Johnson years labor's influence on national policy increased substantially.[44] This influence subsequently decreased during the Nixon, Ford, and particularly the Reagan and Bush administrations.

The first major Social Security legislation since the late 1930s was passed in 1950. These amendments changed the benefit formula making it possible to become eligible for benefits sooner. They also extended the system to cover most of the nonfarm self-employed and many farm workers (Pratt 1976, p. 33). Due in part to the limited proportion of the population in covered jobs and in part to the time it took to qualify, in 1950 only 16 percent of the elderly were eligible for OASI pension benefits while OAA was providing benefits to 23 percent of the elderly (Ball 1988b, p. 31).[45] This legislation increased pension benefits by approximately 77 percent, but all this did was restore purchasing power to its 1940 level (Kingson 1987, p. 25).[46] These changes set a pattern of incremental reform that would continue through the late 1960s (Light 1985, p. 37). The 1950 amendments were a major turning point. The changes made at this point assured that in future years it would be the social insurance approach as opposed to the public assistance approach that would be emphasized in protecting the elderly.

Over the years additional components were added to the Social Security program. In 1956 disability insurance[47] was added and in 1965 hospital insurance for the elderly was added (Schulz 1988, p. 122).[48] In 1956 women became eligible for actuarially reduced old-age pension benefits at age 62 and in 1961 men became eligible for the same benefits (Lammers 1983, p. 93).

In 1972 the indexing of OASI pensions was enacted.[49] In the same year an adjustment was made in the formula used to compute the pre-retirement earnings figure for the purposes of calculating the worker's starting OASI pension benefit. Each year of earnings was to be adjusted using a wage index. As a result the final estimate of pre-retirement earnings would be based on the worker's wage relative to the average wage in the year in which that wage was earned (Ball 1988b, p. 22).

Another major piece of legislation enacted in 1972 was the creation of the Supplemental Security Income (SSI) program. The SSI proposal had originally been a small part of a much more ambitious effort to replace the existing public assistance program with the so-called Family Assistance Plan (FAP). Had the effort been successful Aid to Families with Dependent Children (AFDC) would have been replaced with what was essentially a guaranteed income program. The FAP plan was hotly debated and finally rejected. The only part of the original proposal that did pass was the SSI program which replaced OAA with a guaranteed income program.[50] The FAP proposal got all of the attention during the debates and as a result the SSI program was passed with hardly any debate (Bowler 1974, p. 47). With this legislation as with the legislation on indexing Social Security pensions, most of those who testified were technical experts (Derthick 1979, pp. 339–368). This was a particularly clear illustration of the considerable influence on policy exercised by technical experts from the SSB and subsequently from the Social Security administration during the postwar period (Amenta and Skocpol 1988, p. 121).

Richard Nixon's first term (1969–1973) was a period during which major advances were made in Social Security reform. Of particular note were: (1) the dramatic increase in the size of Social Security pensions, (2) the indexing of pensions and the wages used to compute pension benefits, and (3) the creation of the SSI program. Why such liberalization during a Republican administration? One explanation is that Social Security was such a popular program that both parties wanted to get credit for liberalizing reforms in anticipation of reaping electoral advantage. Both parties wanted the support of the senior vote. In addition, the Nixon administration decided that the indexing of Social Security pensions would help depoliticize the Social Security issue and contain program costs (Derthick 1979, pp. 349–357). As Democrats generally came out looking more generous in connection with the election year debates over how much to increase Social Security pensions, there was a certain logic to Republican support for indexing.

While the 1939 legislation did introduce benefits for dependents, it was quite restrictive, limiting benefits to wives over age 64 and to children under age 16. Since then, provisions for dependents have been gradually liberalized to include divorced spouses[51] as well as all children up to age 18 (age 21 if still in school) and dependent disabled children of any age (Kingson 1987, p. 61). In 1977 the Supreme Court rejected the provision that had required that men prove they were financially dependent on their wives to become eligible for survivor benefits based on a deceased wife's employment history.[52] Very few men take advantage of this provision, however. In late 1987 there was only 1 widower for every 207 widows receiving survivor benefits (Schulz 1988, pp. 138–139).[53]

The spouse benefit (not available until the spouse is at least age 62) associated with the Social Security old-age pension is 50 percent of the covered worker's "basic benefit." In recent years many women have found that 50 percent of their husband's benefit often turns out to be larger than 100 percent of the benefit due on the basis of their own employment history. One result of this provision is that retired women who choose to be counted as dependents end up with the same Social Security old-age benefit as married women who never contributed to the system.[54] The spouse of the deceased is entitled to a widow's (widower's) benefit equal to the amount due the retired worker as a single individual.

In 1977 OASDI was facing a short-term financing problem due in large part to the weak economy.[55] There was a great deal of writing, particularly in the popular press and in the publications of conservative think tanks, about the Social Security "crisis." Claims were made that unless drastic measures were taken the Social Security system would soon go bankrupt (Kingson 1984, p. 135). Such claims capitalized on the public's misconceptions about the Social Security trust funds and how pay-as-you-go social insurance systems are financed. The 1977 amendments to the Social Security Act made a number of changes designed to deal with the short-term financing problem and to reduce the magnitude of the long-term financing problem. The most important of these was the creation of a new cost-of-living-adjustment (COLA) formula that corrected the flaw in the old formula that had overcorrected for inflation (Meyer 1987, p. 15).[56]

It was not until the Reagan era that a serious effort was made to reduce rather than further extend Social Security benefits. Particularly important in this context were the 1981 and 1983 amendments. In the 1981 amendments survivor benefits to youths age 18–21 who were full-time students were dropped. Also dropped for new retirees was the minimum benefit provision (Lammers 1983, p. 112). The original Social Security legislation created a "minimum benefit" of $10. This benefit was paid to recipients whose benefit using the standard formula fell below this level (Schulz 1988, p. 130).

The 1977 amendments did not take into consideration the severity of the economic downturn during the early 1980s that brought with it yet another Social Security short-term financing "crisis." The 1983 legislation again solved the short-term financing problem, but in addition made a more serious effort to deal with the long-term financing problem.[57]

There is evidence to suggest that the emphasis on the "crisis" of Social Security during the late 1970s and early 1980s was part of a more general effort by some conservatives to undermine confidence in and support for Social Security with the ultimate goal of reducing the nation's commitment to a variety of New Deal and Great Society programs. As one example, Stuart Butler and Peter Germanis (1983) of the conservative Cato Institute openly called for "guerrilla warfare" against the Social Security system.

After enactment of the 1983 legislation, the Social Security debate shifted to such issues as generational equity and the anticipated burden due to the eventual retirement of the baby boom generation (Longman 1987; Kingson et al. 1986; Lamm 1985). There are many reasons that the generational equity debate emerged during the 1980s. Among the most important are: large federal deficits, population aging, increasing economic inequality among age groups, income stagnation, the loss of faith in government institutions, and interest group competition (Kingson and Williamson 1991, p. 38). While the most vociferous advocates for greater generational equity claim to be interested in a more equitable distribution of resources between the elderly and other age groups, particularly poor children, most give a great deal more attention to the issue of reducing spending on Social Security than to the issue of increasing spending on poor children (Kingson 1989, p. 361; Binney and Estes 1988; Minkler 1986).[58]

Since the late 1980s there has been a great deal of debate about the recent buildup in OASI trust fund reserves and about the link between these reserves and the federal budget deficit (Williamson and Pampel forthcoming). This buildup is due in large measure to the Social Security amendments of 1983. Some Social Security experts argue that the current effort to build up a large trust fund reserve is the only prudent policy given the anticipated burden starting about 2017 due to the retirement of the baby boom generation (Rivlin et al. 1990; Ball 1990).[59] Others argue, to the contrary, that it would make more sense to return to the prior emphasis on the pay-as-you-go approach (Moynihan 1990; Myers 1989).

Those favoring a trust fund buildup see this as a way to increase savings and investment, policies that should contribute to long-term economic growth. If the size of the national product grows substantially between now and 2017, it will be easier to pay for the retirement of the baby boom generation. Those who back proposals to reduce the size of the payroll tax so as to reduce or eliminate additional increases in the size of the trust fund reserves generally argue that due to current budget deficits, these Social Security monies are being spent to finance current consumption rather than being invested in ways that contribute to long-term economic growth. Independent of whether an effort is made to build up a large trust fund reserve, one point most economists can agree on is that the entire cost of the retirement of the baby boom generation will have to be paid for out of the national product of that era (Aaron et al. 1989, p. 10).[60]

Current Policy

The 1983 amendments specified that for the first time some people would be required to pay taxes on a portion of their Social Security pension. If an individual's income was above $25,000 ($32,000 for couples),[61] he or she would be required to pay income tax on one-half of the Social Security pension benefit (Tomasson 1984, pp. 254–255).[62] Prior to this the entire social security benefit was tax exempt independent of one's unearned income. The 1983 amendments called for a future increase in the age of eligibility for full pension benefits from 65 to 67. This increase will take place very gradually between 2000 and 2027 (Ball 1988b, p. 24). Also in the 1983 amendments was a provision that COLAs are to be based on either the increase in prices or the increase in wages, whichever is lower during years in which the trust fund falls below a specified level.[63]

The 1983 amendments marked the first time that Social Security benefits were cut for a substantial fraction of recipients.[64] The decision to tax half the benefits for those with incomes above $25,000 per year amounted to a cut in benefits.[65] But even more people were affected by the decision to shift the date for the COLA from July to January on a permanent basis. This had the effect of reducing pension benefits by approximately 2 percent (Light 1985, p. 37).

Over the years amendments have been added bringing additional groups into the system. Today the system is almost universal; it includes many domestic and farm workers, most of the self-employed, and all new federal employees. By the early 1980s, 92 percent of male workers and 73 percent of female workers were fully insured.[66] In 1982, 92 percent of those age 65 and over received at least some income from Social Security (Kingson et al. 1986, p. 86).

While the "minimum benefit" is being phased out for new retirees, a "special minimum benefit" introduced in 1972 remains. This benefit is for those who have held long-term jobs in covered employment, but at very low wages (Bernstein and Bernstein 1988, pp. 21–22). In addition, the tilt in the regular benefit formula continues to favor low-income workers. In 1982 low-income retirees received benefits equal to about 53 percent of their pre-retirement wages in contrast to 27 percent for those earning the maximum covered wage (Light 1985, p. 39).

The current federal income tax code exempts those with very low incomes from paying any federal income tax. In view of this, the charge has been made that it is inappropriate to require the payment of Social Security taxes by those with the same low incomes. But Congress has been reluctant to exempt the poor from the payroll tax. One reason is that such a shift in policy might contribute to a redefinition of Social Security as a form of welfare; it would undercut the view that these pension benefits have been earned as a result of contributions made over the years. In 1975, however, Congress enacted an "earned income credit" for low-income workers with children. This tax credit provides an income bonus to these low-wage earners that offsets their Social Security payroll contributions (Schulz 1988, p. 171). One of the arguments made on behalf of this legislation was that it would offset the work disincentive associated with the Social Security payroll tax.

Currently insured persons are eligible for actuarially reduced pension benefits as early as age 62. In 1980 some 65 percent of men and 76 percent of women chose to receive early benefits.[67] There is also a 3 percent increase in benefits for each year a worker delays the receipt of benefits between age 65 and 70. For there to be no actuarial loss due to this delay, the yearly increase would have to be closer to 9 percent. This may be one reason that very few workers select this option.[68]

Conclusions about how generous the American Social Security pension system is relative to other industrial nations depend on how we measure generosity. One of the most common measures is pension effort, the ratio of spending on public pensions to a nation's GDP (Pampel and Williamson 1985). Despite substantial increases in pension spending since the end of World War II, by this measure the United States still ranks low relative to many industrial nations. In 1985 the United States spent 7.2 percent of its GDP on OASDI pensions in contrast to 6.7 percent in Britain, 11.8 percent in Germany, and 11.2 percent in Sweden (OECD 1988a, pp. 140–141).

Another way to compare nations is with a measure of pension adequacy. The most common measure here is the ratio of the average pension at retirement to the wage of the average worker just prior to retirement. By this replacement ratio measure, the United States does better; it falls slightly below average for single workers and slightly above average for married couples when comparisons are made with the other industrial nations.[69]

Why does the United States rank lower with respect to pension effort than with respect to replacement ratio? One important factor is that relative to other industrial nations the United States has a young age structure. As a result it has a lower proportion of elderly, making it possible to replace an above average proportion of pre-retirement wages (at least for married couples) while spending a below average fraction of the GDP on old-age pensions.

The tax schemes used to finance the OASI programs differ from country to country. In the United States the program is entirely paid for by a highly visible payroll tax. This visibility creates resistance to increases in benefit levels. Wilensky (1981, p. 346) finds the strongest antitax and antiwelfare movements in nations such as the United States that rely heavily on visible taxes. In Sweden, by contrast, the old-age pension tax is much less visible, being paid almost entirely by the employer. Furthermore, in Sweden and in several other European countries old-age pensions benefits are in part paid for out of general tax revenues, a form of taxation that makes more extensive use of less visible forms of taxation such as the value-added tax (VAT).

Accounting for Developments in the United States

Since the United States government was spending about three times as much on Civil War related pensions as the British government was spending on its national old-age pension system during the years just prior to World War I (Rubinow 1913, p. 404), it is relevant to ask why the United States did not follow the lead of most European nations by enacting a public pension system during the Progressive Era (1906–1920). One reason is that the political corruption associated with the Civil War pensions came under attack by progressive social reform groups advocating clean government, civil service reform, and the establishment of government regulatory agencies (Seager 1910, p. 145; Skocpol and Ikenberry 1983, p. 102).[70] Their fear was that any national pension program would end up being used as a source of spoils in connection with political patronage much as the Civil War pensions had been used.

While Britain also had a period of extensive patronage politics during the early part of the nineteenth century, this had changed by the end of the century. Various civil service reform efforts led to the formation of a national civil service to deal with social welfare issues that were relatively independent of political patronage (Orloff 1991, p. 246). Selection of administrators was based on having the appropriate credentials (often a degree from Cambridge or Oxford University) and experience rather than being a ward boss on the winning side in the most recent election. Similarly, at the turn of the century both Germany and Sweden had much more professional, independent, and institutionalized civil service bureaucracies than did the United States.

In the United States there was no comparable development of an independent national civil service dealing with social welfare issues. The substantial democratization during the Jacksonian era took place prior to the development of an impartial professional national civil service (Orloff 1991, p. 247). This was a major reason that patronage politics became so institutionalized as part of the political process (Quadagno 1988a, p. 13). Each time a new party was elected it would remove most of those holding appointive office and replace them with those who had been loyal supporters during the previous election. Instead of social programs such as the Civil War pension system being administered by a relatively independent civil service, it was administered by political appointees who obtained their positions more on the basis of party loyalty than administrative expertise (Skocpol and Ikenberry 1983, p. 92). Given that these same people were often responsible for getting the party's candidate elected again the next time around, it is not surprising that ways were found to use these pension benefits as a source of political spoils. One strategy was sending around staff to certify veterans as eligible for pension benefits just before elections.

During the post-Civil War era political parties were not as clearly organized along class lines as was the case in some European countries. They were to some measure organized around regional lines; for example, the South became solidly Democratic shortly after the Civil War and remained so until well into the middle of the twentieth century. Similarly, prior to the Roosevelt era the North was almost as solidly Republican, particularly outside of major urban areas. In the northern cities with ethnically diverse populations, voting and political affiliation were often organized along religious and ethnic lines. Instead of being used to articulate the demands of a particular social class, party affiliation served more of a "symbolic-expressive" function, and for those playing an important role in efforts to get out the vote there were likely to be patronage jobs or economic benefits in the event of victory (Skocpol and Ikenberry 1983, p. 93). This explanation of why the United States did not enact old-age pension legislation during the Progressive Era points to the relevance of the experience with Civil War pensions as a negative referent. The resistance that the Progressives mounted against the idea of a national old-age pension program was a clear reaction to the patronage politics that came to be associated with the Civil War pensions.[71]

Efforts to account for the relatively late date of enactment of this legislation in the United States have often made reference to the strength of such national values as rugged individualism, voluntarism, self-help, thrift, and a preference for a form of laissez-faire free market capitalism with minimal state intervention (Birch 1955, p. 27; Kaim-Caudle 1973, p. 184; Rimlinger 1971, p. 62). Some have gone further and have traced these values to structural characteristics of colonial and nineteenth century America, pointing to the abundance of land, the high demand for labor, and the fluid social structure (Rothman 1971, pp. 156–159; Williamson 1984, p. 377; Turner 1920). This classical liberalism was particularly evident in the support for social Darwinism during the late nineteenth century. One argument made in this connection was that relief for the elderly would undermine the incentive for the nonaged to work and to be thrifty (Hofstadter 1944, pp. 18–19; Trattner 1974, p. 81).

There is no doubt that many Americans, particularly those in the middle class, have held and continue to hold rightist values on social welfare issues. The same could be said for Britain, Germany, and Sweden during the early part of this century. However, it would be hard to make the case that a leftist ideology was behind Germany's decision to become the first to introduce a public pension system.[72] Similar arguments can be made for Britain and Sweden. Given the strength of rightist ideology and the relative weakness of leftist ideology in these countries at the time when their public pension programs were introduced, we must be cautious when attempting to explain the late date for the introduction of the American Social Security program in terms of the nation's ideological values.

Orloff and Skocpol (1984, p. 733) point out that in many respects at the turn of the century public policy in Britain was more consistent with the tenets of economic liberalism than was policy in the United States.[73] Many of the values typically used to account for the late enactment of pensions in the United States were at least as strong in Britain during the early part of the century, and Britain did enact a pension scheme in spite of these widely and strongly held values.

Turning to the post-World War II period, it is easier to explain why there has been a dramatic increase in spending on old-age pensions than it is to account for why spending on these pensions remains at a low level relative to many other industrial nations. The increase can be accounted for in terms of such factors as economic growth, demographic change, the trend toward earlier retirement, the increased political influence of the senior movement, and competition between the major parties for the senior vote.

The low level of spending on public pensions in the United States relative to countries such as Sweden and Germany can be attributed to a number of factors. One is the difference in age structure. In 1985, 12.0 percent of the United States population was age 65 or over in contrast to 14.5 percent in Germany and 16.9 percent in Sweden (U.S. Bureau of the Census 1987, p. 46). Another consideration is the relative strength of organized labor. In the United States a much smaller fraction of the labor force is unionized then in Germany or Sweden, and labor is not as unified at the national level. Labor's influence in connection with pension policy is facilitated by a variety of corporatist structures in Germany and Sweden that do not exist in the United States.

We also find a difference between the United States and countries such as Sweden and Germany with respect to cultural values, particularly those associated with individualism and self-help as well as distrust of politicians and big government. OASDI programs receive strong public support in all industrial nations, but distrust of public spending runs higher in some countries than in others, and it tends to run particularly high in the United States (Coughlin 1980, pp. 52–74).[74] While there was at least some welfare state backlash during the 1970s in several European countries, the backlash was particularly strong in the United States (Wilensky 1976, pp. 14–21).

The case of the United States raises serious problems for those who seek to offer an account for the introduction of public pensions based on industrialism theory. Of particular note is the evidence that the United States, one of the most industrialized nations in the world at the end of the nineteenth century, did not introduce its first national public pension program until the mid-1930s. Clearly, the timing of the introduction of public pensions was influenced by factors other than the level of industrial development alone.

However, it is also the case that the decision to introduce a public old-age pension scheme was influenced by the economic and social changes associated with industrialization and economic growth. With industrialization and the development of a market economy came changes in family support systems, demographic changes, and a trend toward wage dependency (Achenbaum 1983, pp. 7–11; Rimlinger 1971, p. 209). The shift from a large number of small producers to a smaller number of very large producers also contributed to the need for old-age pensions.[75] At the same time the nation's level of industrialization made it economically feasible to provide public pensions for a substantial retired population.

As we have seen from our prior analysis of developments in other countries such as Germany, Sweden, and Britain, the industrialism perspective is more useful for offering an account as to why public pension schemes were needed than the specific timing of the introduction of these schemes. This suggests that industrialization was an important precondition, but it is only one of several factors that must be taken into consideration when attempting to account for why public pensions were introduced when they were.

It took the Depression of the 1930s to get the United States to enact social security legislation (Orloff 1991, p. 248). No other single factor was more influential than this economic factor. The Depression made it obvious that none of the prior alternatives would be adequate in the event of severe economic dislocation.

The sharp increase in spending on Social Security pensions that has taken place since the end of World War II was made possible by the prolonged period of economic expansion that the United States experienced (Lammers 1983, p. 98). It was at the same time made increasingly necessary by the graying of the age structure and changes in family structure (Achenbaum 1983, pp. 55–56). This economic expansion provided the resources needed to pay for pension coverage to a greater proportion of the population at increasingly generous pension levels. At the end of the 1970s this trend ended. In the early 1980s there was evidence of a concerted effort to roll back spending on Social Security and to limit future expenditures. It is of note that this shift was at least in part a response to the economic stagnation of the 1970s, the problems with inflation, and the dramatic budget deficits of the 1980s. Clearly, the performance of the economy has been a major determinant of Social Security spending trends.

While support for increases in Social Security benefit levels eroded in the early 1980s, spending on Social Security continued to increase. The age structure of the nation continued to shift and with the increasing proportion who were elderly came demographic pressure for increases in spending on Social Security pensions. This was not a new factor, the change in the nation's age structure had been an important source of pressure for increased spending since the end of World War II.[76] The age structure argument is another example of the utility of the industrialism perspective in helping to account for Social Security pension policy developments over the years.

Theorists in the social democratic tradition often compare the United States with nations such as Sweden to support the argument that nations with a strong labor movement and many years of social democratic control of the government tend to spend more on public pensions than do nations like the United States that have relatively weak labor movements and little or no history of social democratic control over the government (Stephens 1979). Consistent with the social democratic perspective we find that the United States spends much less on public old-age pensions than does Sweden.

Quadagno (1988a, p. 181) offers a variant of the conventional social democratic that takes issue with the "weak labor" explanation as being too simplistic. She like Stephens (1979, p. 150) attributes the late introduction and the circumscribed nature of the Social Security Act to the relative lack of organization among mass-production industrial workers prior to 1935. The American labor movement was dominated by the AFL, representing the craft union faction of the movement, that until the early 1930s was opposed to and by 1935 was only weakly supportive of federal old-age pension legislation.[77] Given this, it is difficult to make the case that the delay in enactment of federal old-age pension legislation was a reflection of a weak labor movement. Quadagno correctly argues that it is not possible to do justice to the complexity of the American case without taking into consideration the different agendas of various labor factions.

Nevertheless, it would also be a mistake to conclude that organized labor has had no influence on public pension policy in the United States. While organized labor was not given an important role in the formulation of the original Social Security Act, unions did work with groups such as the Eagles in successful efforts to get state level old-age pension schemes enacted during the 1920s. While these programs provided benefits to only a small fraction of the elderly, they gave some legitimacy to the idea of public old-age pensions and provided some experience that influenced the shape of the eventual federal level legislation; for example, the criticisms made of the early noncontributory state pensions contributed to the decision to go with a contributory federal old-age pension program.

When we look at the major debates, such as those around enactment of Medicare legislation, it is clear that organized labor has been an important actor during much of the post-World War II period (Light 1985, p. 75; Marmor 1981, p. 112); however, it was only one of several important pressure groups that have participated in the policymaking process (Marmor 1973). Thus we find support for the influence of labor, but it must be qualified. There were many powerful groups other than organized labor that were advocating increased spending on Social Security programs during this period.

In some ways developments since the end of World War II are consistent with the social democratic perspective, but not all of the evidence is consistent. Today the United States ranks near the bottom of the distribution of industrial nations with respect to the proportion of the GDP spent on old-age pensions (OECD 1988a, pp. 140–141). This would be expected given that the country also ranks low with respect to any commonly used measure of organized labor strength. However, it is also of note that some of the most important postwar gains with respect to public pensions were made during the Nixon administration, a period when organized labor had particularly little influence on public policy.

According to the social democratic model, the growing power of organized labor is the driving force behind increased government spending on public pensions. While there have been major developments with respect to coverage and comprehensiveness and major increases in spending on public pensions since the end of World War II, it would be hard to make the case that these developments are primarily a response to the increasing power of labor; this is particularly true when we focus on the dramatic changes between the mid-1960s and the mid-1970s.

Theorists in the neo-Marxist tradition often emphasize the social control aspect of pension systems. It is clear that company pension systems, particularly the early noncontributory systems, were introduced with very explicit social control goals in mind. The enormous political influence of the large monopoly corporations that had emerged by the early 1920s was one important reason that company pensions, a form of welfare capitalism, were tried prior to the federal public pension alternative.

Big business did not support the idea of a national old-age pension program until it was clear that the company pension alternative was not by itself going to be able to meet the nation's pension needs. These pension programs were becoming too great a burden for even large corporations to bear. In addition, the massive unemployment of the 1930s was leading an increasing number of workers to question the legitimacy of the existing economic order. Big business had a major stake in the existing social and economic order and consequently wanted the federal government to step in to make sure workers had a clear stake in maintaining that order. The Social Security Act of 1935 was part of the government response that many in big business sought.

While representatives of the working class did not play a direct role in shaping the Social Security Act of 1935, strikes, protests, and mass marches, many of which were working class based, did play an important role in convincing elites of an impending political crisis (Jenkins and Brents 1989, p. 894). These actions set the stage for the legislation by convincing elites that something needed to be done about the problem of old-age security.

At least some of the industrialists who supported the enactment of social security legislation were concerned about the increasing strength and militancy of the socialist movement and organized labor during the Depression (Bernstein 1968, p. 273). They viewed the Social Security Act as a means to contain the spread of socialism and to control labor unrest more generally (L. Olson 1982, pp. 44–45; Piven and Cloward 1971, pp. 88-89).[78] A major goal of this legislation was to reduce unemployment to a level that was politically more acceptable. To this end the legislation was designed to encourage retirement (Graebner 1980, pp. 184–189) and thus open up jobs for younger workers (Schulz 1988, p. 122).

Big business indirectly, if not directly, had a substantial say in the shaping of the Social Security Act (Quadagno 1984).[79] Most of those on the committee that drew up this legislation shared a big business outlook on what type of pension legislation was needed. In line with this business perspective, the Social Security pension system was structured so as to have relatively little impact on the distribution of income (Cates 1983, p. 24). However, some compromises were made that represented responses to other interest groups. Of particular note in this context was the decision to go with a federal-state OAA program that allowed each state to set its own OAA benefit levels. This was a concession to pressure from southern congressmen who were representing the southern white planter constituency, farm owners who employed large numbers of low-wage, primarily black farm workers. The OAA title was designed so as to assure control over the welfare system in the South by the local white power structure.[80]

The shift from the state-administered OAA program to the federally administered and funded SSI program in 1972 can be accounted for, at least in part, by the change in the southern economy that had taken place since the mid-1930s. The economy had become much more like that of the North with respect to industrialization and wage labor. Even the agricultural sector had become much more mechanized. A substantial fraction of young adults who previously would have been agricultural workers had migrated to cities, often in the North. This change in old-age assistance policy reflected the changes that had taken place in the South with respect to the social organization of production (Quadagno 1988b, pp. 252–261).

Migration left behind a rural black population that included many who were illiterate, widowed, and elderly (Marshall 1978, p. 118). This segment of the rural poor had become a burden that the southern congressmen were now all too willing to share with the federal government. Given that the federal government would now be picking up all or most of the cost of providing assistance to these people, control by federal administrators was not as problematic as it would otherwise have been. This shift offers support for a neo-Marxist interpretation of events to the extent that changes in the social organization of production had an impact on social welfare practices.

Useful as it is in accounting for the timing and content of the original Social Security legislation, the neo-Marxist perspective does not adequately account for the extent of the increase in spending on old-age pensions since the end of World War II. The increases in spending may have contributed to the legitimacy of the state and it may have reduced the level of conflict between capital and labor somewhat, but it is not clear that such great increases would have taken place if a need for increased legitimacy and industrial harmony had been the only causal factors. While Social Security continues to serve certain social control functions, such as providing an incentive to leave the work force by age 65, it would be difficult to argue that the program has in recent years been increasing capital's control over labor. Of particular note in this context was the decision in 1972 to index Social Security pensions; this change removed a degree of flexibility that one would expect that capital would have preferred not to have given up.[81]

During the 1970s we heard a great deal about the fiscal crisis of the state and the contribution of spending on social welfare programs to that crisis. According to many commentators one of the major sources of this crisis was spending on Social Security's old-age pensions. Is it contributing to the fiscal crisis today? It is more difficult to make that case today as the Social Security system is presently being used to build up reserves to be used in the future. The system is taking in more than it is paying out in pension benefits.

The link between nineteenth century military pensions and tariff policy points to the influence of industrialists on pension policy. To the extent that increased spending on pensions was favored by northern industrialists who sought protection from the import of European manufactured goods, we have evidence of the economic interests of capital driving pension policy. While this is consistent with a neo-Marxist analysis, the cross-class coalition that was made between northeastern industrial interests and midwestern veterans seeking larger pension benefits is as consistent with a neo-pluralist analysis as with a neo-Marxist analysis.

The neo-pluralist perspective is useful in accounting for many aspects of pension policy development in the United States. The conflict during the nineteenth century over military pensions was as much a regional dispute as it was a class dispute. Southern interests based on the export of agricultural products were pitted against the interests of northern industrialists. Efforts to extend and liberalize the military pensions were supported by one regional elite and opposed by the other.

This regional split over the issue of public pensions was to continue up through enactment of the Social Security Act in 1935. Roosevelt knew he needed the support of southern Democrats to get this legislation enacted. The opposition to federal level old-age pensions by southern congressmen in the 1930s was in large measure linked to the interests of southern-landed elites, much as it had been one hundred years earlier. Compromises had to be made to get the support of these congressmen and senators. The most important of these provided for local (which in the South meant white) control over the OAA program and the exclusion of agricultural and domestic workers from coverage by the OAI program. Both compromises helped minimize the impact of the legislation on low-wage labor markets in the South. As most blacks were excluded, the programs had little impact on wage rates for domestic or agricultural workers.

The efforts of cross-class organizations such as the Eagles on behalf of state level pensions during the 1920s lend support to a neo-pluralist interpretation of public pension policy development. At the same time the Eagles were acting as advocates for the aged they were also dealing with an internal organizational problem, declining membership. Their effort to improve the economic situation for the aged was a vehicle for increasing membership in their organization. Many of the new members were drawn from their coalition partners in this effort, organized labor.

The cultural and ethnic diversity within the working class related to massive waves of immigration during the late nineteenth and the early twentieth century helps account for the lack of unity in the labor movement and more specifically for the split between the craft unions and workers in the mass-production industries. It also helps account for why the AFL preferred to form a coalition with various middle-class interest groups within the Democratic Party rather than attempting to form an independent labor party (Mink 1986, p. 18). The tendency for the craft-dominated AFL to identify more with those above them than those below them in the class distribution in turn had implications for labor's stand on public pension policy. The leadership of the AFL was supportive of public pensions along the Wisconsin (antiredistributive) model (Quadagno 1988a, p. 108). Soon after it was formed the CIO, in contrast, was calling for replacement of the OASI by a flat pension of $60 per month ($90 for elderly couples) paid in large part out of general tax revenues (Cates 1983, pp. 58–59).

Similarly, the senior movement of the 1930s was made up of a large number of cross-class movements such as Upton Sinclair's End Poverty in California (EPIC) movement, Robert Noble's California State Pension movement, and the largest of all, the Townsend movement (Holtzman 1963, p. 87; Williamson et al. 1982, pp. 82–86). The Townsend movement became a national movement explicitly pushing for very generous old-age pensions. While Townsend himself was not in any way involved in the drafting of the Social Security legislation, the senior movement was an important element of the political context of the era putting pressure on the Roosevelt administration to do something about the pension needs of the nation's elderly.

Since World War II a number of interest groups have become active in advocacy efforts on behalf of the elderly. We have already mentioned the role of organized labor. Also important have been a number of professional organizations (e.g., American Nurses Association) and trade associations (e.g., the American Association of Homes for the Aging) representing groups that provide services to the elderly as well as organizations such as the American Association of Retired Persons (AARP), the National Council of Senior Citizens (NCSC), and the National Council on the Aging (NCOA) that are dedicated to advocacy on behalf of issues of concern to the elderly (Light 1985, pp. 76–77; Lammers 1983, pp. 58–59).

A major impetus to interest-group politics was enactment of the Older American Act in 1965. This act led to the creation of more than 3,500 state and area agencies and related service providers comprising a nationwide "aging network" (Estes 1979, pp. 72–73). Organizations representing these agencies (e.g., National Association of State Units on Aging) have been very active in interest group activity around aging related policies. While many of these organizations have been more interested in federal funding for programs linked to the Older Americans Act than in increased spending on old-age pensions, they have produced thousands of workers who are committed to the idea that society should be doing more for the elderly.

During the 1960s and early 1970s Congress frequently increased Social Security benefits and in other ways liberalized the program. What influence that the senior organizations had during the mid-1960s was due in large measure to being part of a coalition that included other more powerful groups such as organized labor (Williamson et al. 1982, pp. 100–101). By the 1980s there had been an important change. Some of the senior organizations such as the American Association of Retired Persons, the NCSC, and the NCOA became very influential with Congress, in part due to the quality of the research their policy analysts carried out in connection with proposed legislation and in part to their ability to on short notice mount effective letter-writing, telephone, and petition campaigns. The senior organizations still worked as coalition members on Social Security related issues, but now found themselves senior members of these coalitions. This was in part due to their increase in size and resources and in part due to declines suffered by some of their former coalition partners, most notably organized labor (Day 1990, pp. 99–104).

In the early 1980s the Reagan administration made an effort to cut back on Social Security spending, both present and future (Myles 1988, p. 283). It met with an outpouring of criticism from the aged. Around the Social Security issue the aged and other supporters of Social Security had become a very powerful cross-class interest group. Even conservative Republicans who wanted to roll back as much of the welfare state as feasible, realized that the risks associated with a direct attack on Social Security benefits were too great.

Theorists in the neo-pluralism tradition have emphasized the role of political competition as a factor driving up Social Security spending since the end of World War II. Most analysts agree that Republicans and Democrats vied with one another over this period to take credit for election year increases in spending on Social Security pensions. Representative Wilbur Mills had a reputation of being conservative with respect to welfare state spending, but in 1972 when he was seriously considering a run for the presidency, he used his influence to push through one of the largest one-time adjustments ever made in the size of these pensions.

One line of argument that is sometimes used to account for American exceptionalism emphasizes ethnic and particularly racial cleavages. Some commentators point to the shift in attitudes toward the poor, including the elderly poor, that took place when the ethnic composition of the poor changed in response to the massive immigration from southern and eastern Europe during the latter part of the nineteenth century. These immigrants differed from native-born Americans, a large proportion of whom were from a British cultural background. The new immigrants often differed in ethnicity, religion, and native language. Many ended up in the big cities in ethnic ghettos. These areas were well known for ethnic favoritism and political corruption. The massive immigration of the late nineteenth century and the early twentieth century was part of the reason for the opposition to public pensions by the Progressives.

There is no doubt that considerations of race influenced the drafting of the Social Security Act of 1935. As mentioned earlier the southern congressmen took great pains to make sure that the OAI title excluded farm and domestic labor and thus most southern blacks. They also made sure that administration of the OAA title was firmly in the hands of the local white power structure. The southern congressmen may not have been able to exert as much influence as they did, if organized labor had been much stronger than it was in the South. This in turn may have been possible had the AFL been more willing to accept black union members. The exclusion of blacks undercut the potential influence of the working class throughout the country and this was particularly true in the South. The racial cleavage in American society has undercut working class solidarity, and it may be an important reason why organized labor has had relatively little influence on social policy, including public pension policy.

Some of the most important work that has been done attempting to account for the late introduction of public pensions in the United States has emphasized the role of state-related factors. Of particular note in this context is the argument that the increase in the degree of democratization in the early nineteenth century, prior to the emergence of an independent professional civil service to deal with social welfare issues, led to a variety of corrupt practices in connection with Civil War military pensions. This legacy of patronage, corruption, and lack of civil service reform left the government without either the legitimacy or capacity to administer a national pension program (Orloff 1991, pp. 246–247).

The federal as opposed to unitary structure of the American state was another influential structural characteristic. It led to a split in decision making about social welfare issues such as public pensions between two levels of government, the state government and the federal government. Given the different economic structures of the southern as opposed to the northern states, it is not surprising that regional differences emerged with respect to preferred old-age pension and public assistance policies. This federal structure made it feasible for southern congressmen and senators to insist that the OAA program be administered at the state level. It also led to dramatic differences between states with respect to OAA benefit levels and eligibility criteria.

The influence that southern legislatures had on the shape of Social Security legislation was due to more than the federal structure of the government. Also important were some nineteenth century decisions about the ways in which congressional committees were structured and the leadership selected. One was the 1822 decision to establish a number of standing committees and give them the power to decide which bills would be debated and voted on by the House or Senate as a whole. A second was to give the leadership of these committees to members of the majority party with the most seniority.

Within a few years after the Civil War the Democrats had taken control of the South and maintained complete control from the mid-1870s until the mid-1940s. During the late nineteenth century in most southern states barriers were erected to political participation by the poor, particularly poor blacks. As a result the South became a de facto one party region. Southern Democrats typically ran for re-election without serious opposition, and, as a result, were returned to office again and again, resulting in more seniority for southern than northern Democrats. This in turn gave them control over a disproportionate share of the key committees with which Roosevelt had to deal.

By the late 1930s organized labor had become a significant political force, but it never formed a labor party and it never obtained control over the Democratic Party. One reason is the structure of the American electoral system, more specifically the use of primaries, the presidential system, and the use of single-member districts (Stephens 1979, p. 150). This electoral system creates a strong incentive for interest groups to coalesce with the existing two-party political structure. Organized labor came to exercise some power within the Democratic Party, but to actually come to control the party it would have been necessary for labor to have organized at the level of local electoral districts across the country and to have run candidates committed to labor's agenda in these districts. Organized labor never did so (Stephens 1979, pp. 151–152).

As Quadagno (1988a, pp. 176–177) points out, it is an oversimplification to refer to "the state" as a unitary entity. It often turned out that different components of the state were involved in the formulation of Social Security legislation on different sides of the same issue. In the case of the 1950 amendments to the Social Security Act, as just one example, "the state" as represented by a conservative Congress did its best to minimize program expansion while "the state" as represented by the technocrats on the SSB were pushing for program expansion. The pattern was similar with much Social Security legislation.

During the early years the chairman of the SSB was very influential in setting Social Security policy and one goal was to minimize the amount of cross-class income redistribution (Cates 1983, pp. 19–20). Derthick (1979. p. 22) argues that the SSB would have been much more progressive in its policies were it not for the very conservative political context in which it was forced to operate. Cates (1983, p. 150) takes issue with her and makes a convincing case that the leadership during the early years was strongly opposed to more redistributive policies. One example of this conservatism of the SSB was the opposition to "blanketing-in" proposals. Such proposals would have extended coverage to those workers who were too old in 1937 to earn sufficient work credits to qualify for a social security pension (Cates 1983, p. 37).

Conclusion

In this chapter we attempt to explain two aspects of American exceptionalism with respect to public pension policy: (1) the late date for the introduction of the first national old-age pension program and (2) the low proportion of national income that is spent on public pensions today relative to spending levels in other industrial nations. We also discuss the reasons for the marked increase in spending on public pensions between the end of World War II and the mid-1980s.

In our assessment of the late date for the introduction of the nation's first national old-age pension legislation we emphasize the influence of the Civil War pension system and the extent to which patronage politics played a role in connection with that system. We also emphasize the emergence of monopoly capitalism and the influence that big business had on both the timing and content of the original legislation.

A number of factors have contributed to the dramatic increase in spending on old-age pensions that has taken place during the postwar years. Among the most important have been: (1) extension of coverage to a larger share of the population, (2) the increase in the real value of these pensions, (3) the graying of the age structure, (4) economic growth, (5) efforts by both parties to take electoral advantage of the pension issue, and (6) the increasing influence of the senior vote.

Despite this growth, however, the United States continues to spend a small share of its GDP on public pensions relative to other industrial nations. One reason is the lack of a strong labor movement during the postwar period. Another is the young age structure of the United States relative to most of these countries. Yet another reason is the nation's cultural values which emphasize laissez-faire liberalism, individualism, the ethic of self-help, and distrust of government. In this connection there was less support for the more egalitarian and more universalistic pension policies that Sweden and many other European countries introduced in the immediate post-World War II period.

In this chapter we consider several theories of public pension policy development and find each useful in accounting for part of the historical evidence, but no one theory stands out as accounting for most of the evidence. We emphasize two different historical periods, the period leading up to enactment of the original Social Security legislation and the postwar period. Explanations linked to the state-centered and the neo-Marxist perspectives prove to be much more useful in connection with the former period than in connection with the latter. The reverse is true with respect to explanations linked to the industrialism and social democratic perspectives. The utility of each of these alternative theoretical perspectives is very much influenced by historical context.

The neo-pluralist perspective, in contrast, is of considerable utility in connection with developments during both of these periods. Some of the arguments are similar across both periods, for example, those pointing to the importance of cross-class coalitions. But others vary with historical context. In connection with the period leading up to the original 1935 legislation we emphasize the impact of ethnic cleavages in the labor movement and regional-based voting blocks in Congress. In connection with the postwar period we emphasize the impact of a much stronger and more institutionalized senior movement as well as electoral competition between Republicans and Democrats for the senior vote.

6

Brazil

In 1923 Brazil introduced a public pension program, becoming one of the first Third World nations to do so. Today Brazil has one of the most comprehensive public pension systems in the Third World; while the benefits for many are modest, a high proportion of the population is covered. Brazil is one of a very few Third World nations that have found a way to extend public pension coverage to the rural population. In some respects public pension policy developments in Brazil are similar to those in other Latin American countries; in other respects the Brazilian case is quite distinctive. For both reasons, where appropriate, comparisons will be made with other Latin American countries.

The Brazilian case is of interest for a variety of theoretical reasons. Up to this point our analysis has focused on the development of pension policy in the industrial nations. Most theories of old-age security policy are derived from more general theories about the welfare state formulated to account for developments in these nations. One goal of this book is to assess the relevance of theories and explanations derived from this literature to developments in Third World nations. Of particular interest are the qualifications and modifications of these theories called for in connection with their use in the context of the Third World.

Brazil has been selected as a case that is intermediate between Nigeria and India with respect to the degree of institutionalization of its democratic structures. This will prove of interest when we attempt to assess democracy's direct impact on pension policy as well as its importance as a contextual factor affecting the impact interest groups such as organized labor have on policy in these countries. Given the diversity among Third World nations with respect to level of economic development and the potential implications of this variation for spending on social programs, we have made it a point in our selection of countries to consider a range on this dimension as well. Brazil is at a substantially higher level of economic development than either India or Nigeria, and it has experienced a much more rapid rate of economic growth throughout much of the past century.[1]

During the past several decades public policy in Brazil has been strongly influenced by a highly elaborated set of corporatist structures. For this reason the case is useful for assessing explanations of pension policy development derived from corporatist theory, particularly the authoritarian variant of corporatist theory.

In our analysis of pension policy developments in Brazil we focus on the following four research questions: (1) To what extent has the evolution of pension policy in Brazil been shaped by corporatist structures? (2) To what extent have democratic structures had an impact on developments in Brazil? (3) What role has organized labor played in shaping pension policy developments? (4) To what extent are the patterns of pension policy development in Brazil similar to those in other Latin American countries?

Brazil's historical legacy has had a profound impact on the evolution of old-age pension policy. For this reason we begin with an historical overview which focuses on events that had implications for the timing and structure of Brazil's original pension program and for the way in which pension policy has evolved over the years. We briefly consider events during the colonial period (1500–1822) and the era of the empire (1822–1889). We consider the Old Republic (1889–1930), the Vargas era (1930–1945), the populist era (1945–1964), and the era of military rule (1964–1985). We then turn to a more explicit focus on comparisons with other Latin American countries and conclude with a theoretical assessment of developments in Brazil.

The Colonial Era and the Empire

The original Portuguese explorers came to Brazil in 1500, and for the first 50 years the major export was dyewood. In the mid-1500s they began sugar cane cultivation and by 1570 they were importing African slaves in quantity (Schwartz 1986, Boxer 1964, p. 2). During the sixteenth century Portugal was a major world power in the arena of international trade. Based on Brazilian production Portugal was able to dominate the world sugar market (Frank 1969, p. 152).

Brazil's first aristocracy was largely made up of the owners of these large plantations and the merchants who handled trade with Portugal (Roett 1984, p. 17). During this period the foundation was laid for Brazil's future economic relationship with Portugal and the European nations more generally. Brazil became a primary products exporter controlled by and dependent on Portugal for most manufactured goods. Most forms of manufacturing were prohibited by Portugal's mercantilistic policies (Robock 1975, p. 18). From the colonial era until well into the twentieth century the Brazilian social and economic structure was shaped by its role in the world economy as a primary products exporter (Topik 1987, p. 5).

During the seventeenth and eighteenth centuries Portugal steadily lost political and economic power relative to other European nations. One reflection of this change was the increase in control that Britain came to exert over trade with Brazil. While Portugal maintained formal sovereignty over the colony, Britain was able to extract trade policies that were much to its benefit. One example was the Portuguese Crown's call for the termination of textile production toward the end of the eighteenth century (Frank 1969, p. 161). This increased the market for British textile exports.

In 1808 the Portuguese king was driven from Lisbon by Napoleon's armies, and he moved the court to Rio de Janeiro making Brazil the center of the Portuguese empire (Roett 1984, p. 25). The court remained in Rio for 13 years and during this period the size of the Brazilian civil service increased substantially, in part due to an increase in the number of patronage jobs (Roett 1984, p. 117). After

Napoleon's defeat the king returned to Lisbon, leaving his son Pedro I as regent of Brazil. Within a year it became clear that the Brazilian aristocracy was unwilling to accept a shift back to the status of colony. Sensing the inevitability of independence, in 1822 Pedro I declared Brazil a sovereign country with himself as emperor. His decision to keep Portuguese elites at the top of the nation's highly centralized bureaucracy to the exclusion of the local Brazilian aristocracy was unpopular and led to his abdication within a few years. His son, Pedro II, became the next emperor and ruled from 1840 to 1889 (Daland 1981, pp. 45–48).

The Empire lasted from 1822 until 1889. Many manufacturing and commercial enterprises were now allowed to operate with relatively little regulation. During this period Brazil became much more of a patrimonial state; that is, a paternalistic bureaucratic authoritarian state controlled by an administrative elite (Roett 1984, p. 19). The state encouraged capitalist development, but maintained control over certain key social and economic functions. Potentially powerful groups were co-opted by the state through patronage and a variety of other social structures promoting dependency on the government (Malloy 1979, pp. 12–16). While patrimonialism was present during the colonial period, it now became much more institutionalized. One form it took was the creation of a much stronger bureaucratic web tying the states to the central government (Uricoechea 1980, pp. 180-181).

During the empire democratic structures began to emerge due in large measure to pressure from the rural elite for a greater degree of representative government (Love 1979, p. 5). The Constitution of 1824 called for a Chamber of Deputies made up of representatives who until 1881 were elected using a two-stage indirect process. Elections were first held for electors who then met in an electoral college to elect those who would serve in the Chamber of Deputies.[2] By contemporary standards the process was corrupt. Through the use of patronage and fraud the cabinet had no difficulty getting the people they wanted, typically those affiliated with the party of the cabinet, elected to the Chamber of Deputies (Graham 1990, pp. 71–72).

Pedro II was able to remain in office as long as he was due in part to his ability to play off one segment of the elite against the other. Over a period of 49 years he had 36 different cabinets (Daland 1981, p. 48). He frequently alternated between Liberal Party (formed in 1831 and favoring modernization as well as a strong central government) cabinets and Conservative Party (formed in 1837, representing the rural oligarchy, and favoring a decentralization of power) cabinets. Only a small fraction of the population was eligible to vote; for example, in the 1886 election less than 1 percent of the population voted (Love 1970, p. 7).[3] These political parties represented the interests of different segments of the elite as defined by regional and personal rivalries.

During the empire at the national level government administrators and the military came to be powerful interest groups. Almost all important positions in the military and civil service were filled by men from the families of the national aristocracy. Most of them did not have large land holdings, and for this reason they were highly dependent on the Emperor for their status and power. The first government pensions were introduced during this period. Not surprisingly, these pensions provided for the military and civil servants, the two groups whose loyalty was most crucial to the emperor (Malloy 1979, pp. 40–41).

Toward the end of the empire Brazil experienced the beginnings of industrialization, but the economy continued to be dominated by agriculture.[4] In 1819 approximately 31 percent of the population were slaves; the proportion decreased to 15 percent by 1872 (Ludwig 1985, p. 54). There was no evidence of labor union activity during this period due in part to the low degree of industrial development and in part to the existence of slavery until 1888 (Alexander 1965, p. 66).

The Old Republic (1889–1930)

With the cooperation of the military the republican faction of the Brazilian elite was able to overthrow the emperor and establish a republic in 1889 (Roett 1984, p. 28). One reason for the success of the republican faction was the increasing economic importance of the coffee industry. A sharp increase in export revenues derived from coffee exports increased the influence of the rural landed aristocracy relative to the largely urban national elite that had been generally supportive of the monarchy (Love 1971). The republicans believed that imperial interference in the economy was hindering economic growth (Topik 1987, p. 2).

One change was a substantial decentralization of political power from the central government to the states (Roett 1984, p. 28). As a result elites at the state level came to exercise more influence then they had during the empire. This meant more influence for large landholders, state level bureaucrats, and the state militia (Erickson 1977, pp. 11–12). A system known as *coronelismo* assured that the rural oligarchy retained its power. In rural areas local strongmen or colonels, who were usually latifundists, were able to translate their economic power into political power (Topik 1987, p. 8). Those elites who exercised the most control in the economically most important states came to exercise a great deal of control at the national level (Erickson and Middlebrook 1982, p. 216).

During the era of the Old Republic Brazil became one of the most decentralized nations in Latin America, but the national administrative bureaucracy remained in place and continued to expand. This provided jobs for the middle class and helped to minimize dissent from this increasingly influential segment of the population (Gomes 1986, p. 95). The result was what has been described as a prematurely large public bureaucracy. The extent of the bureaucratization contributed to chronic inflation, government inefficiency, and persistent budget deficits (Schmitter 1971, pp. 369–370).

As part of the transition from the empire to the Old Republic the emperor was replaced with an elected president, but the government remained an authoritarian oligarchy.[5] There were no nationwide political parties, and candidates for president selected by the incumbent coalition were rarely seriously challenged (Malloy 1979, pp. 22–23). The Constitution of 1891 supposedly liberalized voting requirements, but there was only a small increase in the proportion of the population eligible to vote. Typically less than 3 percent of the population participated in presidential elections during this period (Topik 1987, p. 8; Love 1970, p. 9).[6] While there was a shift in the relative influence of the rural versus the urban factions of the national elite, the groups making up the oligarchy during the Old Republic were basically the same groups making up the oligarchy during the empire (Roett 1984, p. 28).

During the Old Republic Brazil underwent a great deal of urbanization, but it was not being driven by industrialization, but much more by commercialization. The cities grew because wages were higher than in the rural areas. The jobs were for the most part linked to the agricultural export sector. They tended to be service sector, not industrial sector, jobs. Despite this urbanization, in 1920 some 84 percent of the population still lived in rural areas (Topik 1987, p. 8).

During this period Brazil experienced rapid economic growth. Between 1900 and 1930 the per capita income grew at an annual rate of 2.1 percent per year. This growth was due primarily to the increase in agricultural exports, particularly coffee (Gomes 1986, pp. 30–33).[7] The coffee industry made extensive use of immigrant labor, and this immigrant population in turn contributed to the market for inexpensive consumer items produced by Brazil's emerging light industries. Despite the growth of light industry, in 1920 agricultural products accounted for 80 percent of exports (Robock 1971, p. 18).[8]

During this period Brazil began to undergo "delayed dependent capitalist development" (Malloy 1979, pp. 10–15). It was delayed in that the process did not get started until long after it had begun in Britain and in a number of other European countries. It was dependent in that it was shaped by Brazil's dependent position in the world economic system. The industrial nations of Europe and North America were often in a position to undercut the prices of less efficient local Brazilian producers. These nations were also a source of outside investment capital that tended to be directed toward the development of the infrastructure for coffee production and export rather than the development of local industries that would compete on world markets (Furtado 1963).

The Constitution of 1891 guaranteed workers the freedom of association. In the same year there were strikes among cigarette makers and railroad workers in São Paulo. In 1903 railroad workers and longshoremen formed unions (Alba 1968, p. 255). Between the turn of the century and the early 1920s the working class rapidly increased in both size and militancy. During the late nineteenth and early twentieth centuries there was massive immigration to Brazil from Portugal, Italy, Spain, and Germany.[9] These workers brought with them radical European ideas about unionization and played a major role in connection with the establishment of the union movement in Brazil (Alexander 1965, p. 67).[10] During the early part of the century the union movement was controlled by anarcho-syndicalists, but by the late 1920s the communists and socialists had become more influential (Alexander 1965, p. 68; Alba 1968, p. 256).

The most effective strikes tended to be those that disrupted exports or urban services. As coffee processing and export did not involve industrial laborers, strikes among industrial workers tended to have little impact on the overall economy. Given subsequent developments, it is of note that during the era of the Old Republic labor unions were autonomous vis-à-vis the state, but subject to sporadic government repression (Erickson and Middlebrook 1982, p. 240; Schmitter 1971, p. 141).

Prior to 1919 there was no government sponsored social provision for the general population. Before this time those in need, including the elderly, were generally provided for by: (1) their family, (2) mutual-aid associations, or (3) private charity organized by the Catholic church (Malloy 1979, p. 6). Mutual-aid societies began to emerge around the turn of the century (Alba 1968, p. 255). They were in many respects similar to the friendly societies common in Britain during the nineteenth century and were the first organizations to appear among workers. They provided old-age and other social insurance benefits and were financed by contributions by the insured. Mutual-aid societies were as much a middle-class as a working-class phenomenon (Conniff 1975). They were not unique to Brazil; at the time mutual-aid societies could be found throughout Latin America (Mesa-Lago 1978, p. 19).

In addition to these voluntary organizations, a number of large industrial companies such as the railroads set up their own pension funds for employees. These company funds were financed by mandatory employees contributions in some cases supplemented by fines levied on workers for breaking company rules. The benefits were similar to those of the mutual-aid societies, but membership was mandatory for certain categories of employees. A variety of benefits were dispensed by these company funds, including retirement benefits for older workers (Malloy 1979, pp. 36–37).

In 1919 the Brazilian government enacted legislation requiring industrial employers to provide industrial accident insurance for their employees. However, this was done through private insurance companies, and thus it did not constitute a government funded or administered social insurance program. The first social insurance legislation that involved active government participation (*Lei Eloy Chaves*) was enacted in 1923. This legislation called for the creation of a fund that would provide retirement and survivors pensions to railroad employees. It did not establish a government program; it did not even establish an industry-wide program. Each company was required to establish its own fund with its own benefit levels and eligibility criteria.

The *Lei Elov Chaves* called for the establishment of company retirement and survivors' pensions (*Caixa de Aposentadoria e Pensões* or CAPs). Retirement benefits were to be paid to workers age 50 and over with 30 years or more of service. They were also to pay funeral expenses and pensions to surviving dependents. CAPs were to be financed from three sources: (1) mandatory employee contributions, (2) matching employer contributions, and (3) a matching government contribution.[11] The contributions by the employer and the government were to be determined by the size of the employee contributions which varied with income and varied from one CAP to another. The decision to establish separate funds for each company each with its own benefit levels and eligibility criteria reflected Brazil's patrimonial tradition and presaged the corporatism of the Vargas era.

Within a few years similar legislation had been passed calling for funds that would cover workers in other industries such as dockworkers (Gersdorff 1962, p. 198). It is no accident that the early legislation covered a few key sectors of the working class which included those who were most essential to the nation's export-oriented economy and those who provided vital public services. It covered those workers whose strikes caused the greatest hardship to the export industry and to the urban population.

These pensions did not involve income distribution from the rich to the poor or even from the middle class to the working class. Because pension benefits were to be proportional to prior contributions and thus prior incomes, the system in effect set up a transfer from younger to older workers in the same income and social class strata (Malloy 1979, pp. 42–43).

The Brazilian government's decision to enact public pension legislation was influenced by its participation in the Versailles peace conference at the end of World War I. As part of that conference there was much discussion about the need to deal with the problems of workers. In this context the signatory nations committed themselves to a ten-point program that among other things called for the creation of the International Labor Organization (ILO). This contact reinforced the tendency to look to Europe for ideas about how to deal with the labor question.

The Versailles peace conference offered reformist suggestions about how to manage relations between the state and the working class. The Russian Revolution offered an unattractive (to Brazilian elites) radical alternative. While the decision to introduce social insurance legislation was influenced to some degree by the growing influence of the working class in Brazil, it was much more a peremptory move to deal with the situation before it became a serious threat to the status quo (Malloy 1976, p. 43).

While this legislation was influenced by prior European social insurance legislation, it was also influenced by recent social insurance legislation in Chile and Argentina (Malloy 1991, p. 13). The prior experience with mutual-aid societies was yet another important influence. Also important was the experience with the mandatory pension funds that a number of companies had already introduced.

The early pension legislation covered only workers in the service sector, but it covered white-collar as well as blue-collar workers as it called for inclusion of all workers in covered companies. This inclusion of both low and high paid employees provided a form of vertical integration in that both working-class and middle-class workers came to have a similar vested interest in the same company pension plan. It tended to discourage horizontal integration of the working class in that workers with basically the same jobs in different companies were not part of the same pension system. Improvements in benefit levels or liberalization of eligibility requirements for workers in one company would not directly benefit workers in another company.

The Vargas Era (1930–1945)

The "Revolution of 1930" marked the initiation of the 15 year dictatorship of Gétulio Vargas, a major watershed in Brazilian political development.[12] This authoritarian regime emerged in part as a reaction to the perceived failures of the previous period of relative (albeit oligarchic) democracy (Malloy 1979, p. 18). More directly, it was a response to the regime's inability to deal with the financial crisis brought on by the Crash of 1929 and the subsequent worldwide depression that sharply reduced Brazil's export earnings (Normano 1935, p. 240). In addition, the previous regime was not viewed as adequately dealing with the problem of the "dangerous classes" (Erickson and Middlebrook 1982, pp. 217–218; Collier 1982, p. 66).[13]

Vargas, a loser in the presidential election of 1930, took control of the government in a coup d'etat. He was backed by young military officers and a faction of the oligarchy that included more of those representing the urban and the industrial elites and fewer representing the rural elite (Alexander 1965, p. 69). This "revolution" was the outcome of conflict between different factions of the Brazilian elite (Collier 1982, p. 63). It did not result in the complete displacement of one faction by the other, rather it produced a shift in the relative influence of the different factions. It increased the influence of the central government and the civil service bureaucracy. At the same time it reduced the power of large rural landholders, the group that had the most influence during the Old Republic.[14]

During the early Vargas years the regime was supported by some unions (Alexander 1965, p. 69). During the early 1930s there was an upswing in union activity and there were frequent strikes. But Vargas soon began taking action to repress independent union activity. This included the prohibition of strikes, closing down union publications, and the jailing of union leaders (Alba 1968, p. 256). He also used other more indirect mechanisms to control the labor movement that proved very successful. A law calling for the registration of unions was one aspect of a more general effort to redefine the relationship between the state and the unions. The state had long considered organized labor an enemy and now, at least officially, the state sought to become labor's patron and protector, albeit at the cost of also becoming its regulator (Alexander 1965, p. 69).

Vargas created a variety of inducements in an effort to redefine the relationship between the state and the labor movement. The goal was to create a new type of labor movement that was dependent on the state. Instead of being controlled by a political party, it was to be controlled by incorporating the unions into the state apparatus. Registered unions could operate legally and union creation was even encouraged, but strikes and political activity by unions were prohibited. The unions became primarily government agencies for the distribution of social services. Particularly during the early Vargas years these co-opted, dependent, and severely restricted unions proved to be very useful to the government as a mechanism for state control of the labor movement (Collier 1982, pp. 66–70).

In 1937 as Vargas was nearing the end of his term of office, he decided to replace the Constitution of 1934 with a new constitution that would allow him to remain in office. This new constitution was modeled in part on the Italian fascist constitution. It called for the establishment of the *Estado Novo* (New State), which lasted until 1945 when Vargas was forced out of office. Reflecting the influence of fascist ideology, the *Estado Novo* declared that class conflict must end (Alexander 1965, p. 71). The state was to adjudicate any conflicts that might arise between workers and employers. Toward this end the *Estado Novo* entirely reorganized the Brazilian system of labor relations.

To be officially recognized all unions had to once again register with the government, but this time the unions had to agree to a much more restrictive set of provisions that gave the government a great deal of freedom to replace union leaders it did not approve of and in other ways control union activities (Alexander 1965, p. 72). The new system was designed to more thoroughly co-opt and control the labor movement.

Both employees and employers were to be separately organized into parallel hierarchical structures (Erickson and Middlebrook 1982, p. 218). For workers the basic unit was the local union (the *sindicato* or syndicate).[15] These local unions were organized at the state level into federations and then several, but never all, of the state level federations were grouped to form confederations (Roett 1984, p. 105). As a result each occupational category was represented at the national level by several confederations.[16]

The *sindicato* system was intentionally organized in such a way that the unions would not become powerful nationally. Contributing to this goal were: the hierarchical federation and confederation structure, the restrictions on union activity mentioned earlier, and a provision giving very small unions as much influence in federation elections as very large unions. The government often found it expedient to organize a large number of small local unions that could be easily controlled. Its control over the votes of the small unions was one mechanism by which it controlled the federations and the labor movement more generally.

The *sindicato* system reflected the corporatism that was pervasive throughout the Vargas era, particularly during the *Estado Novo*. The reference here is to authoritarian corporatism which is quite distinct from the democratic corporatism we have discussed in earlier chapters, particularly in connection with Sweden.[17] Corporatism was not new to Vargas, it can be traced back to policies of the Old Republic, among them the way in which the original old-age pension systems were structured.

Corporatism can be traced back further to Brazil's Iberian Catholic cultural heritage (Erickson 1977, p. 4). A Papal encyclical in 1891 viewed corporatism as preferable to the conflict implicit in both the socialist and the capitalist models for dealing with the consequences of the industrial revolution (Camp 1969, pp. 30–31). Corporatism was also consistent with Brazil's authoritarian patrimonial tradition reaching back to the colonial era.

In the 1930s the Brazilian elite saw in corporatist doctrine the justification for policies that would allow the nation to modernize with minimal impact on the class structure; more specifically, it would make it possible to industrialize in such a way as to minimize the influence of the emerging working class. The authoritarian variant of corporatism being advocated by the Vargas regime offered Brazilian elites an attractive alternative to the disruption and conflict they feared from both socialism and laissez-faire capitalism. The claim was that class harmony could be achieved by requiring that state agencies mediate any labor–management conflicts (Erickson and Middlebrook 1982, pp. 215–218).

During the Vargas era the working class was co-opted and rendered relatively powerless. One mechanism for this was the *sindicato* system; another was social insurance policy. At the core of the Brazilian social insurance system (*previdência social*) was the old-age pension scheme now extended to include a much larger proportion of the urban labor force. This expansion was carefully crafted so as to contribute to the co-optation and control of the labor movement. By decentralizing the funds and giving each company the right to establish its own eligibility criteria and benefit levels, the government effectively divided the urban working class and undercut efforts at autonomous class-based challenges.

The number of occupational categories covered by *previdência social* increased substantially during the 1930s. This gave an increasing proportion of the labor force a vested interest in the status quo and at the same time created many white-collar jobs for those needed to administer the new pension funds.[18] Between 1930 and 1938 the Vargas regime established a social insurance system that remained pretty much unchanged up through 1966. It covered many in the middle class and the organized sectors of the working class.[19] During the Vargas era there was a great deal of progress with respect to social security legislation, but in large measure the benefits went to the middle class and the more affluent segment of the working class (Thompson et al. 1982, p. 345).

In 1933 a new type of social insurance institution was introduced. It was the *Instituto de Aposentadoria e Pensões* (LAP). The IAPs organized the social insurance and pension funds by occupational category on a national basis rather than on a company by company basis. While the IAP integrated workers from different companies into one national level fund, the social insurance system remained highly fractionalized in that workers in different occupational categories participated in different funds. Thus it did not facilitate a horizontal integration of the working class. The IAPs were very much in the corporatist tradition. Each IAP was administered by an executive officer appointed by Vargas. Each IAP also had a council that included representatives of labor and management, but the labor representatives were selected from above and loyalty was a major criterion in the selection process.

Malloy (1979, pp. 80–81) makes a convincing argument that the Brazilian social insurance system had short-run success in undercutting class-based pressure on the government from labor, but with some unintended long-run consequences. In particular, the corporatist structure of the social insurance organizations brought representatives of the working class into the administration of these funds. While these labor representatives were selected for their loyalty, it did give them access to high level government bureaucrats. Eventually this translated into pressure on the government to respond to particularistic needs of the workers covered by the IAPs. As more groups were incorporated into the social insurance system, there was pressure to respond to the needs of an increasing number of different occupational groups. While Vargas was at first largely successful in his efforts to use the nation's social insurance system as a mechanism for controlling labor, the way he organized the system over the long-run provided organized labor with an important power resource.[20]

Government social insurance technocrats had a substantial impact on developments during the 1930s and early 1940s.[21] Toward the end of the Vargas regime government technical experts came up with a proposal to reorganize social insurance in a single social insurance institution.[22] The so-called ISSB[23] plan was to cover all employed persons. They were clearly influenced in their thinking by the desire to emulate the universalistic approach being advocated by Beveridge and other international experts on social insurance policy. The emphasis was on broad coverage and program unification as well as the standardization of benefits, contributions, and eligibility criteria.

There was, however, another agenda as well. By the mid-1940s Vargas came to believe that labor was getting too strong. This was in part due to the control the syndicates had come to exercise over the administration of pension funds. The proposed ISSB reforms would reduce the opportunities for patronage and in so doing undercut the influence of labor leaders who were using their positions on these funds and the patronage it gave them access to as a source of power. But as it turned out, by the time the ISSB plan was introduced, Vargas no longer had the power to assure that it would be implemented (Malloy 1976, p. 46).

The opposition to ISSB was particularly strong from those who were already members of the existing social insurance institutions, which included many in the urban middle class and a substantial fraction of the urban working class. In addition to opposition from labor there was strong opposition from the private insurance industry. There was also opposition from the large bureaucracy that had grown up around the CAPs and IAPs; many people feared that they would loose their patronage jobs (Malloy 1991, p. 25). In addition, there were politicians and union leaders whose power was linked to positions they held on the CAP and IAP boards. Previously incorporated groups now exercised sufficient influence on the state that they were able to block pension policy initiatives that were viewed as threatening to their interests. The ISSB plan was decreed into law by Vargas in 1945, but the enabling legislation needed to put it into effect was not passed. Shortly thereafter Vargas was deposed and the ISSB plan shelved; however, the ISSB plan was not forgotten as some of the ideas did show up in legislation enacted between 1960 and the early 1970s.

The Populist Era (1945–1964)

In 1945 Vargas was forced out of office in a coup organized by the military and a group of political elites who favored a more democratic Brazil. This ushered in an era of populist democracy that lasted until 1964.[24] There was a fear that Vargas was about to cancel the upcoming elections in order to remain in power (Roett 1984, p. 31; Alexander 1965, p. 77). The Constitution of 1946 calls for politically competitive multiparty elections, but it also retained the Vargas era system of corporatist control over the labor unions (Erickson and Middlebrook 1982, p. 219).

The end of World War II brought with it a consensus that it was time for Brazil to shift away from authoritarianism and to become a much more democratic society. This view was held by influential elite factions in many other Latin American countries as well. Vargas had never developed a political party to mobilize support for his regime. But in 1945 when it became obvious that elections would have to be held, he organized not one, but two political parties.

During this era of populism the urban working class was politically mobilized as it had never been before (Malloy 1976, p. 44); yet, little effort was made to institutionalize the link between the voters and the government. Once elected, the focus of the president was more on responding to the needs of his "clientele" (ward bosses) than those of the voters. Given the clientelistic nature of the Brazilian political system, one need these clients had was for access for various forms of patronage so as to assure they would again be in a position to deliver the vote the next time around (Roett 1984, pp. 31–32).[25]

During much of this period Brazil had a factionalized multiparty political system. This factionalization of the major parties reflected and contributed to a trend toward increasingly polarized class-based politics as the populist era progressed (Collier 1982, p. 86).

Between 1945 and 1947 unions were allowed to operate with a great deal more autonomy than they had under the Vargas regime.[26] But the the trend toward increased militancy and the growing influence of the Communist Party within the labor movement led to a crackdown in 1947. Using the Vargas era laws, the government stepped in and took control of the unions replacing radical leaders with safe co-opted leaders (Collier 1982, p. 88). By the 1950s, however, the unions were again able to reassert their earlier autonomy.

During the administration of President Goulart (1961–1964) organized labor came to have a great deal of influence. It was able to obtain positions for several radical union leaders as executive directors of major social insurance funds. This gave them access to a great deal of patronage further increasing their influence (Erickson and Middlebrook 1982, p. 220). Organized labor did not, however, use its influence to broaden social insurance coverage. It did not push for an extension of coverage to urban marginal workers, rural workers, or other as yet uncovered categories of workers. Instead, the focus was on getting the government to respond to the demands of those already covered for improved benefits (Malloy 1979, p. 104). These benefits for the most part went to Brazil's middle class and its more affluent working class leaving a substantial segment of the low-income population with little or no improvements in coverage or benefits.

During the populist era one of the most important and contentious social policy debates dealt with the issue of public pension policy reform. The single most important public pension law during this period was the *Lei Organica* enacted in 1960. The goal of the social insurance technocrats was to reform and rationalize the nation's social insurance system by introducing much more uniformity with respect to eligibility, contributions, benefits, and administration, along lines suggested by international social security organizations such as the ILO. Such changes were opposed by many in the labor movement and Brazilian Labor Party. Labor was opposed primarily to the proposed administrative reforms that would jeopardize its influence and access to patronage (Malloy 1976, p. 44). Many rank and file workers who were members of IAPs with the most generous benefits also opposed change lest their favored status be jeopardized.

The final legislation represented a compromise between those advocating something along the lines of the ISSB plan and those who opposed efforts to rationalize the system and reduce opportunities for patronage. The final "reform" legislation involved a number of concessions which made the program quite inflationary. The final plan did not mandate the administrative unification called for in the ISSB plan, but it did call for an increase in the standardization of both contributions and benefits. Another important provision introduced indexing for pension benefits based on price increases. The new law also extended benefits that had been available to only some IAPs. In the new legislation all covered workers would be eligible to retire after 35 years of coverage so long as they were at least 55 years old (Malloy 1979, p. 101).

One goal of the technocrats had been to reduce labor's ability to use their positions on the boards of these funds as a source of patronage. However, in the final legislation labor's position was actually strengthened. Prior to 1960 the heads of the IAPs had been appointed by the Brazilian president.[27] But this legislation called for the head being elected by the council for the IAP. As labor was already quite powerful on most of these councils, this produced a substantial increase in labor's influence with respect to who was selected (Malloy 1979, p. 103).

By 1963 some of the IAPs were insolvent and a several others nearly so. A number of factors contributed to the fiscal crisis of the social insurance funds such as: (1) excessive administrative costs due to the number of patronage jobs in the IAP bureaucracies,[28] (2) the political basis of many investment decisions and the associated below-market returns,[29] (3) underpayment, nonpayment, and late payment of statutory contributions by employers,[30] and (4) the huge government debt to the social insurance system built up over the years due to underpayment by the government of its statutory contributions to the social insurance system (Erickson and Middlebrook 1982, p. 241; Malloy 1979, p. 120; Gersdorff 1962, pp. 197–204).

The Era of Military Rule (1964–1985)

Brazil's experiment with populist democracy came to an end when President Goulart was overthrown in a military coup referred to as the "Revolution of 1964." This ushered in the era of military regimes led by an alliance of military officers and civilian technocrats. The coup was in large measure a response to the political and economic problems the nation faced.

A symptom of the political crisis was the increasing militancy of organized labor. President's Goulart's regime and populist democracy more generally were blamed for the increasing number of strikes and other forms of working-class militancy (Erickson and Middlebrook 1982, pp. 215–220). A major goal of the new regime was to strip organized labor of its autonomy and influence as quickly as possible. It wanted to demobilize the working class and reassert the autonomous power of the state (Malloy 1976, p. 44).

The coup was also in part a response to the severe inflation and the falling per capita income. Another economic factor was the increasing dependence of the upper and the middle strata of the population on multinational corporations for credit, jobs, and modern technology (Erickson 1977, p. 10). In view of the changing economic structure of the country, many elites favored a move away from cooperation with organized labor and toward greater cooperation with foreign economic interests.

The coup of 1964 resulted in a shift back to a more authoritarian political structure; in some ways it represented a return to the authoritarian politics of the Vargas
era. But there were a number of important differences. For example, during the
Vargas regime organized labor was co-opted; it was made a partner in social policy
as illustrated by labor's role on the boards administering the social insurance funds.
While labor was for many years kept on a short leash, it eventually became influential with respect to social insurance policy. In contrast, the military regimes
governing between 1964 and 1985 made an effort to exclude labor from powerful
administrative positions in the social insurance system. The repression of organized labor during the early years after the coup of 1964 was harsh. Union centrals such as the General Labor Command (CGT) were abolished, the government
stepped in and purged the leadership of more than 500 unions replacing them with
safe government appointees, and many union leaders were jailed (Keck 1989,
p. 256).

While both the 1930–1945 and the 1964–1985 periods can be described as
corporatist, there were differences. During the former period both the labor system and the social security system were organized along corporatist lines. During
much of the latter period only the labor system was organized along corporatist
lines (Malloy 1991, p. 30; Stepan 1978, p. 74).

From the mid-1960s through the early 1970s Brazil experienced rapid industrial development; GNP per capita grew at an annual rate of 9 percent or more
during much of this period (Gomes 1986, p. 257). There were sharp increases in
public spending and marked increases in foreign private investment by large multinational corporations. Not all sectors benefited equally from this development,
however, Cardoso (1973) describes this period as one of associated dependent
development.[31] By the mid-1970s the economy was starting to deteriorate. During
the 1980s economic crisis became chronic and hyperinflation became a major
political as well as economic issue.

Starting in the mid-1970s the military regime began to open up politically. One
form this took was a gradual increase in the number of administrative positions in
the social insurance system filled by elites who were allied with, but not necessarily controlled by, the technocrats (Malloy 1991, p. 34). Again the social insurance
system started to become a source of clientelistic patronage and interest group
politics.

For a variety of reasons, including the deterioration in economic conditions
and the impact this had on support for the military regime, organized labor was
given increasing autonomy during the late 1970s. During 1978 and 1979 there were
a number of major strikes (Gomes 1986, pp. 158–159). The "new union movement" emerged. This movement operated within the old corporatist union structures, but it was able to do so with greater autonomy. Strikes remained illegal, but
the anti-strike laws generally went uninforced (Keck 1989, pp. 252–253).[32]

When the military regime came to power in 1964 social insurance reform was
undertaken as part of the effort to undercut the influence of organized labor. The
authoritarian corporatist controls on mobilization created a situation in which
social insurance technocrats could formulate pension policy based on their views
of what was economically rational with minimal political (read "labor") inter-

ference (Sloan 1984, p. 216). The various IAPs had become power bases for the Brazilian Labor Party (PTB) labor leaders. The decision in 1966 to unify all of the funds into one institute, the National Institute for Social Security (INPS), was a "reform" designed to take power out of the hands of labor representatives and put it into the hands of government social insurance technocrats (Keck 1989, p. 257).

The INPS represented the realization of one of the major goals of the 1945 ISSB plan, the unification of all of the IAPs into one broad social insurance organization. But there were some important differences; one particularly important difference between the INPS and the ISSB plan, was the lack of representation for organized labor on the board of the INPS. The program was to be run by civil servants with no pretense of working-class representation.[33]

During the 1970s a number of social insurance reforms were made which produced substantial movement toward universal coverage and increased centralization (Malloy 1991, p. 32). The military regime used the expansion of social insurance protection to new sectors of the population as a way to foster regime legitimacy (Keck 1989, p. 257). Of particular note in this context was the extension of coverage to the rural sector in 1971 with the creation of Pró-Rural (LeGrand 1989, p. 33; Weise 1970). At this time coverage was extended to virtually the entire rural population, but the program was quite different from that available in urban areas. It was not even partially financed from direct contributions from rural workers. Instead, it was paid for in part by a tax on wholesalers who purchased rural products and in part by a tax on urban employers.

This program is of particular interest as it illustrates that it is possible to extend coverage to rural sector workers in Third World countries.[34] Given the rural character of Brazil, it is reasonable to ask why coverage was not extended to the rural sector at an earlier date. One reason is that it was not until the 1960s that the nation's elites became concerned about the possible consequences of mobilization of the rural population.[35]

Other important changes in the 1970s included the extension of coverage to domestic servants in 1972, to the self-employed in 1973,[36] to the destitute elderly (over age 70) in 1974, and to rural employers in 1976. As one indication of the expansion in coverage during the 1970s, it is of note that the ratio of pensions to the population age 60 and over increased from .08 in 1950 to .16 in 1960, but increased from .19 in 1970 to .70 in 1980 (LeGrand 1989, p. 35).

Due in large part to the severe economic crisis that hit Brazil during the early 1980s, huge deficits emerged in the National System of Social Security and Social Assistance (SINPAS). In an effort to be more democratically responsive, the government submitted its plan for dealing with the crisis to Congress. It was met with immediate and strong opposition from the official opposition party and to a lesser extent from the official government support party as well. There were also protests from organized labor and even employer associations. Congress did not like this proposal and came up with an alternative proposal; however, as a reflection of the limits to democratic institutions at that point in history, the government ignored this opposition and imposed its own program by decree during Congress' Christmas recess. This decree introduced the Ministry of Labor's program which called for an increase in the payroll tax on workers based on a sliding scale and a flat-rate increase in the payroll tax on employers. At the same time the wage base subject to taxation was substantially increased (Malloy 1991, pp. 39–41).

During the early and mid-1980s there were few important changes in the social security laws. However, the indexing of pension benefits did not keep up with price increases. The Constitution of 1988 called for a number of important changes. One of the most important was equal rural and urban coverage. All workers, even rural workers, are now eligible for a pension equal to at least the minimum wage.

The following is a brief overview of INPS pension benefits under the Constitution of 1988.[37] For the urban population men become eligible for old-age pensions at age 65 (women at age 60) if they have been covered for at least five years. There is a special long-service pension for men with 35 years of service (women with 30 years). For those over age 70 there is a means-tested allowance if the person was in covered employment for at least one year. Survivor pensions are available for dependents of covered workers. There is no requirement that workers, urban or rural, must retire to become eligible for old-age pension benefits.[38] A worker who meets the eligibility criteria for more than one of these pensions has a choice, but can receive only one of them. For rural residents there is an old-age pension that pays 50 percent of the rural minimum wage. Virtually all rural employees over age 65 are eligible for this pension. There is also a survivor's pension and a pension for the elderly or disabled destitute, a means-tested pension available to those over age 70. There are also separate old-age pension and survivor's pension programs for rural employers (LeGrand 1989, pp. 67–72; U.S. Social Security Administration 1990, pp. 32–33). The proportion of the population covered by the social insurance system is the highest in Latin America and one of the highest in the Third World. By 1985 the ratio of pensions to the population age 60 and over was .76 and it is reasonable to assume that the proportion of the elderly living in a family receiving such a pension was even greater (LeGrand 1989, p. 35).

The pension benefit for those covered by the standard program for urban workers is equal to between 70 and 95 percent of the worker's average earnings during the three years prior to retirement.[39] Old-age pensions for urban workers are funded in part by a graduated payroll tax of from 8.5 to 10 percent of earnings. Employers are required to pay a 10 percent payroll tax.[40] The government contribution is flexible; it covers the cost of administration and any deficits. All pensions are automatically adjusted monthly to reflect changes in prices. Prior to 1950 Brazilian pensions were based on the reserve principle, but after that fiscal problems necessitated the shift to a pay-as-you-go system (Gersdorff 1962, p. 197).

The period from 1985 to the present is sometimes described as the "New Republic." Since 1985 Brazil has entered a new more pluralist democratic phase. In 1985 José Sarney became the first civilian "elected" president since 1961 and in 1989 Fernando Collor de Mello became the first popularly (directly) elected president since 1961.[41] Brazil currently has a functioning multiparty political system. During this period organized labor has been given a great deal of autonomy, but much of the corporatist union structure from the Vargas era remains in place as do many of the provisions that were used in the past to control labor.[42] Brazil's inflation problems remain very severe and the associated economic crisis makes the nation's fledgling democratic institutions fragile. Since 1985 some changes in public pension policy have been made, particularly in connection with the Constitution of 1988.[43] High level civil servants continue to exercise a great deal of influence with respect to public pension policy, but the relative influence of the organized labor has been increasing.[44]

During the 1970s the number of workers covered by old-age pensions increased dramatically due in part to the rapid expansion of the modern sector of the economy. The persistent economic crisis of the 1980s combined with the increase in the number of workers eligible for pensions has put a great deal of inflationary pressure on the national budget. This is one reason that some Brazilian pension experts are talking a close look at the Chilean experiment with a privatized alternative to social insurance for the funding of old-age pensions.

Comparisons with Other Latin American Nations

Today all Latin American countries have public pension systems that cover at least some segments of the private sector of the labor force (Mesa-Lago 1983, p. 85). However, in many countries, particularly those in Central America, pension coverage is for all practical purposes limited to a fraction of the salaried labor force living in the capital city and a few other major urban centers. Those that introduced their first programs during the 1920s or earlier, such as Brazil, Argentina, and Chile, tend to cover a larger proportion of the population today. In 1980 an estimated 96 percent of the economically active population of Brazil was covered as was 79 percent in Argentina and 67 percent in Chile.[45] In contrast, coverage is less extensive in countries such as Mexico (42 percent) and Columbia (22 percent) that have had their programs in place only since the 1940s (Mesa-Lago 1986, pp. 128, 136).[46] The major reason the figure is so high for Brazil is that nearly the entire rural population is covered.

Many of the countries that introduced their first pension systems substantially after Brazil, such as Mexico (1943) and Columbia (1946), were influenced by more recent social insurance models such as Britain's Beveridge Plan. The original pension schemes in these countries tend to be more centralized and uniform with respect to contribution and benefit procedures. Most of these countries began by providing benefits to certain categories of workers in urban areas. Over time, benefits were extended to other categories of workers and to other geographical areas (U.N. 1970, p. 243). Unlike the earlier schemes the trend was to include the new groups in the original program, not to create new programs or separate funds as new categories of workers were added.

Linked to more comprehensive coverage is the tendency for nations with older pension systems to spend a larger portion of their national products on public pension benefits. Thus in the early 1980s we find Chile (6 percent), Argentina (6 percent), and Uruguay (9 percent) spending a much larger proportions of their GDP on pensions than countries such as Columbia (.8 percent), Mexico (.6 percent), El Salvador (.4 percent), and Honduras (.2 percent).[47] The corresponding figure for Brazil is 2 percent. While this is much above the levels for the Central

American countries cited, it is low relative to Chile, Argentina, and Uruguay. One factor contributing to the discrepancy is the difference among these nations with respect to the percent aged: 4 percent in Brazil in contrast to 6 percent in Chile, 8 percent in Argentina, and 10 percent in Uruguay. Another factor is the variation among these nations in the proportion of social security resources allocated to public pensions. Brazil (45 percent) is lower than Uruguay (79 percent), Argentina (55 percent), and Chile (53 percent) (Mesa-Lago 1986, pp. 128–129).

While no single factor can account for why some countries introduced old-age pensions early and others later, there is evidence that level of economic development was a factor. There was also a general tendency to extend coverage to military officers and high level civil servants prior to extending coverage of any category in the private sector, a trend that parallels that in the industrial nations. When coverage was extended to the private sector, the pattern throughout Latin America has been similar to that in Brazil in that it was first extended to workers employed in critical infrastructure industries such as the railroads, next to a variety of critical urban sectors such as public utilities, and then at a later point to industrial workers (Malloy 1979, pp. 148–149).

Coverage for rural workers and the urban underemployed (marginal workers) is still uncommon in much of Latin America.[48] Where coverage of some rural workers does exist in countries such as Argentina and Chile as well as Brazil, it has tended to be a recent development. In Columbia almost no rural workers are involved in the social security scheme and in Ecuador the rural social insurance scheme makes no provision for old age (Mallet 1980, p. 380).

In many Latin American countries as in Brazil the state played a major independent role in the development of public pension policy. It does not appear to have been merely a passive object of class or interest group pressure (Schmitter 1972).[49] Policies were frequently initiated from the top down as part of a conscious policy of social control. The corporatist nature of pension policy development in Brazil can also be found in Chile, Argentina, and most other Latin American countries. Malloy (1979, pp. 151–152) uses the term *controlled inclusion* to describe the process by which specific categories of workers were brought into state-formulated top-down pension programs in all of the Latin American countries that were early adopters and many that were later adopters of public pension systems.

The corporatist organization of public pension systems and of social insurance systems more generally were part of a politics of accommodation that tended to divide the working class not only in Brazil, but also in Chile, Argentina, and a number of other Latin American countries. These programs privileged certain key segments of the working class making it difficult for organizers to build broad class-based workers' movements. Pressure groups attempting to influence pension policy in these countries are generally organized along occupational lines (e.g., civil servants, peasants, blue-collar workers, white-collar workers) rather than along social class lines (Mesa-Lago 1978, p. 10).

Originally the controlled inclusion of workers on the boards of institutions administering pension fund monies was a mechanism for the state to control workers. But eventually (by the 1950s) in countries such as Argentina and Chile as well as in Brazil these organizations came to provide a context in which the representatives of labor were able to put pressure on the state to increase spending on those sectors of the working class that were already incorporated into the pension system. These groups became increasingly difficult to control and an increasing burden on the economies of these nations. The serious inflation that they began to experience during the 1950s was due in part to the burden of pension and other social insurance spending (Malloy 1979, pp. 155–156).

While there are a number of similarities among the Latin American countries with respect to the development of public pension fund policy, there are also some important differences. Of particular note is a recent pension policy change in Chile, one of the first South American nations to introduce a public pension system.[50] In 1981 Chile introduced a major social security "reform" that in some respects represented a sharp reversal of what had been several decades of liberalization.[51] In 1924 Chile introduced a social security program that established a social insurance scheme for blue-collar workers and a compulsory savings scheme for white-collar workers (Mesa-Lago 1978, p. 25).[52] In some respects the 1981 legislation represented a step back to the lower level of central government commitment implicit in the 1924 policies for white-collar workers. After more than 50 years following the European social insurance model, the decision was made to shift to a form of mandatory individual private insurance (U.S. Social Security Administration 1981).[53] This shift is particularly noteworthy as Chile had one of the most well developed social insurance systems in the Third World. The Pinochet government found the existing pay-as-you-go system funded by employer and employee contributions too expensive.[54]

The response was a change to a variant of the provident fund approach. The new pension system is funded primarily by tax exempt contributions made by the employee to his or her own retirement fund (Arnold 1982, p. 17).[55] In addition, the government subsidizes a special minimum pension for those who would be due a pension below a specified very low level (Scarpaci and Miranda-Radic 1991, p. 31). Upon retirement workers choose between a periodic withdrawal plan and buying an annuity from a private insurance company (Castro-Gutiérrez 1989, p. 57).[56] Thus what the worker is able to withdraw during retirement is a function of contributions and accrued interest. The primary role the government plays in this pension system is the regulation of private institutions responsible for managing these retirement fund monies.

In connection with the shift from a social insurance approach to this privatized alternative, a number of private institutions have been set up to compete with one another for the workers' funds much as mutual funds in the United States compete for Individual Retirement Account (IRA) monies (Scarpaci and Miranda-Radic 1991, p. 31). Today there are 14 such private pension funds (or pension fund administrators). Workers are free to shift their account from one fund to another in an effort to maximize the return earned on their pension investment (Arnold 1982). The Chilean system differs from provident funds in many other nations in that retirement funds are administered by private institutions, not the government. Investment decisions are based on the best interests of the fund's investors which may differ from the needs of the government. If the government wants access to these monies, as it frequently does, it must bid along with various private interests and pay market rates of return. Under the prior system the pension institutions were often required to invest in specified government development projects which typically paid unfavorable rates of return.

So far the new Chilean approach to social security has proven very popular with workers as well as employers. The original plan projected a 5.5 percent per year real return on worker contributions and during the first 10 years the average was closer to 13 percent per year (Koselka 1991, p. 160). The present system is costing most workers less then the traditional approach and at the same time is yielding substantially greater pension benefits (*Pension System in Chile* 1990, pp. 28–31). Advocates of this privatized alternative to old-age provision point out that a substantial fraction of these monies are being invested in job-creating and wealth creating private sector investments. This may help explain the strong performance of these funds in recent years as the Chilean economy has been doing well, but critics point out that final judgment must be reserved until the nation has experienced a period of prolonged economic stagnation.

The Chilean model has not gone unnoticed in other countries (Koselka 1991, p. 160). Certain aspects of the model are presently being adopted in Mexico and plans are being made for introducing schemes influenced by the Chilean model in Argentina, Venezuela, Peru, and Bolivia. In some of these countries (e.g., Mexico) the plan is to add a layer based on the privatized Chilean model to an already existing social insurance based scheme; in others (e.g., Bolivia) workers would choose between the two alternatives with incentives of varying strength to elect the privatized alternative. Interest in Chile's largely privatized model is not limited to Latin American countries; policy experts in Poland have also been giving it serious attention.

Accounting for Developments in Brazil

There is much evidence that state structure, in particular the Brazilian variant of authoritarian corporatism, has had a major impact on the evolution of pension policy. When the first pension program was established in 1923 the government had corporatist social control goals in mind (Malloy 1991, p. 14). During the Vargas regime pension coverage was extended to many new occupational groups and a variety of other structural changes were made all with very explicit corporatist goals in mind. Instead of creating a uniform program for all workers, separate programs were created for each new category of workers covered. To further discourage working-class solidarity separate funds were set up for each company within a particular industry. In addition, both blue-collar and white-collar workers were included in the same pension fund. The key to corporatist control was the specification that these funds were to be administered by a board made up of representatives of employees and employers with an executive officer selected by the government. Moreover, the labor representatives were selected from above, not elected from below.[57]

For many years these structures worked as the Brazilian elite had originally intended. By the mid-1940s, however, organized labor was using its position on boards of the CAPs and IAPs to exert influence on the government. Structures that had been established to control labor were increasingly being used in reverse; labor was now using these same structures to colonize and control parts of the government.

By 1964 labor's autonomy, militancy, and influence on the bureaucracies controlling the old-age pension funds had become a major threat to the interests of the Brazilian elite. The military regime that came to power after the coup of 1964 introduced changes in the corporatist structures used to control labor. The corporatist labor system continued, but the structure of control of the social security system changed. Decision making became much more centralized and labor leaders who had been using their positions of influence on the boards administering the various social insurance funds were replaced by technocrats answerable to the Ministry of Labor (Malloy 1991, p. 30).

During the late 1970s change was in the air, and by the mid-1980s the exclusion of labor from national decision making was starting to break down. Today Brazil is more pluralistic, but much of the corporatist labor legislation from the Vargas era still remains on the books. Brazil's pluralistic democracy is still relatively fragile and the move away from its authoritarian corporatist heritage is not yet complete. It is possible that there will eventually be a shift to something close to the democratic corporatist structures found in many European countries, but it is too early to make that determination.

Since 1889 Brazil has alternated between authoritarian regimes and more democratic regimes. The major reforms in old-age pension legislation and in social insurance legislation more generally have taken place during the authoritarian periods (1930–1945, 1964–1985). There have been few reforms in pension legislation during the most recent democratic period (since 1985). During the populist era the most significant action was organized labor's successful opposition to a major reform proposal that would have substantially extended pension coverage, but also would have reorganized the administration of social insurance in such a way as to eliminate many positions held by labor leaders. These positions were used as sources of patronage which gave these labor leaders an important clientelistic power base.[58]

It is of note that the first old-age pension system was introduced in 1923, during the somewhat democratic era of the Old Republic. However, if we take into consideration the small proportion of the population eligible to participate in elections during the Old Republic, the lack of working-class pressure for public pensions, and the very clear Bismarckian intent of the original legislation, it is difficult to make a convincing argument that it was a response to pluralistic democratic pressures or to democratic state structures.

Organized labor had an impact on the evolution of pension policy in Brazil, but it was more in the Bismarckian sense than in the social democratic sense. The original legislation in 1923 was formulated with the social control of labor very much in mind. This was even more so with respect to developments during the authoritarian regimes. During the populist era labor again did have an impact, but it was in a negative sense of blocking efforts to extend coverage to new groups, an exercise of power that is more consistent with the neo-pluralist than the social democratic perspective.

Brazil and a few other countries that were among the most economically developed of the Latin Amencan countries were also the first to enact old-age pension legislation. Thus there does seem to have been at least some relationship between level of development and the decision to enact such legislation.[59] In Brazil the first groups covered were not the industrial workers, but workers in infrastructure activities central to agricultural exports such as railroad workers and dockworkers.[60] Next covered were infrastructure workers central to Brazil's increasingly urban society, those working in key public utilities. This pattern is not consistent with the industrialism perspective as it is ordinarily formulated.

The industrialism perspective is, however, useful in accounting for some important developments during the 1970s and 1980s. During the 1970s the real value of pension benefits increased substantially. This was possible due in part to the young age structure of the covered population, the increase in the number of workers paying in relative to those receiving pensions, and increasing incomes due to rapid economic growth. The economic recession of the 1980s produced a stagnation if not a contraction in the size of the formal sector, the sector from which the government obtained most of the money to finance the social security system. As a result the government could not afford to fully index pensions, and they tended to decline in real value during this decade.

More recent formulations of the industrialism perspective have emphasized the bureaucratic and demographic consequences of economic development rather than the level of economic development alone (Wilensky 1975). In view of this it is of note that a much larger proportion of the Brazilian population is covered by the social insurance system than in other Latin American countries that have had such a program for a much shorter period of time; this may in part be due to the long-term consequences of bureaucratic incrementalism. In general, the old-age pension schemes were among the first social insurance programs introduced, and it is also the case that countries with older schemes tend to spend more on the old-age pension component. For example, Brazil, which established its first old-age pension program in 1923, allocates 45 percent of its social insurance spending to pensions; in contrast, Guatemala, which established its first scheme in 1969, allocates only 14 percent to pensions (Mesa-Lago 1986, p. 128).

Uruguay and Brazil both introduced their first old-age pensions early in the century, but in 1980 Uruguay was spending 79 percent of its social security monies on old-age pensions (versus 45 percent in Brazil) and 11 percent of its GDP on social security (versus 5 percent in Brazil). One factor contributing to this difference is the difference in age structure. In Brazil only 4 percent of the population was over age 65 in contrast to 10 percent in Uruguay (Mesa-Lago 1986, p. 128). The proportion of the Brazilian population over age 65 has increased since the turn of the century, but it remains low relative to some Latin American countries and relative to all Western European countries. Due to this demographic trend, spending on public pensions has increased less in recent decades in Brazil than in the Western industrial nations (Montas 1982).[61] This evidence is consistent with the more recent formulations of the industrialism perspective.

There is some evidence that Brazil's dependent position in the world economy had an impact on the structure and evolution of pension policy. The first categories of workers covered were those who were in the best position to disrupt the flow of the agricultural exports that Brazil was so dependent on for foreign exchange and economic growth more generally. Thus Brazil's dependent position in the world economy seems to have had an impact on which categories of workers were covered first.

Looking at the era of military rule from 1964 to 1985, we find the system being "reformed" in such a way as to substantially decrease labor's influence in connection with the administration of the funds. This was part of the regime's more general effort to reduce the influence of labor. At the same time those representing the interests of the multinational corporations that Brazil was becoming increasingly dependent on were being given greater influence. There is little doubt that the effort to control labor during this period, in part by reducing labor's influence in connection with the social insurance organizations, was linked to the effort to improve Brazil's business climate for national and multinational industries.

During much of the past century however, Brazil's economic elite has been less than unified. While the state has typically served the interest of certain sectors of the economic elite, the cleavages among elites have been too great to fit a simple neo-Marxian model. Thus we must be cautious when using the social control variant of the neo-Marxist monopoly capitalism perspective to interpret Brazilian pension policy developments. While social control motives were clearly behind many of the policy developments we have considered, much of the evidence is more consistent with the corporatist variant of the state-centered perspective.

Conclusion

Brazil was one of a small number of Latin American countries that introduced their first old-age pension schemes prior to the United States. Today, while benefits remain low by Western European standards, particularly for the lowest paid workers, the Brazilian social insurance scheme covers almost the entire population. We have assessed the relevance of a number of general theories of pension policy development which have evolved from studies based almost exclusively on the Western industrial nations. Several of these general theories have been useful in accounting for certain aspects of pension policy development in Brazil, but the Brazilian context is sufficiently different from that of the industrial nations that some of these theories prove more useful when appropriate adjustments are made.

It seems that the most extensive reforms and the greatest efforts to expand coverage were made during the more authoritarian regimes rather than during the more democratic regimes. During the populist era labor did show an interest in social insurance policy, but it was primarily in terms of rather narrow particularistic interests in improved benefits for themselves. Most of the pressure for reform in the sense of introducing uniform eligibility criteria and benefit formulas, reducing inefficiency and administrative costs, and extending coverage to new segments of the population, came from civil service technocrats, not from organized labor or leftist politicians.

Brazil is much like Germany in that implementation of pension systems occurred during authoritarian periods as a means of social control; it is much like Britain in that democratic pressures attempted to limit expansion in the early stages among those who already had benefits. Brazil has perhaps only recently reached the stage where the existence of democratic procedures and diverse interest groups will drive further spending. This may occur with the future growth of the aged population.

The modernization of the Brazilian economy brought with it structural changes such as increased urbanization, increased dependence on electric utilities, and increased dependence on the railroads, changes that made the economy vulnerable to certain key groups of workers. These changes seem to have been more important than industrialization as determinants of the timing for the introduction of Brazil's first pension schemes. The rapid growth of the Brazilian economy during the postwar years provided the economic resources that made possible the increases in spending that did take place, but there is no evidence of the emergence of an influential gray lobby. Given Brazil's relatively young age structure, if anything, demographic trends have to this point helped contain public pension spending increases. Today, however, the nation's age structure is starting to change rapidly and this will have major pension policy implications in the years ahead.

Brazil's authoritarian corporatist state structure during much of the past 60 years has had a major impact on pension policy development. While some analysts would interpret much of our evidence as supporting a social control variant of the neo-Marxist perspective, we view the Brazilian state as quite autonomous during most of this period and thus emphasize an interpretation that is more consistent with the state-centered perspective. Organized labor has had an impact on policy over the years, but more in a corporatist than a social democratic sense. The major impact has been that policies have been introduced and designed so as to minimize working-class solidarity and mobilization.

7

India

India with a total population in excess of 850 million has the second largest elderly population in the world.[1] The nation has been a pioneer with respect to social security policy development in South Asia. Its provident fund approach to old-age social security provision has had an impact on policy in such nations as Malaysia, Singapore, Sri Lanka, Indonesia, and Nepal, all of which have adopted provident fund schemes (Thompson 1979, pp. 123–128).[2] But not all nations in the region followed the Indian example, some such as Pakistan and the Philippines adopted social insurance schemes while others such as Bangladesh, Burma, and Thailand have yet to adopt national programs to deal with the economic needs of the elderly.

There have been many studies of the problems of nation-building and national integration in the newly independent nations which emerged during the post-World War II era (Weiner 1967; Huntington 1968; Bell and Freeman 1974). This literature has given some attention to the role of social welfare policy as part of the effort to promote national integration, but very little attention has been given to the role old-age social security programs have played in this process. In this chapter we extend the literature in this tradition with our assessment of the extent to which the introduction of old-age security programs in India was motivated by the desire to foster national integration. Given a substantially greater degree of income inequality than in the industrial nations (World Bank 1991, pp. 262–63) and an ethnic diversity comparable to that of the Holy Roman Empire (Rudolph and Rudolph 1987, p. 64), India is a particularly appropriate case in which to assess the relative impact of class and ethnic cleavages on old-age security policy development. The nation's relatively well developed democratic institutions and the strength of its communal cleavages make India a particularly appropriate Third World nation for assessing the utility of the neo-pluralist perspective. Its colonial legacy and the size of the state sector make it appropriate for assessing the utility of the state-centered perspective as well.

In this chapter we focus on the following set of interrelated questions about the development of old-age security policy in India: (1) Why was the first program introduced when it was? (2) Why has the provident fund approach been emphasized? (3) What has been the relative role of cleavages based on class as opposed to those based on language, ethnicity, region, caste, and religion? (4) How important a role has the state played relative to that of various class and nonclass interest groups?

India's colonial legacy has had a major impact on the evolution of its old-age social security policy and for this reason we begin our analysis with an overview of the historical context from which these policies have emerged. We then trace policy developments up through the present and discuss the major old-age income security programs in place today. We conclude with a theoretical assessment of the historical evolution of India's old-age security policies.

Early History: Sixteenth–Nineteenth Centuries

The first Europeans to reach India during the modern era[3] were the Portuguese who arrived in 1498 and continued to dominate trade with India throughout the sixteenth century (Wolpert 1977, p. 135; Spate 1957, p. 161).[4] Portuguese traders were soon followed by the Danish, French, Dutch, and British traders (Rothermund 1988, pp. 11–14; Fersh 1965, p. 58). At the outset each country selected different ports and thus different spheres of influence, but competition for control of the India trade soon emerged. British trade with India was monopolized by the East India Company which started operation early in the seventeenth century (Singhal 1983, pp. 235–236). By the middle of the eighteenth century Britain had emerged as the undisputed European power in India[5]; however, it would be another one hundred years before the British were able to claim sovereignty over the entire subcontinent.

The expansion of British (the East India Company's) territorial claims was gradual and the result of a series of treaties and wars with the largely autonomous states that made up what we today call India (Singhal 1983, p. 291).[6] The British ruled indirectly in many areas. Approximately 600 "native states" making up approximately one-third of the land mass of the colony continued to be ruled by hereditary princes (Fersh 1965, p. 54).[7] It was not until the Revolt of 1857[8] that the British Crown took direct control over the Indian colony (Karunakaran 1964, p. 7). Prior to this point it was nominally the East India Company, not Britain that controlled territory in India (Griffiths 1965, p. 362). After this revolt was suppressed there was virtually no organized resistance to British rule for the rest of the century (Spate 1957, p. 161).

Throughout most of its history India had been subdivided into a very large number of autonomous princely states ruled by hereditary rajas. Periodically, as during the Gupta dynasty (320–540) and the Mughal dynasty (1526–1707), one ruler was able to wield control over a substantial portion of modern day India, but large areas in southern India were not included even in the Mughal Empire. Furthermore, in many of those areas that were under nominal control of the Mughal emperor, at the local level power was exercised by relatively autonomous hereditary princes (Griffiths 1965, p. 226). Given this history one must be cautious when making generalizations about India prior to British rule when the relevant political history as well as many social practices were regional or local rather than national (Fersh 1965, pp. 54–57).

In India during the Mughal dynasty and presumably earlier, the primary source of support for the aged was the joint family.[9] This pattern continues today in a modified form, particularly in rural areas. In the traditional Hindu family the old-est male member of the family occupies a position of authority and high status.[10] Yet, even during the Mughal era an effort was made to provide for the destitute elderly who had no family for support. Many were able to obtain some help from craft guilds or various socio-religious organizations (Employers' Federation of India 1970, pp. 7–8).

The Indian states had been actively engaged in trading with other nations as far away as Africa and China long before the first Europeans arrived (Rothermund 1988, pp. 8–9). They were major exporters of cotton and silk cloth to Africa (Wolpert 1977, p. 247). During the seventeenth and early eighteenth century India continued to produce large quantities of cloth for export and some of the Indian factories employed several hundred workers (Griffiths 1965, p. 301).

During the eighteenth and nineteenth centuries British rule had a disruptive impact on the Indian economy, particularly the village economy. Some scholars argue that the average standard of living in India was lower at the end of the nine-teenth century than it was at the start of the century (Nair, 1979, p. 252).[11] Others argue that extreme poverty was common in India even in the sixteenth century, prior to significant European involvement in the Indian economy (Griffiths 1965, p. 477). While there is debate among scholars as to how much of India's pervasive poverty today can be attributed to the impact of British rule, there is general agree-ment that the British did have an adverse impact on the village economy.

Prior to the era of British rule most Indian villages were almost entirely self-sufficient. Each village had its cultivators and its artisans; little by way of markets or goods from outside the village were required. The peasants were poor by con-temporary standards, but they were not subject to the swings of world commodity markets. As the British obtained political control over territory they began to set the prices (typically very low prices) that would be paid for various products.[12] This impoverished many workers who had no alternative to accepting these very low prices and the corresponding low wages (Griffiths 1965, p. 367). The British encouraged specialization among cultivators and a shift to cash crops for export to Britain. There were periods when this specialization benefited the local economy as when the demand for cotton was high during the American Civil War, but it also made the village economy highly vulnerable to the devastating impact of swings in world commodity markets.

The industrial revolution in Britain created both a demand for raw materials and a need for export markets for finished goods. Given India's dependent colo-nial position, the impact of Britain's industrial revolution on India was in many respects negative (Nair 1979, p. 252). In addition to being organized around the supply of British industry, the Indian economy was also structured to provide a ready market for British manufactured goods. Village artisans were unable to com-pete with cheap imported goods such as brass and copper utensils. Similarly, handi-craft weavers were unable to compete with the prices of British mill cloth (Griffiths 1965, p. 473).[13] This forced down wages and then produced massive unemploy-ment (Spate 1957, p. 166). As the artisans left the villages the cultivators who remained became increasingly dependent on the outside market to provide the money needed to buy imported utensils, tools, and the like. A money economy replaced a barter economy making the peasants more vulnerable to the adverse consequences of swings in the world economy (Griffiths 1965, p. 473).

Starting in the 1850s a few mills were built, but even at the end of the century 90 percent of the demand for mill cloth was being met by imports from Britain which is of particular note given that India had once been a major exporter of textiles (Wolpert 1977, p. 248). Many factors contributed to India's relative lack of industrialization during the late nineteenth century. One of the most important for the textile industry was Britain's unwillingness to allow the protective tariffs that would have encouraged Indian industrialists to make the necessary capital investment in enterprises capable of locally producing textile machinery (Rothermund 1988, p. 54).

The Era of the Independence Movement

The Indian National Congress was founded in 1885 (Cumming 1932, p. 39). The first meeting involved only 70 delegates (Spear 1965, p. 170); while the number did increase over time, it did not become a mass-based political party and movement until Gandhi became its leader in 1920 (Nair 1979, p. 253). During the early years it was primarily an annual gathering of urban middle-class Indian moderates interested in discussing various social and political reforms they hoped the British might consider (Hardgrave and Kochanek 1986, p. 49; Singh 1966, p. 23). The group was well educated and included many businessmen and lawyers, but there were no representatives of peasants or the lower classes (Powell-Price 1955, p. 586). During the early years there was no call for Indian independence, no call for the introduction of social insurance programs, and no call for the use of militant tactics to obtain desired reforms.

After the turn of the century the expression of dissatisfaction with British rule became increasingly open (Fersh 1965, p. 60). At the 1905 meeting of the Indian National Congress the moderate reformist tone of the discussion shifted. Japan's recent military victory over Russia gave more militant members reason to push harder for reforms (Griffiths 1965, p. 295). In 1906 Congress[14] made its first demand for Indian self-government and it authorized the boycott of British goods as a political tactic (Cumming 1932, pp. 52–53). While the organization was becoming increasingly militant, it was still not a mass-based political organization.

India made a substantial contribution to the British war effort during World War I including sending thousands of troops to Europe. Many Indians expected that in return for this support India would be granted independence, and they were disillusioned when it became clear that the British were unwilling to move in this direction.[15] One of the consequences of the war experience was the recognition among Indians that Britain was only one among many approximately equal European powers. Another was a shift toward a much less respectful view of British culture and Western civilization more generally (Spear 1965, p. 182). This diminished view of Britain emboldened those seeking independence and after the war the independence movement gathered steam. Mobilization efforts were facilitated by discontent among peasants and among the urban working class due in part to the economic dislocation caused by the sharp economic contraction at the war's conclusion (Nair 1979, p. 253; Weiner 1964, p. 102).[16]

Gandhi is credited with organizing the first successful nationwide strike in India (1919), and by 1920 he was the undisputed leader of Congress (Singh 1966, p. 26). He convinced Congress to shift to a self-conscious policy of noncooperation with the British (Griffiths 1965, p. 305). Gandhi was able to transform Congress from an assembly of urban middle-class professionals into a mass based political movement with support from all strata (Fersh 1965, p. 61). Particularly crucial was his success in attracting most of India's major interest groups including the peasants (Wolpert 1977, p. 301). Even as late as the 1980s, 76 percent of the Indian population lived in rural areas (Hardgrave and Kochanek 1986, p. 18). During the 1920s Congress became a major political force. In 1942 it was declared an illegal organization and its leaders were jailed for demanding Indian independence.

After India became an independent nation in 1947, Congress remained the most powerful political party. Ever since independence India has had a multiplicity of political parties most of which are regional in character. Some 85 political parties participated in the first general election in 1952. Between 1952 and 1991 the only periods during which Congress did not control the Parliament was from 1977 to 1979 and again from 1989 to 1991. Collectively, opposition parties have captured more than half of the vote in most national elections since independence, but due to disunity they have rarely been able to displace Congress; however, Congress itself split in 1969 and again in 1978.[17]

The polity in India has for the most part been pluralistic, but there was a period between 1975 and 1977 when Indira Gandhi attempted to substitute a more authoritarian corporatist regime. Nevertheless, her efforts were rejected by voters in 1977 when she was voted out of office and control of government shifted from Congress to the Janata Party (Rudolph and Rudolph 1987, p. 252). Shortly thereafter Indira Gandhi was expelled from Congress, but she soon formed a new party called Congress (I) which regained control of Parliament in 1980 and retained it until 1989 when the party then under the control of Indira's son Rajiv Gandhi lost the general election.[18] The domestic agenda of Congress has in many respects been social democratic; for example, it has consistently supported public ownership of a number of major industries in the modern sector of the economy. During general elections Congress has emphasized the need to provide for India's poor; however, for a variety of reasons including limited funds, government policy has not always been consistent with this rhetoric. Today Congress is more commonly classified as a centrist than a social democratic party.

The development of organized labor in India was much influenced by Congress and the independence movement more generally. In 1890 the Bombay Mill Hands Association was formed (Sinha 1980, p. 24). Some scholars point to this organization as India's first labor union. Others are more cautious pointing out that it was a very small organization without union dues or the various regulations that typify unions. Labor organization did not start taking on the characteristics of a union movement until the end of World War I (Varma 1964, p. 153).

In 1920 the All-India Trade Union Congress was formed. This was the first national labor organization. It was formed so as to provide representation for

India in the International Labour Organization (Sinha, 1980, p. 26). While the proportion of workers who belonged to unions was still small in 1920, the unions were starting to have some political influence (Sinha 1980, p. 26).[19] The proportion of workers joining unions continued to increase up through the mid-1970s reaching approximately 4 percent of the total labor force and approximately 25 percent of the organized (modern) sector of the economy, which is about where it stands today (Hardgrave and Kochanek 1986, p. 177; Mamoria and Mamoria 1983, p. 123).

The evolution of the labor movement during the 1920s, 1930s, and 1940s was closely linked to the more general movement Gandhi was leading for national independence (Weiner 1964, p. 101). The independence movement contributed to an environment that was conducive to the growth of the union movement, but the broader goals of the independence movement also tended to undercut commitment to the narrower set of concerns that are typically the focus of union organizing. From the 1920s through the 1940s union membership was rapidly expanding, but some scholars argue that this was more a reflection of the struggle for independence than a class struggle. Discontent was expressed toward Indian managers and owners, but the strongest discontent was reserved for the British rulers (Weiner 1964, p. 102).

The potential influence of unions has been undercut by the large number (approximately 25,000 today) and intense competition among unions, competition which is encouraged by legislation allowing groups as small as seven workers to form their own unions (Hardgrave and Kochanek 1986, p. 177; Varma 1964, p. 153). At the national level India's labor movement is organized into eleven labor federations, but the deep partisan cleavages make it impossible for labor to speak as one voice on behalf of labor's interest (Rudolph and Rudolph 1987, p. 25). Workers in the same organization often have a choice as to which union to join. This competition for membership keeps union dues low and dues collection procedures lax, reducing the influence of the unions. Trade union members have little loyalty to individual unions. They switch unions frequently and often join more than one. The average Indian union has about 800 members (Mamoria and Mamoria 1983, p. 136). Given the small size of unions, the lack of substantial economic resources, the fierce competition among unions, and the relatively small size of the organized sector, it is not surprising that organized labor's impact on pension policy over the years has been modest.[20]

Organized labor does not represent the interests of the nation's massive poor population. Most likely to be unionized are the more affluent urban wage earners holding white-collar or industrial jobs.[21] Union members are concentrated in the organized sector of the economy that includes only 15 percent of the population (Johri 1982, p. 108). These workers are more concerned with legislation that will benefit themselves than with efforts to help the the least well-off (Weiner 1964, p. 100).

The unions have made a number of demands in connection with India's provident fund schemes. Some have been met, others have not. The unions have pushed for extending coverage to a greater proportion of the work force. They have also pushed for higher benefit (and therefore contribution) levels. These demands have pushed for higher benefit (and therefore contribution) levels. These demands have generally been supported by the government in large measure because the provident fund monies are invested in government securities and thus provide a significant source of investment capital. However, the demand by some labor leaders that the provident fund schemes be converted into social insurance programs has not been supported by the government (Johri 1967, p. 185).

Due to the control that the central government has been able to exercise over wage agreements, demands for better wages and working conditions are more often directed at key government officials than at management (Hardgrave and Kochanek 1986, p. 177). When Congress has been in power the Indian National Trade Union Congress has generally been regarded as an arm of the government. It seems to be more an organization to control labor and mobilize labor around the agenda of Congress than an organization to articulate the interests of labor and pressure Congress on behalf of organized labor. The union leadership tends to take the view that it is in the best interest of workers to support policies that will facilitate long-term national economic growth rather than pushing for maximum short-term wage gains.

The pace of industrialization picked up significantly during World War II (Rothermund 1988, pp. 74, 118; Spear 1965, p. 216), but even at the end of the war less than 2 percent of the labor force was employed in the industrial sector (Nair 1979, p. 254).[22] Between 1900 and 1947 there was almost no increase in real per capita income, but since independence the average annual real growth rate has been approximately 1.3 percent (Hardgrave and Kochanek 1986, p. 21). Between 1950 and 1980 real per capita income increased by 50 percent (Rothermund 1988, p. 172).

As the nation began to industrialize, it also began to urbanize, increasing from 11 percent urban in 1901 to 24 percent by the early 1980s (Hardgrave 1984, p. 18).[23] With industrialization and urbanization it became increasingly evident that the traditional joint family was not able to provide adequate old-age security for workers in certain sectors of the economy, such as the organized sector. Industrialization and other related changes such as urbanization and increased dependence on money wages contributed to the pressure for more social security legislation (Sinha 1980, pp. 23–26).

The nation's first social insurance legislation was the 1923 Workmen's Compensation Act (Johri 1982, p. 109).[24] This act called for a lump sum payment to disabled workers; it did not provide a pension or any other form of continuing income (Cohen 1953, p. 11).[25] This legislation did, however, become a model for similar legislation in a number of other Asian nations. The 1925 Provident Fund Act led to the creation of provident funds as a mechanism to provide for old age and disability, but it only covered civil servants and government railroad workers (Sinha 1980, p. 109). Here again the benefit paid at retirement or upon disability was a lump sum with no continuing pension.

A number of factors contributed to the relatively long period between enactment of this early social insurance legislation and enactment of the first old-age social security legislation (1948) for the private sector. Particularly important was the struggle for independence. One might have expected the British to have introduced more by way of social insurance legislation in an effort to control labor; however, as most of those who were mobilized in connection with the independence movement were not employed in enterprises that could easily have been included in provident fund or social insurance schemes, it is unlikely that such efforts would have significantly tempered demands for independence. Given the economic demands on Britain first due to the Depression and then to World War II, it is not too surprising that colonial administrators made so little effort to formulate and introduce new social security programs.

By the early 1930s most railroad workers were working for companies that had introduced provident fund schemes, but only about 30 percent of railroad employees were covered. The lowest paid workers were generally excluded. Despite the focus on the war and on efforts to maintain order in the face of an increasingly powerful independence movement, colonial administrators were starting to formulate plans for provident fund schemes during the 1940s (Mamoria and Mamoria 1983, p. 57). During the early 1940s model schemes were formulated and circulated to major employers primarily in the industrial sector. Some employers introduced such schemes, but any such action was strictly voluntary.

British rule left India with a number of important political legacies; it provided experience with an independent judiciary, a free press, an apolitical military, and parliamentary democracy (Moorhouse 1983, p. 225). The various institutions and bureaucratic structures associated with British colonial rule contributed to the emergence of a strong central government during the post-independence period (Rudolph and Rudolph 1987, p 1). Prior to British rule the subcontinent had been divided into several hundred autonomous and semiautonomous states reflecting a great deal of diversity with respect to language, religion, ethnicity, and cultural traditions. More than a hundred years of British rule did much to unify these territories, making possible the modern state of India (Griffiths 1965, p. 226). English became a national language shared by the most formally educated Indians.[26] This was particularly important to unification given that 16 major languages are spoken in India.[27] During the last 30 years of British rule the independence movement provided yet another source of unification. The struggle against the British did much to promote nationalism and at least temporarily unify groups that had traditionally been split by strong cleavages based on religion, language, caste, and region (Jeffrey 1986; Hardgrave 1984, p. 26; Griffiths 1965, p. 237).

While overall British rule contributed to the unification of India, a number of long-standing cleavages remained. Many of these cleavages were reinforced by British policy that called for separate representation for various population subgroups such as the untouchables, Muslims, Anglo-Indians, and Sikhs. Such policies contributed to the development of organized interest groups along occupational, religious, caste, tribal, regional, and linguistic lines (Weiner 1964, pp. 98–103). However, these cleavages are so deep and long-standing that it would be inappropriate to overemphasize the role of the British in accounting for the number and the strength of the cleavages that exist today (Singh 1966, pp. 8–10; Fersh 1965, p. 57). These cleavages are a major reason that today social policy is much more influenced by interest group than strictly social class politics.

Policy Developments Since Independence

In 1948 the Coal Mines Provident Fund and Bonus Scheme Act was enacted. It was India's first national private sector provident fund plan. As the name suggests it covered only workers in the coal-mining industry (Sinha 1980, p. 110). The popularity of this act led to demands for similar legislation covering other industries (Johri 1982, p. 109). The outcome was the much more comprehensive 1952 Employees' Provident Fund and Miscellaneous Provisions Act. This act was similar to the 1948 legislation, but it applied to several different industries. When introduced it covered workers in only 6 industries, but the number increased to 173 by the late 1980s (Bhattarai 1989, p. 484).[28]

Analysis of the debate prior to enactment of the 1952 legislation reveals that many would have preferred the social insurance approach common in the industrial nations, but that alternative was rejected because of the potentially heavy burden on the economy (Cohen 1953, p. 15). Fear of corruption was another reason to prefer the provident fund approach to the social insurance approach (Sinha 1980, pp. 144–145).

Even the provident fund approach was at first opposed by organizations such as the All India Manufacturers' Organization that were concerned about the financial burden on employers and the possibility of a negative impact on the nation's rate of economic growth. Similarly, workers were concerned about the employees' contributions which many viewed as an unacceptable tax on their already low wages. The provident fund idea was, however, strongly supported by a number of high level technocrats in the Indian Administrative Service (Sinha 1980, pp. 109–110, 144).[29] Despite prior opposition from some quarters, soon after enactment the program proved popular with covered workers.

In 1971 a survivor's pension referred to as the Employees' Family Pension Scheme was added to the Indian social security system (Mamoria and Mamoria 1983, pp. 61–63). It represented a significant innovation in two respects. It was India's first old-age social insurance legislation. In addition, it was the first social security program to which the government made a contribution (Hoskins 1971, p. 28). This legislation called for the payment of a survivor's pension based on the income of the deceased.

The 1972 Gratuity Act can be viewed as a modest victory for labor in that it took a benefit which previously had been at the discretion of the employer and made it a part of the social security system. Traditionally many employers had paid a gratuity at retirement as a reward for long and loyal service. Whether the gratuity was paid and the size of the payment was entirely at the employer's discretion. This legislation transformed the benefit in that it now became the subject of collective bargaining between labor and management (Sarma 1981, p. 225).

In 1976 the Employees' Deposit-Linked Insurance Scheme was added (Johri 1982, p. 109). It is a form of life insurance. It covers the same workers who are covered by the Employees' Provident Fund Scheme and calls for a variable lump sum benefit to the designated survivor based on the balance in the worker's account at the time of death. This legislation had the effect of almost doubling the amount paid to survivors (*International Benefit Guidelines* 1989, p. 114).

Today India's Employees' Provident Organization includes three major programs: (1) the Employees' Provident Fund scheme, (2) the Employees' Family Pension scheme, and (3) the Employees' Deposit-Linked Insurance scheme. The Employees' Provident Fund is by far the largest of the social security programs providing income benefits to the aged. It is administered by a Central Board of Trustees that is made up of representatives of government, labor organizations, and employer organizations (Bhattarai 1989, p. 485). Workers contribute 8.33 percent of their wages and the employer makes a matching contribution (U.S. Social Security Administration 1990), p. 118). There is also a small additional tax on employers to cover the cost of administering the program. Workers ordinarily become eligible for benefits at age 55, and as a requirement for receiving the benefit they must retire from covered employment (Sarma 1981, p. 205). The old-age benefit is paid as a lump sum; the size of this benefit is determined by the contributions from the employer and the worker over the years and by the interest earned on those contributions.

The scheme is fully funded with the monies contributed being invested in government securities that earn interest at a rate set by the central government (Johri 1982, p. 114); however, it is of note that the interest paid over the years has not kept pace with inflation. Establishments with 20 or more workers that have been in operation for five years or more must participate in the program if they are in one of the industries presently included (Sarma 1981, pp. 203–204).[30] Membership in the scheme is optional for employees earning more than Rs 2,500 per month, but it is compulsory for employees earning less than this amount. Once enrolled the employee may elect to continue irrespective of subsequent wage levels; however, the employer may limit coverage to the first Rs 2,500 (*International Benefit Guidelines* 1989, p. 113).[31] There are alternative systems for seaman, miners, railroad workers, and public employees. In the event of death prior to the receipt of the retirement benefit, the monies due are paid to the designated beneficiary. Under certain conditions, most of which would be considered financial emergencies, the worker can withdraw some of the monies before age 55. If funds are withdrawn prior to 15 years of participation, the size of the employer's contribution is reduced (Chowdhry 1985, p. 122).

The Family Pension covers the same workers as does the Employees' Provident Fund and participation for these workers is compulsory (Johri 1982, p. 114). It is financed by equal contributions of 1.16 percent from the employee, the employer, and the central government (Bhattarai 1989, p. 484). For the employer and the employee these monies are diverted from the 8.33 percent contributions made to the Employees' Provident Fund. If the worker dies prior to age 60 his or her beneficiary (usually the worker's widow) gets a lump sum payment of Rs 2,000 and a subsequent family pension of 20 percent of the worker's monthly wage up to a specified limit. The pension is paid until the time when the deceased worker would have been age 60.[32] At age 60 workers cease to be covered by the Family Pension scheme. At that point the worker is eligible for a retirement benefit based on contributions to the scheme over the years.[33]

The Payment of Gratuity Act covers employees in firms, factories, mines, and plantations with 10 or more workers (Bhattarai 1989, p. 486).[34] Employers are only required to provide coverage to employees earning less than Rs 2,500 per month, but the majority voluntarily extend this benefit to all employees (*International Benefit Guidelines* 1989, p. 113). The entire cost of the program is paid for by the employer; there is no contribution from the employee and no contribution from government (Mamoria and Mamoria 1983, p. 64); however, the worker must have been employed by the specified employer for 5 or more years to be eligible for this benefit at retirement or termination. The lump sum benefit is equal to 15 days wages for each year of continuous service with a maximum benefit equal to 20 months of wages (Chowdhry 1985, p. 122). To become eligible for this benefit, the worker must leave the establishment paying the benefit, but the worker can accept work with another employer.

The Employees' Deposit-Linked Insurance scheme covers the same workers covered by the Employees' Provident Fund (Sarma 1981, p. 210). The employer makes a contribution of 0.5 percent of wages to the fund and another 0.1 percent to cover the cost of administration. The central government makes contributions into the fund and to the cost of administration at a level of about one-half that made by the employer.[35] Employees do not make any contributions to this scheme (Bhattarai 1989, p. 485). At death the designated beneficiary receives a death benefit equal to the average balance in the provident fund during the prior three years subject to a maximum benefit of Rs 10,000.

By the mid-1980s 13 million workers were covered by the Employees' Provident Fund (Bhattarai, 1985). This comes to only 7 percent of the total labor force, but approximately 50 percent of those employed in the organized (modern) sector. Coverage is much higher in nations such as Malaysia (about 70 percent) and Sri Lanka (about 50 percent) (Martin 1988, pp. S106–107).[36] Looking at the Indian population age 60 and over we find that about 10 percent have received some form of social security assistance (Groskind and Williamson 1991, p. 110).

However, some states such as Kerala and Uttar Pradesh have introduced pension schemes that extend coverage to substantially more than 10 percent of the population. One estimate is that in Kerala 38 percent of those who are gainfully employed are covered by a state or central governmant old-age social security scheme (Tracy 1991, p. 62).[37] The state level schemes are generally noncontributory old-age pensions for the destitute (Bose 1982, p. 32).

At the national level coverage by the Employees' Provident Fund is being gradually extended to an increasing number of industrial and commercial establishments. But even in urban areas a majority of workers remain uncovered. The self-employed and urban marginal workers, of whom there are many, generally do not have coverage. Given the slow pace of expansion even in urban areas, the prospects for widespread coverage in rural areas are at present quite remote (Thompson 1979, p. 125).[38] This pattern of limited coverage in urban areas and virtually no coverage in rural areas is common throughout Asia. This is starting to change, however. In 1980 Kerala introduced a noncontributory old-age pension scheme for low-income agricultural workers (Tracy 1991, p. 75). At the national level a noncontributory life insurance scheme for very low-income rural workers was introduced in 1988. The scheme provides a death benefit of Rs 3,000 paid for by the central government (Bhattarai 1989, pp. 487–488).

An Evaluation of India's Provident Fund Approach

The provident fund alternative has a number of strengths and a number of limitations as an approach for old-age security in India. Any effort to assess the efficacy of India's provident fund approach must take into consideration the alternatives. Different arguments would be made if it were assumed that the alternative was no public provision at all for the elderly as in Bangladesh and Burma than if it were assumed that the alternative was some sort of social insurance program.

As we look around the world today we tend to find social insurance systems in the industrial nations and provident fund systems in many poor nations. This might suggest that a provident fund approach is all that is possible for poor nations. Yet, as there are comparably poor nations such as Pakistan and the Philippines that have adopted the social insurance approach, it would seem that both alternatives are viable even for poor nations.[39]

As noted earlier, at the time when India's leaders were formulating the nation's first old-age social security program, the social insurance alternative was considered, but it was rejected as being too expensive (Cohen 1953, p. 15). As a number of very poor countries have introduced public old-age pension programs based on social insurance principles since then, it would seem, at least in retrospect, that India could have put together some sort of public pension scheme even in the early 1950s. But at the time the provident fund approach seemed most appropriate given the limited resources available and the small size of the modern sector of the economy.

Once introduced, the program proved popular, creating pressure for expansion to other industries and creating support for additional related provident fund and pension schemes (Sinha 1980, pp. 109–110). It also led to the creation of a corps of government civil servants committed to extending and improving the nation's social security coverage for the aged.

A strength of the provident fund approach is that it has contributed to capital formation. The monies contributed have been invested in government securities. This has assured a steady flow of funds to the government for investment in a number of projects designed to promote economic growth. Rather than being a hindrance to economic growth as some had feared (Sinha 1980, p. 144), it has been a major source of investment capital. The actual impact on economic growth cannot be measured with precision, but it does seem reasonable to conclude that overall it has been positive.

The fear of corruption is one reason some countries delay the introduction of public pension schemes.[40] One aspect of the problem is the fear that pensions will be granted as political favors to those who do not meet eligibility requirements. A related fear is that persons who are capable of being self-supporting will feign disability in order to lay claim to public monies. These issues are less problematic with a provident fund system because the worker only has access to funds previously contributed. As corruption is a problem throughout the Indian civil service bureaucracy, this argument needs to be taken seriously (Hardgrave and Kochanek 1986, p. 85; Sinha 1980, pp. 144–145).

A related argument is that a provident fund is more appropriate than a social insurance scheme when the administrative infrastructure does not exist for the more complex social insurance approach (Dixon 1982, p. 328). This description fits much of India, particularly rural India where most of India's elderly live.

A limitation of India's provident fund approach is that the protection provided to dependents is often entirely inadequate; this is particularly so when the worker retires or becomes disabled after only a few years of coverage. The lack of shared risk, a characteristic of the provident fund as opposed to the social insurance approach, means that the covered worker can only obtain benefits from the system that correspond to prior contributions into the scheme (by the worker and employer) during the covered period. For those who take a job in a covered industry late in life or who are disabled early in life, the benefits can be far from adequate even when we measure adequacy in terms of wage levels among Indian workers.

The provident fund approach provides a lump sum payment rather than a pension upon retirement. This lump sum approach turns out to be popular with many Indian workers who prefer it to the alternative of an actuarially comparable monthly pension. The problem from a social security point of view is that many workers use up these funds in a few years (in some cases a few months or weeks) and end up with little or nothing to live on for the the last years of their lives (Gupta 1986, p. 335). Again the lack of attention to the value of shared risk is at the root of the problem. For those who die soon after retirement, the lump sum makes sense; but for a number of those who end up living for many years after retirement, even a very modest pension might make more sense. In theory at retirement workers can take the lump sum payment and invest it in an annuity with a private insurance firm and thus assure themselves a lifetime pension, but in practice few do so. Given that many of these workers will have compelling immediate economic needs, it is not surprising that so few elect to buy an annuity from the lump sum proceeds.

The provident fund approach is problematic for workers with low wages and irregular work histories. Many of these workers will from time to time be employed in covered industries, but their wages and years of contribution will be so low that the lump sum benefit paid at retirement will be entirely inadequate to provide for old age even if spent as wisely and rationally as could be expected. Most social insurance systems, in contrast, provide a somewhat better return on contributions for the lowest paid workers. When this is done it is often possible to provide at least a minimally adequate retirement benefit to the working poor. The approach is also problematic for rural workers who may not be paid on a regular weekly or monthly basis and who receive much of their remuneration in some form of in-kind payment.

Both a strength and a limitation of the Employees' Provident Fund is that when faced with certain financial emergencies it is possible for workers to obtain permission to withdraw monies from their accounts. It is a little like borrowing against an insurance policy; however, these funds are not replaced. The poorest workers who are most likely to be faced with financial emergencies that have forced them to withdraw funds early are most likely to end up at retirement with a lump sum benefit that is even less adequate than would otherwise have been the case.

The Indian provident fund approach does little to redistribute income from the more affluent to the poor. While social insurance systems typically involve relatively little redistribution, the tendency to provide the lowest income contributors with a better return on prior contributions does involve at least a modest degree of income distribution. But the provident fund approach does not involve even this degree of redistribution. If workers can only take out what they put in, there is no redistribution accept in the very limited sense that those who have been covered prior to retirement will tend to have higher after retirement incomes than they would otherwise have, had the provident fund not existed. Monies that would have been spent earlier in life are now available. This can also be viewed as redistribution across the life span as opposed to redistribution between different income groups.

Accounting for Developments in India

Several factors contributed to the timing of the introduction of India's first national old-age security legislation. Enactment so soon after independence was no accident. It was clearly part of a more general effort to promote national integration, a particularly problematic issue in a nation with such religious, regional, and ethnic diversity. A closely related explanation is that the introduction of old-age security legislation was due in part to the change in state structure, the shift from being a colony to an independent nation. The evidence that so many of the newly independent African and Asian nations introduced such schemes within a few years of attaining their independence supports this conclusion.

Many of the African and Asian nations that had been British colonies prior to World War II ended up introducing provident fund systems soon after independence. Similarly, many of the nations that had been French colonies introduced social insurance systems. There is a pattern suggesting the influence of colonial background. But why did the French favor social insurance and the British the provident fund approach? One possible factor is that France was more interested in extending French culture and French institutions to its colonies.[41] One such institution was old-age pensions based on social insurance principles. However, the difference in colonial background argument offers only a partial explanation as it does not account for the discrepancy between Pakistan (which introduced a social insurance based old-age pension system) and India (with its provident fund scheme), both of which had been part of the same British colony.

When India introduced its Employees' Provident Fund in 1952, many observers assumed that this was only the first step on the road toward social insurance. The assumption being that within a few years India would reach a level of development at which it would be feasible to shift from the provident fund to the social insurance approach. Since the early 1950s India has experienced substantial economic growth. This growth has contributed to the expansion in the number of firms and workers covered by the the Employees' Provident Fund Scheme. It has contributed to an increase in the value of the eventual provident fund benefits. It has been a major factor making possible the addition of other old-age security programs such as the Employees' Family Pension Scheme, the Employees' Deposit-Linked Insurance Scheme, and the Payment of Gratuity Act. Despite this economic growth, however, there is no evidence that India's provident fund approach will be replaced by the social insurance approach anytime soon.[42]

One reason there has been no such shift is that the existing approach has proven to be a major source of investment capital. In addition to being less of a potential drain on scarce government resources, the provident fund approach provides a valuable source of investment capital that can be directed toward a variety of projects designed to promote economic development (Sinha 1980, p. 144). While a scheme based on social insurance principles would also be a source of investment capital, it is common for such schemes to mix social insurance and social welfare goals. In democratic countries there are often political pressures during the early years of such schemes to pay pensions that are more generous than the workers contributions would justify. In contrast, with the provident fund approach workers get out only what they and their employers have put into the system.

Another factor is the opposition from many of those employed in what has become a massive government bureaucracy. Once the Employees' Provident Fund was in place, the bureaucracy needed to administer it became a source of pressure not only to extend coverage, but also to resist radical change. It is easy for those employed in such a bureaucracy to support program expansion as it often means more staff, but a shift to an entirely new program is a potential threat to people's jobs and day-to-day work routines.

In addition, workers who have contributed to these programs over the years have come to constitute an interest group that is opposed to radical change. Many have come to support the idea of a lump sum payment at retirement and would not give this up for a government pension of equivalent actuarial value. Some fear that their contributions will be lost or discounted if a shift is made to the social insurance approach. In many cases the worker's family has come to anticipate the payment of a lump sum benefit at retirement. This large sum of money is often used to buy the family a major consumer item (e.g., a car) that would otherwise be beyond the means of the family. Such a purchase may be viewed as part of the intergenerational exchange. The retired worker provides this major lump sum benefit to the joint family which in return provides support during the retirement years.

While some social security technocrats in the Indian government are interested in extending coverage and improving the adequacy of existing old-age security programs, there are others who urge caution in the expansion of these programs. Were the aged as a group to come to depend on the government as their major source of economic support, the demand on resources would be overwhelming and it could have a devastating impact on the rate of economic growth. The task of providing for India's aged is so immense relative to available resources that the government cannot risk assuming the major responsibility for providing even a minimally adequate standard of living for all of the elderly or even all of the economically needy elderly. The goal seems to be to design programs that will better provide for those without adequate family support without undermining the strong sense that it is the responsibility of the family to provide for elderly parents (Bose 1982, p. 38).

There are a number of reasons why so few rural workers are covered by the Employees' Provident Fund. One is that neither the provident fund approach nor the social insurance approach to income security for the aged works well when attempting to provide coverage to agricultural workers for whom a substantial fraction of remuneration takes the form of noncash in-kind benefits, often grain and other agricultural products. As this is the case for many Indian farm workers, it would be difficult to work out a system of provident fund or social insurance contributions that would be suitable for them. In addition, rural workers receive very low wages. For this reason it is difficult to set aside even a small proportion of earnings for the future in the form of payments into a provident fund.[43] A further problem is that much of rural India lacks the necessary institutional infrastructure for the collection of contributions, keeping of records, and the payment of benefits in connection with a provident fund or social insurance scheme.

As mentioned earlier, a few states have found ways to provide old-age security coverage to at least some of the rural elderly. States such as Uttar Pradesh and Kerala have introduced old-age pensions for the destitute elderly that include those in rural areas (Tracy 1991; Bose 1982). These schemes avoid some of the problems mentioned earlier by not requiring contributions to a provident fund or social insurance scheme as a condition for pension eligibility. Elderly pensioners must instead prove that they have little or no income and no family in a position to provide support. While this approach simplifies bookkeeping, it results in a very modest pension and coverage for only the most destitute.

As of 1988 the central government introduced a program that provides some old-age social security coverage in the rural areas in the form of a Rs 3,000 death benefit financed entirely by the government. But this program is again limited to the poorest of the poor and it does not provide any support beyond the initial lump sum payment (Bhattarai 1989, pp. 487–488). It is likely that it will be quite some time before even this modest program reaches all of those it is designed to help.

Most Indians expect that their families will be the primary source of economic security in old age. Generally this is a reasonable expectation. Even in the cities about 75 percent of the elderly are living with their children (Martin 1988, p. S103). If at all possible children generally do make the effort to provide for their parents in old age. But as the children may themselves be destitute, this is not always possible. Of the destitute elderly without a source of family support, some are able to obtain help from one of several state or central government old-age security programs, but little effort is made to reach those who are in need and eligible for these benefits (Petri 1982, p. 78; Desai and Khetani 1979). Lack of adequate old-age social security coverage is problematic for the landless elderly poor in rural areas (Mahadevan 1986). They are less likely to be adequately provided for by their children than is the case for the elderly with landholdings that will be inherited by those children (Petri 1982, p. 76; Raj and Prasad 1971). Particularly vulnerable during droughts and other such calamities are rural elderly poor widows (Agarwal 1990, p. 341; Bose 1982, p. 28).[44]

The migration of many of the young to urban areas and the associated shift from extended to nuclear family structure is weakening the traditional familial support system for the elderly. But the urban nuclear families tend to maintain traditional Hindu family values which buffer the impact of this migration (Gore 1968). This includes support for parents even when they remain in rural areas and when children are relatively poor themselves (Tracy 1991, p. 70; Nair 1990).

As in the case of the United States it would seem that the timing of the emergence of democracy in India has influenced the development of old-age security policy. In the Indian case democratic institutions have emerged while the nation is still predominantly rural. The political strength of those living in rural areas has as a result contributed to the emergence of a polity based on traditional ethnic, caste, and languages cleavages as opposed to class cleavages (Rudolph and Rudolph 1987, p. 397). India has relatively well developed democratic institutions despite the presence of a substantial amount of election-related violence and fraudulent vote counts in some areas. But the major political parties generally do not compete for votes around old-age income security policy or social security policy more generally. There seems to be agreement that issues other than social security policy are more relevant to most voters' decisions about which candidates and parties to support.

A number of other factors have also undercut the emergence of a polity based on class cleavages. One of the most important has been state ownership of many firms in the modern sector.[45] Approximately two-thirds of those employed in the organized sector work for government-owned firms (Johri 1982, p. 108). This means that a substantial fraction of workers in the modern sector work for state-owned enterprises, not private industry. For employees in these firms, it is representatives of the state, not capital, that they negotiate with for wage increases and improvements in working conditions.

State ownership of major sectors of the organized economy gives the government an important source of revenues. As a result the government is much less dependent than it would otherwise be on revenues extracted from the general population. Some scholars argue that the state in India is a "third actor" in the making of public policy—the other two being capital and labor (Rudolph and Rudolph 1987, pp. 397–400). The reference to the state as a third actor is meant to suggest more than the traditional argument that the state can act autonomously making its contribution to the policymaking process independent of the interests of either capital or labor. The state's direct control over such a large portion of the organized sector has allowed it to do much more than mediate between the interests of capital and labor. The state is itself a major independent actor in the policymaking process which often entirely dominates both capital and labor (Rudolph and Rudolph 1987, p. 23). With these resources the state is in a position to be in large measure self-financing, self-determining, and some would say, self-serving.

As economic conditions have improved, there has been a substantial increase in life expectancy. All other things being equal this would produce a sharp increase in the proportion aged. But due to high birthrates in combination with substantially reduced infant mortality rates, there has been a rapid increase in the number of young people. As a result the proportion of elderly is still relatively low compared to levels in the industrial nations, but it is increasing and it is projected to increase quite dramatically during the next few decades. Traditionally old age begins at 60 in India (Mahadevan 1986, p. 498). In 1961 5.8 percent of the population was over age 60. The figure increased to 7.5 percent by 1981, and it is projected to increase to 10 percent by 2001 (Tracy 1991, p. 68).[46] So far changes in age structure do not seem to have had a major impact on old-age security policy, but this may change in the years ahead as the population begins to age more rapidly.

India has made much economic progress since independence and this has been reflected in an increasingly elaborate and generous set of social security programs for the aged. With industrialization and related changes such as urbanization, expansion of the modern sector, and labor mobility, it has became increasingly evident that traditional reliance on the joint family is not by itself going to be sufficient as a means of providing economic security for the aged, particularly among those employed in the organized sector of the economy (Sinha 1980, pp. 23–26; Bose 1982, p. 38). Economic development has increased the need for social security legislation and has also increased the resources available for such programs.

The evolution of the Indian civil service bureaucracy can be linked in part to the process of industrial development and in part to the British colonial legacy. We mention this factor in connection with our discussion of industrialism because the evidence suggests that the nation's social security technocrats were quite influential in the decision to introduce a provident fund system and in shaping provident fund policy over the years (Sinha 1980, pp. 109–110). These technocrats reflect the development of bureaucratic structures that can be linked to industrialism and economic development.[47]

The industrialism perspective as it is ordinarily formulated not only emphasizes the role of economic development and the various demographic and bureaucratic consequences of this development, it is also explicitly deemphasizes the role of political factors such as the strength of organized labor and leftist parties. The evidence in connection with the Indian case supports the first part of the theory, but with respect to the second part it is mixed. Organized labor was not a major factor with respect to the introduction of provident fund legislation, but it does seem to have had some impact on subsequent developments. The evidence for India calls for at least some modification of the traditional version of the industrialism perspective to allow room for the independent influence of political factors.

India's ethnic, religious, and linguistic diversity are part of the reason that the nation started with a provident fund system and has not shifted to a social insurance system. The fractionalization of the nation into a number of subgroups is consistent with an approach to social security policy that requires each worker to provide for his or her own old age. The shared risk aspect of social insurance and the general tendency in social insurance schemes to provide a better return on contributions for those with the lowest incomes is more likely to gain popular support in a homogeneous society. In this sense various religious, linguistic, and caste interest groups can be viewed as relevant to the shaping of policy. The evidence suggests that these interest groups were more influential in the sense of providing a context that policymakers felt obligated to take into consideration than in the sense of being active as organized groups pushing for specific social security policies.

There are three class-related interest groups of particular note: organized labor, the industrialists, and the small farmers ("bullock capitalists"). In the late 1940s when the original legislation was being formulated, both capital and labor were minor actors. Only 2 percent of the labor force was included in the industrial sector (Nair 1979, p. 254); this had obvious implications for the proportion of the labor force that was organized and for the fraction of the economy dominated by industrialists. Even today private capital has a relatively modest impact on India's national economy and social policy. The private sector continues to be over-shadowed by the public sector due to public ownership of so much of the nation's basic industry and to so much public control over investment capital.

More influential than either organized labor or private capital is the rural sector. Some 76 percent of Indians live in rural areas and 70 percent are employed in the agricultural sector (Hardgrave and Kochanek 1986, p. 12). Of particular note is the increasing power in recent years of the small-scale, self-employed farmers that make up approximately one-fifth of India's rural population. They tend to vote as a block and for candidates who will represent their interests (Chellaney 1990, p. 30) The reference is to small-scale cultivators who rely more on their own family labor than on hired farmhands. They also tend to rely more on human and animal power (hence the term *bullock capitalists*) than on tractors which require a much larger farm to become cost effective.

In general, organizations representing business such as the All India Manufacturer's Organization did not support the idea of introducing provident funds (Sinha 1980, p. 144). The concern was that such programs were too expensive for employers who would be required to contribute to these funds. Given the need to keep costs low to be competitive many of those representing the interests of the business sector argued that such efforts would undercut the nation's rate of economic development. It was economic development rather than social programs that was viewed as the most efficient way to provide for the social welfare needs of the aged.

Between 1920 and the mid-1970s the proportion of workers belonging to unions steadily increased (Mamoria and Mamoria 1983, p. 123). Thereafter, union membership has not increased. Unions have had some impact on old-age social security legislation, for example, in connection with Family Pension legislation in 1971. The unions are also asked to participate on various commissions set up to review the working of social security programs (Gupta 1986, p. 272); however, in general, unions have not been powerful political actors in the formulation of old-age security policy at the national level. One reason has been the relatively small fraction of the labor force unionized, but even more important has been the structure of the labor movement with a very large number of small unions in intense competition with one another for members (Mamoria and Mamoria 1983, p. 136). At the national level many of the unions are organized into 1 of 11 national labor federations, but the deep ideological cleavages between these federations make it difficult for labor to unite for collective bargaining purposes (Rudolph and Rudolph 1987, p. 25).

In Sweden and in several other European countries labor is organized at the national level into a small number of labor federations that have traditionally been able to work together to represent labor as a whole in collective bargaining with the national level representatives of management and representatives of the state. The corporatist bargaining structures that have emerged in these European countries tend to facilitate social policymaking along class lines. In India, by contrast, the central government is such a powerful third actor that the corporatist structures are more a vehicle for the control of labor (as in Brazil during much of the past 60 years) than a vehicle for the representation of labor's interests.

In India the central government presents itself as the protector of the interests of organized labor, not as labor's class enemy. While this may be the way the government wants the relationship to be viewed, the evidence suggests that the government often does not represent the interests of organized labor well; the government has at many points taken steps to undercut labor's ability to function autonomously (Rudolph and Rudolph 1987, p. 24). In India decision making with respect to national social welfare policy as with public policy more generally is highly concentrated in the hands of the prime minister, the Cabinet, and the highest levels of the Indian Administrative Service (Hardgrave and Kochanek 1986, p. 74).[48]

Some scholars argue that if the unions had been strong earlier, it is possible that India would have ended up selecting the social insurance approach rather than the provident fund approach in connection with the provision of old-age retirement benefits (Sinha 1980, p. 25). There may be something to this argument, but it is highly speculative given that organized labor was not even backing the social insurance approach when the foundations of old-age security policy were being worked out in the late 1940s. The issue was not high on the agenda of either organized labor or the average Indian worker. Both labor leaders and the workers were much more concerned about such issues as increasing wages and promoting economic growth. Employees' contributions were viewed by many workers as a tax burden they could ill afford.

The legislation of the early 1970s can in part be attributed to the efforts of labor. The Family Pension scheme introduced in 1971 had been high on the agenda of organized labor ever since a similar scheme was introduced for public employees in 1964. The 1972 Payment of Gratuity Act transformed a termination benefit that had been entirely at the discretion of the employer into a benefit to be negotiated in advance with union representatives.

In some states unions have been stronger than they have been at the national level. One example is Kerala. Since the 1950s in Kerala unions representing agricultural workers have been particularly influential with respect to state level social policies. In Kerala there is a long tradition of trade union activism on behalf of programs for retired workers (Krishnamurthy 1979). The unions played an important role with respect to the Kerala Agricultural Workers' Act of 1974 which among other things introduced a provident fund scheme for agricultural workers (Tracy 1991, p. 71). They also played a role with respect to the Kerala Destitute Pension Scheme (1961) and Agriculture Workers' Pension Scheme (1980).

Union strength is only one aspect of working-class strength. Another frequently cited aspect is social democratic or leftist party strength. As the domestic agenda of Congress is in large measure social democratic, it is appropriate to give some credit for developments since independence to this source. However, as India's political parties are not organized along class lines as they are in many Western industrial nations, we must be cautious about interpreting the impact of Congress as an indicator of working-class strength. Also given that at the national level Congress has been in power during almost the entire period since independence, it is not possible to make comparative statements about developments when Congress as opposed to the opposition was in power.[49]

If organized labor was not pushing for enactment of the Employees' Provident Fund prior to its enactment, who was behind it? Enactment of this legislation was in large measure due to the successful effort of a relatively small group of high level civil servants, social security technocrats in contact with their counterparts at the International Labour Organization and in various government positions in other nations, particularly Britain. Related to this is the colonial legacy argument which is supported by evidence that planning was going on for a provident fund system several years before the nation became independent (Mamoria and Mamoria 1983, p. 57).

There is general agreement that British rule had an adverse impact on the Indian economy during the nineteenth century and the first several decades of the twentieth century. The British viewed India as a nation to be used as a source of low priced raw materials and as a market for British manufactured goods. No effort was made to protect or to develop local industry India's position in the world economy today is at least in part due to its colonial legacy. A case can be made that were it not for this legacy India might today be much more advanced industrially.[50] Were that the case, social provision for the aged might well be more generous than it is. The nation might even have opted for social insurance pensions as opposed to the provident fund approach that characterizes so many of the former British colonies.

Since independence foreign investment in India has been closely regulated by the government and limited in scale. India's emphasis on self-sufficiency (Chellaney 1990, p. 27) has minimized dependency on the rich industrial nations. The nation's focus on diversity with respect to both trading partners and export products has contributed to this same goal. While India does carry a substantial foreign debt, in the early 1980s the cost of this debt was only 11 percent of exports, about one-third the debt burden that Brazil was facing (Rudolph and Rudolph 1987, pp. 11, 395). India is today largely self-reliant for both technological and consumer products (Nayar 1983). India's governing elite has not been foreign controlled during the post-independence period (Hardgrave and Kochanek 1986, p. 15). In short, it would be difficult to make the case that old-age security policy in India is presently being shaped by economic interests outside the country.

Conclusion

In this chapter we have argued that concern over the issue of national integration and the structural shift from being a colony to an independent nation were among the most important factors influencing the timing of the introduction of the nation's first old-age security legislation. The decision to opt for the provident fund approach was influenced in part by the nation's British colonial legacy. This decision was also influenced by the low level of economic development, the need for investment capital, the related fear of any program that could end up making significant demands on the nation's very limited national budget, and concern about corruption which in turn can be linked to the various primordial cleavages that characterize Indian society.

We have presented evidence that unions have had some influence on policy developments, but it is often difficult to differentiate true victories for labor from policies that were introduced because they were favored by the state and happen also to be supported by labor as well. Nationally the labor movement is not unified and as a result the unions do not have a great deal of influence independent of the political parties with which they are typically linked. This conclusion is less true with respect to some states such as Kerala. In any effort to account for old-age social security policy developments in India, cleavages based on ethnicity, religion, caste, and region must be given more emphasis than those based on social class, a concept that seems peculiarly Western in the Indian context.

Approximately 76 percent of Indians live in rural areas. Almost this many work in the agricultural sector. This gives rural India a great deal of political influence. Of particular note is the influence of the self-employed small farmers. Their lack of interest in spending on social programs that are going to benefit primarily those in urban areas is not hard to understand. It is unlikely that these "bullock capitalists" will come to support a shift from the provident fund approach to the social insurance approach any time soon.

While no one theoretical perspective offers a full account of old-age social security policy developments in India, several theories offer at least partial accounts. The industrialism perspective with its emphasis on the role of level of development and related factors such as urbanization and the structure of the labor force is useful; however, a significant limitation of this perspective is its insistence that political factors have no independent role in accounting for policy developments. The development of democratic institutions since independence seems to have facilitated the impact that organized labor has been able to exercise on old-age security policy. But even more important have been the political constraints imposed by the various primordial communal cleavages.

India's large civil service bureaucracy is a factor mentioned by those who emphasize the importance of various aspects of state structure. The role of the nation's civil service technocrats in the formulation of the original provident fund legislation and in the extensions of that legislation over the years was significant. The evidence points to a great deal of concentration of power in the hands of the central government. While government officials do make it a point to consult with representatives of those likely to be most directly affected by proposed legislation, the state is a much more powerful actor relative to capital, labor, and the nation's many other interest groups than is the case in Western industrial nations such as Sweden and Britain.

The importance of India's colonial legacy offers further support for the state-centered perspective. It had profound implications for the decision to base the nation's first old-age security scheme on the provident fund model as opposed to the social insurance model. The colonial legacy argument appropriately emphasizes the consequences of the nation's dependent position during the period of British rule, but the related neo-Marxist dependency theory perspective that has proved useful for the analysis of bureaucratic authoritarian regimes in Latin America such as Brazil is of limited use for the analysis of recent developments in India. Efforts to reduce the control of outside powers on the Indian economy, efforts originating with the struggle for independence, have subsequently carried over into successful attempts to become less dependent on foreign investment and imports.

For the Indian case the state has played a major role with respect to the formulation of the original old-age social security policy and with developments since the early 1950s. With respect to national policy state actors have been much more influential than labor, big business, or any other class-based actors. While we cannot point to any single nonclass interest group that has been a major actor with respect to old-age security policy, the communal cleavages that so divide the nation have certainly created a policy context which has made it all but impossible for state actors to form the consensus that would be needed for a fundamental policy change such as shifting from the provident fund approach to the social insurance approach to old-age security policy.

The lack of the emergence of the aged as a major demographic and political constituency is due in large measure to the nation's high fertility rate. This is one reason there has been very little pressure from this segment of the population for the introduction of a comprehensive national old-age pension system. But this is not to say that interest groups have been irrelevant to policy developments; to the contrary, the bitter antagonism between various religious, ethnic, regional, caste, and language groups has contributed to the emergence of a wide variety of interest groups based on primordial cross-class cleavages (Rudolph and Rudolph 1987, p. 306). The distrust among these groups has been an important factor contributing to the popularity of the provident fund approach with its emphasis on limiting what workers can get from the scheme to what they or their employers have contributed.

While the traditional pluralist perspective is of limited utility in accounting for old-age security developments in India, there does seem to be some support for a modified version of this perspective we refer to as neo-pluralism. If we broaden the definition of interest groups to include civil service and other government employees, the evidence in support of an interest group perspective increases. Similarly, if we take into consideration the nation's cleavages with respect to caste, language, ethnicity and the like, the support further increases. The cleavages among these interest groups have contributed to a policy environment conducive to the provident fund approach, an approach that minimizes the opportunity for the redistribution of resources from one group to another. The fractionalized nature of interest groups has obstructed significant expansion of the system. Currently, however, the demands of India's various interest groups are becoming increasingly problematic for the central government (Kohli 1988, p. 305). The expected growth of the aged population may place further demands on the central government for more spending. Unlike the past, the existence of democratic structures may in the future prove important in facilitating the influence of the aged and other groups.

8

Nigeria

Nigeria's large population and substantial oil resources make it one of the most influential nations in sub-Saharan Africa.[1] In 1961 it became the first African nation to introduce a provident fund plan. The National Provident Fund (NPF) served as a model for similar schemes in several other African nations. While each sub-Saharan African nation has its unique characteristics, such as substantial oil resources in Nigeria's case, they share many characteristics. Most went through comparable colonial experiences, have relatively small modern sectors, and have heterogeneous populations with deep religious, ethnic, and linguistic cleavages. In many ways the development of old-age social security policy in Nigeria is similar to that in other nations of sub-Saharan Africa, but in some respects it differs. For both reasons we will want to make comparisons with developments in other sub-Saharan nations.

Like many sub-Saharan African nations one of the most serious problems that Nigeria has faced since independence in 1960 has been that of national integration (Tordoff 1984, p. 2). Most of the population has had a stronger identification with and allegiance to a subnational unit such as the tribe (ethnic group), state, or region rather than to the nation as a whole. While scholars have given considerable attention to the national integration role of public policy in the health and education sectors, there has been very little prior effort to analyze the link between old-age security policy and national integration objectives.

Ethnic conflict poses one of the greatest threats to national integration that the sub-Saharan nations face. In many of these nations the conflict intensified during the years following independence. This might suggest that ethnic conflict would have been even greater had it not been for the colonial experience, but there is strong evidence suggesting that ethnic consciousness was actually strengthened by the colonial experience (Ayoade 1986, p. 116; Huntington 1968, p. 38). Even class theorists in the neo-Marxist tradition generally acknowledge that ethnic politics plays a major role in public policymaking in Nigeria and other sub-Saharan nations, but they then go on to argue that class factors are also very important. In this context they typically emphasize the influence of ruling elites and of the bureaucratic middle class. Class theorists also point to the role of transnational corporations, economic dependency, and the colonial legacy in efforts to account for the poor record of the sub-Saharan nations with respect to economic development and efforts to establish democratic institutions (Azarya 1988; Ake 1981). In

164

the present analysis we assess the relative importance of class and ethnicity in shaping the development of Nigeria's old-age security policy.

The issue of corruption, particularly civil service corruption, has been a problem in most sub-Saharan nations since independence. While some scholars emphasize the positive functions of this corruption (Huntington 1968, pp. 68–69), it is more common to emphasize the adverse consequences of the problem for regime legitimacy (Young 1988, p. 25). In this chapter we explore the consequences of corruption for the development of old-age security policy in Nigeria.

We focus on a set of interrelated questions about the development of old-age social security policy in Nigeria: (1) Why did Nigeria introduce an old-age social security scheme when it did? (2) Why did it select a provident fund as opposed to a social insurance based pension scheme? (3) Why has there been so little by way of old-age social security policy development since the introduction of the original program in 1961?

Despite its substantial oil resources and revenues, Nigeria remains a very poor nation.[2] For this reason the Nigerian case provides a strong test of the generalizability of explanations of social security policy development linked to the industrialism perspective. Given the pervasiveness of societal cleavages based on ethnicity, region, and religion, Nigeria is also a particularly appropriate African case for the assessment of the neo-pluralist perspective.

As Nigeria's colonial experience has had a major impact on the development of its old-age social security policies, we begin with an overview of the historical context out of which these policies have emerged. We trace relevant developments up through the present. Then, for comparative purposes, we describe the social insurance based old-age pension scheme that has evolved in the Ivory Coast, a French-speaking West African country that is in many respects similar to Nigeria, but differs in a few important respects including its status as a former French colony. We conclude with an assessment of several alternative explanations of old-age social security policy in Nigeria.

The Colonial Era

By the end of the fifteenth century Portuguese traders had reached what is now Nigeria (Dusgate 1985, p. 15). At first they were interested in the pepper, ivory, and gold that could be obtained from the natives (Isichei 1983, p. 93), but they were soon buying slaves, a major item of trade long before these European traders arrived (Hatch 1971, p. 77). In Northern Nigeria Islam was introduced in about 1000 A.D. (Lubeck 1986, p. 8).[3] It was consistent with the Koran to conduct slave raids against pagans (Diamond 1967, p. 7). By the end of the eighteenth century the British controlled two-thirds of the trans-Atlantic slave trade, but they did not make an effort to control significant amounts of Nigerian territory. They were interested in small parcels of land along the coast that were used for trading posts.[4]

While slavery was well institutionalized prior to the arrival of the Europeans, the immense demand for slaves created by the introduction of plantations in the New World had a major impact on the West African economy including what is now Nigeria. Some scholars argue that the demand for slaves encouraged hostilities and frequent slave raids among the various tribes (Hatch 1971, p. 90). This institutionalized animosity among the various tribal groups (today referred to as ethnic groups) may have contributed to the strong distrust and the deep ethnic cleavages that continue to influence politics and social policy today. While a few Nigerian merchants, kings, and chiefs became very wealthy in connection with the slave trade, the impact on the Nigerian economy as a whole was definitely adverse (Hatch 1971, p. 90). Much of the wealth that did come to Nigeria was either hoarded in unproductive assets (such as the iron bars used as a form of money) or spent on a lavish life-style for the few.

Between the early eighteenth century and the end of the nineteenth century Britain controlled what is now Nigeria indirectly through the large trading companies that did business there.[5] In 1899 what had been a sphere of British influence became a protectorate of the British Crown (Ikime 1977, p. 210). As was the case with other African nations, the colony and eventually the state was the creation of Europeans.[6] It was not a geographical entity that those living in the territory identified with. This is one reason that even today many Nigerians continue to have a stronger sense of identity with and allegiance to their ethnic community than with the nation as a whole (Hatch 1971, p. 11).

Both the British and the French made use of existing political authorities to rule their African territories, but they did so in very different ways. The system of indirect rule first introduced in northern Nigeria became a model for many other British territories throughout Africa. The British political officer responsible in a local area took the role of advisor and interfered with the decisions of the native authority as little as possible (Crowder 1972, p. 360). The goal was to govern through the existing rulers who were responsible for the day-to-day administration of the local community in accordance with traditional customs (Kurian 1982, p. 1332).

In contrast to the British policy, the French policy was to make the local chief entirely subordinate to the local French political officer. The chief was merely an agent of the colonial government. The French, unlike the British, made little effort to construct even the local governmental units in such a way that they would correspond to the precolonial political boundaries. Those selected by the French as chiefs were often not those who would have been selected using the traditional criteria and procedures (Crowder 1972, p. 362).

How do we account for the difference in approach to colonial rule? The British were much less concerned with attempting to get the Nigerians to adopt British culture. In contrast, the French were interested in the assimilation of their colonial peoples (Crowder 1972, p. 367). The British assumed that eventually British administration would be taken over by the Nigerians themselves. In contrast, the French tended to assume that their African colonies would indefinitely remain an extra part of France (Kingsnorth 1966).

The British system of indirect rule left intact the traditional structures of provision for the elderly and other needy groups. While it is difficult to make generalizations about a territory that included more than two hundred different tribes (ethnic groups) each with its unique cultural beliefs and practices, the pattern throughout Nigeria and West Africa more generally was to obtain support from one's family, particularly one's children; however, as there were differences in lineage structures and in property inheritance patterns, there was variation with respect to who provided care for dependent elders. In general, immediate family members provided for the elderly (Ijere 1966, p. 469; Aire 1974, pp. 411–412). If this source of support was not adequate, members of the broader extended family were responsible. In a few of the large city-states such as Benin tax monies were sometimes available to provide for chiefs, priests, warriors, and the dependent elderly (Oyovbaire 1984, p. 30).

While Nigeria did not come under the political control of Britain until late in the nineteenth century, the economy was strongly affected by the British presence long before this (Hatch 1971, p. 169). The export of slaves and subsequently of palm oil dominated the Nigerian economy throughout the nineteenth century making it vulnerable to swings in world markets (Isichei 1983, p. 98). The British expected colonial governments to pay their own costs. In response to this imperative the colonial administration encouraged a shift from subsistence farming to cash crops for export. This helped generate the needed revenues, but it also made the economy more vulnerable to swings in world markets.

One of the first acts of the British after pacifying the indigenous population at the end of the nineteenth century was the expropriation of much land. As this land had traditionally been controlled by elders, the policy undercut both the authority and the economic well-being of the aged (Oyeneye 1990, p. 19). Thus British colonialism affected both the absolute and the relative well-being of the elderly, particularly elderly males, from very early on.

After World War I Britain put a tariff on palm oil exports to Germany so as to assure British industry an adequate supply at a favorable price (Hatch 1971, p. 178). During the Depression of the 1930s duties were placed on Japanese imports so as to reduce competition for British producers. These examples illustrate ways in which the British manipulated the Nigerian economy with an eye toward the needs of the British economy.

After World War II British industry continued to dominate the Nigerian economy. A few huge firms such as the United Africa Company dominated the import-export business (Cohen 1974, p. 38). During the early 1960s most of the funds for industrial development came from outside the country. What emerged was a small capital intensive modern sector that expatriated a substantial portion of profits to Britain and other industrial nations (Cohen 1974, pp. 38–40). The influence of these transnational monopoly corporations did not end with independence in 1960—it continues today (Graf 1989, pp. 92–93).

Independence was attained in 1960 through a gradual and nonviolent process. While there was a group of Nigerian nationalists pushing for independence, no mass movement formed that united all Nigerians in a struggle for independence. Instead the timing and details of independence were worked out in negotiations among elites (Andrain 1988, p. 220). In 1955, a few years before Nigeria as a whole was granted its independence, Britain began granting a great deal of self-rule to each of Nigeria's three major regions (Falola and Ihonvbere 1985, p. 254). As a result, at the time of independence the regional governments were almost as powerful as the federal government. This contributed to Nigeria's subsequent difficulties around the issue of national integration (Okoli 1980, p. 114).

The first political party in Nigeria was the Nigerian National Democratic Party (NNDP) founded in 1922. The NNDP called for Africanization of the civil service, more spending on education, policies designed to stimulate economic development, and self-government for Lagos. The National Council of Nigerian Citizens (NCNC) (formed in 1944) called for democratic self-government for all of Nigeria (Nelson 1982, pp. 36–37). There is no evidence, however, that these or any other major political parties were pushing for the introduction of pensions or provident fund programs prior to independence.

Trade unionism in the modern sense can be traced to the formation of the Railway Workers' Union in 1932 (Ananaba 1969, pp. 16–18). Until enactment of the Nigerian Trade Unions Ordinance in 1938, union membership was for the most part limited to three unions: (1) the Civil Service Union, (2) the Railway Worker's Union, and (3) the Nigerian Union of Teachers (Yesufu 1982, pp. 96-98). While unions members were for the most part confined to the small modern sector of the economy, this sector was sufficiently influential that a successful general strike was called in Lagos in 1945 that involved at least 30,000 workers (Ananaba 1969, p. 44).

While the number of workers who were union members increased rapidly during the 1940s and 1950s, less than 2 percent of the labor force was unionized at the time of independence. Thus the influence of organized labor on old-age social security policy would have been modest even if the unions had been pushing for some sort of public pension program or for a national provident fund plan. But there is no evidence that the issue of old-age social security was on the agenda of organized labor at the time when the decisions about the original provident fund scheme were being made. The labor force was very young due to the nation's high fertility rate and as a result workers were concerned with more immediate issues such as present wages rather than with the more long-term issues such as old-age retirement benefits.

Developments Since Independence

At independence Nigeria was divided into three regions (Oyovbaire 1984, p. 61). Each was dominated by a political party that had very little influence outside of that region (Kirk-Green 1986, p. 49).[7] There were in addition a number of much smaller and less influential parties in each region. A parallel set of splits existed with respect to language and ethnicity. In each of these three regions there was one dominant ethnic group, and the dominant language in the region was the language of that ethnic group. But again each region included a number of other much smaller ethnic and sub-ethnic groups, many of which had their own languages.

Scholars differ with respect to their estimates of the number of different ethnic groups in Nigeria with most falling in the range between 250 and 400.[8] The range for estimates of the number of different languages is similar (Sanda 1987, p. 169; Nelson 1982; Coleman 1958, p. 15).[9] This extreme ethnolinguistic fractionalization has been a major factor in Nigerian politics and policy over the years.[10] Nigerians typically identify with different subethnic levels depending on the context (Wolpe 1974, p. 231; Post and Vickers 1973, pp. 26–27). A person may identify as being Yoruba when in London, Egba when in Lagos, and Egbado when in Abeokuta.[11]

Independence resulted in the removal of the British institutions of social control. The result was an outpouring of communal antagonism that eventually led to the breakdown of constitutional government. The term *tribalism* has often been used to describe this conflict, but it is now common to use less pejorative terms such as *communalism* (Wolpe 1974, p. 231) or *ethnic conflict* (Post and Vickers 1973, p. 11).

In an effort to reduce the regionalism that contributed to the civil war between 1967 and 1970 when the Eastern Region attempted to become the independent nation of Biafra, the original three regions have been replaced in stages by an increasing number of states; today there are 30.[12] The goal of this shift has been to reduce the intensity of regional conflict and to encourage crosscutting groupings that vary depending on the issue (Odetola 1978, p. 143).

Democratic national elections were held in 1959, 1964, 1979, and 1983, but corruption was pervasive. At the time of independence Nigeria had the institutional trappings of democracy, hut there was little genuine acceptance of the fair elections aspect of the model (Cohen 1974, p. 261). The colonial experience had been highly authoritarian, providing little by way of direct experience with democratic institutions (Andrain 1988, p. 220; Bretton 1962, p. 181). Given the extreme distrust of the various ethnic and regional[13] groups for one another, there was a great deal of pressure to achieve electoral victory by whatever means necessary. In some cases this meant buying votes, rigging elections, or physical violence directed against those who supported opposition candidates (Falola and Ihonvbere 1985, p. 108; Post and Vickers 1973, p. 3).

The issue of expanding the social security system came up during the 1979 election campaign. The Unity Party of Nigeria (UPN), a party with a democratic socialist orientation led by a Yoruba, Chief Awolowo, included a promise to expand social security coverage as a plank in its platform (Dudley 1982, pp. 187–188; Andrain 1988, p. 237). Awolowo (1966, p. 112) had long been on record in favor of a government pension for all persons over age 65 who could demonstrate economic need. In the 1979 election the UPN lost, but it did get strong support in four Yoruba-speaking states. Given the nature of Nigerian politics it is, however, difficult to separate the ethnic vote from the vote for the UPN's program. Furthermore, this pension proposal was not a major part of the UPN's program, and it was not a reason that many people voted either for or against the UPN.

The UPN was not the only party to bring up the issue of old-age social security in the 1979 election. The National Party of Nigeria (NPN), a right of center party, also promised more protection for the aged (Dudley 1982, p. 192). However, this was a vague promise that does not seem to have been an important part of the party's platform. The NPN won the general election, but there was no evidence of any movement on the old-age social security issue prior to the coup in 1983 in which the civilian government was replaced by a military government.

Ever since independence Nigeria's major political parties have tended to represent ethnic and regional as opposed to class interests.[14] The old-age security issue has not been an important factor in Nigerian elections; it was not a salient issue even in the 1979 election. Since independence Nigeria has alternated between rule by democratically elected leaders (1960–1966, 1979–1983) and military rule (1966–1979, 1983–present), but there is no evidence that more attention was paid to old-age social security policy during periods of civilian rule and greater democratization.

The fractionalization of political parties along regional and ethnic lines also characterizes the labor movement (Cohen 1974, p. 114; Kilby 1967, p. 494). For many years organized labor was highly fragmented and efforts to unify unions into a strong union central were not successful.[15] One source of the weakness of the Nigerian labor movement has been the existence of a large number of very small unions; this was particularly true prior to 1978. Union membership was often limited to those employed by a single employer or government department (Sklar 1963, p. 23). During the 1960s the number of unions was increasing rapidly; as a result the size of the unions remained small despite a substantial increase in union membership (Tokunboh 1985, p. 97). By the mid-1970s there were more than 700 unions, but only 2.5 percent of the total labor force was organized (Kurian 1982, p. 1339; Yesufu 1982, pp. 100–101). The laissez-faire union policy in Nigeria resulted in a proliferation of small weak unions. Except for a few brief periods (e.g., the General Strikes of 1945, 1964, 1971, 1975, and 1981), the labor movement has been divided into a number of uncooperative and hostile groups (Graf 1989, pp. 92–93; Cohen 1974, p. 70; Tokunboh 1985, p. 107).[16]

Since the late 1970s there has been substantial consolidation in the Nigerian labor movement. In 1978 the military government reorganized approximately 700 small unions into 42 larger industrial unions which were placed under the jurisdiction of the Nigerian Labour Congress (NLC) (Otobo 1986, p. 340).[17] There was general recognition by the unions that the extreme degree of fragmentation in the labor movement was a problem (Tokunboh 1985, p. 93). The military government sought the formation of the NLC as a way to avoid the emergence of a hostile union central and as a mechanism to help build support for its economic and social policies. Although formed through the government's initiative the NLC officials are democratically elected and do have some autonomy (U. S. Department of State 1987). Nonetheless, the government does not hesitate to cancel union elections and disband governing bodies when it wants to do so.

Another source of weakness in the Nigerian labor movement has been the involvement of rival international unions.[18] In the period immediately after independence there was a flurry of activity on the part of several international labor unions seeking to gain a foothold in Nigeria. These international unions were in competition with one another and brought in substantial outside monies. But they also put pressure on the unions they affiliated with not to cooperate with unions affiliated with their rival international unions (Otobo 1986, pp. 343–344). These international unions and the monies they could supply made it possible for a number of unions to survive that might otherwise have been forced to merge with other unions for a more centralized and powerful labor movement (Cohen 1974, p. 99). Today Nigerian unions are not allowed to affiliate as members of non-African international unions, but some do have fraternal relations with one or another of these international unions as nonmembers.[19]

During periods when military regimes have been in power Nigeria has been ruled by an authoritarian bureaucratic oligarchy. Power has been concentrated in the hands of high level military officers and government technocrats. Also influential during such regimes has been the business elite. When civilian governments have been in power a more diverse, but still highly limited set of interest groups have had influence on policy. Even during the periods of increased democratization the government would be more accurately described as a competitive oligarchy than as a pluralistic democracy. During such regimes power has been concentrated in the hands of local business elites,[20] senior civil servants, high level military officers, and a few key professional groups such as lawyers, academics, and physicians (Andrain 1988, pp. 22–34). Those representing the large rural population and those representing organized labor have had little influence during either military or civilian regimes.

Nigeria's National Provident Fund

No government social security provision for the elderly was made prior to independence.[21] However, in 1961, shortly after independence, the NPF was introduced. The NPF was and still is essentially a compulsory savings scheme designed to provide some economic assistance to covered workers at the time of retirement. The employer and the employee make periodic contributions, but there are no government contributions. The benefit, ordinarily paid as a lump sum upon reaching retirement age, is generally equal to the total contributions plus interest earned on those contributions. Nigeria's provident fund is administered by a management board made up of representatives of employees, employers, and the government (ISSA 1989, p. 95; *Social Security in Africa* 1983, p. 55).

Covered workers contribute 6 percent of wages below a specified level. The employer makes a matching contribution. As the upper limit for employee contributions is only 4 naira per month, the maximum yearly combined contribution in 1987 came to about U.S. $24 (ISSA 1989, p. 97). Given the meager size of this annual contribution it is not surprising that the eventual lump sum benefit upon retirement does not offer a great deal by way of old-age security provision. In 1976 the government tried to increase the maximum combined monthly contribution from 8 to 20 naira, but there was such a strong negative reaction from the public that the new policy was soon rescinded (ISSA 1982, p. 47).

If a covered worker dies prior to receiving this retirement benefit, the monies are paid as a lump sum death benefit to the worker's next of kin. If a covered worker becomes seriously ill for an extended period of time or becomes unemployed for a year or more, it is possible to obtain permission to withdraw up to half of the funds (and accrued interest) in the account (*Social Security in Africa*

1983, p. 55; ISSA 1980a, p. 202).[22] When such withdrawals are made, the lump sum available upon reaching retirement age is much less than it would otherwise have been.

NPF coverage is confined for the most part to wage and salary employees in the modern sector working in urban areas. There is almost no coverage for the vast majority of the population, particularly those living in rural areas (ILO 1977, p. 10). Many factors contribute to the low coverage in rural areas (Ijere 1978, p. 25). One is the belief among many policymakers that in the rural areas the traditional forms of social support are more appropriate and effective (Aubry 1974, p. 17). Due to the lack of an appropriate social welfare infrastructure in rural areas, the cost of administering a provident fund system in such areas would be high. This is due in part to the scattered settlement patterns and in part to poor communication links between many of these areas and the urban centers (ILO 1977, pp. 40–41). Most important of all is the very low per capita income in these areas and the low proportion of remuneration in the form of money income (Ijere 1978, p. 25). It is difficult to set up a system for social insurance or provident fund contributions for poor subsistence farmers and agricultural workers who receive a substantial fraction of their remuneration in the form of crops (Moreau 1974, p. 20).[23]

Establishments with fewer than 10 workers are not required to participate in the NPF. Local, state, and federal government employees who are covered by the Pensions Ordinance of 1951 are exempted from the NPF as are casual workers, the self-employed, aliens, and most rural workers, and diplomats (*Social Security in Africa* 1983, p. 54). Also excluded are teachers and administrators of universities and colleges as well as primary and secondary schools; these groups are covered by various alternative superannuation schemes (ISSA 1961). Until 1978 public sector employees were covered by the NPF, but they are now covered by a separate scheme (U.S. Department of State 1983, p. 1).

Nigeria was the first African nation to introduce a national provident fund scheme for private sector workers, and within a few years several other countries such as Zambia, Uganda, Tanzania, Ghana, and Kenya had introduced similar schemes (ILO 1977, p. 10). But Nigeria was not the first to introduce a national old-age social security plan. Several other countries had previously introduced social insurance based old-age pension schemes—for example, Equatorial Guinea (1947), Burundi (1956), Rwanda (1956), and Zaire (1959) (Mouton 1975, pp. 4–8). In opting for the provident fund approach, Nigeria was if anything going against the trend to adopt social insurance based pension systems.

One reason to opt for the provident fund approach is that it calls for a simple administrative infrastructure (ILO 1977, p. 5). Some argue that such schemes are more appropriate for nations with high illiteracy rates such as Nigeria.[24] This would, however, be a more compelling explanation of Nigeria's decision were it not the case that more than twice as many sub-Saharan African nations have introduced social insurance pension schemes as provident fund schemes.[25] In many nations adopting social insurance pension schemes literacy rates were lower than in Nigeria (e.g., Senegal, Mali, Central African Republic). It is also of note that the former French colonies, which are not more developed than the former British colonies, have all opted for social insurance schemes (Ijere 1978, p. 64). While these nations have also had difficulty extending coverage to rural workers, their social insurance based old-age schemes have proven as viable as the provident fund schemes.

While the basic structure of Nigeria's provident fund scheme has remained intact over the years, the program is periodically reviewed and minor changes have been made. Originally the provident fund was administered only out of the main office in Lagos. A decentralization process began in 1973 and now there are state offices throughout the country which has greatly improved access (U.S. Department of State 1983). The substantial increase in NPF participation between 1979 and 1982 was due more to these administrative changes than to pressure from labor unions or leftist political parties.

Industrialization has contributed to urbanization and both have contributed to a shift toward wage labor. This shift has made an increasing proportion of the population vulnerable to swings in the economy and in need of social security programs of various sorts (Sanda 1987, p. 173; Aire 1974, pp. 412–413). Although the number of workers covered by the NPF has steadily increased during the past 25 years, most Nigerians continue to rely primarily on traditional measures, particularly support from children (Peil 1991, p. 98; Sanda 1987, p. 174). The majority continue to live in rural areas where the traditional sources of social security are all that is available.[26] A substantial proportion of even those living in urban areas depend primarily on the traditional measures linked to the extended family (Ijere 1966, p. 463).

In Nigeria as in other nations with provident fund schemes the lump sum payment of the retirement benefit is popular, but it does leave many recipients with less than adequate protection (ILO 1977, p. 38).[27] The benefit sometimes amounts to several years of wages, but these monies are often used up quickly leaving the recipient without sufficient funds to maintain an adequate standard of living (Mulozi 1982, p. 88). Inflation also causes problems. One estimate is that between 1971 and 1981 the real value of funds in the NPF decreased by 70 percent even after adding in accrued interest. Due to the poor record in keeping pace with inflation, many workers consider the NPF more a form of taxation than a savings plan (O'Reilly 1982, p. 6).

Many of those covered by the NPF find the provident fund approach preferable to the social insurance alternative, but there has also been a great deal of dissatisfaction with the way in which the program has been administered; this was particularly true prior to decentralization (ISSA 1980b, p. 8). A common complaint is that it is very difficult to obtain information about the value of one's account. Another is that it often takes a long time to obtain one's provident fund benefits upon retirement (Aire 1974, p. 415). Another frequent criticism is that many employers are slow in remitting contributions to the NPF. Some firms evade provident fund payment by underreporting the number of employees or the amount employees are paid.[28] Yet another problem is that employees are often not given information about payment schedules and how to transfer accounts when changing jobs (U.S. Department of State 1983, pp. 2–3).

There is evidence suggesting that if given the option a majority of workers would not participate in the NPF (George 1987, p. 23). In response to these and other criticisms, in 1983 the civilian government announced plans to eventually convert the NPF into a comprehensive social insurance program. One proposed shift would be from the lump sum payment to regular payments over a period of 10 years. However, these long-term plans were contingent upon favorable economic and political developments which never materialized. Since these plans were announced the civilian government was overthrown and the economy remained weak. No such change is currently under active consideration.

By the mid-1980s more than 2.5 million workers were covered by the NPF (ISSA 1989, p. 97). This came to about 8 percent of the economically active population age 15 to 54. However, another 3 million workers were covered by one of the pension programs for government workers (Ogunshola 1979). Thus we can estimate that approximately 20 percent of the economically active population is covered by the NPF or some sort of public pension (Tracy 1991, pp. 102–103).[29] This is a small fraction of the total labor force, but it does include a substantially larger proportion of those employed in the modern sector.

While the NPF has been expanding over the years, the various state and federal pension systems continue to cover more workers. Thus in the Nigerian context these government pension schemes constitute a significant part of the government's total old-age security effort. Federal and state workers in higher level positions (pensionable employees) who have been covered for 15 years or more are generally eligible for retirement at age 60 with a gratuity benefit equal to 100 percent of their final salary and a (noncontributory) pension equal to 30 percent of that salary. Those who retire with 35 or more years of covered service are eligible for a gratuity equal to 300 percent of their final salary and a pension equal to 70 percent of that final salary (Oyefeso 1988).

In Nigeria as in many other African nations the provident fund scheme was originally viewed as a first step toward the development of a social security system that would eventually include a social insurance based old-age pension system (Mouton 1975, pp. 24–25; Mulozi 1982, p. 85). But as these provident funds schemes have become institutionalized, it has become evident that the shift from a provident fund to old-age pensions is difficult to make, in part for technical reasons (such as how to treat contributions already made into the provident fund), but more importantly for political reasons. A variety of vested interest groups have grown up around the provident funds and they vigorously oppose proposals to shift to pension fund schemes (ILO 1977, pp. 28–29). Rwanda is an exception; it did shift from a compulsory savings scheme to a pension scheme (ILO 1977, p. 39). In a few countries including Ghana and Kenya there has been some discussion of such a shift, but it does not seem likely that the shift to the social insurance approach will come anytime soon in these countries. Tanzania, however, is in the process of making a gradual shift from a national provident fund to a social insurance program (Dixon 1986, p. 106).[30]

While Nigeria is not considering a shift to the annuity approach any time soon, the ultimate goal, at least so far as some high level civil servants are concerned, is to convert the scheme into a social insurance program (ISSA 1980b, p. 4). Illustrating one way this could be done, Zambia has introduced the option of either an annuity or a lump sum payment in connection with its provident fund system (Mulozi 1982, p. 94). However, to date the annuity (pension) option has not proved popular; the vast majority of eligible Zambian workers select the lump sum alternative (ILO 1977, p. 38). Despite such evidence, during the 1980s the management board of the NPF was considering an eventual shift from a lump sum payment to an annuity approach (ISSA 1982, pp. 47–48). However, there is general agreement among the key civil servants that the NPF would have to establish a track record for the efficient collection of contributions and payment of benefits before any such conversion could be seriously considered.

Public Pension Policy in the Ivory Coast

Our primary focus in this chapter is on the development of old-age social security policy in Nigeria. To this end it is useful to make comparisons with developments in other sub-Saharan nations. Of particular interest are the public pension systems that have been introduced in the French-speaking nations. In this section we discuss the public pension program in the Ivory Coast, a former French colony located approximately 400 miles west of Nigeria. The social insurance based public pension program in the Ivory Coast is similar to that in several other West African nations that were once French colonies.[31]

In general old-age pension schemes in French-speaking Africa began as systems set up for civil servants. The Lamine-Gueye Law of 1950 called for coverage of African nationals in the civil service that was "more or less" comparable to that available for the French civil servants (Ejuba 1982, p. 102). As these countries gained independence, they found themselves administering pension schemes that resembled the French scheme. The Ivory Coast became independent in 1960 and in the same year introduced an old-age pension scheme for the general population.

In 1968 the Caisse Nationale de Prévoyance Sociale (National Fund for Social Contingencies—CNPS) was created (Bakayoko and Ehouman 1987, p. 72). The CNPS is an independent public agency managed by a joint employer-employee board. The CNPS includes an old-age pension program as one of several social insurance programs. The CNPS covers employees in the private sector, but many employers do not yet participate in the program.[32] The program currently involves only a fraction (440,000 workers in 1984) of the nation's population of approximately 10 million (Bakayoko and Ehouman 1987, p. 72). One reason is that more than half of the population lives in rural areas and agricultural workers are excluded as are the self-employed and the numerous urban marginal workers. Another reason is that many workers, even those working for employers for whom coverage by the social security system is "compulsory," are not covered (Musiga 1982, p. 320). In the Ivory Coast as in many African nations there is a substantial gap between the theoretical scope of coverage as specified in legislation and actual coverage.

There is a 1.6 percent tax on the worker's earnings[33] and a corresponding 2.4 percent payroll tax paid by the employer.[34] Contributions are paid into a Reserve

Fund administered by the CNPS. Half of the funds are placed in development banks for investment in several different sectors of the economy (Bakayoko and Ehouman 1987, p. 80). The other half are invested in government securities.

The full old-age pension is paid at age 55, but an actuarial reduced pension is available as early as age 50.[35] Workers must cease all wage-earning activity to become eligible for this pension (Kouassi 1991, p. 134). The standard pension is calculated by multiplying 1.33 percent of the worker's average earnings[36] by the number of years of coverage. There is a provision for a survivor's pension[37] equal to 50 percent of the deceased's pension, but there is no spouse benefit.[38]

To become eligible for the standard old-age pension benefit, the worker must have worked at least 10 years in a company covered by the CNPS program. There is an "old-age settlement" payable to workers age 55 or older who are ineligible for the standard pension because they have less than the required number of years of covered employment (U. S. Social Security Administration 1990, p. 133). This settlement is equal to the total of all contributions paid into the fund by or on behalf of the worker. There is also a "solidarity pension" for retired workers who worked for the company for 10 years or more, but who are ineligible for the standard pension because their employer was not covered until after they retired (Kouassi 1991, p. 135)

The Ivory Coast does not have independent unions in the Western sense. But some bargaining does take place between a government controlled organization for employees (The *Union Générale des Travailleurs de Côte d'Ivorie*) and another representing employers (The *Union de Côte d'Ivorie*). One of the issues these organizations negotiate is the size of the lump sum retirement benefit that is based on the worker's final earnings and number of years of service (*International Benefit Guidelines* 1989, p. 133). Thus in the Ivory Coast many workers in the organized sector get what amounts to a retirement gratuity benefit in addition to their social insurance pension.

In the Ivory Coast as in Nigeria old-age provision is for most of the population a family responsibility. Only a small fraction of the elderly are eligible for an old-age pension. As in Nigeria coverage is restricted for the most part to urban workers in the modern sector of the economy. The proportion of the total population covered by the old-age social insurance program (CNPS) in the Ivory Coast today is very similar to that covered by the National Provident Fund program (NPF) in Nigeria.

Accounting for Developments in Nigeria

In our efforts to account for old-age social security developments in Nigeria, we must take into consideration similar developments at about the same time in other sub-Saharan nations. In the early 1950s most of these nations were still European colonial territories and only one (Equatorial Guinea) had a national old-age social security program. During the 1960s many of these nations became independent and shortly thereafter introduced either provident fund systems or social insurance based pension systems. There was a clear link between attaining independence and the establishment of these and other social security programs.

Another explanation for the decision to introduce a government administered national provident fund is that it was part of an effort to legitimize the central government (Tracy 1991, p. 101). In many nations, as in Nigeria, at independence most of the population identified more strongly with regional and local ethnic (tribal) groupings than with the nation as a whole. The tendency to identify with one's ethnic group rather than with Nigeria has been the source of a great deal of intergroup conflict. The introduction of provident fund systems and old-age pension systems can be interpreted as efforts to justify the existence of a national level government and to a lesser extent to give a potentially disruptive segment of the population a vested interest in government sponsored social welfare institutions (Williamson and Pampel 1991, p. 36).

This second explanation is a variant of the neo-Marxist social control thesis (Piven and Cloward 1971; O'Connor 1973). However, the argument here differs from Piven and Cloward's formulation in that the focus is on the generally more privileged workers in the modern sector to the exclusion of the much larger group of workers in the informal urban sector and the rural agricultural sector. It also differs to the extent that those who framed the original provident fund legislation were much more concerned about ethnic and regional conflict than about class conflict.

In Nigeria as in many of the other countries an effort was made to introduce democratic political institutions in connection with the transition to independence. But lack of prior experience with and acceptance of democratic institutions resulted in very weak democratic structures (Cohen 1974, p. 261). Given the newness and tentativeness of those democratic structures, it is not possible to account for the introduction of Nigeria's provident fund in terms of the increase in the level of democratization. Many nations that were not even briefly democratic were among those introducing provident funds or old-age pension systems. Furthermore, there is no evidence of greater expansion of provident fund coverage in Nigeria during periods of civilian (more democratic) government (1961–1966, 1979–1983).[39]

Between the end of World War II and independence, the Nigerian economy experienced considerable economic growth which continued up through the start of the Biafran Civil War in 1967. After the end of the war the economy began to grow even more rapidly and continued to do so throughout the 1970s, but it was now highly concentrated in the oil industry (Kirk-Greene 1986, p. 57). In 1960 some 80 percent of Nigeria's export revenues came from agricultural products, but by the mid-1980s about 90 percent came from oil (Oyefeso 1988, p. 1).[40] Similarly, by the mid-1980s approximately 70 percent of government revenues were derived from the oil industry (U.S. Dept. of State 1987, p. 5). While oil was providing much needed monies for development projects, it was a highly capital intensive industry that directly involved only a small fraction of the population.

In the early 1980s there was a sharp drop in the price of oil which had an adverse impact on the economy (Kirk-Greene 1986, p. 45). Between 1980 and 1988 oil revenues decreased from $25 billion to $7 billion, and this reduced the nation's per capita GNP to less than half what it had been in 1980. The government had become greatly overextended due to substantial overestimates of the oil revenues that would be available. The reduction in oil revenues had strong repercussions throughout the Nigerian economy.

During the early 1980s due in part to the rapid rate of increase in per capita income during the 1970s, there was much talk about a possible shift from the provident fund approach to the social insurance approach to old-age social security policy. While such proposals are still discussed, it is generally recognized that no such proposals will get beyond the talking stage until there is a substantial improvement in the Nigerian economy. It is not only the low per capita income and the related lack of fiscal resources that undercuts proposals for greater government involvement in old-age security programs, but also the instability of the economy due to the dramatic impact on government revenues of fluctuations in the world oil market (Tracy 1991, pp. 102, 113).

While we have had much to say about the impact of level of development, economic growth, and economic instability on the relative lack of old-age security policy development in Nigeria, it is also important to look at this relationship in another way. Since 1961 the NPF has grown to cover a substantial proportion of the workers in the organized sector. The forced savings involved has created a substantial pool of money to invest in projects that create jobs and promote economic growth. Some of this money has gone for loans to finance the construction of private housing and some has been invested in private corporations (ISSA 1989, p. 99).

Nigeria's low per capita income in 1961 contributed to the decision to introduce a provident fund as opposed to a social insurance based system, but when comparisons are made with other sub-Saharan nations, the evidence does not suggest a strong relationship between level of development and the choice between these alternatives. Similarly, there is no clear trend with respect to the timing of the introduction of old-age social security systems and level of development, except in the sense that as a group the sub-Saharan African nations are among the least developed nations in the world and as a group they were also among the last to introduce old-age social security programs.

Except for the years of the Biafran Civil War (1967–1970), the 1960s and particularly 1970s were characterized by rapid economic growth (World Bank 1983a, p. 135). Workers were drawn to the major urban centers such as Lagos and this increased the need for modern social security programs (Sanda 1987, p. 173; ILO 1977, p. 4). The growth in the number of people covered by the provident fund since it was introduced in 1961 seems in part to have been a response to economic development and the increasing need for coverage in the modern sector (ISSA 1980a, p. 197).[41]

In our analysis of old-age social security development explanations emphasizing Nigeria's dependent position in the world economy must be used with caution and qualification. In Nigeria the legacy of dependency is in large measure the legacy of colonialization. Economic dependency did not end in 1960 when the nation became politically independent; large multinational corporations continued to control certain key sectors of the Nigerian economy (Cohen 1974, p. 38). However, outside economic investment has also contributed to the nation's growth. It would be risky to argue that the nation would today be more developed or that the old-age security system would be more developed had there been little or no foreign investment since independence.[42]

Nigeria has a very high fertility rate and as a result the population is heavily concentrated in the younger age categories. This is one of the reasons that so little attention is given to government social welfare programs for the aged. This age structure creates a great deal of government and societal interest in focusing scarce public funds on health and education programs for the young as opposed to the elderly (Adeokun 1984).

The provident fund approach is particularly well suited to a nation that is faced with deep ethnic cleavages and the associated distrust of government officials who are members of a different ethnic group (Williamson and Pampel 1991, p. 35). With such a scheme there is less concern about one group or another getting more than its fair share as the system is based on individual accounts structured so that the benefits are strictly limited to prior contributions (plus interest). It is also true, however, that there are many African nations, such as the Ivory Coast, that have introduced social insurance systems despite deep and long-standing ethnic cleavages. The common historical legacy of tribal conflict in much of sub-Saharan Africa linked in part to slave trading and raiding of prior centuries is one source of these contemporary cleavages.

While Nigeria's ethnic cleavages were not a major determinant of the decision to introduce a provident fund scheme, these cleavages have been and will continue to be a source of resistance to proposals calling for a shift from a provident fund to a social insurance based pension scheme. That is, ethnic politics is relevant to efforts to account for what can be described as the lack of development in old-age social security policy since 1961 (Tracy 1991, p. 107). The evidence suggests that despite the efforts of the current regime to sharply reduce the extent to which political parties are defined along ethnic and regional lines, ethnic politics will be a significant determinant of future developments. Similar arguments can be made for the relevance of interest group politics based on language, religion, and region.[43]

Colonial background played a major role in subsequent old-age social security developments in Nigeria. The decision to introduce a provident fund as opposed to a social insurance pension was clearly linked to the nation's British colonial background. The former British colonies tended to introduce provident fund schemes (ILO 1977, p. 10) and the former French colonies such as the Ivory Coast tended to introduce pension schemes (Mulozi 1982, p. 83). This explanation and evidence are also consistent with a cultural diffusion explanation of old-age social security policy development.

Strong civil service backing was a major reason the NPF was introduced in 1961, and the civil service has continued to be one of the most influential actors shaping NPF policy since then. Under military rule high level civil servants have been often more than advisors and administrators; they have been the primary policymakers. Government officials consulted with representatives of regional governments, trade unions, and employers' associations prior to introducing the NPF scheme (International Social Security Association 1961).[44] But there is no evidence that it was introduced in response to pressure from any of these groups or from the general population. The decision was in large measure made by civil servants who were aware that old-age pension schemes had been established in several new African nations and that provident fund schemes had been established in India and other former British colonies (Tracy 1991, p. 104).

Once the NPF was introduced, the program itself became a structural factor inhibiting the introduction of a social insurance based pension scheme. Any such scheme soon develops a constituency of bureaucrats, managers, and covered workers who favor the status quo and oppose any proposals for radical change. They fear that somehow they will be adversely affected by the change. This is basically a policy legacy or state structure argument, but it is also consistent with an interest group politics perspective.

From the outset there were problems of corruption in the Nigerian civil service bureaucracy (Sanda 1987, pp. 170–171; Harbison 1962, p. 204).[45] These problems seem to have grown worse over time (Lubeck 1986, p. 42; Kirk-Greene 1986, p. 44).[46] The argument has been made that pension systems are more difficult to establish during periods of concern over possible civil service corruption (Orloff and Skocpol 1984). This argument could potentially be used to help account for the decision to go with a provident fund scheme as opposed to a pension scheme in Nigeria. However, it is important to keep in mind that there were similar problems of corruption in many other African nations that introduced old-age pension schemes at about the same time Nigeria was introducing its provident fund plan. The corruption argument is more relevant in connection with efforts to account for the relative lack of old-age social security policy development over the three decades since the original program was introduced (Tracy 1991, p. 107). People are less likely to push for a shift to a pension system if they do not trust the government to pay the old-age pensions or to pay pensions commensurate with the contributions made over the years.

Had organized labor been more unified and more influential, it is entirely possible that Nigeria would have introduced a comprehensive public pension program to provide old-age security. But given the fractionalization of organized labor, it is not surprising that there has been relatively little pressure from labor to shift from a provident fund system to a more comprehensive social insurance approach to income security in old age (Tracy 1991, p. 108). Changes have been made in Nigeria's provident fund scheme since it was introduced in 1961, but there is no evidence that organized labor has played a significant role in these policy changes. Even if organized labor had been a more influential interest group, old-age social security policy was not an issue that was high on labor's agenda, particularly during the 1960s and 1970s (Tracy 1991, p. 108).[47]

However, organized labor was not entirely without interest or influence with respect to old-age security issues. During the 1980s the NLC was one of the groups backing the proposed shift from a provident fund to a public pension system. In addition, it is now common for employers in the organized sector to provide gratuity payments in addition to the NPF benefit upon retirement for long-term employees. These gratuity payments are usually union negotiated (*International Benefit Guidelines* 1989, p. 172).

The predominantly rural nature of Nigeria has inhibited efforts to increase the role of the government in providing old-age security benefits. While Nigeria has undergone substantial urbanization since independence, it remains a predominantly rural nation with four-fifths of the population living in rural areas (World Bank 1983b, p. 69). Given the strength of family support systems in the rural areas, this reduces the pressure on the government to make more of an effort at social provision for the elderly. As most proposals for old-age social security policy reform would only reach workers in the urban modern sector of the economy, the vast majority of the population would be excluded from the benefits of any such policy change.[48] This is one reason most Nigerians have little interest in such proposals.

Were an effort made to extend old-age security coverage to a significant fraction of those in the informal urban sector or in the rural sector, the government would run into a series of problems due to lack of experienced administrative personnel, inadequate information processing systems, and poor communication facilities (Mouton and Gruat 1988; ILO 1977, pp. 40–41). While these problems would increase if coverage were substantially expanded in urban areas, they would become more severe were a serious effort made to extend coverage to the rural sector.

The rural nature of Nigerian society contributes to strongly held traditional values about the responsibility of family, particularly children, to provide for elderly parents when they are no longer able to provide for themselves. This intergenerational support system is working relatively well in both urban and rural areas (Ekpenyong et al. 1986).[49] The general population assumes that it is the responsibility of the family, not the state, to provide for the elderly (Peil 1991). While workers look forward to receiving the NPF lump sum benefit and any other gratuity payments upon retirement, these monies are generally not viewed as the primary source of social provision after retirement. In some cases the monies are useful for the purchase of a plot of land for subsistence farming or for starting up a small business, but for the most part workers look to their children as their primary means of support in old age.

Conclusion

The decision to introduce an old-age social security scheme in 1961 can primarily be attributed to the shift from the status of a colony to that of an independent nation, the need to promote national integration, and the need to legitimize and empower the central government. The decision to go with a provident fund as opposed to a social insurance based program was due in part to Nigeria's low per capita income, but more importantly to the nation's British as opposed to French colonial legacy.

The Nigerian case is of note for how little change there has been in old-age security policy since the introduction of the Nigerian Provident Fund in 1961. Among the factors contributing to the relative lack of policy development in this sphere have been: a low per capita income, economic instability related to fluctuations in world oil prices, a small modern (organized) sector of the economy, a predominantly rural population, and a very young age structure. As important if not more important is the existence of strong family support networks and the widely held belief that the elderly should and will be taken care of by their children. Also important is a lack of confidence that the government can be trusted to provide old-age support. This lack of trust is related to a number of factors including the serious administrative problems plaguing the NPF over the years and the evidence of pervasive government corruption including ethnic favoritism and patronage.

The historical record for the Nigerian case suggests that the decision to intro-duce a provident fund in 1961 and the relative lack of development in old-age social security policy since then cannot be accounted for in terms of any one over-riding cause or theoretical explanation. Rather, we consider explanations derived from several different theories and find many of them useful in accounting for a portion of the evidence. We make use of the industrialism perspective, particu-larly with respect to the consequences of Nigeria's low level of economic devel-opment. We find a number of arguments related to the state-centered perspective useful both in connection with efforts to account for the introduction of the origi-nal NPF in 1961 and in connection with the relative lack of developments since then. We make relatively little use of class-based theories, but fairly extensive use of neo-pluralist arguments emphasizing the role of societal cleavages based on such attributes as ethnicity, religion, and region.

9

Cross-National Analysis

To this point our focus has been on evidence drawn from a series of historical case studies. For many questions about the origins and the evolution of old-age security policy, qualitative comparative historical analysis is the methodology of choice. This approach allows us to address detailed questions about the ways in which policy has evolved in different countries. It lends itself to the analysis of issues and developments that are unique to a specific country. To approach a full understanding of the evolution of old-age security policy in a specific country, it is essential that we have access to the kinds of information and explanations that only a detailed historical case study can provide.

It would be a mistake, however, to conclude that all interesting and important questions about cross-national variation in pension policy must be based on the comparative historical method alone. It is also desirable to formalize some of the insights of the case studies by developing testable propositions and evaluating them with quantitative data. A quantitative analysis can complement qualitative results by extending the number of nations studied, organizing diverse, often idiosyncratic findings, and checking robustness of the conclusions with a different method.

Our primary emphasis on the case studies in this book extends and revises our previous quantitative work (Pampel and Williamson 1985; 1988; 1989; Williamson and Pampel 1986). The unique and nuanced characteristics of social policy and its determinants found in the case studies of the individual nations were not captured in our previous studies. To come full circle, however, some of the case study insights can now be incorporated to improve our quantitative models.

Each approach has its own strengths and weaknesses, and offers insights unavailable from the other (Ragin 1987, p. 17). Where the case studies provide historical and national details, the quantitative method focuses on narrow components that are numerically measurable. At the cost of narrowness, however, the quantitative analysis can provide more precise estimates and more confident generalizations about spending patterns than are possible on the basis of our historical case study data alone. For instance, we will control statistically for multiple forces and spuriousness in the analyses to follow. The relative effects of age structure, development, class structure, and party rule, each associated with different theories, can be more precisely compared. Without statistical controls, it is hard to determine which variables, all of which in some way seem associated with pension expansion, have effects when controlling for the others. Moreover, with the quantitative results we can more confidently suppose our arguments apply to more than seven nations.

Another advantage of the quantitative methods is the ability to more formally model contextual influences. In particular, we investigate the possible joint influence of the dimensions of state structure (e.g., democratic corporatism and level of democracy) with indicators linked to the different theories of pension policy development. The case studies assume each nation represents a unique constellation of forces of state, economy, class, and interest groups. The quantitative analysis tries to more generally identify, measure, and model state-based contextual sources of national differences in the determinants of pension program development. Translating national context into variables, and allowing them to interact statistically with other determinants, limits the kind of information that can be studied. At the same time, however, it allows for direct comparison of countries in ways not feasible with case studies.

Toward this end, we examine pension spending patterns for 18 industrial nations and 32 Third World nations for the years between 1960 and 1980—a period marked by expansion of existing systems rather than introduction of new systems. Our focus will be on a few key issues that are better addressed using quantitative analysis than qualitative historical analysis. The results cannot be integrated tightly with the case studies which are based on different methods and different methodological assumptions. In some ways, the evidence may lead us to qualify or contextualize some of the conclusions made in earlier chapters; in other ways, the evidence may prove to be consistent with and mutually reinforcing of previous results. Either way, the quantitative results serve to complement the previous findings rather than substitute for them.

The Theoretical Approach: A Review and Extension

A review of the case studies challenges conventional class-based views of public pension policy development. The simple version of the social democratic thesis, which argues that union strength and leftist rule are responsible for the emergence and expansion of pension programs, is clearly inadequate to capture the diversity of findings in the case studies. Similarly, neo-Marxist theories, which see pension development as a form of social control, emerge as important in only a few instances. Both theories err in focusing exclusively on the struggle between capital and labor; one sees the welfare state as a victory for labor, the other as a victory for capital. Neither accounts for the role of nonclass groups and independent state interests that we find important for all case studies. To counter the limited view of the class theories, we argue for a broader, more eclectic explanation.

If the class theories are incomplete, neither are they irrelevant. All of the five theories that guided the interpretation of the case studies receives some support. Most contexts highlighted the importance of pluralist democratic competition and the organization of the state, but others highlighted the importance of class power and conflict. Further, the industrial infrastructure, monopolization of capital, and evolution of political structures emerged as important in certain instances.

The complexity of the case study results mirrors the diversity of findings from numerous quantitative studies. Our own previous statistical studies suggest the size and political influence of aged populations are crucial to the growth of pension spending. These studies focus on the demographic characteristics of the population, finding that the size of the aged population has a strong positive effect on pension spending controlling for other variables. In contrast, other studies emphasize the importance of labor union strength and rule by social democratic parties (Castles 1983, p. 85; Hicks and Swank 1984, p. 99; Stephens 1979, pp. 99–105). The longer the years of left party rule (or the shorter the years of right party rule), and the larger and more centralized the labor unions within a country, the higher the pension spending. Finally, quantitative studies of state influence compete with those of age and class. Studies have included as determinants of spending various state-based determinants such as tax structure, fiscal centralization, federalism, administrative size, corporatist mediation, and coalition governments (Friedland and Sanders 1986, p. 208; DeViney 1983, p. 303; Pampel and Williamson 1989, pp. 65–66). Despite the large number of existing studies and the years or decades of debate, attempts to prove the superiority of one set of variables over the other have ended instead in much disagreement and inconsistency.

All this negates any hope for a simple, direct conclusion in the form of a single organizing proposition to emerge from either the case studies or previous quantitative literature. Summing the instances in which each of the theories receives strong support, and subtracting instances in which they receive little support, would provide a crude, but misleading tally that hides the complexities of the processes behind pension development. Something more than the typical proposition of the form "the greater X, the greater Y" is needed to organize the lessons of the case studies. Rather than as an automatic response to changes in class or age structure, capitalist or industrialist development, or democratic or bureaucratic expansion, pension development must be seen as emerging in special ways to all these forces.

A starting point for developing nuanced propositions that reflect the complexity of the case studies and the quantitative literature is to consider how these separate—and often competing—approaches can be integrated. Pampel, Williamson, and Stryker (1990) suggest the state and its structure might be seen as an important determinant of pension expansion, not in isolation from class and age forces, but in combination with them. State interests and the optimal policy for pursuing those interests may vary with the demands and resources of class and age groups that comprise the state's environment. Likewise, the ability of class and age groups should depend on more than the groups' sizes and interests. It also depends on the mediating role of the state relative to societally generated demands. Both types of forces would be seen as inseparable and equally important in determining pension spending.

Our case study results lend some credence to the view of the joint impact of state and society. In Sweden, state-sponsored corporatist arrangements facilitate the influence of union and business (and perhaps middle-class) desires for a generous, universal pension system. In Germany, trade union influence was simultaneously fostered and tempered by the state bureaucracy. In Britain, the tradition of a professional civil service along with efforts by all political parties to use welfare program legislation to electoral advantage illustrate the combination of the state and society. The lack of corporatist structures, however, undercuts labor impact in Britain. And in the United States, a relatively weak state dependent on patronage politics limited the ability of age and related group demands to translate into new programs, particularly during the early part of the century. Here again, the absence of state participation of organized interest groups limited labor's influence. In each case, then, the nature of the state appears to increase or decrease the effectiveness of group demands for pension programs.

The case studies of Third World nations, while showing qualitative differences from the advanced industrial economies, again suggest the difficulty of separating forces of state and society. In Brazil, neither forces of organized labor nor diverse interest groups were influential in substantially expanding pension coverage. For many years the authoritarian state used pensions more as a means to maintain order than as a response to societal pressure. In Nigeria as well, weak democratic state structures have limited the impact of popular demands for reforms in provident fund policy. In contrast, a democratic tradition in India has meant that organized labor has had at least something to say in determining the shape and generosity of the old-age security system. Thus, the specific state structures important for translating societal demands into old-age security spending in these nations often involve the emergence of democratic institutions rather than the particular form of the democratic state as in advanced industrial democracies. Yet, the same principle of the contextualized relationships between state, society, and old-age security policy applies equally well.

The interactive argument combines elements of several theories in a way that may be better able to explain the results than any single theory alone. While social democratic or neo-Marxist theory are insufficient to account for our findings, it is possible that in combination with state-based theory, the class theories make more sense. Similarly, neo-pluralist theory finds more support in some nations than others. If state theory can help identify the conditions for the effectiveness of age groups, the combination of the two is more valuable than either alone. Though we began with five separate theories, a motive for quantitative analysis is to help integrate them.

What follows is an attempt to identify the dimensions of state context that shape the way demand variables affect pension spending, and to formalize more precisely some of these ideas about the interaction of state and society. Given the vastly different stages of political development between the advanced industrial democracies and the Third World nations, the relevant dimensions of state context will certainly differ. Theoretical specification of the interactive argument is therefore presented separately for the two groups of nations. Results testing the theoretical predictions then follow, first for the advanced industrial democracies, then for the other nations.

Corporatism, Politics, and Pension Spending

A number of dimensions of state context prove relevant to the policy processes determining pension benefits in the case studies for the advanced industrial democracies. Of particular importance is the existence of corporatism. This concept proves useful for the quantitative study of spending, and as a means of linking class and nonclass theories.

Corporatism (alternatively referred to as neo-corporatism, democratic corporatism, or societal corporatism) involves arrangements for class and interest group organization, representation in policymaking, and political mediation. It is defined as the participation of organizational representatives of business and labor in state-sponsored, societal-level negotiation and bargaining over state policy (Schmitter 1974). By officially recognizing, representing, and mediating between classes, corporatist structures reinforce the centrality of class organization to policy bargaining. In the absence of corporatism, state-sanctioned participation of class organizations in public policymaking does not exist. Rather, class and other social groups influence policy by organizing themselves into an unspecified number of nonhierarchial, voluntary, and competitive organizations. No group is officially sanctioned as the formal representative of classes or other designated participants in national policymaking (Schmitter 1974).

More than an arrangement between private actors, corporatism in essence is a state-sanctioned, tripartite collaboration (Panitch 1980, p. 173; Schmitter 1985, pp. 35–37). Because corporatism represents an overlap of state and societal factors, it is difficult to classify as a state-based or societal-based force. Both dimensions are involved and neither is reducible to the other. State and class interests seek out one another and over time more formal procedures evolve for negotiation and bargaining (Schmitter 1985, p. 37). Class representatives gain benefits of legitimacy and monopoly in negotiation; the state gains in the influence over the private sector. The process over time seems to yield tradeoffs in which capital obtains profit-making economic growth and labor quiescence in return for providing full employment and supporting an increased social wage for labor (Cameron 1984, p. 146; Goldthorpe 1984, p. 325).

Stable structures of corporatism alone would not appear to generate welfare spending without external demands from societal groups for more spending. Logically, enhanced state capacity stemming from corporatist arrangements would permit, but not require welfare policy outcomes. Whether or not state capacity is exercised should depend on the economic and social environment in which that capacity exists. Thus, corporatism may emerge as an important determinant of pension spending in combination with—as a facilitator or inhibitor—of changing class or age structure.

This reasoning implies some state contexts are more conducive to certain kinds of interest mobilization than others. Class-related variation in union size, capital strength, and partisan party rule should most influence spending in nations where union and capital interests are articulated within, mediated by, and centralized by corporatist structures. Centralization of class bargaining over policy, even for an age-related program such as pensions, makes classes the dominate cleavage, source of identification, and organizational line of mobilization. Once mobilized for institutional conflict along class lines, political conflict tends to further social solidarity within classes and mobilize labor support for additional spending (Esping-Andersen 1985, p. 229). Thus, emergence of corporatist structures for policy formation demarcates interests in ways that highlight class associations relative to other lines of conflict. Furthermore, even given similar levels of class mobilization, the existence of centralized structures makes bargaining and compromise easier because a limited number of encompassing actors are involved in the process. It also lessens backlash with solid class support for negotiated outcomes and minimizes parochial opposition to larger class goals. Institutionalized corporatist structures should thus make pension spending more responsive to class organization.

Conversely, age structure and nonpartisan variables may prove less important in corporatist contexts and more important in noncorporatist contexts. The lack of centralized structures for mobilization of interests along class lines—indeed, having fragmented class groupings and noncorporatist bargaining—tends to promote emergence of a variety of specialized interests that transcend or cut across class interests. As a result, groups with direct interests in particular programs—the aged for pensions, business for regulatory agencies, labor for unemployment—become more influential in policy outcomes (M. Olson 1982, pp. 48–52). Further, local political processes emerge as more important than national bargaining as groups seek to influence local representatives to support their interests. A fragmented power structure makes it difficult to insulate politicians from parochial demands, or to favor encompassing group interests. In noncorporatist contexts, then, mobilization along nonclass lines is likely to make pension spending less responsive to class strength, and more responsive to size of the aged population.

We can therefore make the following hypothesis: *The influence of class groups increases with corporatism while the influence of the aged population decreases with corporatism.* This already presumes additive influences of class and age groups and concentrates explicitly on how corporatism shapes that influence.[1] In so doing, the hypothesis attempts to integrate the five theories we have been considering. The social democratic and neo-Marxist theories are thus viewed as applying to corporatist nations more than noncorporatist nations. Similarly, the industrialism and neo-pluralist theories are viewed as applying more to noncorporatist nations than corporatist nations. The state theory, limited in this context to state-sponsored corporatist arrangements for negotiation, specifies the scope of the other theories. Although the formal hypothesis simplifies the complex theories, it has the advantage of summarizing in precise terms how they may be made consistent.

Democratic Political Development and Pension Spending

The processes determining pension spending in Third World nations no doubt differ from those in high-income nations. Even assuming that, as in advanced industrial democracies, the structure of the state facilitates the way demand variables translate into pension spending, the relevant state structures should differ for the Third World nations. The advanced industrial nations have highly institutionalized democratic procedures such as fair and regular elections, freedom of the press, and group opposition (Bollen 1983, p. 477). Within generally similar democratic systems, different structures of interest representation may then emerge. Many Third World nations, in contrast, lack essential democratic structures for the organization of (potential opposition) interests. The formation and mobilization of interests into channels of class or age consciousness have less relevance in nations where the opportunity for public expression of group interests is constrained or unavailable. Indeed, since democratic corporatism seldom exists outside the European nations, and its counterpart in nondemocracies as authoritarian corporatism has little to do with mass representation of societal groups,[2] the relevant dimension of state structure among the developing nations relates to the presence of democracy itself.

A review of world variation in the existence of democratic political institutions shows the need to incorporate this variation in one form or another into models of pension spending. Many nations such as in sub-Saharan Africa and Central America have virtually no experience with democracy. Others such as Costa Rica, the Philippines, and Sri Lanka have considerable democratic experience. Our three case studies, for instance, vary greatly in the presence of democratic procedures. According to Bollen's (1980, pp. 387–388) scale of democracy which varies from 0 to 100, scores are 91.2 for India, 60.9 for Brazil, and 49.5 for Nigeria. Muller's (1988, p. 55) measure of years of democratic experience to 1970 assigns values of 22 for India, 15 for Brazil, and 0 for Nigeria.

This cross-national variation in democracy by itself does little to explain variation in pension spending. The mere existence of procedures for mass participation will mean little unless economic and productive changes create group demands for social protection. A necessary, if not sufficient, condition for pension development is the shift to industrial market labor in which old-age insecurity is a serious risk. Without such changes, political procedures may mean little for pension development. Indeed, the direct effect of democracy may be both positive and negative. Authoritarian states may have the capacity to quickly implement expansive social policies when not hindered by political restraints. At the same time, they may have little motivation to act when the masses have limited input into policy.[3]

If the direct effect of democracy is unclear, however, the indirect or interactive influence may be more straightforward. The impact of social and economic changes are likely facilitated by the ability of interest groups to influence policy through democratic pressure. Increased democratic representation of the population through election of democratic leaders and popular participation of the citizenry will make the government more responsive to social and economic change. Economic and demographic change, to the extent that it diversifies interests and mobilizes ascriptive groups, should have stronger effects in democracies where such interests can be more freely expressed and acted on.

This reasoning can be made more concrete when applied to the effects of economic and demographic characteristics on pension spending. While growth of the aged population by itself increases the need for old-age support, this need and the growing pressures for benefits it engenders may better translate into higher public expenditures in the presence of democratic government. We can predict, therefore, that the positive effect of percent aged on pension spending will increase with the existence of democratic procedures. Similarly, economic development, by creating a more specialized labor force, increases the size of the groups unable to work (e.g., unemployed, less educated, older workers in declining industries) at the same time it increases the societal ability to support them. The ability of vulnerable groups to demand surplus wealth directed to their needs increases with democracy. Economic development, like percent aged, might be expected, then, to have stronger effects on pension spending in democracies than in nondemocracies.

Along with economic and population structures, years of social insurance program experience may increase expenditures (Wilensky 1975, p. 25). This may reflect expansion of technical knowledge of the government bureaucracy needed to implement new programs easily, the bureaucratic momentum in budgeting that makes limiting spending for existing programs difficult, or the development of influential constituent groups represented by the program All these effects may vary with the level of democracy as well. The power of the bureaucracy to expand the programs it administers might be expected to be greatest when dealing with elected legislatures and executives. We can hypothesize that the effect of social insurance program experience is stronger in democracies than nondemocracies.

In summary, these arguments suggest political enfranchisement is crucial but not sufficient for growth of the welfare state. Certain structural, bureaucratic, and demographic changes are also needed. Political pressures and preferences of populations then combine with changes in the structure of democracy to increase pension spending. Since the ability to affect spending stems in part from the existence of democratic procedures to express public interests, we hypothesize that the processes determining pension spending differ between the Third World democracies and nondemocracies.

Research Design, Data, and Measurement

The preceding theoretical arguments can be used to make predictions—consistent with the qualitative studies—concerning the combined influence of state and society variables on pension spending. The arguments imply that the usual models which assume that the effects of all variables are the same regardless of the level of the other independent variables are flawed. If state and society variables work together, this must be reflected in statistical models.

To translate the interactive arguments into empirical models, we analyze aggregate data on pension spending and a variety of relevant economic, social, political, and state determinants for both advanced industrial nations and Third World nations. Within these groups, the models must allow the effects of demand variables to shift with the level of the state variables (or vice versa). For the advanced industrial nations the relevant contextual state variable is corporatism; for Third World nations the relevant state variable is democracy.

For both groups of nations, the quantitative analyses attempt to maximize diversity in pension spending, state context, and social demands. In contrast to the case studies of a select and small number of nations, the quantitative analysis needs to be based on as many data points as possible. We therefore analyze all nations for which the International Labour Organization has data on pensions and for as many years as are available (i.e., 1960–1980). Once results are obtained for the full sample of nations, it is still possible to draw out the implications of the results for the position of the countries analyzed in the case studies. Still, we begin with an attempt at generality rather than specificity.

The first group of nations to be considered, the advanced industrial democracies, is limited to those with mature welfare states in which political democracy allows the political participation of age and class groups to potentially affect policy outcomes.[4] This group includes the United States, Canada, Japan, New Zealand, Australia and 13 Western European nations.[5] Besides the four nations studied in earlier chapters, the sample adds other nations which represent additional diversity on pension spending and societal characteristics. Despite similarity in democratic procedures, the nations differ greatly in political and state structures. They show substantial differences in years of leftist party government rule, size of the aged population, degree of corporatism, and pension spending.

Because of limitations in the availability of quantitative measures, the analysis covers only the years from 1959 to 1980. The 22-year time period misses much of the historical span covered in the qualitative study, and does not cover changes in the past decade. Still, it includes a period of important change—one characterized by economic growth followed by fiscal crisis, keen competition among groups for resources, and a strained capacity of government to fund higher benefits for a growing aged population. Some nations have responded quite generously to the growth of the aged population and higher demands for retirement benefits while other nations forced cutbacks in retirement benefits. Further, the previous evidence suggests age-based political action in at least some of the nations grew during this time period. Thus, the years to be studied cover periods of both growth and retrenchment of the welfare state.

Combining 18 nations, each with data for 22 years, creates a potential sample size of 396. This offers the opportunity for multivariate analysis of the total sample as well as of temporal and cross-national subgroups.

We rely here on the commonly used measure of pension expenditures from the International Labor Organization (1985, pp. 92–105). While not including all sources of pubic income for the elderly—medical care, housing, or energy assistance are unavailable or measured separately—it does include public retirement benefits for workers and citizens.[6]

The typical measure of pension effort divides pension expenditures by GNP. To control for automatic increases in spending due to increases in the number of pension recipients, we can also divide pension expenditures by percent aged population. This provides a more severe test of the political influence of percent aged by controlling for demographically induced spending increases. It also offers a straightforward interpretation of the meaning of the variable: it is equivalent to pension expenditures per aged person as a ratio to national product per capita, or to average pension benefit relative to the standard of living. We examine both this relative measure of pension benefits and the simpler, more general ratio to national product.

A variety of independent variables have been used by researchers in their studies of pension and welfare spending. We rely on a set of determinants that have been shown in the literature to relate to welfare or pension spending, and that are tied to the various theories we have been considering. The correspondence between theories and indicators is not exact, however. Some indicators relate to two or more theories; conversely, some theories share in the importance they attribute to certain variables. Our goal here is not to match precisely indicator coefficients with theories—our approach is more integrative. Still, the theories we have been discussing provide an initial means to organize and justify the quantitative variables we select. Given detailed literature on this topic, and the use of nearly all the variables in previous studies, we limit discussion to a short description of the variables (see Appendix for a list of data sources).

The focus of industrialism theory on the responsiveness of policy to economic and social changes leads to the use of GDP per capita (in U.S. constant dollars). National product represents changes in the capacity to fund expensive retirement programs as well as the changes in the economy and work force which necessitate retirement at older ages. The theory would also suggest policy responds to short-term economic changes in unemployment and the cost of living. Unemployment is measured as a percentage of the labor force and inflation as the consumer price index.[7] Percent aged is also important in the industrialism literature as it reflects changing size of the population needing pension support in advanced industrial economies (Wilensky 1975, p. 9).

The neo-pluralist theories also attribute importance to percent aged, though more as a political force or interest group than as an indicator of need. In addition, the theory focuses on nonpartisan measures of political participation which reflect the means by which citizen demands translate into policy (Pampel and Williamson 1989, pp. 65–67). One such measure is electoral participation (i.e., voters as a percentage of the population age 20 and over); another is party electoral competition (i.e., index of the equality of votes received among parties receiving votes).

Among these variables, we give particular attention to the size of the aged population. The importance of the aged population in the case studies reflects the organization of elderly interest groups and their role in public policy rather than mere numbers. Ideally, the crude quantitative indicator, percent aged, can capture some of these important influences on pension spending. Pension spending increases directly in proportion to the increased size of the population assuming benefit levels do not decline. More important, to the extent that the impact of the size of the aged population on pension spending varies across societal and political contexts, it reflects in part the organizational factors that are described in more detail in the case studies. In combination with a measure of corporatist context, the effects of percent aged may indirectly reflect the organization of interest groups. Such effects are consistent with the neo-pluralist arguments for consideration of the political impact of the size of the aged population.

The social democratic theories emphasize partisan political strength. For a program like pensions, which includes predominantly middle-class recipients, the distinction between leftist and other parties proves less useful than the distinction between rightist and other parties.[8] The partisan, class-based measure cumulates right party rule since 1945 on the basis of the classification by Castles (1982, p. 59). The theory focuses directly on the strength of classes as well as on their reflection in class-based parties. Labor strength is measured as union density or percent of the labor force belonging to labor unions. For capital strength, we rely on measures of operating surplus over GDP—a crude proxy for profits—and capital formation over GDP (Pampel, Williamson, and Stryker 1990, p. 542). Theories of monopoly capital, which represent the needs of capital as the driving force of welfare spending and attribute less importance to worker movements and political parties, would also focus on the strength of capital.

Given this sample of nations and time periods, another variable, political democracy, is not likely to be important. All nations by the postwar period record high levels of political democracy. As a constant rather than a variable, political democracy can do little to explain variation in pension spending. While differences in levels of political democracy did affect policy in these nations during the turn of the century period, this factor is not useful when attempting to account for differences in spending patterns between 1959 and 1980. It will, however, be very important in analysis of Third World nations.

Finally, our focus on corporatist state context requires a measure that taps national differences in the existence of institutionalized structures for class compromise. Numerous measures, all of which depend to one degree or another on the judgment of experts, are available from the literature. Wilensky (1976, p. 50), Schmitter (1981, p. 294), Schmidt (1982, p. 135), Lehmbruch (1984, p. 66), and Bruno and Sachs (1985, p. 226) all offer related classifications. The scores are based, to one degree or another, on the centralization of labor union federations and employer associations; the existence of national-level collective bargaining; the efforts to develop concerted policies responsive to national requirements; and the negotiation of social policy under government auspices. The measures focus on societal corporatism rather than on sectoral corporatism within particular industries. They also focus on the facilitative role of government in organizational negotiation rather than on authoritarian corporatism in which the state takes on a more directive role. This is not to say the measures are identical. For instance, Wilensky emphasizes central government power; Schmitter emphasizes the associational monopoly of peak labor and employer associations; and Schmidt emphasizes commitment to an ideology of social partnership between labor and capital. Still, the individual scales are designed to measure the same general concept and differ in emphasis more than purpose.

The similarities of the scales allow them to be usefully combined or averaged. A factor analysis on all five scales shows a principal components factor of one dimension. The factor loadings for each of the individual measures allow us to create a single, combined scale (Pampel, Williamson, and Stryker 1990, pp. 540–541). The scale has the advantages of (1) providing a summary of similar and related variables, (2) minimizing idiosyncratic results inherent in the use of individual variables that may include measurement error, and (3) simplifying tests of already complex interactive hypotheses.

The scores for the corporatism scale are presented for each of the nations in Table 9–1. The scores are highest for the small central European and Scandinavian nations which tend to be centralized, structurally integrated, and corporatist. The English-speaking nations occupy the opposite of the classification; they are decentralized and fragmented in state structure. Other Western European nations fall somewhere between the extremes. Figures on percent aged and two measures of pension spending show only a modest direct relationship with the scale (the correlations are, respectively, .42, .45, .35). However, the factor scale, when treated

Table 9–1. Nation Values of Corporatism, Percent Aged, and Pension Spending

Nation	Factor Score	% Aged 1960	% Aged 1980	Pen/GDP 1960	Pen/GDP 1980	Pen/Old 1960	Pen/Old 1980
Austria	1.56	12.0	15.1	4.6	8.8	38.4	58.3
Norway	1.55	11.1	14.3	2.4	7.5	21.7	52.2
Sweden	1.42	12.0	15.9	3.6	9.7	29.7	61.0
Netherlands	1.14	8.7	11.2	3.6	11.2	41.4	99.7
Denmark	.67	10.6	14.0	3.7	7.8	35.1	56.0
Finland	.50	7.3	11.5	2.2	6.2	30.5	54.1
Germany	.39	10.8	14.8	6.0	9.5	55.4	64.3
Belgium	.38	12.0	14.0	3.0	6.6	25.4	46.8
Switzerland	.11	10.2	13.3	2.1	7.5	20.4	56.6
Japan	−.12	5.7	8.6	0.2	2.2	4.1	25.0
Ireland	−.51	11.2	11.0	2.3	5.3	20.6	47.8
New Zealand	−.74	8.7	9.1	3.5	6.7	40.5	73.5
Australia	−.78	8.5	9.1	2.2	3.8	26.1	42.0
Italy	−.85	9.1	13.0	3.1	9.8	33.7	75.2
France	−.94	11.6	13.8	2.6	7.7	22.7	55.9
United Kingdom	−1.16	11.7	14.6	3.0	4.8	25.6	32.7
United States	−1.30	9.2	10.9	2.3	3.9	25.1	35.7
Canada	−1.31	7.5	8.9	1.9	2.9	25.3	32.4

Note: GDP = gross domestic product; Pen = pensions.

as a measure of an independent underlying dimension of class organized and mediated policymaking, may facilitate or inhibit the influence of other determinants of welfare spending.

Results for the Industrial Nations

If our arguments are correct, the models require more than simple additive effects of demand variables and corporatism. The interaction of the two would better characterize the process of determining pension spending. For comparison, however, we first present the more typical additive model. The independent variables include the demand variables relating to economic product, age structure, political participation, party competition, partisan rule, union density, and fiscal conditions. Also included is the measure of corporatism and significant country effects. The model pretty well reflects the results of previous studies (see Table 9–2, column 1 for the unstandardized coefficients, column 2 for the standardized coefficients).[9] Percent aged has the strongest effect while GDP, percent voting,[10] inflation, profits, and capital formation have smaller effects in the expected direction. A high percentage of the population over age 65 increases pressure for spending, as does high political participation. High inflation and economic product drive up spending while high profits and investment reduce spending. Right party rule has a strong effect, but in the opposite direction found by other studies. The positive effect of rightist rule may reflect the bourgeois character of pension programs in many nations.

Table 9–2. Unstandardized Coefficients for GLS Estimates of Additive and Interactive Models of Pension Spending: Advanced Industrial Democracies

| Variable | Pensions/GDP | | | | Pensions/Old | | | |
| | Additive | | Interactive | | Additive | | Interactive | |
	b	B[a]	b	bxz[b]	b	B[a]	b	bxz[b]
Intercept	−.094		−.118		−.834		−8.13	
GDP/Pop	.337†	.198	.220†	.058	2.26†	.183	1.94†	−.549
% Aged	.376†	.380	.194†	−.119*	1.24*	.172	−.035	−1.25†
Elec. Comp.	−.042*	−.117	−.020*	.001	−.167*	−.065	.042	.060
% Vote	.043†	.260	.044†	.028†	.436†	.363	.412†	.200*
Right Rule	.083†	.298	.109†	.055†	.680†	.336	.910†	.495*
% Union	.005	.030	.004	−.013	−.049	−.048	.006	−.075
Unemploy.	.023	.022	.036	.031	.274	.036	.362	.186
Inflation	.011†	.170	.016†	.008†	.073†	.156	.105†	.052†
Profits	−.051†	−.128	−.051†	−.032†	−.436†	−.150	−.436†	−.160*
Capital Form.	−.039†	−.069	−.033†	.007	−.209†	.051	−.252†	.087
Corporatism	.056*	.024	−.043		.194	.011	.107	
Country Effects								
Belgium	−.239†		−.205†		−3.12†		−2.86†	
Italy	.123		.381†		1.58		4.67†	
Japan	−.072		−.117†		−2.66†		−4.58†	
Netherlands	.398†		.473†		5.07†		5.21†	
New Zealand	−.141		.074		2.48		3.52†	
Switzerland	1.06†		.943†		10.9†		7.76†	
R²-OLS	.904		.928		.874		.905	
df	378		368		378		368	

*p < .05; †p < .01.

[a]Standardized coefficients; [b]Coefficients for multiplicative interaction terms.

Note: GLS = generalized least squares; GDP = gross domestic product; Pop = population; Elec. Comp. = electoral competition; % vote = percentage voting; Right Rule = right party rule; % Union = percentage of the labor force belonging to labor unions; Unemploy. = unemployment rate; Capital Form. = capital formation.

Neither corporatism nor union density have strong direct effects on pension spending, in part because they are closely related.[11] The results thus provide little support for the social democratic theory.

The additive model provides only a starting point for the analysis. Multiplicative interaction terms of the corporatist scale times each of the other variables in the model are added to the basic equation in Table 9–2. The differences in processes determining pension spending are analyzed by adding to the equation multiplicative interaction terms of corporatism by each of the other independent variables. The coefficients for the multiplicative terms will show how the effect of the demand variable changes for different levels of the state variables. Hence, the state variable can be seen as providing the contexts in which the demand variables operate differentially. The full model (in columns 3 and 4) thus includes 27 variables—10 additive terms, corporatism, 10 multiplicative terms, and 6 dummy variables. The interaction terms significantly increase the variance explained (F = 12.3).

The coefficients for the interaction terms represent the change in the effect of each variable for a one standard deviation increase in the interacting corporatism dimension. The additive terms represent the effect of the dynamic variables on pension spending when corporatism has a zero value (in other words, at the mean of the factor score). Therefore, the estimated effect of each variable for any single nation or any value on the corporatism dimension can simple be obtained by multiplying the interaction term by the appropriate corporatism z-score and adding that value to the additive effect. The interaction term coefficients parsimoniously summarize much information, can be used to calculate separate models for individual nations, and avoid the arbitrary groupings of nations that are sometimes created when continuous interaction terms are not used.[12]

Interpreting the meaning of the individual interaction coefficients does indeed show evidence in support of the interactive hypothesis for percent aged and some of the class variables. The results show quite clearly that the strong positive impact of percent aged weakens at higher levels of corporatism. At the midpoint of corporatism, a 1 percent increase in percent aged raises pension spending as a percent of GDP by .194. At 1.55 standard deviations above the mean, at the approximate value of Austria and Norway, the effect of percent aged falls to .009. For noncorporatist countries like the United States or Canada, the effect of percent aged nearly doubles, from .194 to .349. Thus, the institutional variation in the responsiveness of pensions to demographic structure appears substantial: the aged are more influential in noncorporatist societies where classes are not organized to participate in processes of policy formation.

The model for the relative pension measure, which is standardized for changes in the size of the recipient population, is presented in the last columns of Table 9–2. If the effect of percent aged on this variable varies across contexts, it would suggest that the political influence of the aged, above and beyond demographic change alone, is shaped by the class character of policymaking processes. In fact, the negative interaction term for percent aged is significant for this dependent variable. The additive effect is considerably smaller (the standardized coefficient is less than half the size of the coefficient for absolute pension spending) since the demographic relationship is removed. Still, the effect of percent aged becomes strong and positive for the noncorporatist nations, strong and negative for the corporatist, and zero for those in the middle. Because corporatist structures are not directly responsive to the political clout of the aged, whereas policymaking for pensions in noncorporatist contexts is likely to bypass class to organize and respond to the politics of age, the politically based influences of age structure emerge as important only for the noncorporatist nations. In highly corporatist nations, the low responsiveness to growth of the aged population may result in a negative effect of percent aged as the elderly population grows faster than the benefits per person.

Turning now to the results for class variables, we find mixed support for the hypothesis. First, in support of the predictions, the negative effect of profits on pensions increases in absolute value with corporatism. Although the long-run effects of economic growth are to increase spending, the short-run effects of economic fluctuations, as shown by the negative effect of profits, differ. In the short run, a downturn in profits is countered in part by fiscal stimulus, apparently in the form of increased public transfers. Capital most favors expanding spending when threatened economically, and needs it least during financial prosperity. The interactive results suggest that the expansion of pension spending in response to downturns in profits is stronger in corporatist nations. In other words, the ability of capital to realize its short-term interests with regard to profits appears strongest in corporatist nations.

Second, the positive effects of rightist parties is stronger in corporatist nations. The effects of right rule, suggesting support of bourgeois parties for a largely middle-class pension programs, are strongest where labor has a more important role in corporatist negotiation. The structures thus move rightist parties more left-ward in their policies. Otherwise, there is little evidence of either the additive or interactive effect of union density.

The model for all countries combined contains within it more specific models for the four countries considered in our individual case studies. Separate models for individual nations cannot be estimated since the number of variables approaches the number of cases available for any single country. Instead, when the corporatism score for a nation is substituted into the interactive equation, the equation is reduced to additive coefficients for that nation. Not all the differences across nations are significant, but those that are can be interpreted more concretely than the coefficients in Table 9–2.

Table 9–3 shows the unstandardized coefficients for our case study nations for both dependent variables. Sweden shows small effects of percent aged on pension spending over GDP. The negative effect on relative pensions shows that pension spending has not kept up with demographic aging for this corporatist nation. The other nations show stronger and positive effects of percent aged, reflecting the lower levels of corporatism. The United States, compared to Germany and the United Kingdom, shows the strongest effect of percent aged. Conversely, the effects of right rule, profits, inflation, and GDP are stronger in Sweden than the other nations. Class-conscious policy debate and responsiveness to fiscal change in corporatist nations show in these effects.

Table 9–3. Implied Models for Selected Countries

Independent Variables	Pensions/GDP				Pensions/Old			
	Swed.	Ger.	UK	US	Swed.	Ger	UK	US
GDP/Pop	.291	.186	.157	.142	2.61	2.26	2.53	2.67
% Aged	.023	.263	.323	.353	−1.56	.690	1.31	1.64
Elec.comp.	−.019	−.021	−.021	−.021	.115	.007	−.023	−.038
% Vote	.084	.028	.014	.043	.656	.296	.196	.144
Right Rule	.188	.077	.050	.035	1.51	.623	.375	.247
% Union	−.015	.012	.018	.021	−.086	.050	.087	.107
Unemploy.	.081	.018	.003	−.006	.589	.254	.161	.113
Inflation	.028	.011	.007	.005	.168	.075	.049	.035
Profits	−.097	−.032	−.016	−.008	−.631	−.343	−.263	−.222
Capital Form.	−.023	−.037	−.041	−.043	−.146	−.302	−.346	−.369

Note: Unstandardized coefficients calculated from Table 9–2.

Abbreviations as in Table 9–2.

In summary, the results provide additional support and clarification for some of the arguments made in earlier chapters. They are consistent with the view that there are multiple paths to higher pension spending. In some nations, the upward trend is demographically driven, and in some nations it is class driven. English-speaking nations with a long history of democracy, fragmented classes, and more influential special interests are highly responsive to demographic change and age-based political forces. Other nations, particularly Sweden, with strong social demo-cratic rule, seem only slightly responsive to demographic change and more attuned to class power. Germany falls between the extremes and reflects a combination of forces. Although it is likely that we have not identified the exact configuration of national differences most relevant for policy concerns, there is substantial evidence that policymaking processes for pensions do indeed differ.

These results put a particular slant on the typology presented in Chapter 1 that distinguished liberal, radical, conservative, and social democratic nations. While we do not use the exact scheme of Esping-Andersen (1990, p. 52) and Castles and Mitchell (1990, p. 21), their typologies overlap with corporatism. The nations high on the corporatism scale are those described by Esping-Andersen as social demo-cratic, those low on the scale as liberal, and those in the middle of the scale as conservative. Similarly, our scale reflects Castles and Mitchell's distinction between radical (New Zealand, Australia, the United Kingdom) and liberal (United States and Canada) nations. The fact that the coefficients differ for the four nations, and each of the four nations represents a different type of context, indicates some con-vergence in approaches to understanding pension spending.

Regardless of whether corporatism or some other similar typology is used, our approach narrows controversies among divergent theories of pension development. Rather than competing, the class and demographic-based theories may be comple-mentary once the scope of each is specified. Class, demographic, and state theo-ries are all correct, but must be delimited in application to particular contexts or nations. Thus, what have been previously, but not completely correctly, been viewed as competing theories can be integrated.

Results for the Third World Nations

Unlike the study of advanced industrial democracies, where a variety of measures are available for all the nations, the study of Third World nations is made difficult by lack of data. Figures on pension spending are not routinely available for mul-tiple time points. Some countries have no programs, many others do not collect or report spending levels, and still others have such primitive programs that standard accounting categories for reporting them do not apply. Rather than attempting to maximize the sample by accepting dubious figures or invalid pension spending measures, our strategy is to rely on relatively small subset of nations with com-plete, more reliable and valid measures.

In choosing the nations for analysis, we again rely on figures presented by the ILO. Excluding the 18 advanced democracies and the socialist nations of Eastern

Europe (where in 1980 welfare spending meant little in isolation from broader government control of the economy and income distribution), this leaves 32 nations with acceptable measures of pension spending and most of the independent variables. The nations are not representative of all nations in the world, but they do cover all regions, levels of development, and degrees of political democracy. By region, the distribution of nations is as follows: sub-Saharan Africa (12), Middle-East (4), Asia (5), and Latin America (11). Of the three nations we studied earlier, data are available for India and Brazil, but not Nigeria.

The time span for which pension spending and other economic variables are available is from 1960 to 1980. However, yearly series are rarely gathered. Instead, figures are generally presented at five-year intervals, requiring that we limit the analysis to 1960, 1965, 1970, 1975, and 1980. With five time points and 32 nations, there are 162 cases—enough for multivariate analysis.[13]

Because the quality and availability of data in developing nations are limited, we must focus on a relatively small set of easily measured economic, demographic, and political variables. Other political and social characteristics, such as party domination, political participation, corporatism, or union strength are seldom measured accurately and, indeed, may have little meaning in low income nondemocracies. The measures of demographic and economic change on which we concentrate are percent aged and GDP per capita.[14] Another variable, years of social insurance program experience (SIPE) summed over five programs—work injury, old age, sickness, family allowance, and unemployment—is also useful for this sample (Wilensky 1975, p. 24). Since many of these Third World nations have adopted new programs during the time span of study, SIPE does not merely increase by a constant over time, as in the advanced industrial nations, but also shows variability across nations and over time.[15]

The best available measure of democracy comes from Bollen (1980, pp. 387–388), who has created a six component scale reflecting political competitiveness and political liberties. The scale, which varies between 0 and 100, has been shown to be unidimensional, valid, and reliable. However, the measure is available for only the two earliest time points—1960 and 1965. The effects of democracy at the beginning of the time period are likely to influence expenditures in the future even if democratic procedures change in later time points. Still, given possible changes in levels after 1965, it is useful to divide nations into two broad categories. A dividing point of 67.7 on Bollen's scale was used to distinguish low democracy nations from high democracy nations.[16]

First, we examine the trends and levels of expenditures and their determinants over the time span 1960–1980. Since it is possible that democratic context specifies the models—that is, the relationships differ for democracies and nondemocracies—it is worthwhile to examine the trends separately for these two groups. Table 9–4 presents the means for expenditures and the determinants for 1960 to 1980 for each group (values for the 18 industrial nations are presented for comparison).[17]

Expenditure levels for the pension programs comprise a not unexpectedly small part of GDP. In 1960, less than .2 percent of GDP was spent for old-age security programs. From 1960 to 1980, however, the democracies and nondemocracies

Table 9–4. Means on Pension Spending and Determinants by Year and Political and Economic Characteristics

Variable	Low-Income Nondemocracies		Low-Income Democracies		High-Income Democracies	
	1960	1980	1960	1980	1960	1980
Pensions/GDP	.018	.297	.155	.932	2.9	6.7
Pensions/Old	.005	.099	.037	.210	29.0	53.8
GDP/Pop.	583	825	1221	2146	3017	7320
% Aged	2.78	2.90	3.68	4.43	9.9	12.4
SIPE	28.8	93.2	52.8	121.3	114.2	211.0
Democracy	48.4	48.4	82.3	82.3	97.6	97.6
N	19	19	13	13	18	18

Note: SIPE = social insurance program experience; other abbreviations as in Table 9–2.

diverge. For nondemocracies, only small increases occur; for democracies, expenditures as a percent of GDP grew markedly. The gap between the two groups of nations has widened substantially.

Perhaps the divergence stems from higher economic growth and greater demographic change among the democracies rather than from the democratic political environment itself. The trend in real GDP per capita, however, shows growth in both groups of nations. Percent aged better tracks expenditures, since the nondemocracies show little increase, whereas the democracies show a more important change. Yet, the gap in spending between the democracies and nondemocracies grows more than the gap in percent aged.

Table 9–5 presents the main effects of the variables for the developing nations. Initially, the variables include real GDP (logged), percent aged, and SIPE. Democracy alone has no additive effects in the equations and is not included until the interaction terms are included. As in the last section, we present GLS estimates that correct for serial correlation over time and heteroscedasticity across nations.[18]

The results show the dominance of percent aged and SIPE. The effect of percent aged is, as we would expect, stronger for pensions over GDP than for relative pensions. These additive effects may misspecify the process of spending by averaging quite different processes in democratic and nondemocratic nations. Columns 2 and 4 test for the interactive effects of democracy by including the appropriate interaction terms. The variance explained rises substantially with the interaction terms, especially for pensions over GDP (the F-tests for increment in explained variance are 10.6 and 6.4, both significant at the .01 level).[19] Further, the results make theoretical sense: the variables show stronger effects in democracies. For SIPE, the effects increase threefold in democracies. Similarly, the effects of real GDP are larger in democracies than in nondemocracies. Democracy alone does not raise pension spending, but in conjunction with other variables it facilitates the growth of the welfare state.[20] To summarize, the evidence supports the arguments for the facilitative effects of democracy. The demographic and bureaucratic variables directly affect pension spending. However, we also find meaningful dif-

Table 9–5. Unstandardized Coefficients for GLS Estimates of Additive and Democracy Interactive Models of Pension Spending: Third World Nations

Independent Variables	Pensions/GDP		Pensions/Old	
	Additive	Interactive	Additive	Interactive
Intercept	−.909	−.344	−.124	−.098
ln GDP/Pop	.049	.036	.007	.013
	.067	.049	.040	.073
% Aged	.156†	.025	.007†	−.001
	.397	.064	.074	−.011
SIPE	.004†	.002†	.002†	.001†
	.279	.140	.464	.290
Democracy = 1		−.952*		.028
		−.929		.114
Dem x ln GDP/Pop		.018		−.022
		.128		−.652
Dem x % Aged		.136†		.012
		.613		.225
Dem x SIPE		.006†		.001†
		.570		.395
R^2(OLS)	.573	.666	.410	.495
df	156	152	156	152
n,t	32,5	32,5	32,5	32,5

*p <.05; †p <.01.

Note: Standardized coefficients are below unstandardized coefficients.

Dem = democracy; other abbreviations as in Table 9–2 and Table 9–4.

ferences in effects across levels of democracies that are consistent with predictions of the theory.

Comparisons with the Case Studies

Like the qualitative results, the quantitative results are consistent with the view that there are multiple paths to higher pension spending. In the discussion to follow, we note some similarities between the case studies and quantitative results. As we have noted, the different assumptions and goals of qualitative and quantitative analysis makes a tight fit between the two types of results difficult if not impossible. The concepts important for the case studies cannot always be measured quantitatively or generalized to a large number of nations. Discussion of convergence and divergence in the two approaches highlights the benefits of both approaches.

First, the role of the state is most facilitative of pension spending in Sweden. The high degree of corporatism, rather than being directive or autonomous in generating expansion of pension spending, is more important in facilitating class compromise. Under corporatist arrangements, the state officially designates monopolistic representatives of labor and capital and cooperates with the class groups in negotiating social policy. In this role the state contributes to the importance of classes in pension policy. According to the quantitative results, Sweden shows not only a high level of spending, but also the strongest effects of class variables. Corporatism or state action may not directly cause the increase in pension spending, but it indirectly promotes the influence of class groups. It is in highly corporatist nations like Sweden that class organization can translate most effectively into pension spending.

Second, Germany presents another variant on the role of the state. The institutional structures for class compromise are different in Germany than in Sweden. Indeed, the influence of labor is both facilitated and tempered by a variety of bureaucratic structures and labor legislation that assume labor's involvement, but circumscribe its autonomy. As a result, the quantitative results show effects of class that are smaller than in Sweden. The lesson is that the German state, while strong, is also less corporatist and less responsive to class demands than highly corporatist Sweden.

Third, the United States represents a state that is neither facilitative nor directive. It has seldom if ever sponsored corporatist bargaining and did not initiate legislation until after nearly all other advanced industrial nations had. Further, the lack of centralized class organizations to participate directly in bargaining over national policy results in the influence of a variety of specialized interest groups. Although diverse and fragmented class interests initially prevented the passage of legislation, age-based interests successfully expanded benefits (primarily for middle-class contributors and recipients) during the postwar period. The quantitative results show much the same. The effect of age structure is strong and the effects of class structure are weak for a nation such as the United States without any form of corporatist organization.

Fourth, Britain shows a mixture of characteristics of the other nations. The episodic rather than continuous or institutionalized nature of corporatism, however, ultimately limited the impact of labor on pension spending in Britain. The general lack of the facilitative or directive state, and the low or episodic existence of corporatism, makes Britain similar to the United States in it outcomes and its processes. The quantitative models capture the similarities, but not all the differences between the two countries. Britain differs from the United States in the relatively more equitable distribution of benefits. The heritage of social radicalism not present in the United States and the brief periods of collaboration between labor and capital after World War II and during the 1960s may account for the differences.

Turning to the three Third World nations shifts the discussion from the role of the state in the organization of democratic interests to the existence of the democratic procedures themselves. Less democratic nations by definition have a directive state that is more responsive to its own interests than to the interests of the mass citizenry. Democratic nations are more likely to have a facilitative state in which political participation of the citizenry translates into higher pension spending.

Nigeria represents the former case. The implementation of the Nigerian Provident Fund, while in part the legacy of colonial rule, stemmed from an attempt of leaders of a newly independent nation to legitimate central government control. Once the provident fund was implemented, the existence of a self-interested bureaucracy, combined with the lack of democratic procedures, has limited the ability to fund a more comprehensive social insurance program. The contradiction apparent in other nations with a history of directive states (e.g., Germany) is present to a lesser degree in the experience of an authoritarian state like Nigeria: state interests led to program initiation before demand was high in order to increase its own power, but paradoxically led later to resistance of self-interested state employees to demands for further change. The quantitative results for nondemocracies capture the resistance to higher pension spending if not the early state-building pressures for program initiation.

Brazil illustrates some of the same patterns as Nigeria because of the long experience with military rule. Yet, Brazil has also had longer periods of democratic rule as well as a more industrialized economy and larger working class. The authoritarian state implemented pension programs as a form of social control early on, but resisted labor demands for implementation of more comprehensive programs in later periods. The state has been more directive than facilitative. Although demands from labor groups for more benefits grew particularly strong during the brief periods of democratic leadership, they had limited influence given the lack of a democratic tradition. The quantitative results likewise predict limited effects of group demand variables on pension spending in Brazil because of the country's low score on the measure of democracy.

Of the Third World nations, India shows the longest and most continuous experience with political democracy. The quantitative results predict a greater impact of societal forces on spending in India than in less democratic nations (at the same level of development, demographic aging, and social insurance program experience). The direct impact of democracy by itself is, however, limited. Because of longer experience with pension programs, a higher level of development, and a larger aged population, Brazil has a more generous program than India. The case studies show the circumstances in India are considerably more complex than implied by the quantitative models. Old-age policy has not emerged yet as an issue over which parties compete in the electoral process. In the early stages of system development of India, democracy perhaps presented an obstacle to pension development. In fact, competing groups in a democratic environment may have limited the opportunity to expand from a predominantly provident fund system to a social insurance system. Here, the qualitative and quantitative evidence do not correspond closely. Other factors likely need to be included in the future quantitative models to capture more of the complexity apparent in the case studies.

We hope to avoid pushing the consistency between the two results so far as to distort the actual findings. Our point is to indicate some of the similarities of the two types of results rather than to insist that they are identical. That some convergence in the findings exists, even if not complete, increases our confidence of the findings and suggests that the ideas presented in the book be given further consideration in future analysis of both qualitative and quantitative data.

Conclusion

This chapter extends and formalizes some of the insights of the case studies by developing testable propositions about the determinants of pension spending and testing them with quantitative data. The quantitative results help extend potentially idiosyncratic case study findings to a larger number of nations. By checking conclusions with different methods, their robustness or reliability is increased. As the case studies provide a nuanced and multidimensional explanation of pension development in the individual nations, the quantitative study intended to complement the case studies must, to some degree, also reflect the complexities of the processes. Like the case studies, the quantitative study must recognize the diversity of findings across the multiple nations. It must also consider how national context shapes the importance of various determinants and the validity of various theories.

Our attempt to incorporate theoretical diversity and contextual influences on pension spending into a quantitative study proceeds by examining the interactive or joint influence of state and societal forces on pension spending across the advanced industrial democracies and Third World nations. The state and its structure is seen as an important determinant of pension expansion in combination with the forces of societal demand, not in isolation from them. State interests and the optimal policy for pursuing those interests is taken to vary with the demands and resources of class and status groups that comprise the state's environment. In this way, state characteristics or national contexts can be seen as specifying which of the societal forces are most important in particular nations. The models can therefore capture some of the cross-national variation in the determinants of pension spending and the differential validity of the theories.

The state contextual characteristics relevant to pension spending have shifted over the last century for the nations studied. The study of more recent periods with quantitative data, however, allows us to concentrate on a subset. For the advanced industrial democracies, we consider how societal corporatism—arrangements for policy negotiation and compromise under government auspicious among centralized and monopolistic labor federations and employer associations—affects the influence of demand variables. Our guiding hypothesis is that the influence of class groups increases with corporatism while the influence of the aged population decreases with corporatism. For Third World nations, we consider how the existence of procedures for political democracy shape the impact of economic and demographic changes. Our guiding hypothesis is that economic and demographic characteristics are more influential in democracies than in nondemocracies. Conversely, autonomous state forces, independent of socioeconomic change, are more influential in nondemocracies. Both hypotheses thus suggest that structural, economic, and demographic change is necessary but not sufficient for welfare spending; variation in existence of structures for the expression of the interests—such as corporatism or political democracy—stemming from these changes is crucial as well.

To test the hypothesis for the advanced industrial democracies, we examine data on pension spending over GDP and pension spending per aged person for 18 nations over the years from 1959 to 1980. Measures of independent variables include GDP per capita, percent of the population age 65 and over, voter turnout, political party electoral competition, years of rule by rightist parties, union membership as a percent of the labor force, business profits, capital investment, unemployment, and inflation. The variables reflect forces of industrial economic and social change, macroeconomic indicators relevant to policy, nonpartisan political structures and interests, demographic structures, class-based political influences, and class size and strength. The variables roughly match arguments of the industrialism, neo-pluralist, social democratic, and neo-Marxist theories.

The variables are first used to predict both measures of pension spending in models that assume constant relationships across all nations. Nearly all variables have effects in the expected direction, thus indicating some support for all the theories. More important, the statistical model is then extended to allow the effects of the variables to vary by national differences in the level of corporatism. The results show clear evidence that the effects of the variables differ across varied corporatist contexts. Using the model coefficient to compute predicted models for the four countries studied in this book—Sweden, Germany, the United Kingdom, and the United States—illustrates the point. The size of the aged population has little influence and the class based characteristics such as profit levels have more influence in Sweden, the most corporatist nation among the four. In the least corporatist nation, the United States, changes in the size of the aged population are very influential; class effects are less important.

For the Third World, data on 32 nations every five years from 1960 to 1980 are used for the analysis. Although the pension spending dependent variables are the same, the independent variables are limited by data availability. Variables relating to class structure and political organization have little relevance for many of the nations with a small industrial economy or limited political democracy. Hence, we concentrate on those measures available for a diverse set of developing nations. Specifically, the measures include economic development, percent aged, and social insurance program experience. Each variable is then allowed to vary with democracy by estimating separate models for nations classified as democracies and for those classified as nondemocracies. The results support the predictions. That the effects of percent aged and social insurance program experience are increased by democracy suggests the existence of legitimate political procedures for expression of interest increases the ability of groups and changes in society to impact pension spending. In this way, the context of government rule—in this case the existence of democratic political procedures—shapes the process of pension determination.

Based on these findings, competing theories may be seen as complementing one another. Interests potentially may be mobilized in a number of ways, but the actual emergence of influential interest groups depends on historical forces that lead to corporatist bargaining in advanced industrial democracies or to democratic procedures in Third World nations. The institutional context thus conditions the impact of variations in class formation, age structure, and age and class resources on pension spending. Both class and demographic theories may be correct, but must be delimited in their application to particular contexts or nations. While still preliminary, we hope this effort can lead to further integration of what have previously—but not completely correctly—been viewed as competing theories.

Despite our efforts, it is impossible to identify a single state characteristic or societal context that shapes the process of pension determination. We have over-simplified by focusing on one characteristic of developed countries—corporatism—

and one for Third World nations—political democracy. Nonetheless, this is an advance on nearly all previous quantitative research which assumes the effects of societal demand to be the same in all societies. Clearly, our qualitative and quantitative analyses belie this notion. Our efforts in this regard are an important, if incomplete, step in this direction.

Appendix: Sources of Data

Variable	Source
Pension expenditures	*The Cost of Social Security*. 1985 and various years. Geneva: International Labour Office. Table 8.
Gross domestic product (GDP), consumer prices, exchange rates	*World Bank World Tables*, Volume I. 1983. Baltimore: Johns Hopkins. Economic Data Sheet I.
Percent aged, population	*United Nations Demographic Yearbook*, various years.
Percent voting, electoral competition	*The International Almanac of Electoral History*. Thomas T. Mackie and Richard Rose (eds.). 1982. New York: Facts on File.
Leftist rule, rightist rule	*Political Parties of Europe*, Volumes 1 and 2. Vincent E. McHale (ed.). 1983. Westport, Conn.: Greenwood Press. *Political Handbook of the World*. Arthur S. Banks and William Overstreet (eds.). 1984. New York: McGraw-Hill.
Unemployment	*OECD Main Economic Indicators*, various years. Paris: Organization for Economic Cooperation and Development.
Union membership	National Yearbooks.
Profits, capital formation	*OECD National Accounts*. 1984. Paris: Organization for Economic Cooperation and Development.
Social insurance program experience (SIPE)	*Social Security Programs Throughout the World*. 1981. Washington, D.C.: Social Security Administration.
Democracy	Bollen (1980).

10

Toward an Empirical and Theoretical Synthesis

While the seven historical case studies presented in the preceding chapters each involved some comparative analysis, the focus was on accounting for developments in a specific country, and relatively little effort was made to generalize about old-age security policy. In the previous chapter an effort was made to test several hypotheses derived in part from these historical case studies, but due to the constraints of available data, that analysis was limited to a few key issues. In this chapter our goal is to synthesize the findings of both the qualitative case studies and the quantitative analysis. While the emphasis will be on generalizations derived from the case studies, where appropriate these generalizations will be based on or qualified in light of our quantitative analysis.

In Chapter 1 we outlined five general theoretical perspectives that were extensively used both to interpret policy developments in the case studies and to interpret cross-national variation in pension spending patterns in our quantitative analysis. While we have not limited ourselves to explanations associated with these perspectives, many of our arguments can be linked to one or another of them. In view of the centrality of these perspectives to our analysis, they are used as the basis for the organization of the discussion of this chapter. Here we take a systematic look at the contexts in which each of these general theoretical perspectives has proven most useful in accounting for old-age security policy developments. We argue that all of these perspectives are useful in accounting for some developments, but the utility of each varies greatly depending on the historical and national context.

The Social Democratic Thesis

The current orthodoxy among sociologists on the issue of old-age security and the welfare state more generally is that policy in these spheres is the outcome of class conflict. The most widely held view is embodied in the social democratic thesis that social security policy as it has evolved in the industrial nations, particularly since the end of World War II, reflects the outcome of this struggle between labor and capital (Hewitt 1977; Cameron 1978; Stephens 1979; Castles and McKinlay 1979; Williamson and Weiss 1979; Shalev 1983; Korpi 1983; Myles 1984; Hicks and Swank 1984; DeViney 1984; Friedland and Sanders 1986). According to the social democratic thesis, the introduction of new programs, increases in spending on existing programs, and progressive structural improvements in pension programs all reflect the success of labor in its struggle with capital. Labor is assumed to favor an increase in commitment to such changes and capital is assumed to favor a reduction in such commitments or keeping any increase in commitment to a minimum. Social democratic theorists generally attribute differences in pension quality and in spending levels to differences between nations with respect to the strength of socialist parties and trade unions. What we have described is the most common variant of the social democratic thesis which we will refer to as the "simple" version of the thesis to differentiate it from another contextualized variant that combines elements of class theory and corporatist theory.

The historical evidence presented in connection with three of our industrial nation case studies (Germany, the United Kingdom, and the United States) fails to support the argument that organized labor and leftist political parties have been the dominant actors in the evolution of public pension policy. In these countries organized labor and leftist parties had little impact on the shape of the original legislation and had at most a modest impact on the dramatic developments that have taken place during the postwar period. In the three Third World nations we consider there is little evidence that organized labor played a role in the formulation of the original old-age social security schemes, and again labor seems to have had a relatively little impact on policy developments since the end of World War II.

Furthermore, the evidence presented in these case studies and the quantitative analysis can be interpreted as a challenge to the simple version of the social democratic thesis. This evidence serves to refute the social democratic argument that the development of pension policy, particularly in the industrial nations,[1] was in large measure a response to pressure from organized labor and leftist political parties. Clearly, factors other than these were important both with respect to the decision to introduce these programs and with respect to the subsequent evolution of these programs.[2]

A common social democratic response to this line of analysis is that these countries fail to meet the conditions specified in the social democratic thesis. They are not countries in which a large fraction of the workers are organized in a highly centralized national union central, neither are they countries in which social democratic parties have controlled the government for long periods of time during the postwar period. This argument tends to be particularly persuasive with respect to the United States. According to this argument a major reason the United States spends such a small share of its GDP on public pensions is that the labor movement has been weak and social democratic control of the government entirely absent.

But this argument misses the point. Despite the ranking of the United States relative to Sweden and Germany, it does have a highly developed pension system. The program has undergone a great deal of evolution during the postwar period that has little to do with the factors emphasized in social democratic arguments. The test of the influence of these factors within nations does not support the cross-national presuppositions of the social democratic thesis.

Among our case studies there is, however, one important exception to the preceding generalization—Sweden. Since the 1930s organized labor in Sweden has had a strong influence on the Social Democratic Party which in turn has had a strong influence on the expansion of pension benefits as well as social welfare benefits more generally (Olsson 1990).[3] Even in the case of Sweden, however, we must be careful not to overstate the role that unions and the Social Democratic Party have played.

The original proponents of old-age pensions in Sweden were liberal social reformers such as Adolf Hedin. One reason that pensions did not come to Sweden sooner was the opposition from various interest groups, particularly the farmer's block (Tomasson 1984, p. 231). While the Social Democrats eventually agreed to support the pension scheme enacted in 1913, they were quite critical of the proposal and considered it a major compromise rather than an unqualified victory; therefore, the introduction of old-age pensions was not a victory for organized labor or the Social Democratic Party (Baldwin 1989, pp. 20–21).

In Sweden during the post-World War II period, the more conservative political parties have at times attempted to outdo the Social Democrats with respect to proposals for pension policy reform. Parties of both the right and the left have favored pension reform and have attempted to use advocacy of pension benefit increases for electoral advantage (Olsson 1990, pp. 104–105; Baldwin 1990b, pp. 137–138). Thus the role of pension policy as an issue in political competition was almost as important a factor as the actual Social Democratic control of the Swedish government.

While the Swedish government has been controlled by the Social Democratic Party for most of the period from 1932 to the present, there have been a number of other factors that have contributed to the increase in spending on pensions. Of particular note in this context has been the nation's high standard of living. Reflecting the importance of economic factors, the first effort to contain the postwar expansion of spending on public pensions took place in 1981 in response to the stagflation Sweden experienced along with most other industrial nations (Coughlin and Tomasson 1991, p. 155).

In Germany organized labor and the socialists were in favor of pensions long before the original scheme was enacted in 1889. But it was not state pensions that they wanted to see introduced. They wanted pensions that would be administered by the unions rather than employers or the state (Zöllner 1982, p. 12). Organized labor was concerned that state-run pensions would increase the state's control over workers and in the process undercut the influence of organized labor.

During the post-World War II era there was a marked increase in Germany's commitment to old-age pensions. Today Germany spends a larger share of its GDP on public pensions than Sweden, but the evidence does not suggest that this is due to a stronger union movement or to more prolonged Social Democratic control of the government. While labor has had influence, due in part to its inclusion on corporatist boards responsible for the formulation of pension policy reform legislation, much more important in the German case has been the increase in support for more generous programs from the middle class. The middle class came to view pension reform and liberalization as in its own best interest (Baldwin 1990a, pp. 11–12). Other groups including more conservative political parties such as the

Christian Democrats were also advocating policies aimed at liberalization of old-age pension benefits. In addition, the nation was undergoing dramatic economic growth and an equally dramatic graying of its age structure (Esping-Andersen, Rainwater, and Rein 1988, p. 342; OECD 1988a, p. 33).

In Britain several of the leaders of the early pension movement were drawn from the ranks of organized labor, but the public pensions issue was not a major item on labor's agenda (Parrott 1985, pp. 91–92). While organized labor in the end did support the Old Age Pensions Act of 1908, the support was late in coming. Members of the newly organized Labour Party supported pension legislation, but at the time they did not have much political influence. To answer questions about why pension legislation was not enacted sooner in Britain, we must consider the influence of such pressure groups as the friendly societies, the Charity Organization Society, and the insurance industry (Ogus 1982, p. 177).

During the post-World War II period Britain experienced a great deal of pension policy development and liberalization. During this period there was a sharp increase in spending on old-age pensions, and the Labour Party was a strong supporter of this trend. While organized labor and the Labour Party deserve some credit for postwar developments, this credit must be shared. One of the major reforms during this period was the introduction of an earnings-related pension in 1959. While the original proposal for an earnings-related pension was formulated by the Labour Party, the idea was quickly picked up by the Conservative Party and the eventual legislation enacted was the Conservative's proposal, not Labour's proposal (Hannah 1986, p. 58).

In the United States it was not until the 1920s that support for public pensions began to grow. During the 1920s the United Mine Workers supported the idea, but the American Federation of Labor opposed it (Achenbaum 1986, p. 13). It was not until the Great Depression of the 1930s that organized labor became solidly unified in its support of introducing a national public pension scheme (Rimlinger 1971, p. 209).

While the Roosevelt administration was under considerable pressure to introduce a national old-age pension system, organized labor was only one of many groups calling for such a program. He was also under pressure from various old-age groups such as the Townsend movement (Achenbaum 1983, p. 36), from big business with their bankrupt company pension plans (Skocpol and Ikenberry 1983, p. 120),[4] and from those concerned with increasing signs of social disorder and anarchy around the country (L. Olson 1982, pp. 44–45), and from many other groups disturbed about the consequences of very high rates of unemployment and the extreme poverty among the elderly.

The Social Security Act of 1935 represented an attempt to deal with all of these issues. It was prepared with more input from big business than from organized labor, and it can as appropriately be described as a program designed to pacify and control labor as it can be described as a victory for labor in its competition with big business for control over government resources (Piven and Cloward 1971, pp. 35–36). It is important not to confuse what this program has become with the far more modest program enacted in 1935.

The United States experienced a marked expansion in coverage and pension benefit levels during the post-World War II era (Schulz 1988, p. 123). By this time organized labor was strongly behind expansion. It would not be appropriate, however, to attribute all or even most of the gains during this period to the efforts of organized labor as there were a number of other sources of pressure to expand coverage and benefit levels. Both Republicans and Democrats found it politically expedient to support increases in Social Security spending and did so regularly. While the Democrats could be counted on to support more generous increases, both major parties supported increases during this period.

The original public pension legislation in Brazil in 1923 was formulated by the government in large part as a measure to control labor; it was not a proposal that organized labor helped formulate and it cannot be viewed as a victory for labor (Malloy 1976, p. 43). Similarly, increases in spending levels and in coverage during the postwar years were not due in any large measure to pressure from organized labor

There is no evidence that organized labor played a major role with respect to the introduction of India's national provident fund plan in 1951, but organized labor does seem to have had some influence with respect to reforms that have taken place since then. Of particular note in this context was the Employees' Family Pension scheme introduced in 1971 and the 1972 Gratuity Act (Sarma 1981, p. 225). Both of these programs were strongly backed by organized labor.

Nigeria introduced its provident fund scheme in 1961 at a time when it was enjoying a period of relative democratization. However, neither organized labor nor leftist political parties were at the time pressing the government on the old-age social security policy issue. While union leaders along with a variety of other interested parties were consulted by those formulating the original provident fund plan (International Social Security Association 1961), there is no evidence that organized labor had a significant impact on the shape of the final legislation. Over the years the program has been expanded to cover a somewhat larger proportion of the labor force, but again there is no evidence that this expansion is in response to demands from organized labor (Ijeh 1983, p. 21).

The Neo-Marxist Perspective

A second major class theory of pension policy development shares with the social democratic perspective the view that policy outcomes represent the outcome of conflict between capital and labor. But the neo-Marxist perspective does not assume that new programs, improvements in existing programs, or spending increases necessarily represent victories for labor. This second class theory emphasizes the extent to which pension programs have been used to reduce the pressure for changes that would bring about a substantial shift in the distribution of income. It also emphasizes the extent to which old-age security policy is driven by the imperatives of the market and of the world economy. Whereas scholars in the social democratic tradition tend to view public pension programs as contributing to a more egalitarian society, those in the monopoly capitalism tradition tend to question this assumption. Some argue that such programs are generally not redistributive between classes, others argue that any short-term reduction in inequality that may result is typically offset by a long-term tendency to undercut the pressure for greater equality.

In the neo-Marxist tradition considerable attention is given to the ways in which pensions and other social welfare programs have been introduced or expanded with an eye toward the social control of labor; however, welfare benefits may be used for labor control according to other perspectives as well. The state, for instance, often has interests in labor quiescence. What is crucial about the neo-Marxist perspective is the assumption that the state is tightly controlled by an economic elite. Since evidence on state motives is often more difficult to obtain than evidence of labor control, we must interpret the labor control thesis of the neo-Marxist perspective carefully.

One reason Bismarck introduced a public pension system was to give a large number of workers in key sectors of the economy a vested interest in the political and economic status quo. They would be less inclined to support the call by radical socialists for an overthrow of the existing order if it might mean the loss of credits that had been earned toward an old-age pension (Schulz et al. 1974, p. 109). While labor control was clearly one of Bismarck's goals, given the strength and autonomy of the German state in the late nineteenth century, this evidence is more consistent with the state-centered perspective than the neo-Marxist perspective.[5]

While the threat of socialist agitation was less of a problem in Sweden at the turn of the century than it was in Germany, the Swedish elite was well aware of developments in Germany and other major industrial nations. One reason for their support of the pension idea was to help pacify the Swedish working class (Heclo 1974, pp. 179–180). While the Swedish state may not have been as autonomous as the German state at the turn of the century, labor control was also less of a reason for this legislation in the Swedish case.

Based on the neo-Marxist perspective we would expect the original Swedish pension program to have had little real impact on the distribution of income, and this is just what we find. The original Swedish old-age pension scheme was entirely paid for by a tax on employees. There was no contribution from employers and none from the nation's progressive income tax. However, during the postwar era we find quite the reverse. The pension system was much more redistributive; virtually the entire cost was born by the employer and the state.

At first British industrialists opposed the idea of introducing a system of public pensions; however, by the time the legislation was passed support had increased substantially. A significant proportion had become concerned about the efficiency of British workers relative to workers in other nations competing with Britain in world markets (Ogus 1982, p. 160). A number of studies pointing to the squalid living conditions faced by many British workers raised fears that poor health and other social ills associated with extreme poverty were adversely affecting Britain's ability to compete successfully. Industrialists who agreed with this line of reasoning had reason to support the introduction of public pensions and other forms of social insurance.[6] It is also consistent with the neo-Marxist perspective that in Britain, as in Germany and Sweden, the benefit level for public pensions was set very low in an effort to minimize any work disincentive.

In the United States the Social Security Act of 1935 was passed in the middle of the Great Depression, at a time when many were questioning the legitimacy of the existing economic institutions and arrangements. Labor unrest and protest were increasing (L. Olson 1982, p. 44). The pension system eventually enacted turned out to be far less redistributive than those being called for by the most radical labor and aging movement leaders, but it was enough to gain a great deal of public support and to undercut the level of support for those the Roosevelt administration considered dangerous radicals.

Also consistent with the neo-Marxist perspective is the evidence that a major goal of the pension component of the Social Security Act was to provide an incentive for older workers to move out of the labor force (Williamson ct al. 1985, pp. 73–78). This would open up jobs for younger workers and help bring unemployment rates down to a politically more acceptable level (Graebner 1980, pp. 184–189). The assumption was that if unemployment rates could be reduced, the extent of radical social agitation would also decline.

In Brazil during the hearings just prior to enactment of the nation's first old-age pension legislation there was much discussion about the "labor question" and the need for a program that would pacify labor so as to prevent the mobilization of an urban working class in Brazil similar to that which had emerged in the industrial nations of Europe (Malloy 1979, pp. 80–81). As in Sweden, the actual pressure on the government from organized workers was much less intense than in more industrial nations such as Germany, but the Brazilian economic elite was aware of international trends and they were very interested in undercutting any mobilization of the working class before it got well under way.

Economic dependency, colonial legacy, and world system position have had an impact on old-age social security policy development in some of the countries considered, particularly the Third World countries. Arguments emphasizing these factors often fall within the neo-Marxist perspective although some also fall within the state-centered perspective. The impact of these factors on social policy tends to be indirect and for this reason it is sometimes difficult to assess their strength.

In Brazil the first workers to be covered by public pension legislation were those in occupations central to the nation's agricultural export economy. Coverage came much sooner to railroad workers, dockworkers, and to maritime workers than to industrial workers (Gersdorff 1962, p. 198). The late coverage for industrial workers was due in large measure to Brazil's position in the world economy as a nation heavily dependent on agricultural exports. From the colonial era to the present Brazil has held a dependent position in the world economy (Frank 1969, p. 148; Topik 1987, p. 5). This has had implications for long-term economic development which in turn has had implications for monies available to spend on public pensions, but no precise estimates can be made as to what the impact of dependency has been on the nation's level of development, and estimates of the impact on pension spending are necessarily even less precise.

India's status as a British colony had a long-term detrimental impact on the economy. The British stifled the growth of industries that would compete with British industries and promoted policies that made the Indian economy heavily dependent on British imports (Nair 1979, p. 252; Wolpert 1977, p. 248). The adverse impact of colonial status can be traced back at least to the eighteenth century, but it is also true that the British helped develop India in many ways, building a railroad system, modern ports, a modern university system, and the like. While it would be impossible to say precisely what the net negative impact was after taking into consideration the many positive contributions that the British made, there is general agreement that India was a less developed nation at the time of its independence than it would have been had it not been a British colony or if it had obtained its independence at a much earlier point in history.[7] If India had been substantially more developed it is possible that a pension system would have been introduced rather than a provident fund system. It is also possible that the old-age social security scheme would have been introduced several decades earlier and the current benefit levels might be more generous.

Nigeria's dependent position in the world system has undoubtedly had an adverse impact on the nation's long-run economic development. As in the case of India the net impact was negative, but again it would be a mistake to neglect the many positive contributions that the British made to the nation's economic development.[8] Had the British granted Nigeria its independence at a much earlier point in time, it is possible that the nation would be more developed today and in a position to provide more generous old-age social security options for its population. However, it is also possible that earlier independence would have been associated with more internal ethnic conflict rather than more economic growth with the result that old-age social security policy development might not have been more developed than it is today.

While any conclusions about the impact of either Nigeria's or India's colonial experience on contemporary levels of economic development are necessarily speculative, it is clear in both cases that the experience of having been a British colony did have an affect on the type of old-age social security scheme that was eventually introduced (Williamson and Pampel 1991). A very high proportion of former British colonies, India and Nigeria among them, opted for provident funds as opposed to social insurance based pension systems (Parrott 1985, p. 210). Given the resistance to shifting from one type of scheme to another once it has been institutionalized, this difference has had a major impact on old-age social security policy development and it is likely to continue to have a major impact into the indefinite future.

As it is today, at the turn of the century Sweden was highly dependent on external markets for its goods. Several analysts have suggested that this vulnerability to external markets made Sweden sensitive to the need to provide a social welfare net for its people early on. This is one reason the nation has looked so favorably upon public pensions and other social insurance programs.

On the basis of the dependency theory perspective we would expect industrial nations such as Sweden and the Netherlands that are heavily dependent on foreign trade to spend relatively more on old-age pensions than nations such as the United States and Germany that are less heavily dependent on foreign trade. In general, this does seem to be the case. However, not all of the evidence is consistent with this explanation. It does not adequately account for why Japan, a nation that is very heavily dependent on foreign trade, is at the very bottom of the list of industrial nations with respect to spending on old-age pensions, nor does it account for the high spending level in Germany, a nation that has a relatively large internal market and is less dependent on foreign trade than are a number of countries spending far less on pensions.[9]

We find evidence in support of a number of arguments that can be linked to the neo-Marxist perspective, but none prove to be useful in accounting for developments in all seven countries. Furthermore, none of these arguments by itself offers an adequate explanation of developments for even one country across the entire time span considered in our case studies. The neo-Marxist arguments tend to be most useful in accounting for developments surrounding the introduction of the original programs, but less useful in accounting for post-World War II policy developments.

The Industrialism Perspective

The evidence suggests that economic development and industrialization had little impact on the timing of the introduction of pension programs among the industrial nations considered, but pension programs were generally introduced in the industrial nations sooner than in Third World nations. The sustained economic growth that the four industrial nations experienced between the end of World War II and the middle of the 1970s was a factor influencing the trend toward more comprehensive and generous pension benefits. The historical evidence for Brazil, India, and Nigeria suggests that level of development influenced the timing of the introduction of old-age social security programs in these Third World nations relative to those in the industrial nations. It also suggests that the economic expansion that has taken place during the post-World War II era has contributed to the extension of coverage and to the liberalizing reforms that have occurred particularly in Brazil and India.

When we compare the dates the first national old-age social security programs were enacted for the seven countries considered in our case studies, we find that there is a general tendency for the least developed to be late introducing such programs. Industrial nations such as Germany (1889), Sweden (1913), and Britain (1908) enacted programs sooner than Brazil (1923) and much sooner than India (1952) and Nigeria (1961). However, there are some anomalies with respect to order of enactment that cannot be accounted for based on level of development alone. One is that the United States introduced its first program much later (1935) than less industrial Sweden; even Brazil had its first scheme before the United States.[10] A second anomaly is that several nations including Germany introduced pension schemes long before Britain, even though Britain was clearly the most industrial nation in the world at the end of the nineteenth century.[11] The evidence suggests that level of economic development influenced the timing of the introduction of old-age social security schemes, but it was only a contributing factor, not a determining factor.

On the basis of industrialism theory we would expect the more industrialized nations to spend a greater share of the national product on public pensions. There is some support for this in that in 1980 the spending on public pensions for the four industrial nations ranged from 6.3 percent of GDP (Britain) to 12.1 percent (Germany) (OECD 1988a, pp. 140–141). The corresponding figure for Brazil was 2.5 percent.[12] These figures closely parallel those for GNP per capita.[13] However, there is by no means a perfect correspondence between GNP per capita and pension spending. In the early 1980s the United States ranked as one of the top industrial nations with respect to GNP per capita, but it was one of the lowest with respect to pension expenditures. Japan is another such anomaly, spending only 2.3 percent of its GNP on public pensions in 1980, less than the 2.5 percent spent by Brazil despite its much larger GNP per capita ($10,100 vs. $2,200) (ILO 1985).

It is consistent with Wilensky's (1975) version of industrialism theory to look to various demographic correlates of economic development in an effort to account for differences between nations with respect to social security spending policy, but this option offers no simple explanation for the discrepancies we have observed. For example, in 1900 the proportion of the population over age 65 was much higher in Sweden (8.4 percent) than in Britain (4.7 percent) or Germany (4.9 percent) (Laslett 1985, p. 217); based on age structure alone one would have expected Sweden to have introduced its pension program prior to Britain or Germany.[14]

There is, however, some demographic evidence that does support industrialism theory. There is a strong association between percent aged (a demographic consequence of industrialization) and the proportion of a nation's GDP spent on public pensions. For 1980 the ranking of the seven countries with respect to percent aged age 65 and over was: Sweden (15.9 percent), Germany (14.8 percent), Britain (14.6 percent), United States (10.9 percent), Brazil (3.5 percent), India (3.0 percent), and Nigeria (2.4 percent) (World Bank 1983b). The ranking by proportion of the GDP spent on pensions was very similar although not identical.[15]

During the post-World War II period there were dramatic increases in spending on public pensions in the four industrial nations, increases made possible by the substantial economic growth that these nations experienced.[16] Similarly, the increases in the number of workers covered by public pensions in Brazil and the national provident funds in Nigeria and India would not have taken place were it not for economic growth which contributed to the increase in the size of the modern sector. In all three of the Third World countries the size of the wage dependent population was increasing and the proportion of elderly was increasing; but it was the economic growth they all experienced that made it possible to extend coverage and increase the size of contributions to these old-age social security schemes.

It is generally agreed that the emergence of public pensions throughout the industrialized world during the late nineteenth and early twentieth century was at least in part a response to the changes associated with the industrialization these nations were experiencing (Zöllner 1982; Gilbert 1966). A similar argument can be made concerning the emergence of old-age social security programs in many Third World nations, particularly since the end of World War II (e.g., Sinha 1980, pp. 23–26).

The technological, scientific, and educational advances associated with industrialism have had a significant demographic impact on all nations undergoing the process of industrialization. More specifically, the reduction in fertility and increase in life expectancy have had an impact on the age structure of many of these nations. The graying of the age structure has in turn contributed to the emergence and subsequent evolution of pension policy.[17] In the industrial nations the increasing number of elderly was recognized during the early years of pension policy development, but the trend was given a great deal more attention during the post-World War II era due to the increasingly rapid growth of this segment of the population (U.S. Senate 1981, p. 3).

The increase in per capita national product experienced during the past one hundred years in all nations that have experienced at least a modest level of industrialization has not only contributed to an increase in life expectancy and a graying of the age structure, it has also made it economically feasible for many of these nations to consider the introduction of old-age social security systems. Prior to the increase in economic surplus associated with industrialization, most nations had neither the necessary economic resources nor the bureaucratic infrastructure required to administer old-age pension systems.

In many areas, at least some workers who had left the agricultural sector to take jobs in factories were able to return to the farm during periods of slack industrial employment. But with further industrialization an increasing proportion of the population became wage dependent and unable to find adequate means of support to deal with loss of income due to old age, failing health, or long-term unemployment. During the early stages of industrialization many older workers remained in the less wage dependent agricultural sector and were as a result protected, at least to some degree, from the swings of national and international business cycles, but this changed as the industrialization process progressed.

The relevance of the economic dimension is underscored by the policy changes that took place during the late 1970s and early 1980s in many of these countries in response to the stagflation experienced by most industrial nations. Between the mid-1970s and the early 1980s Germany, Britain, Sweden, and the United States all made changes in the procedures used to adjust pensions for price or wage increases. These changes represented cost containment efforts (Alber 1988, p. 120; Zeiter 1983). In the United States the Reagan administration also made an unsuccessful effort to put limits on cost of living adjustments, but in 1983 it did get legislation passed that resulted in taxes being paid on one-half of Social Security benefits for those with incomes of over $25,000 per year.[18] It is unlikely that these efforts to contain spending on Social Security would have taken place were it not for the slow economic growth these nations experienced during the late 1970s and early 1980s.

One of the most extensively used theories of welfare state development during the 1960s and early 1970s was industrialism theory (Kerr et al. 1964; Wilensky 1975). In recent years the tendency has been either to neglect this perspective or to refute it. While our evidence would not allow us to accept this theory to the exclusion of all others, it does suggest that industrialism and economic development must be taken into consideration as part of our effort to account for cross-national differences in pension policy development.

The major focus of industrialism theorists has been on such variables as level of development and rate of development as well as the bureaucratic and demographic correlates of the industrialization process. However, it is also of note that theorists in this tradition generally argue that political factors, particularly partisan politics, have had little if any independent impact on pension policy and welfare state spending more generally in the industrial nations (Wilensky 1975). The relative lack of support for the social democratic thesis is consistent with this aspect of industrialism theory. However, the historical evidence we have presented does call this aspect of the theory into question to the extent it suggests that pension policy has often been influenced by various forms of interest group politics.

The Neo-Pluralist Perspective

The analysis presented in our four industrial nation case studies makes extensive use of the interest group pressure thesis. In each of these countries both the formulation of the original pension program and the changes since World War II have been strongly influenced by interest group pressure from a variety of sources. While the evidence in support of the thesis is weaker for the three Third World nations, we do find some support in these countries as well. Well developed democratic structures may be necessary for a fully developed version of interest group pluralism, but we do find some evidence of interest group politics at work even in countries such as Brazil and Nigeria with less well developed democratic institutions.

In late nineteenth century Germany, Bismarck was unable to get his proposal enacted in its original form because of opposition from the members of the Reichstag representing the middle class. His original proposal called for a noncontributory scheme so as to emphasize the beneficence of the state. He wanted workers to view themselves as dependent on the state for a pension in retirement; he did not want them to view this pension as an earned right (Myles 1984, p. 34). What he wanted was allegiance to the state and support for the political and economic status quo. But the members of the Reichstag representing the middle class would not go along with the idea of a noncontributory pension. It violated their liberal values which placed a high premium on the work ethic and self-reliance. They felt it was important that workers be expected to contribute to their own old-age pensions. They insisted on and got a modification in Bismarck's proposal; the version eventually enacted was a contributory scheme.

Looking at the post-World War II expansion of the German old-age pension scheme, we find the major political parties of the left and the right attempting to outdo one another with respect to pension policy liberalization in an effort to obtain electoral advantage (Tomasson 1984, pp. 223–225). Each party was responding not only to the potential votes of the elderly themselves, but also to the potential votes of various other interest groups that wanted to see more done for the elderly including the unions, the middle-aged children of pensioners, and various health care and social service providers for the elderly.

In Britain a variety of interest groups were active in the pension debate from the outset. Blackley organized a pressure group called the National Providence League that was successful in getting the government to set up a committee to study the pension issue in 1885 (Fraser 1973, pp. 139–140). In 1899 Booth and others formed the National Committee of Organized Labour on Old Age Pensions, a relatively small pressure group whose ideas had a major impact on the eventual scheme enacted in 1908.

Efforts to account for why Britain did not introduce a pension scheme earlier than it did must emphasize the role of various interest groups. Of particular note was the strong opposition to public pensions from the friendly societies; for many years these societies viewed public pensions as an invasion of their turf. Similarly, the Charity Organization Society opposed public pensions preferring the private charity approach (Ashford 1986, p. 178). Also opposed to public pensions were other powerful vested interests including the private insurance industry. The early history of British pension policy is one of competition among relatively small and well focused pro-pension pressure groups led by highly committed articulate social reformers, several other organizations resisting such efforts as invading their turf, and to a lesser extent, business and labor interests.

During the post-World War II era national organizations of pensioners began to participate in the political process; for example, the National Federation of Old Age Pension Associations had considerable influence in connection with the regular pension increments between 1950 and 1974 (Pratt forthcoming; Beer 1965, p. 342). However, politicians of all stripes became increasingly aware of the popularity of the pension reform issue and the wide variety of groups supporting such reforms. Of particular note was the success of big business and the private insurance industry in shaping the 1959 reforms so that contracting out would be one of the options in connection with the new earnings-related pension.

The early history of the pension movement in Sweden was quite similar to that in Britain in that it was dominated by social reformers and the government commissions formed to study the issue. Of particular note was Adolf Hedin who introduced a motion in 1884 calling for the first government commission to study the idea of old-age pensions. This commission came up with a public pension proposal that was defeated due to its opposition by a powerful interest group, the provincial governors. In 1891 a second commission was formed. It too came up with a pension proposal that was defeated in large measure due to opposition from the farm block which represented the nation's largest group of employers (Wilson 1979, p. 6).

The Swedish stand out with respect to the extent to which an effort was made to include all major interested parties in the various commissions set up to study the pension issue. Eventually in 1912 one of these commissions was able to work out a compromise supported by the major interest groups and it was enacted. The inclusion of representatives of the farm block, of the Social Democrats, and of industry including the insurance industry was essential to getting the final proposal enacted by the Swedish Riksdag (Heclo 1974, pp. 190–192).

A number of factors contributed to the expansion of spending on public pensions during the post-World War II era. Organized labor played a major role through its influence on the Social Democratic Party that was in power during most of this period. However, time and again we find evidence of pension reforms being structured in such a way as to increase benefits for white-collar and other middle-class workers. During this period the middle class became a very influential interest group (Baldwin 1988).

Other important interest group related factors in the Swedish case were the graying of the nation's age structure, the high degree of ethnic homogeneity, and attempts by political parties of both the left and the right to use the pension issue to political advantage (Michanek 1964). While old-age pensioners were only one of several interest groups that were active during this period, they were among the most influential with respect to old-age social policy (Olsson 1990, p. 91).

As in Britain and Sweden social reformers were the first to bring the pension issue to the attention of policymakers in the United States. Of particular note in this context were Isaac Rubinow and Abraham Epstein. Also important were such organizations as the Fraternal Order of the Eagles which began to push for old-age pensions at the state level during the 1920s (Lubove 1968, p. 136). The Great Depression led to the growth of a number of organizations calling for the intro-duction of old-age pensions. In 1933 Upton Sinclair formed a group he called End Poverty in California (Achenbaum 1978, p. 129). Subsequently, Francis Townsend formed what came to be called the Townsend movement; it started in California, but soon became a national movement with several hundred thousand followers.

While Roosevelt did not invite the leaders of these various pressure groups and social movements to participate in the formulation of the Social Security Act of 1935, their activities contributed to the perceived need to enact pension legisla-tion (Pratt 1976, p. 23). In the formulation of this legislation there were a variety of interest groups that had to be taken into consideration. The title dealing with the Old Age Assistance program called for individual state programs rather than a national program so as to obtain the support of southern legislators who wanted to be sure not to undercut work incentives for low-wage (African-American) agricul-ture workers (Quadagno 1988a, pp. 115–116).[19] The title for old-age pensions did not cover agricultural workers. To obtain support from the business sector the payroll tax and thus the benefit level had to be kept low. Due to opposition from organi-zations representing the interests of physicians no health care component was included (Anderson 1951, p. 90). In short, the legislation represented the results of many compromises with a variety of interest groups.

Since the end of World War II the proportion of the population covered by Social Security pensions has increased considerably as has spending on pensions and the level of the benefits provided. Consistent with the pattern in Germany, Sweden, and Britain, both the Republicans and Democrats have supported propos-als to liberalize pension policy and to increase benefit levels. With the graying of America in recent decades the elderly have become an increasingly important voting block that politicians of all political persuasions are careful to cultivate (Wallace et al. 1991, pp. 96–97; Williamson et al. 1982). The elderly are not the only people supporting increased Social Security benefits, however. There is typically strong support from those who are middle aged, many of whom prefer to have their par-ents dependent on a government program rather than directly providing economic support to their elderly parents (Neugarten 1974).

There is support from a variety of interest groups that provide various social service and health care services to the aged such as the professional associations for social workers, nurses, nursing home administrators, and gerontologists (Marmor 1973). There are also the various organizations of the aged such as the American

Association of Retired Persons (AARP) and the National Council on the Aging (NCOA). In short, there have been a variety of interest groups pushing on behalf of the aged and relatively few opposing such demands. Prior to the 1980s the strength of the interest groups advocating on behalf of the aged was indicated by the steady flow of new programs aimed at the elderly and the frequent increases in benefit levels. After the 1980 election the strength of the aged and the interest groups on their behalf was reflected in their relative immunity from the welfare state program cuts initiated during the Reagan era.

When the first pensions were introduced during the 1920s Brazil was nominally a republic, but electoral participation was so restricted that it would more appropriately be described as an authoritarian oligarchy. The introduction of pensions for certain key sectors of the economy represented an effort to pacify and co-opt those whose cooperation was most needed (Schmitter 1971, p. 150). It did not represent a concession to direct pressure from the aged, the unions, or any other interest group.

In general, interest groups are able to function much more effectively in democratic than in authoritarian states. Nevertheless, after the various pension programs were in place, a restricted form of interest group pressure did occur included representatives of labor, management, and the state. Even though those selected to represent labor were more answerable to the state than to rank and file workers (Gersdorff 1962, p. 204), over time these representatives were able to use their access to high level government officials to exert pressure for benefit increases. As the nation's pension system was decentralized into a large number of separate pension schemes for different categories of workers, the pressure was typically to increase benefits for a particular category of workers, not for workers in general.

In 1945 government social security technocrats proposed a reorganized social insurance system called the ISSB plan that was to include all employed persons; it called for a substantial increase in the proportion of the population covered and for a much more uniform set of rules governing benefits and contributions. The proposal was strongly opposed from a variety of groups. Most important was the opposition from the already existing social insurance institutions which included many who were middle class as well as more affluent members of the working class, particularly in urban areas. There was also opposition from the civil servants who had jobs in the bureaucracies administering the existing pension funds (Malloy 1979, pp. 84–86). Thus even under the authoritarian Vargas regime a limited form of interest group politics did function and did influence pension policy. During the period of relative democratization between 1945 and 1964 interest groups influenced pension policy, but the pressure took the form of efforts to block proposals to extend benefits to new groups; the preference was to increase benefits to those already covered.

In India the bitter antagonism between various religious, ethnic, regional, and caste groups has inhibited the development of class-based interest groups. The result has been a variety of diverse pressure groups attempting to influence government policy (Weiner 1964, pp. 98–103). Given the heterogeneity of Indian society and the distrust of outgroups, a shift from an emphasis on the provident fund approach to an emphasis on the social insurance approach to old-age security seems unlikely.

With the provident fund approach each person gets out what he or she puts in, and this helps deal with fears that one group is going to get more out than its due at the expense of some other group.

While there is much evidence that Indian society is divided into many nonclass-based interest groups, there is little evidence with respect to the relative impact that these various groups have had on old-age social security policy. The one exception to this generalization is the large civil service bureaucracy which forms an influential interest group and which has had a substantial role in the formulation of old-age social security policy (Sinha 1980, pp. 109–110).

The evidence for Nigeria is in some ways similar to that for India. Both nations are sharply divided with respect to ethnic, linguistic, religious, and regional groupings (Nelson 1982, p. 90). These cleavages crosscut divisions based on class reducing the influence of class-based politics and provide the basis for various forms of nonclass interest groups (Post and Vickers 1973; Wolpe 1974). In Nigeria as in India, civil service bureaucrats were influential in the formulation of the nation's original provident fund scheme. There is no evidence that specific interest groups have been influential with respect to the modest policy changes that have been made since the original plan was introduced in 1961, but it does seem clear that no shift to the social insurance approach is likely in the near future. The deep cleavages in Nigerian society would constitute a major barrier to any such policy shift.

The effects of democracy alone are mixed. In some cases, primarily among the industrial societies at the turn of the century and the Third World countries in more recent years, democratic freedoms impeded the emergence of a centralized system. For instance, diverse groups with interests in more particularistic pension schemes early on had more influence resisting changes in Britain or India than in Germany or Brazil. In other cases, particularly during the post-World War II period among the industrial countries with mature pension systems, democratic competition for votes often centered on multiple parties supporting expansion of popular pension programs targeted toward the middle class. By itself, democracy neither promotes nor hinders pension development, but it does heighten the impact of interest group activities.

The State-Centered Perspective

Our historical case studies offer a number of instances in which state actors and structural characteristics of states have been important determinants of old-age security policy. These findings offer support for the argument that we need to take into consideration the state as an autonomous agent in our efforts to account for cross-national differences in policy. We have focused on such structural considerations as level of institutionalization of democratic structures, the presence or absence of a highly professional civil service corps, and the presence or absence of corporatist structures for mediation of the interests of labor, capital, and the state.

Any effort to account for why Germany was the first nation to introduce a national pension scheme must take into consideration a major structural factor; it was a new nation with a population whose traditional allegiance was to smaller units making up the new nation. This status as a new nation magnified the concern of the ruling elite about the disruptive potential of the emerging urban working class. A pension program and other social insurance programs were viewed by Bismarck and the ruling elite he represented as a mechanism to undercut the socialist movement and to legitimize the state in the minds of these industrial workers.

The German case offers particularly crucial support for the state-centered perspective because it was such a paradigmatic instance of an autonomous state during the period of the German Empire. State structures were also important during the post-World War II era. Of particular note in this context was the impact of democratic corporatist structures. In addition, the highly developed German civil service has been a key actor in the formulation of pension policy throughout most of the past century.

Toward the end of the nineteenth century Britain had much more developed democratic institutions than did Germany. One consequence of this is that a wider variety of interest groups were active in the political process in Britain. The resistance to the idea of public pensions from such organizations as the Charity Organization Society and the friendly societies is one of the reasons that it took longer for pensions to be adopted in Britain. Bismarck had fewer interest groups that were strong enough to block legislation he wanted to see enacted.

When attempting to account for why it was that Britain enacted pension legislation so much sooner than the United States a number of structural differences are relevant. In Britain a national public welfare bureaucracy was created by the Poor Law of 1834 and later in the century a great deal of attention was given to the issue of civil service reform. At the turn of the century no such national civil service bureaucracy was in place in the United States (Orloff and Skocpol 1984, p. 742). This infrastructure difference made it easier for the British to seriously consider introducing a national pension scheme. In Britain patronage politics in the wake of electoral victories had not been the norm since early in the nineteenth century. In contrast the spoils system in the aftermath of an electoral victory was still very much the norm in many areas of the United States at the turn of the century; government administrative and social service positions were for the most part filled by one's supporters rather than career civil servants. This spoils system and the fear of graft in connection with a public pension system was one of the reasons the Progressives were strongly opposed to the introduction of a national pension plan for the United States (Skocpol and Ikenberry 1983, pp. 102–113).

Sweden's well developed civil service corps has played a major role with respect to both the formulation and implementation of the nation's pension policy from the outset. During the early years opposition from a few powerful civil servants contributed to the delay in the introduction of the original program. Over the years Swedish policymakers have depended heavily on civil service experts for advice about how to reform pension policy. Civil service experts have also played a major role in many Third World nations including Brazil, India, and Nigeria.

Among the structural factors frequently cited by those attempting to account for pension policy developments in Sweden is the "remiss" system in which commissions are established to conduct a study prior to major public policy decisions (Woodsworth 1977, p. 23). These commissions are structured in such a way that all of the major interested parties are represented. The policies that emerge from such commissions typically have the support needed for enactment because many of the needs of the various interested parties have been taken into consideration in the formulation of the committee proposal.

In both India and Nigeria provident fund plans were enacted very soon after independence. This was also true of many other former colonial territories in Africa and Asia. This evidence suggests that the structural change from colonial status to status as an independent nation was an important determinant of why these old-age social security programs were introduced when they were. It would seem that there is a common need for new nations to obtain legitimacy for the national government. Such programs also give key sectors of the population a vested interest in the new regime and its programs.

In our analysis we have given a great deal of attention to the relationship between corporatist structures and the evolution of pension policy. We have found it useful to distinguish between two very distinct categories of corporatism—democratic corporatism and authoritarian corporatism.

Authoritarian corporatism has proven particularly useful in our efforts to account for pension policy developments in Brazil. Here the reference is to state structures designed to mediate conflicts between labor and capital in such a way as to assure state control over labor (and to a lesser extent over capital). To this end pension programs were structured in such a way as to undercut the influence of independent labor unions, socialist parties, and other such organizations dedicated to fostering working-class solidarity.

Democratic corporatism has proven useful in our efforts to account for postwar pension policy developments in Germany and particularly Sweden. Here the reference is to voluntary institutional arrangements designed to assure labor a significant voice in the formulation of social and economic policies that impact the well-being of workers. These structures call for labor giving up some of its autonomy, but this decision is voluntary and it is done in a context in which capital gives up some of its autonomy as well. These democratic corporatist structures make it possible for highly centralized unions, highly centralized employer organizations, and top government officials to work out social and economic policies more quickly than would otherwise be the case (Wilensky 1976). The actors in such decision-making structures are less likely to see themselves as engaged in a zero-sum game. Due to better communication and greater trust, solutions can often be worked out in which all major parties see themselves as winners.

In Britain there have been brief periods, such as the immediate postwar period, during which democratic corporatist structures have been in place and have shaped pension policy, but such structures have not been an important factor shaping policy developments in the United States. In neither Nigeria nor India do we find well developed corporatist structures, nor do we find evidence of a strong link between the structures that do exist and the evolution of old-age security policy.

The conclusions that emerge from our case studies provide a guide for the quantitative analysis in Chapter 9. The case studies challenge conventional class-based views of old-age security policy development and lead us to argue for broader, more eclectic explanations that emphasize neo-pluralist and state-centered perspectives. That some contexts highlight the importance of pluralist democratic competition, others the importance of class power and conflict, and still others the organization of the state suggests the need to formalize how context shapes the importance of various factors. Our quantitative analysis attempts to combine elements of the several theories in a way that can be tested more formally. Besides extending the study to a larger sample of nations (18 as opposed to 4 industrial nations, 32 as opposed to 3 Third World nations), the quantitative analysis provides some additional theoretical insights.

We find that corporatist state structure is more important as a determinant of pension spending in combination with forces of societal demand than in isolation from them. For our sample of 18 industrial nations we find that national context must be taken into consideration in any effort to specify which societal forces have the most influence on pension spending levels.

In nations that are high in democratic corporatism such as Sweden and Austria various class effects have a substantial impact on pension spending levels. In contrast, there is little evidence of class effects in nations such as the United States and Britain that have low levels of democratic corporatism. This quantitative evidence offers at least qualified support for the social democratic thesis and class theory more generally, so long as it is applied to nations that have well developed democratic corporatist structures.

Similarly, we find that in the least corporatist nations age structure (percent aged) has much more influence than it does in our most corporatist nations. Our interpretation of this evidence is that in high corporatism nations such as Sweden class actors have more influence on pension policy than do various nonclass interest groups such as the elderly. In contrast, in low corporatism nations such as the United States class actors have much less influence and other nonclass actors such as the aged have more influence. As our actual measure, percent aged, can be alternatively interpreted as a measure of demographic pressure (as viewed from the industrialism perspective) or the relevance of the senior vote (as viewed from the neo-pluralist perspective), our quantitative analysis is most appropriately viewed as lending support to a qualified version of both of these perspectives. We say qualified because the evidence points to substantial influence of percent aged for some nations (the least corporatist), but relatively little influence in others (the most corporatist).

In the analysis of pension spending for our sample of 32 Third World nations we are unable to assess the extent of any interaction between corporatism and other indicators for lack of an adequate quantitative measure of corporatism for these nations. However, we have been able to address the issue of state structure as reflected in a measure of level of political democracy. Our results in many respects parallel those for the industrial nations. Again we find evidence of interaction; that is, we find evidence that national context as measured by level of political democracy has an influence on the impact that other key variables such as social insurance program experience and percent aged have on pension spending levels. We find that percent aged and social insurance program experience have

more influence in the more democratic of these Third World nations. Our interpretation of this evidence is that more democratic regimes are more responsive to
pressure for spending increases from civil service bureaucrats and from the aged
more generally.

The quantitative analysis based on these 32 Third World nations allows us to
test for interaction effects that can not be adequately tested on the basis of our
three historical case studies. It is of particular note that this analysis has led to
evidence calling for the qualification of our findings as to the relevance of democratic structures to old-age security policy. We found little evidence of any such
relationship in our three case studies, but a relationship did emerge when we considered evidence from the much larger sample of 32 Third World nations.

Conclusion

Comparative historical studies typically focus on two or three countries. In the
present study we stretch the comparative historical approach to its limits with our
consideration of seven countries. This allows us to see more variation and forces
us to confront more anomalous cases than would have been true had our study
been limited to two or three countries. Of particular note has been the complexity
introduced by adding three Third World nations to a study that also includes four
industrial nations. But even with seven countries there is too little variation to
adequately address some issues. For this reason we have also included some quantitative analysis based on samples of 18 industrial nations and 32 Third World
nations. Some questions call for studies based on qualitative comparative historical data; some call for studies based on multivariate statistical data; and some such
as those we have considered call for studies based on both types of evidence.

In this chapter we summarize the most important theoretical generalizations
that can be made on the basis of the evidence presented in the previous chapters.
We do not attempt to present the many explanations and interpretations that do
not lend themselves to generalization beyond the specific national context. Our
task here is much more limited. It is to look for theoretical generalizations that
can be made that apply to several of these countries and that might upon further
investigation prove generalizable to other nations as well.

The single most important generalization based on the case study evidence is
that the support for the simple version of the social democratic thesis, one of the
most widely studied and thoroughly documented relationships in the pension policy
literature, is at best weak. Our case study evidence suggests that with the notable
exception of Sweden, organized labor and leftist political parties have had relatively little impact on the evolution of pension policy. However, our quantitative
results show that the social democratic thesis and class theory more generally do
receive support in high corporatism nations such as Sweden. This qualifies our
prior rejection of class theory as applied to the analysis of cross-national variation
in pension spending levels (Williamson and Pampel 1986; Pampel and Williamson
1985; 1988; 1989).

Some arguments and explanations which have evolved out of prior studies based primarily on the industrial nations can with appropriate contextual adjustments be used to cast light on developments in Third World nations as well. One example is the argument that ethnic cleavages can undercut the extent to which old-age security policy is shaped by class cleavages. This has been true in the United States; it has also been true in India and Nigeria. As another example, the social control thesis, which evolved out of studies that focused on developments in the industrial nations (Williamson et al. 1985), can, with appropriate contextual modifications, be used to interpret policy developments in Third World nations such as Brazil and India.

It is generally useful to consider a combination of explanations drawn from a variety of different theoretical perspectives even when attempting to account for developments during a comparatively short period of time in one country. This becomes particularly true when we attempt to explain developments in several different countries over extended time periods. While it is common for scholars to treat these different theoretical perspectives as contradictory, we find it more useful to treat them as complementary. Across countries and across time within a country, the relative utility of the explanations derived from different theoretical perspectives does vary; national and historical context make a difference.

In the analysis presented in this book we have found the social democratic perspective to be of limited utility except in connection with policy developments during the postwar period in nations with well developed democratic corporatist structures. The neo-Marxist perspective has been most useful in the analysis of developments in connection with the introduction of the original old-age security programs, while the industrialism perspective has proven most useful in connection with developments during the post-World War II period. The state-centered perspective has proven useful both for the analysis of developments in countries with well developed corporatist structures and in those with relatively underdeveloped democratic structures, while the neo-pluralist perspective has proven most useful in the context of nations with more well developed democratic structures.

NOTES

Chapter 1

1. Old-age security policy has been a subject of study by scholars representing many disciplines. The use of various class theories has been particularly pervasive among sociologists, but less so among those representing other disciplines.

2. In recent years it has become fashionable to inveigh against the use of general social theories in comparative historical analysis (Stinchcombe 1978; Tilly 1984; Skocpol 1984). We find ourselves in agreement with Kiser and Hechter (1991, p. 23) in their assertion that this trend in favor of almost exclusive dependence on inductive analysis has gone too far.

3. For example, the analysis of why there was so much variation among countries with respect to labor's impact on old-age security policy.

4. For example, the systematic measurement and analysis of the strength of interaction effects.

5. Also referred to as the developmental or socioeconomic perspective (Wilensky et al. 1985, p. 5).

6. Industrialism theorists view such programs as redistributive. Thus economic growth is viewed as contributing to increased spending on public pensions and other social insurance programs that reduce the extent of income inequality.

7. For example, Wilensky (1975, p. 138) used a modified version of Blondel's (1969) categories to classify the nations of the world into four categories: (1) liberal democratic, (2) totalitarian (East Block socialist), (3) authoritarian oligarchic, and (4) authoritarian populist. He concluded that type of political system has at best a very weak net impact on social security spending (Wilensky 1975, p. 27).

8. Wilensky (1975, pp. 42–47) used an indicator based on the ideology of the ruling party or coalition for a 15-year period (1950–1965).

9. For the last three variables our source is Jackman (1975, chapters 4 and 6). He uses three dependent variables: (1) Social Insurance Program Experience, (2) a Social Welfare Index, and (3) a coefficient of intrasectoral income inequality.

10. The emphasis on social control was particularly strong in the 1960s and early 1970s (Gough 1979, p. 11; Piven and Cloward 1971).

11. By the time of the First International; Marx supported legislative efforts at least as a short-term strategy (Stephens 1979, p. 10).

12. However, neo-Marxists do make the point that the state must be somewhat autonomous in order to adjudicate when conflicts arise within the ruling class (Gough 1979, pp. 41–42; Miliband 1969).

13. There are so many variants of the neo-Marxist perspective that it is all but impossible to make definitive statements acceptable to all who consider themselves neo-Marxists. Thus the description of "the neo-Marxist perspective" that follows serves to indicate what we mean when we refer to the neo-Marxist or to the monopoly capitalism perspective; it is not meant as a definitive statement on the subject.

14. The neo-Marxist perspective shares with the industrialism perspective the functionalist assumption that the welfare state is a response to certain functional imperatives. In the case of the neo-Marxist perspective, it is a response to the needs of capital (or the dominant class or the ruling class); in the case of the industrialism perspective, it is the needs of a technological society.

15. In other writings, however, Marx argued for an expansion of democracy (Carnoy 1984, p. 51). This suggests that he believed that the state can, at least in part, be subject to popular control from below. What has come to be viewed as the traditional Marxist view on democracy would more accurately be described as the Leninist view. Lenin ([1917] 1965, pp. 8–9) took a very strong stand against the potential of bourgeois democracy which, in his opinion, only seems to allow influence and control of political institutions by the working class.

16. Some such as Poulantzas (1973; 1978) have shifted their views over time.

17. In the case of public pensions the transfer is from one age group (young adults and the middle aged) to another (the elderly) within the same social class rather than from one social class to another.

18. Industrialism theory also assumes that there is an egalitarian impact.

19. Contrast the argument in *Regulating the Poor* (Piven and Cloward 1971) with that in *The New Class War* (Piven and Cloward 1982).

20. World system theory tends to be identified with the work of Wallerstein (1980), but it can be viewed as a more recent development of dependency theory which has a long history.

21. The British impact was viewed as positive in that it contributed to the destruction of the old stagnant order and laid the foundations for a Western type society (Marx [1853] 1979).

22. It is of note that some neo-Marxists reject the Leninist interpretation and offer an argument similar to Marx's view on India. Warren (1980, p. 7) concludes that the net impact of capitalist intervention in Third World nations has generally been positive. He points out that it has often contributed to economic development, to the development of democracy, and to the creation of a political environment favorable for the development of socialism.

23. We refer to a slightly narrower version of this perspective as "the interest-group politics theory" in some of our previous work.

24. He does not, however, use the expression "neo-pluralism" to describe his perspective, and he makes little explicit reference to interests groups, preferring the term "distributional coalitions."

25. The "free-rider" problem refers to the difficulty in getting individuals to pay dues or in other ways make sacrifices for the collectivity if they are not forced to do so. It is often to the advantage of the individual not to participate in collective action when it is possible to enjoy the benefits of that action without incurring the personal costs that participation entails.

26. The effect of this process on government spending is particularly evident in election years (Tufte 1978).

27. Public choice theory assumes that people are rational utility maximizers and voter choice is described as being analogous to market choice (Mueller 1979). An extensive literature has emerged in this tradition that deals with the behavior of self-interested groups (Buchanan and Tullock 1980), voters (Downs 1957), political parties (Schlesinger 1984), and public bureaucracies (Niskanen 1971).

28. The neo-pluralist perspective can also be linked to the state-centered perspective to be outlined in the next section. The state (or various government agencies) may act as a special interest group making decisions designed to increase its power rather than being

a neutral arbitrator between the conflicting demands of various interest groups (Skocpol 1985, p. 4).

29. The perspective will, however, be of limited value for the analysis of developments in countries that rank low with respect to political democracy and related civil rights such as freedom of the press. It will also be of limited utility in very poor countries as there will be little by way of surplus for the government to allocate.

30. Particularly prominent in the call to "bring the state back in" have been Theta Skocpol (1985) and her colleagues (Skocpol and Amenta 1986; Skocpol and Ikenberry 1983).

31. Wilensky (1976) argues that there tends to be greater resistance to tax increases in countries that emphasize direct taxes such as income taxes based payroll deductions than in countries that emphasize less visible taxes such as the value added tax.

32. The reference here is to constitutional or institutional procedures for electoral participation, fair elections, and the like.

33. Democratic corporatism is viewed by some as a variant of industrialism theory (Wilensky 1976). This interpretation is based in part on the assumption that corporatist decision-making structures are a characteristic of the post-industrial condition that all or most industrial societies are moving toward. Democratic corporatism is viewed by some proponents as an alternative to pluralism, but many pluralists view it as a variant of pluralism (Williamson 1989, pp. 60–63).

34. Sometimes referred to as neo-corporatism or societal corporatism (Schmitter 1974).

35. Sometimes a reference is made to bipartite bargaining and sometimes to tripartite bargaining in connection with democratic corporatism. The former generally refers to bargaining between the representatives of labor and capital without the active participation of representatives of government. Government involvement can take many forms: it may organize the bargaining between labor and capital, it may participate in that bargaining, or it may be obligated (formally or informally) to act on the agreements worked out between labor and capital.

36. Both labor and capital are expected to make compromises. Typically labor is asked to moderate its wage demands and to refrain from strikes. Such compromises are viewed as contributing to long-term economic growth. Employers in return are expected to support policies that contribute to full employment and increases in the social wage.

37. Wilensky (1981, p. 359; 1976, p. 26) and Stephens (1979, p. 100) present evidence that countries with more corporatist decision-making structures tend to spend more on social security programs.

38. Also referred to as state corporatism (Schmitter 1974).

39. The Catholic connection is not just a coincidence. Most of the early (late nineteenth century) advocates of corporatism were Catholic social theorists concerned about the class conflict they saw emerging in response to the industrial revolution. They were critical of liberal capitalism and of the revolutionary socialist alternative; both were viewed as contributing to class conflict. They were, however, more antiliberal than anticapitalist. They were advocates of an organic consensual model of society (Williamson 1989, pp. 25–26).

40. The Esping-Andersen (1990, pp. 52–53) typology differentiates among three categories of welfare state regimes: (1) liberal, (2) social democratic, and (3) conservative. The Castles and Mitchell (1990, p. 13) typology adds a fourth category by subdividing Esping-Andersen's "liberal" welfare state regimes into two separate categories, "liberal" regimes such as in the United States and "radical" regimes such as in the United Kingdom. Castles and Mitchell (1990, p. 16) argue that the radical welfare state regimes emphasize more redistributive policies and lower expenditure levels than do liberal welfare state regimes.

41. Other countries in this category include: Austria, France, and Italy (Castles and Mitchell 1990, p. 13). Countries in this category tend to spend a relatively large proportion of national income on social welfare programs and tend to rank relatively low in benefit equality. The term *benefit equality* refers to the size of the gap between the highest and the lowest benefit paid.

42. Other countries in this category include: Australia, Finland, Ireland, and New Zealand (Castles and Mitchell 1990, p. 13). This term is used because many of these regimes were strongly influenced during the early years of the century by the "social liberals and laborists" who at the time were often referred to as radicals. Countries in this category tend to spend a relatively small proportion of national income on social welfare programs, but tend to be relatively high in benefit equality.

43. Other countries in this category are: Norway, Denmark, and Belgium. These countries tend to spend a relatively large proportion of national income on social welfare programs and tend to be relatively high in benefit equality.

44. Other countries in this category include: Canada, Japan, and Switzerland. These countries tend to spend a relatively small proportion of national income on social welfare programs and tend to be relatively low in benefit equality.

45. In 1989 their was a substantial gap in GNP per capita between Brazil ($2,540) on the one hand and India ($340) and Nigeria ($250) on the other (World Bank 1991, pp. 204–205).

46. On the basis of Bollen's (1980) scale of democracy, a scale that runs from 0 to 100, we find that the scores for our countries cover a broad range: 91 (India), 61 (Brazil), and 50 (Nigeria).

47. For example, it is commonly assumed that due to differences in level of development the industrial nations introduced their old-age pension systems before those in the Third World. While this is true as a general statement, there are exceptions that call for explanation such as the evidence that Brazil and Chile instituted their first public pension schemes many years prior to the United States and Switzerland.

Chapter 2

1. For the period between the end of World War II and reunification in 1990, we trace developments in the Federal Republic of Germany.

2. The Holy Roman Empire also included states and territories outside of what was to become Germany. It included territory in France, Netherlands, Poland, Austria, Italy, and Czechoslovakia. The French Revolution and the Napoleonic wars provided the *coup de grâce* for an already decaying Holy Roman Empire (Ramm 1967, pp. 1–43).

3. It is also referred to as the Second German Empire, the Second Reich, or the Kaiserreich.

4. At the end of the eighteenth century the Holy Roman Empire included over 300 political units in what would eventually become Germany including 51 free cities. Approximately one-third of the territory belonged to the church and was ruled by powerful bishops and abbots. Some of these states were highly autocratic while others were in effect constitutional monarchies. Prussia, which became the most powerful German state, was an absolute monarchy (Ramm 1967).

5. Bismarck was from a Prussian Junker background. Prussian military officers and high level civil servants were recruited almost entirely from among the Junkers (Passant 1959, p. 13).

6. An alternative and more traditional interpretation is that this agrarian recruitment to fill civil service positions gave the Junkers a great deal of influence with government policy makers relative to that of other groups such as big business (Bohham 1984, p. 210; Gillis 1968, p. 127).

7. As with the Prussian Chamber of Deputies the Reichstag had no control over military or foreign policy and could not remove the chancellor who was appointed by the kaiser (emperor) and served at his pleasure. Prussia made up over 80 percent of the population and thus held the vast majority of the seats in the Reichstag.

8. Ferdinand Lassalle was the president of the General German Workers' Association which considered itself a political party (Alber 1988, p. 5). The Social Democratic Party was called the Socialist German Labor Party until 1891; thereafter, it was called the German Social Democratic Party.

9. This legislation was originally enacted for a period of two and one-half years. It was repeatedly renewed until 1890 (Snell and Schmitt 1976, pp. 196–197).

10. The government was not, however, ever successful in completely eliminating the socialist newspapers, and the Social Democratic election organizations were allowed to function (although not without disruption) at least in the larger cities (Snell and Schmitt 1976, pp. 201–203).

11. In the aftermath of the 1848 revolution in France, the General German Workers' Fraternity was founded in Berlin. It was subsequently banned in 1854. This was the first German political worker's organization. The Printers' Mutual Improvement Society founded in 1862 was the first actual trade union organization (Zöllner 1982, pp. 10–11).

12. For example, the General German Workers' Association focused its efforts on the issue of universal suffrage in state and municipal elections, not on issues such as higher wages and better working conditions for labor (Snell and Schmitt 1976, p. 189).

13. At the start of the century approximately 85 percent of the population had at least some rights to farmland, but by the middle of the century the figure was down to 60 percent (Zöllner 1982, pp. 5–6). Early in the nineteenth century the Prussian serfs were emancipated, but there was no distribution of feudal lands. Many continued to work on the Junker estates as hired farm labor, but a substantial number were forced to migrate to the towns and cities in search of employment. In 1830, 80 percent of German workers were employed in the agricultural sector; this declined to 20 percent by 1895 (Mann 1968, p. 201).

14. Opinions varied among different sectors of the business community. Those representing heavy industry strongly supported enactment of social insurance legislation, while many in smaller industries opposed the idea (Ullmann 1981, p. 143).

15. From the fourteenth century on guild members made contributions to the guild that were used to pay for hospitals and funerals as well as for food and lodging for elderly guild members (Zöllner 1982, p. 20). These early benefit schemes for miners made no provision for old-age pensions. It seems that the low life expectancy was the major reason for this (Tampke 1981, p. 72).

16. This was a contributory scheme between 1825 and 1868; thereafter, contributions by those covered were not required.

17. One reason the unions opposed this legislation is that they correctly viewed it as an effort to pacify the proletariat. Another is that they viewed it as an effort to reduce the pressure for across the board wage increases for all workers by targeting special benefits to those most in need (Baldwin 1990a, p. 2).

18. Bismarck's fears concerning the growing influence of the socialists within Germany were to some extent influenced by happenings outside the country; events such as

the Paris Commune of 1871 made him sensitive to the revolutionary potential of the socialist movement (Kohli 1987, p. 132).

19. Humanitarian concerns did play a part, but Bismarck's opposition to proposals calling for a shorter work day, increased wages, and improved working conditions suggests that the main motive behind his legislation was to control labor (Hertz 1975, p. 360).

20. Another compromise he made with the Liberals was the agreement to decentralize the administration of the pension scheme. The Liberals did not want a highly centralized scheme as it would further strengthen Bismarck and the kaiser (Katzenstein 1987, p. 181).

21. Bismarck had wanted a flat-rate benefit scheme (Esping-Andersen et al. 1988, p. 341).

22. The program excluded most white-collar workers and all of the self-employed, including independent farmers.

23. The total tax on employers and employees came to 1.7 percent on earnings up to 40 marks per week (Kaim-Caudle 1973, p. 138).

24. In 1891 the average pension came to approximately 18 percent of the average worker's wage (Zöllner 1982, p. 31).

25. By 1901 salaried employees had formed an organization to press for similar social insurance coverage for white-collar workers, most of whom were excluded from the original pension legislation (Alber 1988, p. 6).

26. By 1912 the Social Democrats had become the largest faction in the Reichstag (Alber 1988, p. 7), but they were kept out of power by a coalition of bourgeois parties.

27. Germany was the first country to add survivor's benefits (Flora and Alber 1981, p. 53).

28. An exception to this generalization was the decision in 1916 to reduce the pension eligibility age for blue-collar workers from 70 to 65 (Zöllner 1982, p. 42). This meant blue-collar workers would be eligible at the same age white-collar workers had been eligible since 1911. This decision has been interpreted as an effort to keep the workers behind the war effort.

29. However, during the last years of the Weimar Republic the balance between contributions and monies being paid out as pensions was severely disrupted by the Great Depression which started in 1929. The government response was to reduce the size of the benefits, but even with these reductions pensioners were better off than they had been, due to the severe deflation and the related drop in the cost of living (Kohli 1987, p. 134).

30. Germany was one of the first European nations to extend coverage to the self-employed (Baldwin 1990b, p. 268).

31. The German Labor Front was not limited to blue-collar workers; it also included white-collar workers and managers.

32. In 1981 there were 9.5 million union members in West Germany and of these 83 percent were members of the 17 industrial unions of the DGB federation. In the mid-1980s the DGB (formed in 1949) represented approximately one-third of all West German workers (Markovitz 1986, p. 12). There is a separate union for white-collar employees and yet another for civil servants.

33. The term *co-determination* is also sometimes used to refer to the participation of workers on the works councils of individual factories.

34. These works councils are not just organized at the factory level. In the case of conglomerates they are often organized at several levels from individual factories all the way up to the conglomerate level. The roots of these works councils can be traced back to the nineteenth century; many factories had similar organizations at the turn of the century (Katzenstein 1987, pp. 125–129).

35. The works councils have considerable influence on the shop floor, but they cannot be used to organize workers or to act as political advocates on behalf of workers (Markovitz 1986, p. 419).

36. If we include white-collar unions and the DBB (the German Civil Servants' Federation), we can get an estimate of the percent unionized of close to 40 percent of the labor force; this higher figure is somewhat misleading, however, because unions outside of the DGB have very little influence. The DBB, for example, is more a lobbying organization than a union in the traditional sense.

37. Pension benefits were increased by approximately 60 percent (Hockerts 1981, p. 328).

38. Some scholars offer a corporatist interpretation of this aspect of the legislation arguing that the goal was to assure that pre-retirement status differences were again clearly reflected in the structure of pension benefits (Esping-Andersen 1990, p. 25). But others point out that this legislation ended the privileged position of white-collar employees. After 1957 pension entitlements under the blue-collar and white-collar schemes were equalized (Alber 1988, p. 23).

39. This meant that in the computation of the worker's average lifetime wage used to compute the pension benefit, prior wages are adjusted for changes in wage levels. This turns out to be a much more favorable adjustment than one based on changes in price levels (inflation).

40. This early retirement provision seems to have been in part a response to the recession of 1967 and its impact on unemployment rates among the elderly (Kohli and Rein 1991, pp. 11–12).

41. At age 65 men and at age 60 women could retire with only 15 years of coverage. An important change was also made with respect to the calculation of the number of years of coverage. Workers were credited not only for years in the paid labor force, but also for substitute periods of unemployment, military service, and the like (Esping-Andersen et al. 1988, p. 337).

42. The 1989 legislation calls for the termination of this practice.

43. Coverage for farmers was added in 1957 and all as yet uncovered salaried workers were added in 1967.

44. In 1985 the amount spent in Germany was at about the same level as in Sweden (11.2 percent), but greater than in the United Kingdom (6.7 percent) or the United States (7.2 percent) (OECD 1988a, pp. 140–141).

45. However, for those who retire early a retirement test has been introduced. Benefits are reduced for those who work more than 75 days per year or earn more than 30 percent of the earnings ceiling used for contributions purposes (Eska 1980, pp. 111–112). In the other direction a substantial incentive has been added to encourage workers to delay retirement. Persons who delay to age 66 or 67 are given a 7.2 percent per year increase in the size of the eventual pension payment (Tomasson 1984, pp. 221–227). It is of note that even with this substantial incentive less than 1 percent of eligible workers choose to delay the receipt of pension benefits (Tracy 1979, p. 42).

46. Unless specified otherwise, the sources for the information describing the West German old-age pension program as of the late 1980s are: Federal Minister of Labor and Social Affairs (1989), International Benefits Information Service (1989a), and *International Benefit Guidelines* (1989).

47. The 1989 legislation calls for extending this to three years per child.

48. For the purposes of computing the size of the pension it is assumed that the parent who leaves (or remains out of) the labor force for the year following the birth of a child

earned 75 percent of the average worker's wage (Federal Minister of Labour and Social Affairs 1989, p. 55).

49. Also of note is the policy of government contributions to the pension system to compensate for the contributions not made during these substitute periods.

50. Unless specified otherwise, the information on the 1989 reforms is drawn from Federal Minister of Labour and Social Affairs (1990).

51. The reason is that the higher tax burden associated with increases in spending on social welfare programs has over the years eroded the proportion of the German worker's gross wages left after taxes (net income). This has put pensioners at an advantage as their pensions have been incremented on the basis of changes in gross income rather than changes in net income.

52. Several trends are viewed as contributing to the impending increase in the pension burden. One is the increase in the number of years workers spend getting educated or trained for their jobs. Another is the trend toward early retirement. A third is the trend toward lower fertility. These are all in addition to the trend toward an increase in life expectancy (Federal Minister of Labour and Social Affairs 1990, p. 4).

53. The projections are less dramatic for the total number of persons age 65 and over per 100 persons age 20 to 64. The projected increase is from 23 in 1985 to 40 in 2025 (U.S. Bureau of the Census 1987, p. 62).

54. The figure was about the same in Britain (4.7 percent) and the United States (4.1 percent), but it was substantially higher in France (8.2 percent) and Sweden (8.4 percent) (Laslett 1985, p. 217).

55. Kerr et al. (1964, p. 37) does, however, point out that during the early stages of industrialization different nations have different types of industrial elites that must be taken into consideration. They point out that the traditional (dynastic) elite in countries such as Germany tend to be more paternalistic than in countries such as Britain where the elite is dominated by liberal (laissez-faire) values. It would be consistent with Kerr et al. to attribute the earlier introduction of pensions in Germany to the differences between the two countries with respect to the values of the industrializing elites.

56. Between 1950 and 1987 the real compound annual growth in GNP per capita for West Germany was 4.0 percent. This can be contrasted with 2.6 percent for Sweden, 2.2 percent for Britain, and 1.9 percent for the United States.

57. The decline was from 53 to 38 percent when both male and female workers are considered together (OECD 1988a, p. 144).

58. In fairness to proponents of this perspective, it should be noted that it was formulated to account for developments during the postwar years. It was never intended for use in accounting for the original decision to introduce social insurance programs. However, attempts to apply the perspective to developments during this earlier era point to a more general limitation of the perspective. It does not offer an adequate account for how organized labor and social democratic parties influence social welfare policy when they represent small parliamentary minorities (Steinmetz 1988, p. 4).

59. Alber (1983, p. 167) presents evidence that overall social security spending (a broader measure than pension spending alone) increased at a more rapid rate when a coalition led by the Social Democrats was in power than when a coalition led by the Christian Democrats was in power. Given that pension spending is a substantial fraction of overall social security spending, it is likely that the trend was similar for pensions as well.

60. For the industrial nations the spending levels ranged from 5.3 percent (Japan) to 15.6 percent (Italy). For the United States the figure was 7.2 percent; for United Kingdom, 6.7 percent; and for Sweden, 11.2 percent (OECD 1988a, p. 11). How do the results change if spending on private occupational pensions is taken into consideration as well? In the

years ahead spending on private occupational pensions will become increasingly important, but as of 1980 the inclusion of data on occupational pensions does not change the rank ordering among the four industrial nations we are focusing on or in any other way alter our basic conclusions. To these estimates we would add approximately .5 percent for Germany, .5 percent for Sweden, 1.0 percent for the United Kingdom, and 1.4 percent for the United States (Esping-Andersen 1990, p. 84). Also see Rein and Rainwater (1986).

61. Esping-Andersen's (1990, pp. 49–50) index is based on the following indicators: (1) the ratio of the minimum pension to the net (after tax) earnings of the average worker, (2) the ratio of the standard pension to the net earnings for a single person, (3) the number of years a worker must contribute to the system to be eligible for a pension, and (4) the proportion of the spending on public pensions financed by contributions from individuals, as opposed to the government or employers. Each of these four components is then weighted by the proportion of the population of pension age actually receiving a pension.

62. It is of note, however, that Esping-Andersen's measure does not consider many structural aspects of pensions, and Germany has made a number of important structural changes since the data Myles used were collected. These changes have, for example, gone a long way toward improving the adequacy with which the special needs of women are taken into consideration.

63. However, there are some neo-Marxists such as Offe (1984, p. 153) who argue that today capitalism cannot exist without the welfare state. O'Connor (1973) and others make a similar point. It is not the existence of the welfare state that is difficult to account for, rather it is the rapid and sustained expansion of the welfare state that is difficult to account for from this perspective.

64. Some scholars, such as German sociologist Karl Hinrichs (personal communication 1991), argue that if we focus on policy-specific democratic corporatism, Germany would rank among the most corporatist nations with respect to pension policy. This may be a factor contributing to Germany's high level of pension spending.

65. We have reservations about Esping-Andersen's (1990) decision to define corporatism in a way that is much closer to authoritarian corporatism than to the democratic corporatism that most scholars consider more relevant to the postwar industrial nations (Schmitter 1974; Williamson 1989).

66. By the nineteenth century Prussian citizens had a great deal of respect for the expert knowledge of civil servants (Ramm 1967, p. 10).

67. While these high level civil servants typically had Junker backgrounds, many saw themselves as representatives of social progress with an obligation to look after the needs of German workers (Zöllner 1982, p. 23). They had also come to accept an ideology in support of industrialism and modernization (Steinmetz 1990, p. 269).

68. By 1913 there were over one million people employed in the civil service (Kosok 1933, p. 106). One reason the civil service bureaucracy became so influential was the nation's late democratization. Another was that the rise of the bureaucracy preceded industrialization and the rise of the bourgeoisie (Schmidt 1989, p. 57).

Chapter 3

1. More successful were the old-age pensions for British civil servants introduced in 1834 (Esping-Andersen 1990, p. 89).

2. Between 1885 and 1914 about 60 percent of adults males were eligible to vote. While this meant many working-class males were still excluded, the number who could vote was much greater than it had been prior to 1885 (Pelling 1968, p. 5).

3. Estimates range from about 25 percent to almost 50 percent of workers (Gosden 1961; Gilbert 1966, p. 166; Hobsbawm 1984, p. 218). The estimates in the 50 percent range include many who were only covered for burial expenses. Estimates in the 25 to 33 percent range refer to those covered for sickness benefits (Johnson 1985, pp. 55–57).

4. The decrease in participation by younger workers can be attributed to a number of factors. The close ties that had characterized the friendly societies were breaking down. An increasing proportion of workers were turning to their unions for the affiliative needs that the friendly societies had previously been meeting. For insurance needs, workers were increasingly turning to private insurance companies.

5. The attitudes of some friendly societies began to change in the 1890s (Treble 1970, pp. 280–288).

6. Blackley originally presented his pension proposal in 1878 (Ashford 1986, p. 178).

7. 20 shillings = £1.

8. The results of this study were reported in a series of 17 volumes, the first of which was published in 1891.

9. In the same year Joseph Chamberlain also presented an old-age pension proposal. His called for a contributory scheme (Collins 1965, pp. 254–255). Chamberlain's proposal did not get as much attention at the time, but may have been a factor in the decision of his son, Neville Chamberlain, to introduce Britain's first contributory scheme in 1925 (Ashford 1986, pp. 178–79).

10. For an excellent review of Booth's work in this connection, see Simey and Simey (1960). His proposal was, however, noticed at the time by a number of leftist leaders (Ashford 1986, p. 178).

11. Some socialist groups were, however, included in the Labour Party.

12. Some scholars argue that British trade unionism can be traced back to the late seventeenth century (Webb and Webb 1920, p. 1). If we drop the criterion of the existence of a continuous existing formal organization, union activity can be traced backed to the early part of the seventeenth century (Brown 1982, pp. 28–29); however, most of the 386 industrial disputes recorded between 1715 and 1800 did not involve continuously existing formal organizations.

13. The Combination Acts of 1799 and 1800.

14. For example, Hunt (1981, p. 193) estimates that 20 percent of the labor force were union members in 1834 in contrast to about 2 percent in 1842.

15. However, the largest and most powerful working-class interest group in Britain at the turn of the century was the friendly societies with well over five million members, not the labor unions with just over one million members (Thane 1984, p. 878).

16. The term *labor aristocracy* is sometimes credited to contemporary scholars, but as Hobsbawm (1964, p. 272) and others (e.g., Gray 1981, p. 64) point out, the term was used extensively during the second half of the nineteenth century.

17. Victorian social commentators described such workers as members of the "respectable" as opposed to "rough" classes (Hobsbawm 1984, p. 219).

18. Chartism refers to a working-class movement that was most active during a 10 year period from the late 1830s to the late 1840s, but it did continue in a moribund form until the late 1850s. The Chartists called for a variety of political reforms such as universal suffrage and the secret ballot. In some areas Chartist candidates were elected to office in local elections (Brown 1982, p. 115). In 1840 there were about 300 Chartist associations in Britain. On occasion they were able to get several thousand people together to protest.

19. The British working class was enfranchised in two stages, first by the Second Reform Act of 1867 and subsequently by the Reform Bill of 1884.

20. This organization was also called the National Committee of Organized Labour for the Promotion of Old Age Pensions for All (NCOL).

21. Pelling (1968, p. 11) mentions a number of other factors that may have influenced the Liberal government's decision. One was the monies available because of the lull in shipbuilding due in part to the destruction of a number of Russian battleships in the Russo-Japanese War. Another was two new cabinet members with an interest in the idea of public pensions, Lloyd George and Winston Churchill. Pelling takes issue with those who argue that enactment of pension legislation was in large measure influenced by the Liberal Party's search for working-class votes.

22. Hay (1975, p. 46) disputes the importance of the 1907 by-elections. He argues that Asquith's cabinet had accepted the idea of a noncontributory pension scheme prior to these by-elections.

23. Some Conservatives did, however, attempt to defeat this legislation by making the proposal so generous that it would end up being unacceptable to Parliament (Read 1982, p. 170).

24. The means test was set at a level that made it possible for a substantial fraction of those over age 70 to qualify. In 1912 about 60 percent of those over age 70 were receiving old-age pensions. Due to longer life expectancy and lower incomes, the majority were women (Hannah 1986, p. 16).

25. The provisions calling for evidence of good moral character and calling for an income test seem to have been influenced by New Zealand's pension program (Ogus 1982, p. 178; Gilbert 1966, p. 215). Relatively few people were actually disqualified on the basis of bad moral character.

26. One reason the impact was modest is that the pensions were paid for out of tax revenues derived primarily from taxes on tea, cocoa, alcohol, and tobacco. These were in large measure consumed by (and thus the taxes were indirectly paid for by) those with low incomes. A relatively small fraction of tax revenues were derived from the death taxes and income taxes levied on the more affluent (Thane 1984, p. 879).

27. As Frederick Rogers, leader of the National Pension Committee, put it, "Well begun—half done!" (Thane 1984, p. 888).

28. The five shillings benefit was about equal to what those on poor relief received (Hannah 1986, p. 16).

29. In contrast, the German scheme varied pension benefits as a function of the worker's prior wages and contributions.

30. In the German scheme both employees and employers made contributions in addition to the modest government contribution.

31. Administration of the German scheme was decentralized.

32. Even with these adjustments, in 1920 old-age pensions had less purchasing power than in 1908 (Gilbert 1970, p. 239).

33. The Widows', Orphans', and Old Age Contributory Pension Act of 1925 was one of Neville Chamberlain's most important pieces of social legislation (Gilbert 1970, pp. 235–251). This legislation had the effect of increasing the number of workers eligible for pensions from a few hundred thousand to over 15 million. For the first time it extended coverage to large numbers of middle-class workers (Pratt forthcoming, chapter 4).

34. The original National Insurance Act (1911) established a compulsory national health insurance scheme and unemployment compensation scheme for workers in seven industries.

35. Female employees became eligible for the contributory pension at age 60.

36. Gilbert (1966, p. 451) points out that civil servants also played a significant role in connection with enactment of the original 1908 old-age pension legislation. Hay (1978,

p. 7), however, takes issue with those who emphasize the independent influence of the civil service on British welfare state development.

37 The formal name for the report is *Social Insurance and Allied Services* (Beveridge 1942).

38. This test was only applied to men aged 65 to 70 (women aged 60 to 65); above these limits there was no retirement test (Ogus 1982, p. 155). In 1956 the formula for reducing benefits was changed from 100 to 50 percent of wages above the specified limit. In 1989 the retirement test was phased out (International Benefits Information Service 1989b).

39. The organization's pressure group activities also included appearances on radio and television and petition drives (Pratt forthcoming, chapter 5).

40. See chapter 5 of Pratt's (forthcoming) book for an excellent discussion of the pressure group activities by the National Federation during this period. He makes a strong case that in the postwar era up through 1975, the National Federation was among the most important actors with respect to pension policy, particularly in connection with the periodic increases in the size of the basic pension.

41. TUC remained committed to the flat-rate approach up until 1957 (Parry 1988, p. 172). During much of the 1950s the Labour Party and TUC could not agree on how to raise the monies needed to improve pension benefits (Baldwin 1990b, p. 233).

42. A useful measure of labor strength is the extent of union centralization. When the labor movement is made up of a small number of large unions and is highly unified at the national level, it is considered highly centralized. In contrast, when it is split into a large number of small unions that are unable to cooperate with one another, centralization is low. Myles (1984, p. 87) gives Britain a very low rating on centralization and gives Sweden a high rating. In addition, a much larger proportion of the work force is unionized in Sweden than in Britain; in 1970, 44 percent of the labor force in Britain was organized in contrast to 75 percent in Sweden (Stephens 1979, p. 115). Union membership peaked in Britain at about 54 percent in 1979, but decreased considerably during the 1980s; by 1985 it was already down to 43 percent.

43. Unless specified otherwise, the information in the section that follows describing the current old-age pension provisions in Britain is drawn from the following three sources all of which are highly recommended as sources for details about the current system: *International Benefit Guidelines* 1989; International Benefits Information Service 1989b; U.S. Social Security Administration 1990.

44. However, Labour had only a thin majority at the time (Dunleavy 1989, p. 257).

45. Highest paid.

46. Adjusted for increases in wage rates over time.

47. Recall that covered earnings include those in a range between the lower and the upper limit used for the purpose of determining contributions.

48. The best 20 years provision is particularly beneficial to women who are more likely to be out of the labor force for a prolonged period of time (Parry 1988, p. 172). In Britain, unlike the United States, all pension benefits are taxed as ordinary income.

49. Pratt (forthcoming, chapter 6) argues that the adoption of SERPS has contributed to "two nations of old age" in Britain. One is made up of the more affluent workers employed by large firms that have contracted out of SERPS and provide employees with occupational pension plans that are superior to SERPS. This group is represented by a variety of well financed interest groups. The second nation is made up of less affluent workers who are covered by SERPS, but no private occupational pension scheme. This group is represented by a variety of less well financed interest groups.

50. The occupational scheme is required to index the GNP for any increase in prices of up to 3 percent per year, the state pays for any inflation adjustment above this level (Wilson 1991, p. 205).

51. As another cost-containment measure between 1998 and 2008 a transition will also be made from the worker's best 20 years to average lifetime earnings (Wilson 1991, p. 204). As yet another, a provision of this legislation calls for reducing the size of the widow's pension due to her husband's SERPS account by 50 percent (O'Higgins 1989, p. 175; Morris 1988, p. 81).

52. See Rein and Rainwater (1986, pp. 50–58) for a second set of estimates that differ slightly from those provided by Esping-Andersen.

53. It is also payable to widows of any age if they have dependent children, and it is adjusted depending on the number of dependents.

54. The British pension system also includes a noncontributory old person's pension payable to those over age 80 who are not eligible for the standard old-age pension, provided they meet certain residence conditions. This pension is payable to those eligible for the standard old-age pension if that pension falls below a specified lower limit. The British pension system also includes an income-tested supplementary pension payable when pension benefits and income from other sources fall below a lower limit (U.S. Social Security Administration 1990, p. 271).

55. This continues an increase that started soon after enactment of the first old-age pension program in 1908. Pensions as a percent of GNP increased from .3 percent in 1910 and 1.5 percent in 1930. The 1985 figure for Britain was lower than that for the United States (7.2 percent), and substantially lower than that for Germany (11.8 percent) and Sweden (11.2 percent) (OECD 1988a, pp. 140–141).

56. The replacement rate for couples in Britain was 47 percent in contrast to 83 percent for Sweden (the top ranked nation), 66 percent for the United States (ranked 5th), and 49 percent for Germany (ranked 11th) (Aldrich 1982, Table 1).

57. The proportion of the population age 65 and over was about the same, just under 5 percent in both countries at the turn of the century (Laslett 1985, p. 217).

58. If we count friendly society membership as a measure of working-class strength in Britain, a case can be made that old-age pensions came later due in part to the influence of working-class opposition to state pensions; yet, this line of reasoning is not consistent with the way in which social democratic thesis is ordinarily used in accounting for welfare state development.

59. However, some Liberals and Conservatives did believe that social legislation was an effective antidote to socialism (Hay 1978, p. 10). While the fear of the socialist movement was less pervasive in Britain than in Germany, many were concerned about the growing influence of unions and the Labour Party.

60. In 1908 there were only 2.5 million union members in Britain (Lloyd 1970, Table 5). In the 1910 general (national) elections (there were two) the Labour Party received less than 10 percent of the vote both times (Lloyd 1970, p. 19).

61. This was no accident. Beveridge himself argued that the state should only provide the minimum pension necessary for basic necessities. His acceptance of nineteenth century liberalism is reflected in the assumption that it is most appropriate to leave it up to workers to provide for themselves for eventual pension benefits above this floor (Baldwin 1990b, p. 122).

62. A case can be made that the shift actually began in 1976 under the prior Labour government (Goodin and Le Grand 1987, p. 149).

63. Between 1950 and 1987 the real compound annual growth rate in GDP per capita

was 2.2 percent. Between 1950 and 1986 the proportion of the population age 65 and over increased from 10.7 to 15.3 percent (OECD 1988a, p. 33; 1988b, p. 11).

64. Between 1951 and 1985 the rate decreased from 31 to 8 percent (OECD 1988c, p. 57; Judge 1981, p. 514). There was a similar trend in Germany, Sweden, and the United States. During the postwar period there was not only a sharp increase in the number of pensioners, but also in the proportion of the elderly who were pensioners. One reason for the decrease in the labor force participation rate was the increase in the magnitude of pensions, particularly the increase relative to the wage of the average worker (Parry 1988, pp. 184–189).

65. Hannah (1986, p. 15) argues that the Liberal Party's support for pensions was influenced by the labor movement's shift from opposition to support for public pensions.

66. While there were socialists within the Labour Party, it was not feared in the same way that the Social Democratic Party was feared by the German elite during the 1880s.

67. Baldwin (1990b, p. 246) argues that while civil servants did play a major role in much of the postwar pension legislation, their decisions were strongly influenced by political and social factors.

68. The evidence suggests that the balance of power has, except in times of crisis, favored the various interest groups within these associations rather than the peak associations themselves (Dunleavy 1989, p. 264).

69. Not all of the evidence from the turn of the century era is consistent with the pluralist perspective. As a result of legislation passed in 1884 many working-class males who were previously excluded from voting became franchised. We might have expected them to push for various social welfare programs such as old-age pensions; however, the evidence suggests that this legislation had little if any impact on the pension movement or the timing of the eventual introduction of pensions (Thane 1984).

70. There are some scholars who would disagree with our interpretation here. They argue that the NFOAPA had little impact on postwar developments (Judge 1981, p. 518; Heclo 1974, p. 260). Their interpretation is that the NFOAPA may have influenced the timing of the pension increases particularly during the 1950s and 1960s, but not the long-run rate of increase.

71. One reason the Thatcher government had such difficulty cutting back on old-age pensions is that a large segment of the middle class benefits from these programs (Goodin and Le Grand 1987, p. 152).

72. The old-age lobby was even able to manage one modest gain during the 1980s, the elimination of the retirement test in 1989 (International Benefits Information Service 1989b).

Chapter 4

1. For Sweden the Middle Ages started with the adoption of Christianity in the twelfth century and ended early in the sixteenth century when Gustav Vasa drove the Danes out and founded the modern state of Sweden. Gustav Vasa is considered the first modern Swedish king (Board 1970, p. 23). At the time Sweden included territory that is now part of Finland. In defeating the Danes Gustav Vasa was able to take control over the territory that is now southern Sweden, territory that had long been under the control of Denmark. During the seventeenth century, Sweden's "Age of Greatness," the nation's territory expanded to include parts of what today are Norway, Germany, and the Soviet Union. During this period it was the major Baltic power (Wallerstein 1980, pp. 211–218). However, Sweden did not have the resources to hold its own over the long run against its Baltic rivals, Prussia

and Russia (Alestalo and Kuhnle 1987, p. 6). It was reduced to its present boundaries by 1809, although it did remain in a loose federation with Norway until 1905.

2. In the fifteenth century the peasants owned about half of the land and the nobility owned about one-tenth (Tilton 1974, p. 563).

3. Gustav Vasa did not hesitate to periodically side with the peasantry in his effort to exercise control over the nobility (Heclo and Madsen 1987, p. 9).

4. Some scholars do, however, argue that the power of the nobility declined sharply during the eighteenth and nineteenth century due in part to the rise in influence of the peasantry. When expedient, the Crown (e.g., Gustavus III) was known to side with the peasantry in an effort to weaken the influence of the nobility (Esping-Andersen 1985, p. 48; Tilton 1974, p. 566).

5. This was also the case in Switzerland and a few small Germanic states (part of the Holy Roman Empire at the time) bordering Switzerland (Metcalf 1987, p. 65).

6. Property and income requirements were dropped for the Lower Chamber by 1909 and by the Upper Chamber in 1918. The 1909 legislation introduced universal male tax-payer suffrage for Lower Chamber elections. Women who were large property owners could vote in elections for the Upper Chamber, but in the popular elections for the Lower Chamber women were excluded until 1921 (Board 1970, p. 31).

7. Gustav Vasa also confiscated all of the vast lands held by the Catholic church and established in its place a Lutheran state church (Tomasson 1970, p. 18). This removed a competing source of national power and greatly added to the wealth of the Crown. Prior to the sixteenth century the Catholic church had played an important role in providing for the elderly poor, the sick, and other needy groups. The Lutheran church that replaced the Catholic church did not have significant wealth and was not in a position to offer substantial support for the elderly poor or other needy groups (Wilson 1979, p. 1).

8. In the first election after the formation of the bicameral Riksdag in 1866, 40 percent of those elected to the Upper Chamber were senior level civil servants.

9. But some historians argue that the Swedish industrial revolution was not in full swing until the 1890s (Anton 1980, p. 2; Lewin et al. 1972, p. 41).

10. During the nineteenth century as a whole Sweden did not develop as rapidly as did Britain, Germany, or the United States, but by the end of the century its rate of economic growth did compare very favorably with these other countries (Scott 1977, p. 378). Between 1871 and 1890 the average annual percentage growth in domestic product was 1.1 percent, but between then and 1910 it was close to 2.4 percent (Korpi 1982, p. 194; Krantz and Nilsson 1975).

11. The figure for Britain was 9 percent (Scase 1977, p. 18).

12. Due to the location of much of Swedish industry in rural areas, the transition from peasant to proletarian was more gradual than in Germany. The cities did not become as overwhelmed with destitute peasants (Esping-Andersen 1980, p. 95).

13. The first organizations of workers would more accurately be described as friendly societies than labor unions in the modern sense. The official goal of the oldest of these new organizations, the Union of Typographers, founded in 1846, was to inculcate "useful-ness and piety" in its members, not to organize workers to push employers for higher wages or better working conditions (Hughes 1970, p. 56). It has been described as a club that provided educational facilities to members (Scase 1977, p. 26). One of the first successful strikes on record was organized by the Journeymen Bakers' Union of Stockholm in 1873.

14. The first modern union was a union of tobacco workers in Malmo formed in 1874. The first national trade union was the Postmen's Union founded in 1886 (Hughes 1970, p. 57). The first Swedish unions tended to be craft unions. In 1912 LO decided to focus on industrial unionism, a decision that led to the dominance of industrial unions and industry-

wide bargaining (Stephens 1979, p. 130). By 1908, 46 percent of LO members were organized into industrial unions as opposed to 26 percent in craft unions (Korpi 1978, p. 64).

15. Due in part to Germany's success in the Franco-Prussian War of 1870–1871, Sweden became in many respects a cultural satellite of Germany between 1872 and 1910. During this period what happened in Sweden often reflected what had happened in Germany a few years earlier (Tomasson 1970, p. 4).

16. Today almost all private companies of any size including multinationals are members of SAF.

17. Today Sweden has six major parties. They are traditionally grouped as the two socialist parties (Social Democratic Party and the Communist Party), the three bourgeois parties (Liberal Party, Conservative Party, and the Center Party), and the Green Party. In 1957 the Agrarian Party was renamed the Center Party.

18. Another source of protection prior to the introduction of public pensions was the benefits for the aged and the sick ironworkers provided by some paternalistic employers as early as the eighteenth century (Scott 1977, p. 450).

19. During the 1880s German social insurance developments were closely followed in Sweden (Montgomery 1939, p. 214).

20. Another similar proposal was prepared by a third commission meeting between 1895 and 1898. While this proposal made it through the Lower Chamber, it ended by being turned down by the Conservative-dominated Upper Chamber. It too would have limited benefits to wage earners.

21. It was not the first national social insurance scheme for Sweden. Sickness insurance had been enacted in 1891 and workers' compensation in 1901.

22. This "remiss" process of extensive consultation with opposition parties and all relevant interest groups has characterized Swedish pension policy throughout the twentieth century (Woodsworth 1977, p. 23).

23. The British Charity Organization Society made similar arguments for similar reasons in connection with the 1908 Old Age Pension Act (Ashford 1986, p. 178).

24. The early German social insurance legislation did get Swedish civil servants and social reformers thinking about the need for similar legislation, but it would not be accurate to argue that the 1913 pension legislation in Sweden was an example of diffusion from Germany (Olsson 1988, p. 7; Kuhnle 1978, p. 26).

25. Some argue that it represented primarily the handiwork of the Liberal Party (Heclo and Madsen 1987, pp. 155–156).

26. In 1870 only 9 percent of the Swedish population was engaged in manufacturing and crafts as opposed to 43 percent in Britain (Scase 1977, p. 18).

27. For the first three decades of the public pension debate the various Royal Workers' Insurance Commissions were dominated by technocratic insurance experts, many of whom were civil servants (Olsson 1990, pp. 85–86). During the late nineteenth century civil servants had a great deal of influence on social policy. One reflection of this influence is the evidence that most cabinet members during this period had been high level civil servants (Therborn 1989, p. 197).

28. The farmers insisted on being covered and they insisted that there be no employer contributions due to the burden such a financing mechanism would put on small farmers (Baldwin 1989, p. 16).

29. The average benefit from the contributory pension in 1930 was approximately $7 per month (Schulz et al. 1974, p. 74).

30. As a result the means-tested supplement was for all practical purposes transformed into a supplementary pension for all low-income workers (Olsson 1988, p. 81).

31. It gave the Social Democrats their first majority in the Lower Chamber.

32. While Sweden was neutral during World War II, the war did have a major impact on social and economic policy. It was not considered politically or economically feasible to undertake any major pension policy reforms while the war was in progress.

33. Today the *folkpension* is alternatively referred to as the universal pension, the basic pension, or as the first tier of the pension system.

34. The benefit for a married couple was 160 percent of that for a single person.

35. Originally the *folkpension* was financed out of general tax revenues and an "earmarked" amount added to the personal income tax. During the 1950s and 1960s this earmarked contribution increased. It was close to being an employee contribution, but it was paid by all taxpayers. In the mid-1970s an employers' contribution was added and soon became the major source of funds with contributions from the other sources falling dramatically (Olsson 1990, p. 145).

36. Another factor contributing to the shift was the split in the Social Democratic leadership. Gustav Möller, for many years the number two person in the Social Democratic hierarchy, lost his battle for party leadership in 1946 after a bitter struggle (Rothstein 1985, p. 152).

37. At first organized labor like the Social Democratic leadership had been reluctant to do away with means-testing (Baldwin 1990b, p. 140). But before long LO came under pressure from pensioners in the trade union movement who favored elimination of means-testing (Olsson 1990, p. 105).

38. But it is also of note that Möller, who was the Social Democratic minister of social affairs (1924–1926, 1932–1951) and one of the major architects of the Swedish welfare state, had long been a strong advocate of universalism (Rothstein 1985, p. 157). There was more continuity in the Social Democratic commitment to universalism than Baldwin's (1988) analysis suggests.

39. The consensus that emerged during the war years in Sweden made it easier to continue the increased state intervention and the higher taxes that had been introduced in response to the war (Baldwin 1988, p. 124).

40. In addition, even blue-collar workers were becoming more affluent and taking on the attitudes and aspirations of white-collar workers (Baldwin 1990b, p. 139).

41. By the mid-1940s means-testing only excluded the most affluent; it was no longer a mechanism for limiting benefits to the poor. Thus most of the middle class would have benefited independent of the decision to phase out means-testing for many program. It was not just the Conservatives, but also the Agrarian Party that backed the universalistic approach from the outset and it may even have been a commission member representing the Agrarian Party who proposed the idea in the first place (Olsson 1990, pp. 102–104).

42. Some scholars take issue with us here. They argue that pensioners were active in connection with the 1946 legislation, but not influential (Heclo 1974, pp. 228–229); however, the bulk of the recent evidence as we interpret it supports the conclusion that they were influential actors (Wilson 1979, p. 9; Olsson 1990, p. 104).

43. Pensioners' organizations were also influential advocates on behalf of indexing (Wilson 1979, p. 10).

44. Prior to 1982 adjustments were made after each 3 percent increase in the monthly consumer price index, and thus several adjustments per year were sometimes called for. After 1982 adjustments were made annually.

45. During the 1950s even the Conservative Party was very supportive of legislation calling for increases in the *folkpension*. One reason was the hope that such increases would undercut the support for introducing a compulsory earnings-related pension (Coughlin and Tomasson 1991, p. 150).

46. These salaried workers argued that their pension benefits had been bought at the

price of lower wage increases. They would be penalized by the scheme the government was at the time considering because it did not take this into consideration (Baldwin 1990b, p. 216).

47. It began to pay its first pensions in 1963, but it was not until 1980 that it was possible to obtain full pension benefits at the regular retirement age of 65 (Coughlin and Tomasson 1991, p. 151).

48. For example, the pension benefit was based on the worker's 15 best years of adjusted earnings as opposed to the worker's entire work history. This provision favored white-collar workers who spend more time than blue-collar workers in school prior to entering the labor force. A similar concession was to require 30 rather than 40 years of coverage to become eligible for full pension benefits. As another concession white-collar workers already covered by occupational schemes were given permission to contract out of the government program, an option that no union exercised due to the favorable terms of the final legislation (Baldwin 1990b, p. 221). Yet another concession was a structure that involved no deliberate redistribution of monies from more to less affluent pensioners.

49. After 30 years the ATP provides a pension equal to 60 percent of the worker's average income. In these computations earnings are adjusted for changes in price levels. When we take into consideration basic pensions and occupational pensions as well, the figure for 1985 was closer to 75 percent of average net earnings.

50. The introduction of the ATP resulted in a new source of inequality among pensioners, between those who were eligible for a substantial ATP and those who were eligible for few if any ATP benefits. This included those who had already retired, those with irregular employment records, and those in certain low-wage industries. In response to this issue in 1969 a pension supplement was introduced. This pension is only available for those who are eligible for little if any ATP benefits (Wilson 1979, p. 24).

51. In 1976 important reforms with respect to retirement age were enacted as well. The standard retirement age was reduced from 67 to 65. Another provision called for enhanced (.6 percent per month) pensions for those who delay the receipt of pensions beyond age 65 (up to age 70).

52. In 1987 under a Social Democratic government and in response to a 1982 campaign pledge, the replacement level was restored to 65 percent.

53. The average annual per capita rate of growth in old-age pensions was 4.4 percent in Sweden in contrast to 2.4 percent in the United States and Germany, and 2.3 percent in Britain. However, it was a lower rate than in some other countries starting from a much lower base—for example, Japan (6.6 percent) and Spain (6.8 percent) (OECD 1988a, p. 25).

54. The replacement rates for couples (the ratio of average old-age pension to average wage in manufacturing) in 1980 was 83 percent for Sweden. This was higher than in the United States (66 percent), Germany (49 percent), or Britain (47 percent). When comparisons were made on the basis of single workers, again Sweden ranked first among all industrial nations (OECD 1988a, p. 50).

55. In 1985 Sweden spent about the same share of its GDP on public pensions as did West Germany (11.8 percent), but it spent a much larger share of the GDP than did the United States (7.2 percent) or Britain (6.7 percent) (OECD 1988a, pp. 140–141).

56. The poverty rates (using the American standard) were much higher in Germany (15.4 percent), the United States (16.1 percent), and Britain (37.0 percent) (Smeeding 1990, p. 12).

57. Most workers in the private sector who are not union members are also covered

by third-tier schemes as many workers will refuse to work for an employer who does not provide this coverage (International Benefits Information Service 1986, p. 9).

58. Of the 9.7 percent of the GDP spent on public pensions in 1980, only .5 percent was due to private occupational pensions. This is the same as in Germany, but far below the 1.4 percent figure for the United States and the 1.0 percent figure for Britain (Esping-Andersen 1990, p. 84).

59. By the mid-1970s ATP assets made up 40 percent of Sweden's capital market (Heclo and Madsen 1987, p. 259).

60. The coalition was led by the Moderate Party, but also included the Liberal Party, the Center Party, and the Christian Democratic Party.

61. This control was due to support from the Agrarian Party for Social Democratic social policy in return for Social Democratic support for farm subsidies (Milner 1989, p. 58).

62. This agreement reinforced certain corporatist tendencies such as the use of centralized bargaining that can be traced back to 1905 (Scase 1977, p. 29).

63. Certain employers' organizations were highly critical when in the 1970s the government became involved in collective bargaining by inviting representatives of labor and capital to meetings a few months prior to the opening of collective bargaining. At these meetings the government would attempt to influence the subsequent bargaining by discussing the economic outlook and announcing the government's tax policy plans. Traditionally the state had been excluded from bargaining between LO and SAF (Lash 1985, p. 220).

64. The Metal Employers wanted to introduce greater wage differentials between high- and low-skilled workers. Employers were finding it difficult to attract high-skilled workers and to get the less skilled to make the effort to upgrade their skills when wage differentials were so small. The Metalworkers' Union was willing to go along with this increase because they feared the loss of highly skilled members to a white-collar union (Lash 1985, pp. 218–222).

65. Between 1870 and 1914 the value of goods manufactured in Sweden increased by a factor of 20 (Tilton 1974, p. 563).

66. The comparison with Germany is not as consistent with the industrialism perspective. In the 1980s Sweden had a higher GNP/capita than Germany, had a higher proportion over age 65, but spent a slightly smaller share of its GDP on old-age pensions (11.2 vs. 11.8 percent in 1985) (OECD 1988a, pp. 140–141; 1988b, p. 11; World Bank 1991, p. 205).

67. One illustration of this has been the shift away from direct contributions from employees to finance public pensions. With the exception of France, no other industrial nation shifts such a large share of the burden for financing public pensions to the employer (OECD 1988a, p. 88).

68. By the early 1980s about 80 percent of white-collar workers were union members as well (Olsson 1988, p. 77).

69. PRO was founded in 1941 and by the late 1980s it had more than 400,000 members (Milner 1989, pp. 76–77).

70. In 1981 SFRF had about 75,000 members (Olsson 1988, p. 80).

71. Some scholars would take issue with us here. They argue that organizations representing the interests of pensioners have had relatively little influence (Heclo 1974, pp. 228–229).

72. Some scholars, such as German sociologist Karl Hinrichs (personal communication 1991), argue that in the sphere of pension policy, corporatist decision-making structures play as important a role in Germany as they do in Sweden.

Chapter 5

1. The United States was not, as is often incorrectly stated, the last industrial nation to enact such legislation. Finland enacted its first public pension program in 1937, Japan in 1941, and Switzerland not until 1946.

2. The first proposal for an old-age pension system was made in 1797 by Thomas Paine ([1797]1945). The nation's first national military pension scheme was enacted even earlier, in 1776. It called for a pension of half-pay for life for soldiers disabled in the Revolutionary War to be paid by the states (Glasson 1918, pp. 20–23). Even more important were the pension laws of 1818 and 1820 that granted military pensions to all (now elderly) Revolutionary War veterans who were in dire economic straits (Achenbaum 1978, p. 84).

3. There was also a reluctance to apply on the part of even those southern veterans who were eligible for military pensions, given the controversy over the issue (Glasson 1902, p. 356; Quadagno 1988a, pp. 33–34).

4. They also estimate that in the northern states 56 percent of native-born white males over age 65 were pensioners in addition to an unspecified number of widows. Some estimates have been much higher with Rubinow (1913, pp. 406–407) and Tishler (1971, p. 89) estimating that two-thirds of native-born white men in the North were pensioners.

5. However, in 1890 U.S. federal expenditures made up only 2.4 percent of the GNP (Borcherding 1977, p. 22).

6. In 1900 approximately 30 percent of those age 65 and over were foreign born (Achenbaum 1978, p. 62).

7. Most southern states did, however, maintain state military pensions for Confederate veterans (Quadagno 1988b, p. 246).

8. In 1927 Epstein founded the American Association for Old Age Security, an influential pension reform group (Pratt 1976, p. 12).

9. The first national pension proposal introduced into Congress (1909) was that of Representative William Wilson (Orloff and Skocpol 1984, p. 729). Wilson had been a coal miner and a secretary of the United Mine Workers union. His bill proposed the creation of what he called the "Old Home Guard." Had the proposal been enacted (it was never reported out of committee), all Americans over age 65 would have been invited to "enlist" in the Old Home Guard if they met the bill's means test. Their duty would be to report once a year to the War Department about the level of patriotism in the local neighborhood. For this effort their "pay" would be $120 per year. The proposal sounds humorous today, but it did represent a serious effort to capitalize on the strong support at the time for generous military pensions. By this time the Civil War pensions had for all practical purposes become old-age pensions, but the American public believed there was a clear distinction between military pensions which were legitimate and honorable, and public old-age pensions which were condemned as "an unholy amalgam of sin and socialism" (Fischer 1978, pp. 170–171).

10. By 1935, 47 old-age pension bills had been introduced in Congress, but none were reported out of committee (Quadagno 1988a, p. 22).

11. Also see Edwards (1979) and Trachtenberg (1982).

12. In the early 1920s union membership peaked at 11 percent of the nonagricultural labor force (Brody 1980, p. 82). The corresponding figure was the same for Sweden, but it was much higher for Germany (30 percent) and Britain (43 percent) (Stephens 1979, p. 115).

13. In 1875 the American Express Company became the first private corporation to pay an employer-financed old-age pension (Achenbaum 1986, p. 200).

14. Prior to the 1920s very few were covered by corporate pensions; one estimate is that only 4 percent of workers were covered in 1915 (Achenbaum 1986, p. 15).

15. Between the early 1920s and 1930 the proportion of the American labor force unionized decreased from 11 to 7 percent (Stephens 1979, p. 115).

16. Quadagno (1988a, p. 71) argues that it began to change its opposition in 1924; Fischer (1978, p. 174) suggests 1930.

17. There were also important developments at this time at the federal level. Of particular note was the introduction of a civil service pension system in 1920 that covered several hundred thousand federal employees (Lubove 1968, p. 126). Also by this time most large cities had pension plans for firemen and policemen (Achenbaum 1986, p. 15).

18. As is the case with most fraternal orders the Eagles was a cross-class organization. It was largely made up of industrial workers, skilled workers, small businessmen, and politicians.

19. It was, however, not until 1929 that the national office of the AFL came out in support of state-level pensions (Pratt 1976, p. 22).

20. Typically industrial and business interests led the opposition to the Eagles sponsored pension proposals (Quadagno 1988a, p. 69). One reason for the opposition was the fear that old-age pensions would cut into a major source of low-wage labor. A second concern was that eventually these pensions would lead to increases in taxes on industry or income. There was also a fear that states without old-age pension programs would be able to price their goods at a lower level and thus have a competitive advantage.

21. A few of the original state pension plans were declared unconstitutional by state supreme courts (Pratt 1976, p. 16). In the early 1930s most old-age pensioners were concentrated in a very few states. Over 70 percent of those receiving state old-age pensions lived in three states: California, Massachusetts, and New York (Quadagno 1988a, p. 72). As of 1935 no southern state had enacted a state old-age pension system. A major reason was the desire to avoid undermining work incentives for low-wage workers, particularly blacks. The concern was not just that the elderly would be less willing to accept low-wage jobs, but that pension monies might also reduce work incentives for other members of an extended family supported in part by these benefits.

22. Not all state pension plans were voluntary, noncontributory, and financed entirely out of county revenues. Starting in 1929 most new schemes were compulsory, an increasing number were contributory, and most included contributions from state revenues.

23. While the Townsend movement became a national movement of the elderly pushing for old-age pensions, in the general population there was not a great deal of pressure for enactment of a national public pension scheme (Weaver 1982, pp. 94–96). Soon after the Social Security Act was passed, however, the Old Age Insurance (OAI) component became popular. By 1936, 68 percent of the population held favorable opinions toward OAI and this increased to 97 percent by 1943 (Tomasson 1984, p. 249; Coughlin 1980, pp. 57–58).

24. Townsend announced his plan in 1933 and the first Townsend club was founded in 1934 (Amenta and Zylan 1991, pp. 253–254). By early 1935 there were about 3,000 Towsend clubs and a total of 450,000 club members (U.S. Congress, Senate Committee on Finances 1935, p. 1047). In 1935 Towsend claimed to have petition signatures from 20 million people who supported his plan (U.S. Congress, House of Representatives Committee on Ways and Means 1935, p. 752).

25. This pension was to be paid for by a 2 percent tax on all business transactions (Amenta and Zylan 1991, p. 253).

26. In 1939, for example, the CIO called for a flat-grant old-age pension of $60 per month for everyone over age 60 to be paid for by taxes on income and wealth (Myles 1984, p. 38).

27. There is much disagreement among scholars as to how strong big business support for the OAI proposal was. Some argue that support was strong (Quadagno 1984). Others argue that big business was for the most part opposed (Berkowitz and McQuad 1980, pp. 90–92; Skocpol and Amenta 1985, p. 572). Yet others argue that big business was divided with support from a "corporate liberal" coalition representing primarily export-oriented industries and opposition from a conservative block representing labor intensive industries oriented toward the domestic market (Jenkins and Brents 1989, p. 893).

28. Ways were often found to pay whites higher OAA benefits than blacks; for example, by paying higher benefits to Civil War veterans and their widows (Quadagno 1988b, p. 246).

29. Epstein was consulted by the CES, but this was more a political gesture. Due to his radical views, he was intentionally not asked to be part of the CES despite being a very prominent member of the pension movement (Pratt 1976, p. 18; Schlabach 1969, p. 138).

30. Only Frank Hering of the Eagles was there. FDR's exclusion of representatives of labor and of the various senior movement groups can be contrasted with the large number of labor and senior movement activists present for the signing of the Medicare legislation and the Older Americans Act during the Johnson administration (Pratt 1976, pp. 18–19).

31. In 1950 only 21 percent of those age 65 and over were receiving OASI pension benefits (Schulz et al. 1974, p. 6).

32. Contributions (taxes) began in 1937. The worker paid 1 percent of his or her wage (on the first $3,000 of annual income) and the employer matched this amount. Between 1937 and 1949 the maximum Social Security tax on the worker was $30 per year (Crystal 1982, p. 6).

33. The insurance provisions are those that closely follow the actuarial principles used in private old-age insurance. The social welfare provisions are those aspects of a pension plan that attempt to make adjustments so as to increase the benefits for those with more need independent of what could be justified on the basis of differences in actual contributions.

34. At the outset Social Security was structured so as to create a substantial trust fund, but even then it was not to be a fully funded system. The original projection was that the trust fund would increase to the point that by 1980 some 40 percent of the annual benefits would be paid out of the interest on these reserves (Munnell 1988, p. 65). By 1939 the plan to build a large trust fund was abandoned in favor of a much smaller trust fund designed to deal with uneven cash flow problems related to the business cycle. The result was a shift to what was essentially a pay-as-you-go scheme. This alternative was acceptable because the taxing power of the federal government stood behind it (Schulz 1988, p. 124). Despite this policy shift, the absolute size of the trust fund did continue to increase until 1956 (Munnell 1988, p. 66).

35. From the outset there has been debate as to the appropriate balance between the principle of equity (as in private insurance) and the principle of adequacy, particularly the adequacy of benefits to low-income beneficiaries (Hohaus 1960, pp. 61–63).

36. Retirees with low incomes could expect a pension with about twice the replacement rate as could those earning the maximum wage for contribution purposes which was $3,000 in 1940 (Myers 1981, p. 262). While some observers have argued that the OAI program redistributes income from those with less to those with more income (Ozawa 1976, p. 216), a more widely held view is that it redistributes income across generations with very little impact on income distribution (Quadagno 1984, p. 634; Fischer 1978, p. 184).

37. Others feared that a large trust fund would encourage extravagant federal spending (Ball 1988a, p. 24).

38. Reflecting this change the name of the program was changed to Old Age and Survivors Insurance (OASI).

39. Such fears were not unreasonable. A federal pension program for workers in the railroad industry embodied in the Railroad Retirement Act of 1934 had recently been declared unconstitutional by the Supreme Court.

40. As an illustration of the shift in language, the Old-Age Reserve Account created in the 1935 legislation was renamed the Old-Age and Survivors Trust Fund in the 1939 legislation. What had been referred to as taxes were renamed insurance contributions in the 1939 legislation (Cates 1983, pp. 31–32).

41. During the 1936 election the Republicans were very critical of the Social Security Act and tried without success to use it against the Roosevelt administration. Conservative groups such as the NAM were highly critical of the payroll tax on employers (Achenbaum 1986, pp. 26–29).

42. While the CIO was pushing for corporate pension funds, the AFL continued to push for improvements in Social Security (Quadagno 1988a, p. 160).

43. A more general argument can also be made that labor's influence was limited by the structure of the American electoral system. Other factors that tended to undermine labor's influence during the postwar era were the cold war and related anticommunist purges within labor and the dramatic shift in the occupational structure with the growth of the largely unorganized white and pink-collar sectors (Stephens 1979, pp. 150–152).

44. However, it was undercut somewhat in 1966 when the powerful United Auto Workers (UAW) union under Walter Reuther's leadership withdrew from the AFL-CIO.

45. Today less than 7 percent of the elderly receive Supplemental Security Income (SSI) (replacement for Old Age Assistance) while more than 90 percent of the elderly are eligible for OASI pensions (Kingson et al. 1986, p. 86).

46. In the late 1940s the average Social Security pension was about $25 per month (Ball 1988, pp. 18–20).

47. At this point the official name for Social Security was changed to Old Age, Survivors, and Disability Insurance (OASDI) (Tomasson 1983, p. 699).

48. The name was changed again, to its current name, Old Age, Survivors, Disability, and Hospital Insurance (OASDHI). The OASDHI program is made up of three separate trust funds and for this reason the programs associated with each are sometimes referred to separately: OASI (Old Age and Survivors Insurance), DI (Disability Insurance), and HI (Hospital Insurance or Medicare). During the early 1980s approximately 83 percent of those receiving cash benefits from the OASDHI program were retired workers and their spouses or survivors. The rest were nonelderly disabled workers and their spouses (8 percent) or the children of deceased and disabled workers (9 percent) (Kingson et al. 1986, pp. 75–76).

49. Prior to 1972 periodic adjustments were made in Social Security benefit levels that compensated for the inflation that had taken place over the years, but until the late 1960s and early 1970s these adjustments did not compensate for increases in living standard for the general population (Schulz et al. 1974, pp. 8–9). The actual indexing of OASI pensions began in 1974. A cost-of-living adjustment (COLA) is made when the consumer price index (CPI) has increased by 3 percent or more during the previous year.

50. SSI also replaced two other public assistance programs, Aid to the Blind and Aid to the Permanently and Totally Disabled.

51. The marriage must have lasted at least 10 years. It is possible to collect this benefit even if the spouse on whose earnings record the benefit is based has not started to collect his or her Social Security pension, but that spouse must be age 62 or older (O'Grady-LeShane and Williamson 1992, p. 70).

52. As a result of Supreme Court decisions in 1975 and 1977 the United States became one of the most advanced nations in the world with respect to the elimination of gender differentiation in connection with eligibility for OASDHI benefits (Tomasson 1984, p. 252).

53. One reason is that there are fewer widowers than widows, but a more important factor is that men generally are entitled to better benefits based on their own employment histories.

54. The dually entitled worker receives his or her "own benefit" which is then supplemented so as to bring the total benefit up to the level of 50 percent of the spouse's benefit. Dually entitled workers did, however, in addition have disability and survivor's protection during their working years.

55. Among the factors contributing to this short-term financing problem were: (1) the sharp increase in the size of the OASI pension benefits contained in the 1972 amendments, (2) the faulty indexing procedure enacted in the same legislation, (3) the unanticipated increase in the number of workers awarded disability benefits, and most importantly, (4) the combined impact of several years (starting in 1973) of high inflation, high unemployment, and lower than expected increases in wage rates (Kingson 1984, pp. 134–135).

56. This legislation also called for periodic increases in the maximum amount of earnings subject to payroll taxation through 1981 and for automatic adjustments based on changes in wage levels thereafter (Kingson 1984, p. 136).

57. The long-term financing problem was due to anticipated increases in life expectancy, declining fertility, and the impending retirement of the baby boom generation.

58. With a few notable exceptions the call for generational equity has come primarily from conservative commentators; however, a few progressives such as Eric Kingson (1988, p. 772) argue that it is in the interest of the elderly to support increased spending on programs designed to improve the future productivity of today's children.

59. Some analysts argue that the anticipated dependency burden associated with the retirement of the baby boom generation is being blown all out of proportion. They point out that if we look at the total dependency ratio, a measure based on the ratio of all nonworking members of society (young and old) to the size of the labor force, the burden will be no greater than it was during the 1950s and 1960s when the baby boomers were children (Schulz et al. 1991, pp. 337–38).

60. Individuals can save for their own retirement and live off of the assets they have accumulated over the years, but it is not possible for an entire society to do so (Thompson 1990). The goods and services that the baby boom generation consumes during retirement will have to be produced at that time.

61. The $25,000 threshold is not just based on earned income, but on adjusted gross income which also takes into consideration asset income (Bernstein and Bernstein 1988, p. 54).

62. While OASI had to this point never been taxed, that was not the intent of the original legislation. Rather it was the outcome of rulings by the Bureau of the Internal Revenue (now the IRS) in 1939 and 1941. As a result of these rulings the benefits were designated as gratuities from the federal government and as such were not subject to federal taxation (Tomasson 1984, p. 250; Lawrence and Leeds 1978, p. 28).

63. Ordinarily the COLA is based on changes in prices.

64. However, the 1977 amendments included an "adjustment" in the benefit formula that resulted in benefit cuts for most future beneficiaries.

65. The monies generated by this tax on Social Security pension benefits are returned to the OASI trust fund.

66. The proportions would be higher were we to include those who had been working in "covered jobs" for less time than it takes to become fully insured. The major groups still excluded from coverage are: (1) federal employees hired prior to 1984, (2) some state and local government workers (as of 1984 approximately 70 percent were covered [Ball 1988, p. 20]), (3) some farm and domestic workers with very low yearly earnings, and (4) self-employed persons with very low incomes (Schulz 1988, p. 123). Also not included are those who make their living in various illicit activities and many illegal immigrants.

67. For a portion of these workers, maybe as much as 20 to 30 percent, the decision to retire is not a choice, as they find themselves out of work with little prospect of employment and no other income alternatives.

68. Legislation has been enacted that will gradually increase the size of this increment from 3 to 8 percent between 1990 and 2010 (Tomasson 1984, p. 252).

69. For single workers the replacement rate for the industrial nations ranged from 29 percent (Denmark) to 68 percent (Sweden) with the United States at 44 percent. For couples the range was from 47 percent (Britain) to 83 percent (Sweden) with the United States at 66 percent (Inkeles and Usui 1988, p. 285). Also see Aldrich (1982) and Myles (1988, p. 269).

70. Another reason is that in Britain, Germany, and Sweden there was no equivalent of the American GAR.

71. This line of reasoning is consistent with the "social learning" theory of policy formation that Heclo (1974, pp. 306–307) outlines.

72. Rimlinger (1971, p. 91), a scholar in the national values tradition, argues that it was the strength of a patriarchal paternalism and the weakness of liberal values that in large measure account for Germany's early introduction of social insurance programs.

73. Also see Weir et al. (1988, p. 12).

74. Coughlin (1980, pp. 57, 152) argues that old-age pension spending has escaped the general American hostility toward public spending, but the low spending levels as well as his own data pointing to greater support in the United States for reducing taxes and cutting services suggest it may not have entirely escaped this hostility.

75. In 1850 approximately 70 percent of manufactured goods were produced in small handicraft workshops. By 1890, 80 percent were produced in factories (L. Olson 1982, p. 29).

76. We take issue with the conclusion of Myles (1988, p. 283) that demographic pressure was not an important factor.

77. In support of this interpretation Esping-Andersen (1985, p. 245) accounts for the existence of a more well developed welfare state in Sweden than in Denmark in terms of the early influence of industrial unions in Sweden while the craft unions maintained much more influence in Denmark.

78. For a critique of Piven and Cloward's interpretation, see Achenbaum (1980).

79. Jenkins and Brents (1989, p. 898) would qualify this statement with the assertion that it was one sector of big business that had a major impact, the "corporate liberal" coalition. Others would go further and claim that this legislation was supported by only a few liberal-reformist businessmen and they did not in any sense represent the views of big business as a whole (Skocpol and Amenta 1985, p. 572).

80. Quadagno's (1984, pp. 645–646) neo-Marxist interpretation is that the Social Security Act of 1935 represented a compromise between monopoly and competitive sector capitalists, that is, between big business on the one hand and small business and southern agricultural interests on the other.

81. On the other hand, as noted earlier, this decision did contribute to a depoliticization of the Social Security program. It made the cost of living increase automatic and thus circumvented what had over the years become a source of competition between Democrats and Republicans to gain political advantage through support of ever higher benefit levels, particularly in election years.

Chapter 6

1. In 1989 the GNP per capita for Brazil was $2,540 in contrast to $340 for India and $250 for Nigeria (World Bank 1991, pp. 204–205). In 1900 Brazil and India had approximately the same per capita income (Gomes 1986, p. 32).

2. There was also a Senate made up of people directly appointed by the emperor.

3. During the empire income criteria were used to severely restrict suffrage; during the Old Republic literacy requirements were used to the same end (Love 1970, p. 7).

4. The aggregation of workers into large industrial enterprises was rare until the turn of the century (Baer 1965, pp. 13–15).

5. It has been referred to as an era of oligarchic democracy (Malloy 1976, p. 43). The Old Republic was, however, somewhat more democratic than the empire; for example, many more government positions were filled by elections, and the proportion of the population eligible to vote did increase (Love 1970, p. 7).

6. In the presidential election of 1894 some 2.2 percent voted; in 1906, 1.4 percent; and in 1930, 5.7 percent, the highest value during the Old Republic (Love 1970, p. 9).

7. Some of the economic growth during the Old Republic was linked to infrastructure activities designed to service the agricultural export sector or to provide urban services—for example, building railroads and electric power plants (Malloy 1979, p. 24). Also important was the growth of light industries designed to produce inexpensive consumer goods for local markets.

8. In 1900 only 2 percent of Brazilian workers were employed in manufacturing; this increased to 9 percent by 1920 (Ludwig 1985, p. 138).

9. The scale of this immigration put downward pressure on wages and in so doing resulted in ethnic conflicts within the working class (Malloy 1979, p. 32).

10. By 1930 over 1,000 "undesirables," mainly union organizers, had been deported (Topik 1987, p. 10).

11. In actual practice the government contributed only a fraction of what was called for and as a result built up a huge debt to the CAPs over the years (Malloy 1976, p. 50). The government contribution was financed by highly regressive indirect taxes on goods and services. Contributions from employers also tended to fall short of the amounts called for (Erickson and Middlebrook 1982, p. 241).

12. Vargas was forced to resign in 1945, but was subsequently elected president between 1950 and 1954. He had his greatest impact during the period of his dictatorship, and for this reason the 1930–1945 period is often identified as the Vargas era.

13. While working-class strike activity was on the decline during the 1920s due in part to the gradual emergence of corporatist mechanisms of social control, some strike activity, particularly from those not yet included in these structures, did continue.

14. Those backing Vargas looked much less favorably upon the liberal political institutions and laissez-faire economics of the Old Republic (Topik 1987, p. 3; Erickson and Middlebrook 1982, p. 214).

15. For each employees' syndicate there was a parallel employers' syndicate.

16. The system was never fully implemented for employers, but for the workers the

system remains pretty much in place today (Roett 1984, p. 105). One important change is that in 1985 it became legal to organize central (national) labor organizations (Keck 1989, p. 252).

17. Schmitter (1974, p. 103) and many other scholars use the expressions state corporatism (authoritarian) and societal corporatism (democratic). Many of the fascist regimes in Europe selectively drew on corporatist theory to justify totalitarian policies. The same was true of many authoritarian regimes in Latin America. In both cases the goal was to justify policies designed to maximize autonomous state power and to minimize the influence that other interest groups, particularly organized labor, were able to exert on the state. These uses of corporatist theory underlie what we refer to as authoritarian corporatism.

18. While the practice of providing jobs in the government bureaucracy to marginal members of the upper strata has a long history in Brazil, it was not until the 1930s that the bureaucracy began to expand at an explosive rate (Roett 1984, p. 117). The practice of providing jobs in the bureaucracy so as to assure middle-class support for the regime was not new, but it became an increasingly serious source of the nation's chronic inflation problem.

19. However, it did not cover the self-employed, urban marginal workers, or the rural population.

20. This was, however, more the power to protect turf and patronage resources than the power to initiate programatic reforms (Malloy 1991, p. 24).

21. During the populist era (1945–1964) their influence decreased, but by the late 1960s they had again become major actors in the formulation of pension policy.

22. The reforms embodied in the ISSB (see n. 23) proposal reflected the influence of contact with social security experts in organizations such as the ILO. The end of World War II brought with it the view that countries around the world should attempt to bring their social security schemes into compliance with internationally defined standards. During the war there were meetings among Latin American social security experts. A certain amount of consensus emerged from these meetings that reform of the region's particularistic social insurance schemes was called for (Malloy 1979, p. 85).

23. *Instituto de Serviços Sociais do Brasil.*

24. Malloy (1979, p. 83) refers to this as the period of populist democracy. Erickson (1977, pp. 2–5) prefers to describe it as a semi-corporative period so as to emphasize that it combined Vargas era corporatist structures with some aspects of liberal democracy. The term *quasi-democratic* has also been used to describe this era.

25. The populist parties of this era made vague promises of social reform, but there was no strong commitment to redistributive policies. They were nationalistic class-alliance parties that sought support from both white-collar and blue-collar workers (Alba 1968).

26. The Constitution of 1946 granted unions the right to strike, but the enabling legislation was never enacted. In addition, the Vargas era law prohibiting strikes was never rescinded. Thus during the populist era there was a clear contradiction between the constitution and specific laws (Erickson and Middlebrook 1982, p. 240).

27. These administrators were selected more for loyalty to the president than for their competence in managing pension funds (Gersdorff 1962, p. 204). This was also true in many other Latin American countries such as Argentina and Chile (Mesa-Lago 1978, p. 11).

28. The problem of overstaffing of these bureaucracies due to the demands of political patronage was endemic throughout Latin America (Maso-Lago 1978, p. 204).

29. Poor investment decisions by political appointees administering public pension funds were common throughout Latin America (Mesa-Lago 1978, p. 3).

30. It was also a common practice for employers to delay sending in contributions collected from employees so as to take economic advantage of Brazil's high inflation rate (Malloy 1979, p. 120).

31. Others refer alternatively to state capitalist development (Baer et al. 1976).

32. However, in 1980 there was a brief crackdown in response to strikes in which many union leaders were purged and sent to jail (Keck 1989, p. 267).

33. The goal of excluding labor from the boards was not the only reason for this legislation. The consolidation of the funds also offered a way to deal with the insolvency several were experiencing (U.N. 1970, p. 243).

34. It has potential implications for countries such as Nigeria and India where very few of those living in rural areas are covered by old-age security programs. Were these countries to consider a similar financing mechanism, an extension of coverage might be possible. But there is another important difference—Brazil has a larger and more well developed organized (modern) sector of the economy making it much more feasible to pay for benefits to rural workers with taxes on wholesalers and urban employers.

35. Another factor is that in rural areas there were alternative means of providing minimal support to the elderly. In old age rural workers were typically given access to small plots of land for cultivation to meet their subsistence needs (Gersdorff 1962, p. 203).

36. Since 1960 coverage for self-employed workers had been optional; in 1973 it became compulsory.

37. Unless specified otherwise, the material describing the current public pension system comes from one of the following sources: U.S. Social Security Administration 1990, pp. 32–33 or *International Benefit Guidelines* 1989, pp. 30–36.

38. However, to become eligible for a pension, workers must quit their current jobs at least long enough for the authorities to verify that they have quit. At that point the workers can in theory go back to work for the same employer, but firms in the formal sector often refuse to accept them back.

39. For those covered by the main program for urban workers, the benefit is 70 percent of this average earnings figure incremented by 1 percent for each year of coverage up to a maximum of 95 percent; however, the rural population and certain categories of the urban population (e.g., the destitute elderly) are covered by separate programs that pay much lower pensions based on the legal minimum wage (LeGrand 1989, p. 36).

40. The rate is 12.5 percent for employees of financial institutions and 19.2 percent for the self-employed. Employers in the industrial and commercial sectors pay an additional tax of 10 percent of net profits (U.S. Social Security Administration 1990, p. 32).

41. In 1985 Neves was indirectly elected president by a tightly controlled electoral college. Sarney became president when Neves became ill and died before actually taking office. Collor de Mello was the first president to be elected by a direct vote since 1961.

42. For example, the government still has the right to set salaries by decree and to prohibit strikes (Alves 1989, p. 63).

43. In 1986 the ceiling for employer contributions was eliminated. The Brazilian Constitution of 1988 called for additional pension policy reforms. The most important was to increase the level of the minimum old-age pension to the legal minimum wage.

44. Evaldo Amaro Vieira 1991, personal communication.

45. Approximately 60 percent of the economically active population of Latin America have old-age pension coverage, but if we exclude Brazil, the figure falls to 43 percent (Castro-Gutiérrez 1989, pp. 41–42; Mesa-Lago 1986, p. 137).

46. Coverage tends to be even lower for nations with more recent pension programs such as those dating from the 1950s in Honduras (14 percent) and El Salvador (12 percent) (Mesa-Lago 1986, pp. 129, 136).

47. These figures were calculated by the authors based on data presented by Mesa-Lago (1986, pp. 128–129).

48. There are several reasons rural workers are often excluded. In addition to being less of a political threat and more poorly organized than certain categories of urban workers, they often own their own homes and have access to small plots of land providing at least a minimal subsistence in time of need (Mallet 1980, p. 380).

49. Pluralists, however, point out that the state has typically also been influenced by a few powerful interest groups (Foxley et al. 1979, p. 151).

50. Unless specified otherwise, information describing the current Chilean system is drawn from one of the following three sources: Scarpaci and Miranda-Radic 1991; *Pension System in Chile* 1990; U.S. Social Security Administration 1990, pp. 52–53.

51. Between 1960 and 1980 due to a decline in fertility and an increase in life expectancy there was a dramatic increase in the ratio of pensioners to contributing workers from 9 per 100 to 45 per 100 (*Pension System in Chile* 1990, p. 4). This is one reason that this pay-as-you-go system was running into very serious financing problems by 1980. Another contributing factor was the strong temptation that existed to evade paying the full amount of compulsory contributions due. Because of these problems, during the 1970s the old scheme was replacing closer to 20 percent of the final salary of covered workers than to the intended goal of 70 percent (Simone 1983, p. 6).

52. For a description of the system that was in place prior to 1981 and is still in effect for many workers, see U.S. Social Security Administration 1990, pp. 52–53. As of 1986 the old system was closed to new entrants. As in Brazil the old system was made up of many separate pension funds; in 1980 there were 32 such funds.

53. Coverage is mandatory for employees, but optional for the self-employed. By the late 1980s approximately 75 percent of the labor force was covered (Miranda-Radic 1991, p. 38).

54. In the 1970s Chilean public spending as a percent of GNP was substantially above average for the Latin American countries (Foxley et al. 1979).

55. Workers are required to contribute 10 percent of wages and they have the option of making an additional tax-free contribution up to a limit that varies with income (*International Benefit Guidelines* 1989, p. 50). Covered workers are also required to make an additional contribution that varies from one fund to another, but ranges up to about 3 percent of wages to pay for disability and survivor's pension insurance and for administrative costs (*Pension System in Chile* 1990, p. 10).

56. Pension benefits are indexed to the consumer price index.

57. While a number of other Latin American countries have had corporatist labor systems and corporatist social security systems, Brazil seems to have been the most corporatist in both spheres (Malloy 1991, p. 21).

58. During this period there was a similar pattern in several other Latin American countries including Chile (Petras 1969, pp. 294–297) and Peru (Astiz 1969, pp. 206–211).

59. However, when Brazil introduced its first old-age pension scheme it was far less economically developed than were the nations of Western Europe when they introduced their schemes. In the mid-1920s Brazil's real income per capita was less than 40 percent of that in Germany during the 1880s and less than 33 percent of Sweden's in 1910 (Clark 1957, pp. 104, 132, 184).

60. The earliest pension coverage went to the military and upper level civil servants (Malloy 1991, p. 15).

61. However, the proportion over age 65 is now increasing rapidly and current projections call for an increase to 9 percent of the Brazilian population by 2025 (U.S. Bureau of the Census 1987, pp. 46–47).

Chapter 7

1. In 1989 approximately 4.3 percent of the population or 36 million people were age 65 or over. China with an estimated 57 million people age 65 and over in 1989 has the world's largest elderly population (World Bank 1991, p. 204; U.S. Bureau of the Census 1987, p. 46).

2. India introduced a provident fund plan for coal miners in 1948 and extended coverage to a number of other industries in 1952. Indonesia and Malaysia both introduced provident funds in 1951; the other countries mentioned introduced their provident fund plans between 1953 and 1958 (Dixon 1982, p. 326).

3. Alexander the Great had invaded the Punjab in 327 B.C.

4. When the Europeans first arrived in India they found a very advanced society. Several factors account for India's inability to protect itself from European dominance. One was the Mughal court's neglect of its navy and the resulting inability to protect its traditional trade with East and Southeast Asia. Another was the decision by most of the Mughal nobility to direct their substantial economic assets toward conspicuous consumption (Nyrop 1985, pp. 28–29).

5. In the Battle of Plassey (1757) Britain eliminated the last serious challenge to its power on the subcontinent. However, France did not give up all of its outposts in India until the 1950s and Portugal held Goa until 1961 (Fersh 1965, p. 67).

6. The armies of the East India Company were for the most part made up of Indian troops led by British officers (Nyrop 1985, p. 35).

7. There were three types of territories: (1) The colony was subdivided into a number of regions called "presidencies" that were administered directly by British governors; (2) there were the 600 or so "native states" each ruled by a hereditary prince who was "assisted" by a British administrator; (3) there were also the so-called tribal territories that were nominally under British control, but in these areas the British made almost no effort to exercise their influence (Fersh 1965, pp. 58–59).

8. This was a major, but unsuccessful mutiny of Indian soldiers employed by the East India Company. It is also referred to as the 1857 Mutiny.

9. The traditional Hindu joint family was made up of a group of brothers and their wives, sons, and unmarried daughters often all living in one large compound (Karve 1964, p. 52).

10. This continues to be true today particularly when the elderly are landholders (Petri 1982, p. 76; Bose 1982, p. 24).

11. Rothermund (1988, p. 172) disputes such claims; he estimates that per capita income actually increased about by about 20 percent between 1860 and 1900.

12. They also exempted British traders from all customs duties eliminating what had traditionally been an important source of local tax revenues (Griffiths 1965, p. 362).

13. Not only did the British remove all import taxes on textiles brought in from Britain, they also imposed heavy excise taxes on textiles produced by Indian industry (Wolpert 1977, p. 248).

14. The Indian National Congress is typically referred to as "Congress" or sometimes as "the Congress," but it is rare to refer to it as the "Congress party."

15. Many Indians had similar thoughts for similar reasons during World War II and were again disillusioned to find that Britain did not have plans to grant India independence as soon as the war ended (Moreland and Chatterjee 1957, pp. 453–459).

16. World War I stimulated the industrial sector of the Indian economy, but that sector contributed only about 3 percent of the net national product. A small group of Indian industrialists did very well during this period, but for the general population the war-induced inflation resulted in a decline in real wages (Rothermund 1988, pp. 73–75).

17. In 1969 it split into Congress (R) for ruling and Congress (O) for opposition. In 1978 Congress (R) split into Congress (I) for Indira and Congress (U) which subsequently evolved into Congress (S). Congress (I) while currently out of power is still the single most powerful party in India at the national level.

18. Rajiv Gandhi was assassinated in the midst of the 1991 election which returned Congress to power.

19. In the view of some scholars India's late start in the development of trade unionism is one reason that relatively little attention has been paid to social security programs over the years (Sinha 1980, p. 25).

20. India's chronic high unemployment and underemployment have further undercut the strength of organized labor. Another factor is the major role the state has played as an employer in the organized sector of the economy (Johri 1982, p. 108).

21. Unionized workers generally earn 10 to 15 times as much as do landless rural workers (Hardgrave and Kochanek 1986, p. 178).

22. At the time of independence the business and industrial sectors accounted for only 5 percent of the nation's income; today these sectors account for over 30 percent (Hardgrave and Kochanek 1986, p. 20).

23. As late as the early 1980s, 70 percent of the labor force was engaged in agriculture (Chowdhry 1985, p. 97). While India's urban population remains small relative to its rural population, the speed of urbanization is starting to accelerate (Hardgrave and Kochanek 1986, p. 17). Since more than 70 percent of India's population lives in rural areas, the problem of providing for the aged is less problematic than it would be were the nation much more urbanized (Petri 1982, p. 76).

24. This legislation called for payment to workers injured in job-related accidents resulting in disability or death. It also called for benefits to some who were disabled with occupation-related diseases. Some scholars do not consider the 1923 Act a true social insurance measure because it placed the entire burden for financing the program on the employer (Mamoria and Mamoria 1983). Those reasoning along these lines generally consider the Employees' State Insurance Act of 1948 the nation's first true social insurance scheme. This 1948 act introduced a compulsory social insurance program for employees in the modern sector that covered such contingencies as maternity, employment injury, sickness, and widowhood (Johri 1982, pp. 110–111).

25. In the 1920s organized labor was more concerned with immediate issues such as loss of income due to work-related injuries than with more future-oriented issues such as economic security in old age.

26. However, as of 1986 only 2.5 percent of the population spoke English in contrast to the 30 percent who spoke Hindi, the most widely spoken language in India.

27. One scholar argues that 135 languages are spoken in India (Chowdhry 1985, p. 96). Most of the 135 can, however, be classified as dialects related to the 16 major languages. Their are 12 languages spoken by a million or more people (Hardgrave and Kochanek 1986, p. 10).

28. The number of factories covered increased from 12,000 in 1961 to 93,000 in 1980 (Mamoria and Mamoria 1983, p. 61).

29. The Indian Administrative Service (IAS) is the successor to the British Indian Civil Service. It is the elite corps of the nation's civil service bureaucracy. Over the years since independence the IAS has become increasingly politicized and corrupted (Rudolph and Rudolph 1987, pp. 2–3).

30. This includes most employers with 20 or more workers (*International Benefit Guidelines* 1989, p. 113) and it includes close to 50 percent of those employed in the organized (modern) sector (Johri 1982, p. 113).

31. India is the only nation with a provident fund scheme that excludes (most)

employees whose earnings exceed a specified level (Dixon 1982, p. 329). It is also the only nation with a provident fund scheme with an earnings floor for contribution purposes (Dixon 1986, p. 108).

32. If the deceased worker is under age 25, the benefit is paid as a lump sum rather than as a pension.

33. The pension is based on contributions from both the employee and the employer as well as the interest on those contributions. Employers may contract out of the Family Pension scheme if they offer an alternative more favorable to employees (Johri 1982, p. 115).

34. The gratuity is a retirement benefit for some, but a termination-of-employment benefit for others as it is often paid to workers of any age who leave the organization after five or more years of service (Johri 1982, pp. 115–116).

35. Of the 20 nations with provident fund schemes only in India does the government make contributions as is illustrated by this scheme (Dixon 1982, p. 329).

36. In the early 1980s, 71 percent of the labor force in Malaysia were reported as contributing to the nation's provident fund scheme (Ministry of Welfare Services 1982, p. 290). However, this figure may substantially overstate coverage as can be illustrated by the case of Sri Lanka. At approximately the same time it was estimated that 51 percent of the population were covered by the nation's provident fund scheme, but only 19 percent were covered by currently active accounts (Samarasinghe 1982, p. 166).

37. Tracy (1991 p. 62) estimates that if we also take into consideration retirement schemes from private sources up to 50 percent of gainfully employed workers may be covered.

38. However, some rural workers who are employed by large plantation enterprises are covered; for example, in Assam the state government has introduced a provident fund scheme for tea plantation workers (Johri 1982, p. 109).

39. Only 21 Third World nations, primarily in Africa and Asia, have introduced provident fund systems and 72 have introduced social insurance schemes (Dixon 1986, p. 33).

40. See Orloff and Skocpol (1984) for a discussion of this fear of corruption argument. They analyze the late introduction of old-age pensions in the United States.

41. We elaborate on this point in the next chapter.

42. The pattern has been similar in other nations. In many cases provident fund schemes were viewed as a first step toward the introduction of social insurance, but once in place provident funds have proven popular and shifts to the social insurance approach have been rare (Dixon 1986, p. 106).

43. A similar argument can be made with respect to most Indian citizens, even those not employed in the agricultural sector. Wages are low and as a result few feel they can afford to make substantial contributions in connection with various social security schemes. Most would prefer to maximize income while young, active, and healthy rather than set aside substantial funds for a distant and uncertain old age they may never live to experience. The low life expectancy in India (57 years at birth) relative to the minimum age of eligibility for provident fund benefits (age 55) lends some credence to this line of reasoning (U.S. Bureau of the Census 1987, p. 13).

44. One reason that elderly widows are often the poorest of the poor is that in many states women do not own property (Mahadevan 1986, p. 501).

45. In addition, a substantial fraction of union members in India are white-collar employees (Rudolph and Rudolph 1987, p. 24).

46. In 1985, 4.3 percent were over age 65, and this figure is projected to increase to 9.7 by 2025 (U.S. Bureau of the Census 1987, pp. 46–47).

47. However, this evidence is also consistent with explanations emphasizing the role of interest groups, historical legacy, and state structure.

48. While policy is initiated from the top, it is common to hold open hearings and to consult with representatives of those groups likely to be most directly affected by the policy under consideration.

49. However, at the state level there is a great deal of variation with respect to the extent of control by Congress. During much of the past 40 years Kerala has had leftist coalition governments. It is significant in this context that Kerala, one of India's poorest states, has been one of the most progressive with respect to old-age security legislation.

50. However, as British rule made some positive economic contributions, an alternative albeit weaker case can be made that India might have been even less developed than it is were it not for the period of British rule.

Chapter 8

1. Approximately one African in five lives in Nigeria, but estimates of the Nigerian population vary widely as there has not been a satisfactory census since 1952. One of the most reliable sources puts the figure at 114 million in 1989 (World Bank 1991, p. 204).

2. The nation's GNP per capita in 1989 was approximately $250 which was about the same as in Uganda ($250) and Zaire ($260), but somewhat below that in the Ivory Coast ($790) (World Bank 1991, p. 204).

3. Although the evidence is sketchy, there is reason to believe that Berber traders were in contact with the savannah peoples of Northern Nigeria trading for ivory and slaves during the first millennium A.D. (Nelson 1982, p. 5).

4. One reason they did not make more of an effort to go inland was the fear of tropical diseases. Another was the fear that they would alienate the African middlemen they depended on to supply slaves.

5. In Nigeria the British were primarily interested in trade; they did not create settler plantations and they invested very little in manufacturing (Andrain 1988, p. 218).

6. Dudley (1973, pp. 22–27) argues that by the start of the twentieth century the processes of diffusion and assimilation had already led to the incipient emergence of Nigeria. He asserts that the boundaries of Nigeria were delimited by Britain after the general patterns of the indigenous cultural geography had been established. Most Nigerians take issue with this claim. Oyovbaire (1981, p. 356), for example, points out that any such homogenization by 1900 was an incidental consequence of British colonial control.

7. In the Western Region there were two major parties, but one of these soon split.

8. By one estimate there are over 300 distinct ethnolinguistic groups in Nigeria each with an identifiable home area (U.S. Dept. of State 1987).

9. Ethnic (tribal) groups and languages are often related, but they are not necessarily coterminous (Nelson 1982, p. 90). Some scholars argue that references to there being several hundred different languages in Nigeria are misleading. Most Nigerian languages can be classified into about ten language groups with most of the others viewed as dialects of these (Ikejiani and Ikejiani 1986, p. 39). English is the official language of Nigeria and is now taught in primary school, but it is spoken well by a relatively small fraction of the adult population (Kurian 1982, p. 1331).

10. With respect to ethnic and linguistic heterogeneity, Nigeria is considered by some to be one of the most heterogeneous nations in the world (Kurian 1982, p. 1331).

11. Margaret Peil (1990, personal communication).

12. Between 1967 and 1991 the number of states increased in stages from 12 to 30.

13. Some scholars argue that regionalism is a more important source of political conflict in Nigeria than ethnic heterogeneity (Okoli 1980, p. 117).

14. One reason that ethnicity is such a strong determinant of political allegiance is the

belief that those in power will give preference to their kin, local community, and ethnic group in the allocation of scarce resources (Joseph 1987, p. 189; Panter-Brick 1970, p. 5). The patterns of patronage and favoritism following electoral victories tend to support such beliefs.

15. In addition to the cleavages between unions with respect to ethnic and regional differences, there were sharp ideological cleavages between the radical and conservative unions. The radical unions have adopted a Marxist world view and a distrust of the government. The conservative unions have adopted a much more pluralistic view of the state.

16. It is common in Nigeria for various labor factions to take different sides on proposed changes in social welfare policy in an effort to upstage or undermine the current leadership of the Nigerian Labour Congress (NLC) (Otobo 1986, p. 352).

17. By the late 1970s the NLC had organized about ten percent of the modern-sector work force, but membership has declined sharply in recent years due in part to several years of austerity and high unemployment levels (U.S. Dept. of State 1987).

18. Some of the most important being: the World Federation of Trade Unions (WFTU), the International Confederation of Free Trade Unions (ICFTU), and the World Confederation of Labour.

19. The NLC is, however, allowed to belong to an African international union, the Organization of African Trade Union Unity (U.S, Dept. of State 1987).

20. Local business elites bankroll political parties and have far more influence than the managers of multinational corporations, who are often treated with suspicion (Margaret Peil 1990, personal communication).

21. The British did, however, introduce a worker injury scheme in 1942. This scheme required employers to take out liability insurance to cover this contingency with private insurance firms. Worker injury schemes were generally the earliest social security measures introduced for non civil servants throughout Africa (Mulozi 1982, p. 95).

22. If the worker is so incapacitated as to be permanently unemployable, the entire balance in the account can be withdrawn.

23. Given how close many in the agricultural sector are to minimum subsistence, it would be necessary to subsidize any provident fund or social insurance program with monies obtained from other segments of the population (Mouton and Gruat 1988, p. 49). Such a program would call for more national solidarity than presently exists in Nigeria.

24. In 1980 Nigeria's adult literacy rate was only 34 percent which is about average for sub-Saharan Africa (World Bank 1983b, p. 69).

25. By the mid-1970s, 41 of Africa's 51 countries had introduced some form of old-age social security scheme (ILO 1977, p. 10).

26. Even when children migrate to urban areas, they feel obligated to do what they can to provide for their parents. Typically, there is a shift from the provision of personal services to economic support (Peil et al. 1989, p. 105). However, the traditional support system is not working as well as it did in the past and as a result an increasing number of the elderly are not being cared for (Olatunji Oyeneye 1991, personal communication).

27. One reason the lump sum benefit is popular is that the sum involved is often enough to start a small business or buy a plot of land. These alternatives are attractive for the protection they provide against inflation. In addition, many workers want to return to their homeland when they retire, and the infrastructure does not exist to get regular pension payments to those living in many rural areas (O'Reilly 1982, p. 6).

28. When employers fall into arrears on payment of contributions or fail to make contributions, the size of the worker's eventual provident fund benefit is reduced. It is

very difficult for the employee to keep track of the status of his or her account, and the Nigerian government does not have the efficient bureaucratic infrastructure needed to keep close tabs on employer compliance. In an effort to maximize profit or save a business that is failing, it is common for Nigerian employers to fall into arrears or attempt to conceal provident fund payments due (Ijeh 1977, pp. 8–10).

29. The figure would increase slightly were we to include coverage by private occupational pensions as well (*International Benefit Guidelines* 1989, p. 171). This figure can be contrasted with a figure of 38 percent for India (Tracy 1991, p. 62).

30. Over the years very few nations have made the shift from national provident funds to social insurance programs. The shift has been made in five nations other than Rwanda and Tanzania: Egypt, Iraq, and three small island nations, Dominica, St. Lucia, and the Seychelles (Dixon 1986, p. 106).

31. Unless specified otherwise, the information presented in this section was drawn from Kouassi (1991), Bakayoko and Ehouman (1987), or U.S. Social Security Administration (1990).

32. There are separate pension systems for several different categories of government employees.

33. The tax only applies to workers between the ages of 18 and 55. There is an earnings cap for contribution purposes, but it is set very high, approximately 45 times the minimum wage (*International Social Security Review* 1986, p. 388).

34. Another way to look at it is that the old-age pensions are financed by a 4 percent tax of which 40 percent is paid for by the employee and 60 percent by the employer.

35. The pension is reduced by 5 percent for each year that it is taken prior to age 55 (Bakayoko and Ehouman 1987, p. 83).

36. They use "revalued" earnings (*International Benefit Guidelines* 1989, p. 133).

37. The survivor's pension is payable to widows over age 50 as well as widows who are invalids or under age 50, but with two or more dependent children. There is also an orphan's pension for dependents under age 16 (Bakayoko and Ehouman 1987, p. 90).

38. There is, however, a supplement for dependent children under age 16.

39. However, some Nigerian scholars do argue that the relative lack of stable democratic government has undercut the development of old-age social security policy (Olatunji Oyeneye 1991, personal communication).

40. The manufacturing sector remains small with heavy industry dominated by multinational corporations (Andrain 1988, p. 238).

41. However, in many areas in Nigeria there has been a great deal of urbanization linked to factors other than industrialization such as the increase in the size of the federal and state government bureaucracies.

42. Marsh (1988) would take issue with us here. In a study of 55 less developed nations he finds a negative relationship between level of foreign investment and subsequent economic growth.

43. In recent years the sharp split between the predominantly Muslim North and the predominantly Christian South has again become a serious problem. It seems that revival of Islamic fundamentalism among the Muslim population in the North is one of the major reasons.

44. Consultants from ILO played a key role in helping Nigerian civil servants set up their provident fund scheme (ISSA 1976, p. 43).

45. The British civil service in Nigeria emphasized efficiency, neutrality, and integrity. But with independence the ethos of the civil service bureaucracy changed. It became an instrument for the acquisition of individual and group resources (Bretton 1962, pp. 86–87).

46. Gowon, who was in power from 1966 to 1975, pledged to rid the nation of corruption; but nepotism, bribery, and graft continued to play a major role in the exercise of influence and authority (Nelson 1982, p. 66). Since independence Nigeria has alternated between civilian and military governments, but corruption has been a consistent problem in both (Joseph 1987; Andrain 1988, p. 241; Falola and Ihonvbere 1985, p. 108).

47. Organized labor has traditionally been suspicious of how government and private pensions are used. One reason for their lack of support for greater involvement in old-age security policy has been a concern about the labor control aspects of such legislation (Sanda 1987). With respect to the proposed shift from the NPF to a social insurance pension scheme, the evidence suggests that the unions have had doubts as to whether a future regime would make good on a current regime's promise of pension benefits (Tracy 1991, p. 114). There is also evidence, however, that some elements of labor would support a shift from a provident fund to a pension scheme (ISSA 1988).

48. Approximately 87 percent of elderly Nigerians live in rural areas (Oyeneye 1990, p. 21).

49. One reason the traditional family support system continues to work as well as it does is that so few people live to be so old they become incapacitated, and those who do tend to die rather quickly (Tracy 1991, p. 107).

Chapter 9

1. The limited time span studied relates to a period of growth in mature, well-established systems among the industrial countries. The processes of implementation of centralized public systems and expansion of mature systems differ, especially in regard to the impact of political democracy. The limited time span studied relates to a period of growth in mature, well-established systems among the industrial countries. The processes of implementation of centralized public systems and expansion of mature systems differ, especially in regard to the impact of political democracy.

2. Authoritarian corporatism, especially as illustrated in the chapter on Brazil, represents more of an attempt by the state to direct or control labor rather than to incorporate it into policy negotiation. Some see even democratic or societal corporatism as harmful to the long-run interests of labor. The degree and means of labor control in societal or democratic corporatism nonetheless differ from the outward control in authoritarian corporatism or fascism. Authoritarian corporatism involves less the organization of labor interests than the consolidation of dictatorial power.

3. We have argued that democracy can inhibit expansion in the early stages of pension system development, but expand it in later stages. The mixture among Third World nations of new and old systems reflects to counterbalancing effects of democracy in this sample.

4. Some of the material that follows assumes advanced statistical knowledge. For those interested in the substantive conclusions more than the technical means used to reach these conclusions, this material may be skipped. The discussion and conclusion sections of the chapter thoroughly summarize the results without reference to statistical detail.

5. Finland, Norway, Sweden, Denmark, the Netherlands, Belgium, Germany, Austria, Switzerland, France, Italy, United Kingdom, Ireland.

6. Our focus on expenditures does not capture all dimensions of the generosity and universality of systems, and others have made efforts to construct more detailed indices (Myles 1984, pp. 63–72; Palme 1990b, pp. 28–35). Still, spending is a necessary if not sufficient condition for a quality system, and worthy of study in its own right.

7. Other theories would recognize responsiveness to these macroeconomic changes, but do not see them as dominant. Instead, certain political structures are necessary for economic changes to be influential on spending.

8. Social democratic theory by name alone implies it is the role of leftist parties that is crucial for policy development. For a program like pensions, however, with large middle-class support, the literature suggests left and center parties are equally likely to support expanded development. Variation in the strength of rightist party opposition thus becomes the prime determinant of actual spending expansion. In fact, left party has no significant effect in our model and has been deleted in favor of the measure of rightist parties. Whether leftist or rightist party is measured is less important to the social democratic theory than is the representation in one form or another of partisan party rule in relation to class-based goals.

9. Generalized least squares estimation adjusts for country-specific autocorrelation and heteroscedasticity (Kmenta 1971, pp. 508–517; Stimson 1985, pp. 926–929).

10. Because it is closely related to percent voting, electoral competition has an unexpected negative effect. Further, the effect is not robust, as it is reduced to insignificance when sensitivity analyses are performed. We do not attribute substantive meaning to the coefficient.

11. The model also includes dummy variables for nations whose spending varies significantly, on average, from the predicted values. Not all the differences across nations in pension spending are captured by national differences on the independent variable. The dummy variables are used to represent country-specific deviations from expected values that are constant over time. Controls for such unmeasured—and unvarying—country effects are necessary for unbiased estimates. Only a subset of the nations show any such deviation. Italy, Switzerland, and the Netherlands spend more on social welfare than might be expected from their political and social composition. Belgium, New Zealand, and Japan spend less than expected. While we are not able to explain the underlying characteristics of these countries that are responsible for the continued overprediction or underprediction of spending levels, control for the nations in the form of time-constant dummy variables at least removes the influence of the unmeasured characteristics from the estimates for the other variables. None of the other 12 nations, including the 4 that formed the basis of the case studies, show such country effects.

12. A number of tests of robustness were performed on the model. With one exception they suggest the results are stable and not due to outlying or influential cases. The exception is that the model changes over time to some degree. The facilitative or inhibitory effects of corporatism are stronger in the 1970s than the 1960s. In this regard, Table 9–2 provides a picture of the average of the two periods. For more details, see Pampel, Williamson, and Stryker (1990, p. 545).

13. Because of changes in the reporting format of the ILO in 1978, 7 of the 32 nations discontinued their reports of pension spending with the 1977 figures. Rather than delete these nations, we used 1977 values on pension spending and on the independent variables rather than the 1980 values. Levels of spending and its determinants are unlikely to change greatly in three years; even less likely is that the relationship between spending and its determinants would change in so short a period. Indeed, if these nations are deleted, the results are not substantially changed. We therefore attempt to retain as many nations as possible despite minor differences in timing of measurement. An analysis of the earlier period can be found in Pampel and Williamson (1989, pp. 91–96).

14. GDP per capita is logged to reduce the skew among this diverse sample of nations. The log transformation implies that the same dollar change in GDP has the strongest effect at the lowest values of development, and levels off at higher values.

15. See the Appendix for a description of data sources.

16. Brazil, Panama, and the Philippines, which experienced loss of democratic free-doms during the period, do not change the results when shifted to another category. Though this measure of democracy does not appear to bias the results, we replicated our findings with a measure of democracy based on years of democratic experience (Muller 1988, p. 55). The results are substantially the same.

17. Of the 32 Third World nations, 19 are classified as nondemocratic: Benin, Bolivia, Burma, the Congo, El Salvador, Ethiopia, Guatemala, Guyana, the Ivory Coast, Kenya, Mali, Mauritania, Morocco, Nicaragua, Niger, Senegal, Togo, Upper Volta, and Zambia. Thirteen nations are democratic: Brazil, Colombia, Costa Rica, Cyprus, India, Israel, Malaysia, Mexico, Panama, the Philippines, Sri Lanka, Turkey, and Venezuela. Clear regional differences exist in these two groups. All but 7 of the nondemocracies and none of the democracies are African. That many nondemocracies come from the same region is not, by itself, a flaw in the classification. Democracy is a concept that is more meaningful theoretically than geographical location.

18. With only five time points, it is not possible to estimate nation-specific estimates of serial correlation. Instead, the mean coefficient across all 32 nations is used.

19. The negative coefficient for the additive effect of democracy has little substantive meaning in these equations. It shows the difference in intercepts between democracies and nondemocracies when values on all other variables are 0. Yet, the zero points on the vari-ables in this equation are not substantively meaningful. Moreover, given that the effect for percent aged and SIPE is greater for democracies than for nondemocracies (rather than parallel), the effects will diverge toward infinity as the distance from the point of intersec-tion increases. Thus, in the presence of interaction, the additive negative effect of democ-racy does not indicate that democracy lowers welfare expenditures.

20. The effects of class variables, which were found to relate to corporatist context in the previous section, are more difficult to study here since measures are either not appli-cable to nondemocracies with a primarily agricultural labor force or not available. Pampel and Williamson (1989, pp. 96–101) examine the effects of economic dependency as a proxy for class relations and find some evidence that these variables interact with democracy as well; however, they do not eliminate the effects of the other variables.

Chapter 10

1. Social democratic theorists have not claimed that the theory could be used to explain developments in Third World nations. Our analysis provides concrete evidence suggesting that it is probably unwise to attempt to do so.

2. The social democratic argument as applied to the introduction of these programs is implicit. It is not explicitly included as part of the perspective as the focus is typically on developments since the end of World War II, not on the politics surrounding the introduc-tion of these programs.

3. With the exception of a brief period during the late 1970s and the early 1980s the Social Democratic Party was continuously in power between 1932 and 1991.

4. In contrast to big business, small business opposed enactment of the original Social Security legislation (Achenbaum 1978, p. 138).

5. However, it is consistent with the neo-Marxist perspective for those analysts who believe that the German state was in the last analysis controlled by economic elites and not autonomous.

6. Not all industrialists had these concerns. The Charity Organization Society was able in 1908 to produce a petition calling for a delay in the enactment of pension legislation that was signed by some 2,000 corporate executives and bankers (Heclo 1974, p. 178).

7. If the territory that is today India had obtained its independence at a much earlier point in time, say at the time the major South American nations became independent, it is entirely possible that India would not today be a single nation. What was once the British colony of India is now four separate countries. Given that it was made up of several hundred princely kingdoms prior to becoming a British colony, it is entirely possible that what is today India would have ended up a rather large number of independent countries. Thus any effort to assess the precise impact on present level of economic development or on old-age social security policy, necessarily becomes very speculative.

8. As in the case of India it is likely that had it not been for the colonial experience, the territory that is now Nigeria might well have become a substantial number of separate independent countries.

9. In 1985 Sweden spent 11.2 percent of its GDP on public pensions; the Netherlands, 10.6 percent; the United States, 7.2 percent; Japan, 5.3 percent; and Germany 11.8 percent (OECD 1988a, pp. 140–141).

10. The United States stands out as being very late, but it is not the only late industrial nation; Switzerland did not introduce its first national pension scheme until 1946.

11. Other nations that preceded Britain include: Austria (1906), Denmark (1891), and New Zealand (1898). Australia introduced its first scheme the same year Britain did (U.S. Social Security Administration 1990).

12. Due to the extensive use of the provident fund approach in India and particularly Nigeria, comparable expenditure figures are not available. However, were provident fund benefits, which extend to less than 10 percent of the economically active population in these countries, treated as expenditures, it is likely that the corresponding expenditure figures would be less than the 2.5 percent Brazilian figure.

13. For 1982 GNP per capita for the industrial nations ranged from $9,700 (Britain) to $14,000 (Sweden); in the same year it was $2,200 for Brazil, $860 for Nigeria, and $260 for India (World Bank 1984, pp. 218–219).

14. In 1900 among Europeans nations France was second only to Sweden in percent aged 65 and over at 8.2 percent of the population and in 1850 France had a higher proportion aged than any other European nation: 6.5 percent (France) vs. 4.8 percent (Sweden) and 4.6 percent (England) (Laslett 1985, p. 217). Thus based on age structure we would have expected France to have introduced a pension system sooner than either Germany or Britain, but this was not the case. The French system was not introduced until 1910.

15. In the case of India and particularly Nigeria, the pension expenditure figures are less meaningful than a more general measure (which is not currently available) that includes provident fund distributions as well. But even were such a measure available, there is little reason to expect a change in the basic relationship reported here.

16. Between 1960 and 1985 spending on pensions increased from 4.4 to 11.2 percent of GDP for Sweden, from 9.7 to 11.8 percent for Germany, from 4.0 to 6.7 percent for Britain, and 4.1 to 11.2 percent for the United States (OECD 1988a, pp. 138–141). Between 1950 and 1987 the average annual growth rate of GDP for these countries was: 2.6 percent (Sweden), 4.0 percent (Germany), 2.2 percent (Britain), and 1.9 percent (United States).

17. By the 1920s in the United States and in several other industrial nations there was concern that population aging was having an adverse impact on productivity (Graebner

1980, pp. 4–10). This concern about productivity was one factor contributing to the perceived need to increase public pension efforts.

18. This amounted to a benefit cut for upper and upper middle income Social Security recipients. The limit was $25,000 for singles and $32,000 for couples.

19. As a reflection of this goal, Old Age Insurance benefits were lower than Old Age Assistance (public welfare) benefits in most states (Quadagno 1984, p. 634).

BIBLIOGRAPHY

Aaron, Henry J., Barry P. Bosworth, and Gary Burtless. 1989. *Can America Afford to Grow Old? Paying for Social Security*. Washington, D.C.: Brookings Institution.

Achenbaum, W. Andrew. 1978. *Old Age in the New Land: The American Experience Since 1790*. Baltimore: Johns Hopkins University Press.

———. 1980. "Did Social Security Attempt to Regulate the Poor?" *Research on Aging* 2:270–288.

———. 1983. *Shades of Gray*. Boston: Little, Brown.

———. 1986. *Social Security: Visions and Revisions*. Cambridge: Cambridge University Press.

Adeokun, L. A. 1984. *The Elderly All Over the World: Nigeria*. Paris: International Center of Social Gerontology.

Agarwal, Bina. 1990. "Social Security and the Family: Coping with Seasonality and Calamity in Rural India." *Journal of Peasant Studies* 17:342–412.

Aire, J. U. 1974. "Problems of Social Security in Nigeria." *Quarterly Journal of Administration* 8:409–425.

Ake, Claude. 1981. *A Political Economy of Africa*. London: Longman.

Alba, Victor. 1968. *Politics and the Labor Movement in Latin America*. Stanford: Stanford University Press.

Alber, Jens. 1983. "Some Causes of Social Security Expenditure Development in Western Europe 1949–1977." Pp. 156–170 in *Social Policy and Social Welfare*, edited by Martin Loney, David Boswell, and John Clarke. Milton Keynes, England: Open University Press.

———. 1988. "Germany." Pp. 1–154 in *Growth to Limits*, vol. 2, edited by Peter Flora. New York: Walter de Gruyter.

Aldrich, Jonathan. 1982. "Earnings Replacement Rates of Old-Age Benefits in 12 Countries, 1969–80." *Social Security Bulletin* 45 (November):3–11.

Alestalo, Matti and Stein Kuhnle. 1987. "The Scandinavian Route: Economic, Social, and Political Developments in Denmark, Finland, Norway, and Sweden." Pp. 3–38 in *The Scandinavian Model*, edited by Robert Erikson, Erik Jørgen Hansen, Stein Ringen, and Hannu Uusitalo. Armonk, NY: M.E. Sharpe.

Alexander, Robert J. 1965. *Organized Labor in Latin America*. New York: Free Press.

Altmeyer, Arthur. 1966. *The Formative Years of Social Security*. Madison. University of Wisconsin Press.

Alves, Maria Helena Moreira. 1989. "Trade Unions in Brazil: A Search for Autonomy and Organization." Pp. 39–72 in *Labor Autonomy and the State in Latin America*, edited by Edward C. Epstein. Boston: Unwin Hyman.

Amenta, Edwin and Theda Skocpol. 1988. "Redefining the New Deal: World War II and the Development of Social Provision in the United States." Pp. 81–122 in *The Politics of Social Policy in the United States*, edited by Margaret Weir, Ann Shola Orloff, and Theda Skocpol. Princeton: Princeton University Press.

Amenta, Edwin and Yvonne Zylan. 1991. "It Happened Here: Political Opportunity, the New Institutionalism, and the Townsend Movement." *American Sociological Review* 56:250–265.

Ananaba, Wogu. 1969. *The Trade Union Movement in Nigeria*. New York: Africana Publishing Corporation.

Anderson, O. W. 1951. "Compulsory Medical Care Insurance, 1910–1950." *Annals of the American Academy of Political and Social Science* 273:106–113.

Andrain, Charles F. 1988. *Political Change in the Third World*. Boston: Unwin and Hyman.

Andrén, Nils. 1961. *Modern Swedish Government*. Stockholm: Almqvist and Wiksell.

Anton, Thomas J. 1980. *Administered Politics: Elite Political Culture in Sweden*. Boston: Martinus Nijhoff.

Arnold, Robin. 1982. "Chile: The First Year of Social Security Reform." *International Benefits Information Service*. August 19, pp. 17–22.

Ashford, Douglas E. 1986. *The Emergence of the Welfare States*. London: Basil Blackwell.

Asitz, Carlos A. 1969. *Pressure Groups and Power Elites in Peruvian Politics*. Ithaca, NY: Cornell University Press.

Aubry, Paul. 1974. *The Achievements of Mutual Benefit Societies in Developing Countries*. Report III, XVIII General Assembly of the ISSA. Abidjan, October–November 1973. Geneva: General Secretariat of the International Social Security Association.

Awolowo, Obafemi. 1966. *Thoughts on Nigerian Constitution*. Ibadan: Oxford University Press.

Ayoade, John A. A. 1986. "Ethnic Politics in Nigeria: A Conceptual Reformulation." Pp. 105–118 in *Ethnicity, Politics and Development*, edited by Dennis L. Thompson and Dov Ronen. Boulder, CO: Lynne Rienner.

Azarya, Victor. 1988. "Reordering State-Society Relations: Incorporation and Disengagement." Pp. 3–21 in *The Precarious Balance*, edited by Donald Rothchild and Naomi Chazan. London: Westview Press.

Baer, Werner. 1965. *Industrialization and Economic Growth in Brazil*. Homewood, IL: Irwin.

Baer, Werner, Richard Newfarmer, and Thomas Trebat. 1976. "On State Capitalism in Brazil: Some Issues and Questions." *Inter-American Economic Affairs* 30 (Winter): 69–92.

Bakayoko, Adama and Sylvestre Ehouman. 1987. "Ivory Coast." Pp. 69–99 in *Social Welfare in Africa*, edited by John Dixon. London: Croom Helm.

Baldwin, Peter. 1988. "How Socialist is Solidaristic Social Policy? Swedish Postwar Reform as a Case in Point." *International Review of Social History* 33:121–147.

———. 1989. "The Scandinavian Origins of the Social Interpretation of the Welfare State." *Comparative Studies in Society and History* 31:3–24.

———. 1990a. "The Middle Classes and the Postwar Welfare State: The French and the German Cases." Paper presented at the symposium on the International Comparison of Social Security Policies and Systems organized by the Research Section of the Ministry of Social Affairs (MIRE) in cooperation with the International Social Security Association (ISSA), Paris, June 13th–15th.

———. 1990b. *The Politics of Social Solidarity: Class Bases of the European Welfare State 1875–1975*. Cambridge: Cambridge University Press.

Ball, Robert M. 1988a. "The Original Understanding on Social Security: Implications for Later Developments." Pp. 17–39 in *Social Security: Beyond the Rhetoric of Crisis*, edited by Theodore R. Marmor and Jerry L. Mashaw. Princeton: Princeton University Press.

———. 1988b. "Social Security Across Generations." Pp. 11–38 in *Social Security and Economic Well-Being Across Generations*, edited by John R. Gist. Washington, D.C.: American Association of Retired Persons.

———. 1990. "Why the Social Security Tax Rate Should Not Be Reduced." *Social Insurance Update*, newsletter of the National Academy of Social Insurance, No. 13, May.

Beer, Samuel H. 1965. *Modern British Politics: A Study of Parties and Pressure Groups.* London: Faber and Faber.

Bell, Wendell and Walter E. Freeman, eds. 1974. *Ethnicity and Nation-Building.* London: Sage.

Bensel, Richard F. 1984. *Sectionalism and American Political Development, 1880–1980.* Madison: University of Wisconsin Press.

Berkowitz, Edward and Kim McQuad. 1980. *Creating the Welfare State.* New York: Praeger.

Bernstein, Barton J. 1968. "The New Deal: The Conservative Achievements of Liberal Reform." Pp. 263–289 in *Towards a New Past,* edited by Barton J. Bernstein. New York: Random House.

Bernstein, Merton C. and Joan Brodshaug Bernstein. 1988. *Social Security.* New York: Basic Books.

Berry, Jeffrey M. 1984. *The Interest Group Society.* Boston: Little, Brown.

Beveridge, Sir William. 1942. *Social Insurance and Allied Services.* New York: Macmillan.

Bhattarai, A. K. 1985. Unpublished memo from the Undersecretary A. K. Bhattarai (of India) to the Secretary of the International Social Security Association in Geneva, May 2.

———. 1989. "Social Security Programs in India." *International Social Security Review* 42:479–488.

Binney, Elizabeth A. and Carroll L. Estes. 1988. "The Retreat of the State and its Transfer of Responsibility: The Intergenerational War." *International Journal of Health Services* 18:83–96.

Birch, A. H. 1955. *Federalism, Finance and Social Legislation in Canada, Australia and the United States.* London: Oxford University Press.

Blackbourn, David and Geoff Eley. 1984. *The Peculiarities of German History.* New York: Oxford University Press.

Block, Fred. 1977. "The Ruling Class Does Not Rule: Notes on the Marxist Theory of the State." *Socialist Revolution* 7:6–28.

Blondel, Jean. 1969. *Introduction to Comparative Government.* New York: Praeger.

Board, Joseph B. 1970. *The Government and Politics of Sweden.* Boston: Houghton Mifflin.

Bollen, Kenneth A. 1980. "Issues in Comparative Measurement of Democracy." *American Sociological Review* 45:370–390.

———. 1983. "World System Position, Dependency, and Democracy: The Cross-National Evidence." *American Sociological Review* 48:465–479.

Bonham, Gary. 1984. "Beyond Hegel and Marx: An Alternative Approach to the Political Role of the Wilhelmine State." *German Studies Review* 7:199–225.

Borcherding, Thomas. 1977. "One Hundred Years of Public Spending, 1870–1970." Pp. 19–44 in *Budgets and Bureaucrats: The Sources of Government Growth,* edited by Thomas Borcherding. Durham, N.C.: Duke University Press.

Bornschier, Volker. 1981. "Dependent Industrialization in the World Economy: Some Comments and Results Concerning a Recent Debate." *Journal of Conflict Resolution* 25:371–400.

Bornschier, Volker, Christopher Chase-Dunn, and Richard Rubinson. 1978. "Cross-National Evidence of the Effects of Foreign Investment and Aid on Economic Growth and Inequality: A Survey of Findings and a Reanalysis." *American Journal of Sociology* 84:651–83.

Bose, Ashish. 1982. "Aspects of Aging in India." Pp. 24–45 in *Aging in South Asia,* edited by Alfred de Souza and Walter Fernandes. New Delhi: Indian Social Institute.

Bowler, Kenneth. 1974. *The Nixon Guaranteed Income Proposal; Substance and Process in Policy Change.* Philadelphia: Ballinger.

Boxer, Charles R. 1964. *The Golden Age of Brazil 1695–1750.* Berkeley: University of California Press.

Bretton, Henry L. 1962. *Power and Stability in Nigeria.* New York: Praeger.

Brody, David. 1980. *Workers in Industrial America.* New York: Oxford University Press.

Brown, Kenneth D. 1982. *The English Labour Movement 1700–1951.* New York: St. Martin's Press.

———. 1985. "The Edwardian Labour Party." Pp. 1–16 in *The First Labour Party 1906–1914*, edited by Kenneth D. Brown. London: Croom Helm.

Bruno, Michael and Jeffrey D. Sachs. 1985. *Economics of Worldwide Stagflation.* Cambridge: Harvard University Press.

Buchanan, James M. and Gordon Tullock, eds. 1980. *Toward a Theory of the Rent-Seeking Society.* College Station, TX: Texas A&M.

Bundesministerium für Arbeit und Sozialordnung, Referat Öffentlichkeitsarbeit. 1988. *Statistisches Taschenbuch 1988: Arbeits- und Sozialstatistik.* Bonn: Bundesministerium für Arbeit und Sozialordnung.

Burch, Philip. 1973. "The NAM as an Interest Group." *Politics and Society* 4:97–130.

Butler, Stuart and Peter Germanis. 1983. "Achieving Social Security Reform: A Leninist Strategy." *Cato Journal* 3:547–556.

Cameron, David R. 1978. "The Expansion of the Public Economy: A Comparative Analysis." *American Political Science Review* 72:1243–1261.

———. 1984. "Social Democracy, Corporatism, Labor Quiescence and the Representation of Economic Interests in Advanced Capitalist Society." Pp. 143–178 in *Order and Conflict in Contemporary Capitalism*, edited by John H. Goldthorpe. Oxford: Clarendon Press.

Camp, Richard L. 1969. *The Papal Ideology and Social Reform: A Study of Historical Development, 1878–1967.* Leyden, Netherlands: E.J. Brill.

Cardoso, Fernando H. 1973. "Associated Dependent Development: Theoretical and Practical Implications." Pp. 142–178 in *Authoritarian Brazil: Origins. Policies, and Future*, edited by Alfred Stephan. New Haven: Yale University Press.

Carlson, Valdemar. 1966. "Institutional Change in a Welfare State." *Journal of Risk and Insurance* 33:587–596.

Carnoy, Martin. 1984. *The State and Political Theory.* Princeton: Princeton University Press.

Carr, William. 1979. *A History of Germany 1815–1945.* New York: St. Martin's Press.

Castles, Francis G. 1982. "The Impact of Parties on Public Expenditure." Pp. 21–96 in *The Impact of Parties: Politics and Policies in Democratic Capitalist States*, edited by Francis G. Castles. Beverly Hills: Sage.

Castles, Francis G. and Robert D. McKinlay. 1979. "Public Welfare Provision, and the Sheer Futility of the Sociological Approach to Politics." *British Journal of Political Science* 9:157–172.

Castles, Francis G. and Deborah Mitchell. 1990. "Three World of Welfare Capitalism or Four?" Discussion Paper No. 21, *Public Policy Program Discussion Papers.* Canberrra: Australian National University.

Castro-Gutiérrez, Alvaro. 1989. "Pension Schemes in Latin America: Some Financial Problems." *International Social Security Review* 42(1):35–61.

Cates, Jerry R. 1983. *Insuring Inequality: Administrative Leadership in Social Security, 1935–54.* Ann Arbor: University of Michigan Press.

Chellaney, Brahma. 1990. "Passage to Power." *World Monitor* 3 (February):24–32.

Chowdhry, D. Paul. 1985. "India." Pp. 93–132 in *Social Welfare in Asia*, edited by John Dixon and Hyung Shik Kim. London: Croom Helm.

Clark, Colin. 1957. *The Conditions of Economic Progress*. Third Edition. New York: St. Martin's Press.

Cnaan, Ram A., Sven E. Olsson, and Terrie Wetle. 1990. "Cross-National Comparisons of Planning for the Needs of the Very Old: Israel, Sweden, and the United States." *Journal of Aging and Social Policy* 2:83–107.

Coates, K. and T. Topham. 1980. *Trade Unions in British Politics*. Nottingham: Spokesman Books.

Cohen, Robin. 1974. *Labour and Politics in Nigeria 1945–71*. London: Heinemann.

Cohen, Wilbur J. 1953. "Social Security in India." *Social Security Bulletin* 16(5):11–15.

Coleman, James S. 1958. *Nigeria: Background to Nationalism*. Berkeley: University of California Press.

Collier, Ruth Berins. 1982. "Popular Sector Incorporation and Political Supremacy: Regime Evolution in Brazil and Mexico." Pp. 57–109 in *Brazil and Mexico: Patterns in Late Development*, edited by Sylvia A. Hewlett and Richard S. Weinert. Philadelphia: Institute for the Study of Human Issues.

Collins, Doreen. 1965. "The Introduction of Old Age Pensions in Great Britain." *Historical Journal* 8:246–259.

Commons, John R. 1935. *History of Labor in the United States, 1896–1932*. New York: Macmillan.

Conniff, Michael L. 1975. "Voluntary Association in Rio, 1870–1945: A New Approach to Urban Social Dynamics." *Journal of Inter-American Studies and World Affairs* 17:64–81.

Coughlin, Richard M. 1980. *Ideology, Public Opinion and Welfare Policy*. Berkeley: Institute of International Studies, University of California.

Coughlin, Richard M. and Richard F. Tomasson. 1991. "Sweden." Pp. 147–164 in *International Handbook on Old-Age Insurance*, edited by Martin B. Tracy and Fred C. Pampel. New York: Greenwood Press.

Crowder, Michael. 1972. "Indirect Rule—French and British Style." Pp. 358–369 in *Perspectives on the African Past*, edited by Martin A. Klein and G. Wesley Johnson. Boston: Little, Brown.

Crystal, Stephen. 1982. *America's Old Age Crisis: Public Policy and the Two Worlds of Aging*. New York: Basic Books.

Cumming, John. 1932. *Political India: 1832–1932*. London: Oxford University Press.

Cutright, Phillips. 1965. "Political Structure, Economic Development and National Social Security Programs." *American Journal of Sociology* 70:539–355.

———. 1967. "Income Redistribution: A Cross-National Analysis." *Social Forces* 46:180–190.

Dahl, Robert. 1956. *A Preface to Democratic Theory*. Chicago: University of Chicago Press.

Daland, Robert T. 1981. *Exploring Brazilian Bureaucracy*. Washington, D.C.: University Press of America.

Dawson, William H. 1912. *Social Insurance in Germany, 1883–1911*. London: Scribner.

Day, Christine L. 1990. *What Older Americans Think: Interest Groups and Aging Policy*. Princeton: Princeton University Press.

Dearing, Mary R. 1951. *Veterans in Politics: The Story of the G.A.R.* Baton Rouge: Louisiana State University Press.

Derthick, Martha. 1979. *Policymaking for Social Security*. Washington, D.C.: Brookings Institution.

Desai, M. M. and M. D. Khetani. 1979. "Intervention Strategies for the Aged in India." Pp. 99–112 in *Reaching the Aged: Social Services in Forty-four Countries*, edited by Morton I. Teicher, Daniel Thursz, and Joseph L. Vigilante. London: Sage.

DeViney, Stanley. 1983. "Characteristics of the State and the Expansion of Public Social Insurance Expenditures." *Comparative Social Research* 6:151–174.

———. 1984. "The Political Economy of Public Pensions: A Cross-National Analysis." *Journal of Political and Military Sociology* 12:295–310.

Diamond, Stanley. 1967. *Nigeria: Model of a Colonial Failure*. New York: American Committee on Africa.

Dixon, John. 1982. "Provident Funds in the Third World A Cross-National Review." *Public Administration and Development* 2:325–344.

———. 1986. *Social Security Traditions and their Global Applications*. Belconnen, Australia: International Fellowship for Social and Economic Development.

Downs, Anthony. 1957. *An Economic Theory of Democracy*. New York: Harper and Row.

Dudley, Billy J. 1973. *Instability and Political Order: Politics and Crisis in Nigeria*. Ibadan: IUP.

———. 1982. *An Introduction to Nigerian Government and Politics*. Bloomington: Indiana University Press.

Dunbabin, J. P. D. 1988. "Electoral Reforms and their Outcome in the United Kingdom 1865–1900." Pp. 93–125 in *Later Victorian Britain, 1867–1900*, edited by T. R. Gourvish and Alan O'Day. New York: St. Martin's Press.

Dunleavy, Patrick. 1989. "The United Kingdom Paradoxes of an Ungrounded Statism." Pp. 242–291 in *The Comparative History of Public Policy*, edited by Francis G. Castles. New York: Oxford University Press.

Dusgate, Richard H. 1985. *The Conquest of Northern Nigeria*. London: Frank Cass.

Edwards, Richard T. 1979. *Contested Terrain: The Transformation of the Work Place in the Twentieth Century*. New York: Basic Books.

Einhorn, Eric S. and John Logue. 1989. *Modern Welfare States*. New York: Praeger.

Ejuba, E. J. 1982. "Social Security Developments in French-Speaking Countries South of the Sahara: Trends Since 1970." Pp. 101–129 in *The ILO/Norway African Regional Training Course*. Geneva: International Labour Office.

Ekpenyong, S., O. Oyeneye, and M. Peil. 1986. "Nigerian Elderly: A Rural-Urban and Interstate Comparison." *African Gerontology/Gerontologie Africaine* 5(12):5–19.

Employers' Federation of India. 1970. *Social Security in India: A Review*. Bombay: Employers' Federation of India.

Epstein, Abraham. 1922. *Facing Old Age*. New York: Alfred Knopf.

Erickson, Kenneth P. 1977. *The Brazilian Corporative State and Working-Class Politics*. Berkeley: University of California Press.

Erickson, Kenneth P. and Kevin J. Middlebrook. 1982. "The State and Organized Labor in Brazil and Mexico." Pp. 213–262 in *Brazil and Mexico: Patterns in Late Development*, edited by Sylvia A. Hewlett and Richard S. Weinert. Philadelphia: Institute for the Study of Human Issues.

Ermisch, John. 1989. "Demographic Change and Intergenerational Transfers in Industrial Countries." Pp. 2–32 in *Workers Versus Pensioners: Intergenerational Justice in an Ageing World*, edited by Paul Johnson, Christopher Conrad, and David Thomson. Manchester, England: Manchester University Press.

Eska, Brunhilde. 1980. "The Social Security System of the Federal Republic of Germany." *Social Service Review* 54:108–123.

Esping-Andersen, Gøsta. 1980. *Social Class, Social Democracy and State Policy*. Copenhagen: New Social Science Monographs.

————. 1985. *Politics Against Markets: The Social Democratic Road to Power*. Princeton: Princeton University Press.

————. 1990. *Three Worlds of Welfare Capitalism*. Princeton: Princeton University Press.

Esping-Andersen, Gøsta, Lee Rainwater, and Martin Rein. 1988. "Institutional and Political Factors Affecting the Well-Being of the Elderly." Pp. 333–350 in *The Vulnerable*, edited by John L. Palmer, Timothy Smeeding, and Barbara B. Torrey. Washington, D.C.: The Urban Institute.

Estes, Carroll L. 1979. *The Aging Enterprise*. San Francisco: Jossey-Bass.

Falola, Toyin and Julius Ihonvbere. 1985. *The Rise and Fall of Nigeria's Second Republic: 1979–84*. London: Zed Books.

Federal Minister of Labour and Social Affairs. 1989. *Social Security*. Bonn: Bundesminister für Arbeit und Sozialordnung, Referat Öffentlichkeitsarbeit.

————. 1990. *Pension Reform '92: Your Pension—Something to Rely On*. Bonn: Bundesminister für Arbeit und Sozialordnung, Referat Öffentlichkeitsarbeit.

Fersh, Seymour. 1965. *India and South Asia*. New York: Macmillan.

Fischer, David H. 1978. *Growing Old in America*. New York: Oxford University Press.

————. 1979. "The Politics of Aging: A Short History." *Journal of the Institute for Socioeconomic Studies*, 4:51–66.

Flora, Peter and Jens Alber. 1981. "Modernization, Democratization, and the Development of Welfare States in Western Europe." Pp. 37–80 in *The Development of Welfare States in Europe and America*, edited by Peter Flora and Arnold J. Heidenheimer. New Brunswick, NJ: Transaction.

Form, William. 1979. "Comparative Industrial Sociology and the Convergence Hypothesis." *Annual Review of Sociology* 5:1–25.

Foxley, Alejandro, Eduardo Aninat, and J. P. Arellano. 1979. *Redistributive Effects of Government Programmes: The Chilean Case*. Oxford: Pergamon Press.

Frank, André Gunder. 1969. *Capitalism and Underdevelopment in Latin America*. New York: Monthly Review Press.

————. 1978. *Dependent Accumulation and Underdevelopment*. New York: Monthly Review Press.

————. 1980. *Crisis: In the World Economy*. London: Heinemann.

Fraser, Derek. 1973. *Evolution of the British Welfare State*. London: Macmillan.

Friedland, Roger and Jimy Sanders. 1985. "The Public Economy and Economic Growth in Western Market Economies." *American Socioloigcal Review* 50:421–437.

————. 1986. "Private and Social Wage Expansion in the Advanced Market Economies." *Theory and Society* 15:193–222.

Furtado, Celso. 1963. *The Economic Growth of Brazil: A Survey from Colonial to Modern Times*. Berkeley: University of California Press.

Gailbraith, John Kenneth. 1952. *American Capitalism*. Boston: Houghton Mifflin.

Galtung, Johan. 1971. "A Structural Theory of Imperialism." *Journal of Peace Research* 8:102–116.

George, Usha G. 1987. "Social Legislation in Relation to Labour in Nigeria: A Critique." *Nigeria Magazine* 55 (January–March):18–25.

Gersdorff, Ralph von. 1962. *Savings, Credit and Insurance in Brazil*. Barbados, West Indies: Government Printing Office.

Gilbert, Bentley B. 1966. *The Evolution of National Insurance in Great Britain: The Origins of the Welfare State*. London: Michael Joseph.

————. 1970. *British Social Policy 1914–1939*. Ithaca, NY: Cornell University Press.

Gillis, John. 1968. "Aristocracy and Bureaucracy in 19th Century Prussia." *Past and Present* 41:105–129.

Glasson, William. 1902. "The South and the Service Pension Laws." *South Atlantic Quar-
terly* 1 (October):351–360.
———. 1918. *Federal Military Pensions in the United States*. New York: Oxford Univer-
sity Press.
Goldthorpe, John H. 1984. "The End of Convergence: Corporatist and Dualist Tendencies
in Modern Western Society." Pp. 315–343 in *Order and Conflict in Contemporary
Capitalism*, edited by John H. Goldthorpe. Oxford: Clarendon Press.
Gomes, Gustavo Maia. 1986. *The Roots of State Intervention in the Brazilian Economy*.
New York: Praeger.
Goodin, Robert E. and Julian Le Grand. 1987. *Not Only the Poor*. London: Allen and
Unwin.
Gore, M. S. 1968. *Urbanization and Family Change*. Bombay: Popular Prakashan Press,
1968.
Gosden, P. H. J. 1961. *The Friendly Societies in England. 1815–1875*. Manchester,
England: Manchester University Press.
Gough, Ian. 1979. *The Political Economy of the Welfare State*. London: Macmillan.
Graebner, William. 1980. *A History of Retirement*. New Haven: Yale University Press.
Graf, William. 1989. "Issues and Substance in the Prescription of Liberal-Democratic Forms
for Nigeria's Third Republic." *African Affairs* 88 (January):91–100.
Graham, Richard. 1990. *Patronage and Politics in Nineteenth-Century Brazil*. Stanford:
Stanford University Press.
Gray, Robert. 1981. *The Aristocracy of Labour in Nineteenth-Century Britain, c. 1850–
1900*. London: Macmillan.
Greza, Gerhard. 1989. "A Wide Consensus in Favor of the Pension Reform," Pp. 1–4 in
Social Report (4–89 e). Bonn: Inter Nationes.
Griffiths, Percival J. 1965. *The British Impact on India*. Hamden, CT: Archon Books.
Groskind, Fred and John B. Williamson. 1991. "India." Pp. 103–112 in *International Hand-
book on Old-Age Insurance*, edited by Martin B. Tracy and Fred C. Pampel. New
York: Greenwood Press.
Gupta, N. H. 1986. *Social Security Legislation for Labour in India*. New Delhi: Deep and
Deep Publications.
Hallendorff, Carl and Adolf Schück. 1929. *History of Sweden*. Stockholm: C. E. Fritze.
Hannah, Leslie. 1986. *Inventing Retirement*. Cambridge: Cambridge University Press.
Harbison, Frederick. 1962. "Human Resources and Economic Development in Nigeria."
Pp. 198–219 in *The Nigerian Political Scene*, edited by Robert O. Tilman and
Taylor Cole. Durham, NC: Duke University Press.
Hardgrave, Robert L. 1984. *India Under Pressure*. Boulder: Westview Press.
Hardgrave, Robert L. and Stanley A. Kochanek. 1986. *India: Government and Politics in
a Developing Nation*. Fourth Edition. New York: Harcourt Brace and Jovanovich.
Hatch, John. 1971. *Nigeria: A History*. London: Secker and Warburg.
Hay, J. R. 1975. *The Origins of the Liberal Welfare Reforms 1906–1914*. London: Macmillan.
———. 1978. *The Development of the British Welfare State, 1880–1975*. London: Edward
Arnold.
Heclo, Hugh. 1974. *Modern Social Politics in Britain and Sweden*. New Haven: Yale
University Press.
Heclo, Hugh and Henrik Madsen. 1987. *Policy and Politics in Sweden*. Philadelphia: Temple
University Press.
Hertz, Frederick. 1975. *The German Public Mind in the Nineteenth Century*. Totowa, NJ:
Rowan and Littlefield.

Hewitt, Christopher. 1977. "The Effect of Political Democracy and Social Democracy on Equality in Industrial Societies: A Cross-National Comparison." *American Sociological Review* 42:450–464.

Hicks, Alexander. 1991. "Unions, Social Democracy, Welfare and Growth." *Research in Political Sociology* 5:209–234.

Hicks, Alexander and Duane Swank. 1984. "On the Political Economy of Welfare Expansion: A Comparative Analysis of 18 Advanced Capitalist Democracies,1960–1971." *Comparative Political Studies* 17:81–120.

Hinrichs, Karl. 1991. "Public Pensions and Demographic Change." *Society* 28 (September/October):32–37.

Hobsbawm, Eric J. 1964. *Labouring Men*. New York: Basic Books.

———. 1984. *Workers: Worlds of Labor*. New York: Pantheon.

Hockerts, H. G. 1981. "German Post-War Social Policies Against the Background of the Beveridge Plan. Some Observations Preparatory to a Comparative Analysis." Pp. 315–339 in *The Emergence of the Welfare State in Britain and Germany: 1850–1950*, edited by W. J. Mommsen. London: Croom Helm.

Hofstadter, Richard. 1944. *Social Darwinism in American Thought 1860–1915*. London: Oxford University Press.

Hohaus, Rinehart. 1960. "Equity, Adequacy, and Related Factors in Old Age Security." Pp. 61–63 in *Social Security: Programs, Problems, and Policies*, edited by William Haber and Wilbur J. Cohen. Homewood, IL: Irwin.

Hohorst, Von Gerd, Jürgen Kocka, and Gerhard A. Ritter. 1978. *Sozialgeschichtliches Arbeitsbuch Band II: Materialien zur Statistik des Kaiserrichs 1870–1914*. Munich: C. H. Beck.

Holtzman, Abraham. 1963. *The Townsend Movement*. New York: Bookman Associates.

Hoskins, Dalmer D. 1971. "Introduction of Survivor Pension Program in India." *Social Security Bulletin* 34 (8):28–30.

Hughes, H. D. 1970. "Trade Unions." Pp. 56–66 in *Democratic Sweden*, edited by Margaret I. Cole and Charles Smith. Freeport, NY: Books for Libraries Press.

Hunt, E. H. 1981. *British Labour History 1815–1914*. London: Weidenfeld and Nicolson.

Huntington, Samuel P. 1968. *Political Order in Changing Societies*. New Haven: Yale University Press.

Ijeh, M. C. 1977. "Alternative Approaches to the Problems of Arrears in Employer Contributions." Pp. 8–15 in *Roundtable Meeting for Member Organizations of the International Social Security Association in English-Speaking Countries of Africa*, Lagos, 30 November–3 December 1976. African Social Security Documentation. Geneva: International Social Security Association.

———. 1983. "Decentralisation of Social Security Administraion." Pp. 19-26 in *Social Security Documentation African Series*. Lome, Togo: African Regional Office of the International Social Security Association.

Ijere, Martin O. 1966. "Indigenous African Social Security as a Basis for Future Planning—The Case of Nigeria." *Bulletin of the International Social Security Association* 19:463–487

———. 1978. *The Development of the African Social Security System*. Lagos, Nigeria: African University Press.

Ikejiani, Okechukwu and M. Odinchezo Ikejiani. 1986. *Nigeria: Political Imperative*. Enugu, Nigeria: Fourth Dimensional Publishers.

Ikime, Obaro. 1977. *The Fall of Nigeria*. London: Heinemann.

Inkeles, Alex. 1981. "Convergence and Divergence in Industrial Societies." Pp. 3–38 in

Directions of Change: Modernization Theory, Research, and Realities, edited by Mustafa O. Attir, Burkart Holzner, and Zdenek Suda. New York: Westview Press.

Inkeles, Alex and Chikako Usui. 1988. "The Retirement Decision in Cross-National Perspective." Pp. 273–311 in *Issues in Contemporary Retirement*, edited by Rita Ricardo-Campbell and Edward P. Lazear. Stanford, CA: Hoover Institution Press.

International Benefit Guidelines. 1989. New York: William M. Mercer International.

International Benefits Information Service. 1986. "IBIS Profile- Sweden." Pp. 1–25. Chicago: Charles D. Spencer and Associates.

———. 1989a. *Germany Reference Manual*. Chicago: Charles D. Spencer and Associates.

———. 1989b. *IBIS Reference Manual—United Kingdom*. Chicago: Charles D. Spencer and Associates.

International Labour Office (ILO). 1977. *Improvement and Harmonisation of Social Security Systems in Africa*. Report II, Fifth African Regional Conference. Abidjan, September–October 1977. Geneva: International Labour Office.

———. 1985. *The Cost of Social Security*. Geneva: International Labour Office.

International Social Security Association (ISSA). 1961. "Nigeria: Establishment of a Provident Fund." *Bulletin of the International Social Security Association* 14:620–622.

———. 1976. *African Social Security Documentation*. Geneva: General Secretariat of the ISSA.

———. 1980a. *Sixth African Regional Conference of ISSA*. Cairo, 16–21 October 1978. Reports and Documents. Geneva: General Secretariat of the ISSA.

———. 1980b. Committee on Provident Funds. *Fourth Meeting of the Committee*. Lagos, 4–6 December 1979. Geneva: General Secretariat of the ISSA.

———. 1982. Committee on Provident Funds. *Sixth Meeting of the Committee*. New Delhi, 8–10 February 1982. New Delhi: ISSA Regional Office for Asia and Oceania.

———. 1988. *Social Security Documentation: African Series. Ninth African Regional Conference*. Casablanca 9–12 November 1987. Geneva: General Secretariat of the ISSA.

———. 1989. Committee on Provident Funds. *Tenth Meeting of the Committee*. Nairobi, 27–29 September 1988. Geneva: General Secretariat of the ISSA.

International Social Security Review. 1986. "Developments and Trends in Social Security, 1984–1986." *International Social Security Review* 4/86:375–460.

Isichei, Elizabeth. 1983. *A History of Nigeria*. London: Longman.

Jackman, Robert W. 1975. *Politics and Social Equality: A Comparative Analysis*. New York: Wiley.

Janowitz, Morris. 1976. *Social Control of the Welfare State*. Chicago: University of Chicago Press.

Jeffrey, Robin. 1986. *What's Happening to India?* New York: Holmes and Meier.

Jenkins, J. Craig and Barbara G. Brents. 1989. "Social Protest, Hegemonic Competition, and Social Reform: A Political Struggle Interpretation of the Origins of the American Welfare State." *American Sociological Review* 54:891–909.

Johnson, Elizabeth S. and John B. Williamson. 1987. "Retirement in the United States." Pp. 9–41 in *Retirement in Industrialized Societies*, edited by Kyriakos S. Markides and Cary L. Cooper. New York: Wiley.

Johnson, Paul. 1985. *Saving and Spending: The Working-class Economy in Britain 1870–1939*. Oxford: Clarendon Press.

Johri, C. K. 1967. *Unionism in a Developing Economy*. Bombay: Asia Publishing House.

———. 1982. "Social Security in India." *Labour and Society* 7:105–135.

Joseph, Richard A. 1987. *Democracy and Prebendal Politics in Nigeria*. Cambridge: Cambridge University Press.

Judge, Ken. 1981. "State Pensions and the Growth of Social Welfare Expenditure." *Journal of Social Policy* 10:503–530.

Juttemeier, Karl H. and Hans-George Petersen. 1982. "West Germany." Pp. 181–206 in *The World Crisis in Social Security*, edited by Jean-Jacques Rosa. San Francisco: Institute for Contemporary Studies.

Kaim-Caudle, Peter R. 1973. *Comparative Social Policy and Social Security*. London: Martin Robertson.

Karunakaran, K. P. 1964. *Continuity and Change in Indian Politics*. New Delhi: People's Publishing House.

Karve, Irawati. 1964. "The Family in India." Pp. 47–58 in *Contemporary India*, edited by Baidya Nath Varma. New York: Asia Publishing House.

Katzenstein, Peter J. 1985. *Small States in World Markets: Industrial Policy in Europe*. Ithaca, NY: Cornell University Press.

———. 1987. *Policy and Politics in West Germany*. Philadelphia: Temple University Press.

———. 1989. "Stability and Change in the Emerging Third Republic." Pp. 307–353 in *Industry and Politics in West Germany*, edited by Peter J. Katzenstein. Ithaca, NY: Cornell University Press.

Keck, Margaret E. 1989. "The New Unionism in the Brazilian Transition." Pp. 252–296 in *Democratizing Brazil*, edited by Alfred Stepan. New York: Oxford University Press.

Keller, Morton. 1979. *Affairs of State: Public Life in Nineteenth Century America*. Cambridge: Harvard University Press.

Kerr, Clark, John T. Dunlop, Frederick Harbison, and Charles A. Myers. 1964. *Industrialism and Industrial Man*. New York: Oxford University Press.

Kilby, Peter. 1967. "Industrial Relations and Wage Determination: Failure of the Anglo-Saxon Model." *Journal of Developing Areas* 1:489–520.

Kincaid, J. C. 1973. *Poverty and Equality in Britain: A Study of Social Security and Taxation*. Hamondsworth, England: Penguin Books.

Kingsnorth, G. W. 1966. *Africa South of the Sahara*. Cambridge: Cambridge University Press.

Kingson, Eric R. 1984. "Financing Social Security: Agenda-Setting and the Enactment of the 1983 Amendments to the Social Security Act." *Policy Studies Journal* 13:131–155.

———. 1987. *What You Must Know about Social Security and Medicare*. New York: Pharos Books.

———. 1988. "Generational Equity: An Unexpected Opportunity to Broaden the Politics of Aging." *Gerontologist* 28:765–772.

———. 1989. "Misconceptions Distort Social Security Policy Discussions." *Social Work* 34:357–362.

Kingson, Eric R., Barbara A. Hirshorn, and John M. Cornman. 1986. *Ties That Bind*. Washington, D.C.: Seven Locks Press.

Kingson, Eric R. and John B. Williamson. 1991. "Generational Equity or Privatization of Social Security?" *Society* 28 (September/October):38–41.

Kirk-Greene, A. H. M. 1986. "West Africa: Nigeria and Ghana." Pp. 30–77 in *Politics and Government in African States, 1960–1985*, edited by Peter Duignan and Robert H. Jackson. London: Croom Helm.

Kiser, Edgar and Michael Hechter. 1991. "The Role of General Theory in Comparative-historical Sociology." *American Journal of Sociology* 97:1–30.

Kmenta, Jan. 1971. *Elements of Econometrics*. New York: Macmillan.

Kohli, Atul. 1988. "State-Society Relations in India's Changing Democracy." Pp. 305–315 in *India's Democracy*, edited by Atul Kohli. Princeton: Princeton University Press.

Kohli, Martin. 1987. "Retirement and the Moral Economy: An Historical Interpretation of the German Case." *Journal of Aging Studies* 1:125–144.

Kohli, Martin, and Martin Rein. 1991. "The Changing Balance of Work and Retirement." Pp. 1–35 in *Time for Retirement*, edited by Martin Kohli, Martin Rein, Anne-Marie Guillemard, and Herman van Gunsteren. Cambridge: Cambridge University Press.

Kollmann, Geoffrey. 1991. "Social Security: Investing the Surplus." *CRS Report for Congress*, January 27. Washington, D.C.: Congressional Research Service, U. S. Library of Congress.

Korpi, Walter. 1978. *The Working Class in Welfare Capitalism*. London: Routledge and Kegan Paul.

————. 1982. "The Historical Compromise and its Dissolution." Pp. 124–141 in *Sweden: Choices for Economic and Social Policy in the 1980s*, edited by Bengt Rydén and Villy Bergström. London: George Allen and Unwin.

————. 1983. *The Democratic Class Struggle*. London: Routledge and Kegan Paul.

Koselka, Rita. 1991. "Chile's Social Security." *Forbes*, October 28, pp. 158–160.

Kosok, Paul. 1933. *Modern Germany*. Chicago: University of Chicago Press.

Kouassi, Prosper Koffi. 1991. "Ivory Coast." Pp. 133–138 in *International Handbook on Old-Age Insurance*, edited by Martin B. Tracy and Fred C. Pampel. New York: Greenwood Press.

Krantz, Olle and Carl-Axel Nilsson. 1975. *Swedish National Product 1861–1970*. Lund, Sweden: CWK Cleerup.

Krishnamurthy, V. 1979. "Social Security Schemes in Kerla." Pp. 273–300 in *Role of Trade Unions in Social Security in Asia and the Pacific: Report of a Regional Seminar*. New Delhi: International Labour Office.

Kuhnle, Stein. 1978. "The Beginnings of the Nordic Welfare States: Similarities and Differences." *Acta Sociologica* 21 (Supplement):9–35.

————. 1981. "The Growth of Social Insurance Programs in Scandinavia: Outside Influences and Internal Forces." Pp. 125–150 in *The Development of Welfare States in Europe and America*, edited by Peter Flora and Arnold J. Heidenheimer. New Brunswick, NJ: Transaction.

Kurian, George T. 1982. *Encyclopedia of the Third World*. Revised Edition, vol. 2. New York: Facts on File.

Lamm, Richard D. 1985. *Mega-Traumas, America at the Year 2000*. Boston: Houghton Mifflin.

Lammers, William W. 1983. *Public Policy and Aging*. Washington, D.C.: Congressional Quarterly Press.

Lash, Scott. 1985. "The End of Neo-Corporatism?: The Breakdown of Centralized Bargaining in Sweden." *British Journal of Industrial Relations* 23:215–239.

Laslett, Peter. 1985. "Societal Development and Aging." Pp. 87–116 in *Handbook of Aging and the Social Sciences*. Second Edition, edited by Robert H. Binstock and Ethel Shanas. New York: Van Nostrand Reinhold.

Lawrence, William J. and Stephen Leeds. 1978. *Federal Income Transfer Payments, Fiscal Year 1977*. White Plains, NY: Institute for Socioeconomic Studies.

LeGrand, Thomas K. 1989. "The Determinants of Male Age of Retirement in Brazil." Ph.D. dissertation. Ann Arbor: University of Michigan.

Lehmbruch, G. 1984. "Concentration and the Structure of Corporatist Networks." Pp. 60–80 in *Order and Conflict in Contemporary Capitalism*, edited by John H. Goldthorpe. New York: Oxford University Press.

Lenin, V. I. [1917] 1939. *Imperialism: The Highest Stage of Capitalism*. New York: International Publishers.

————. [1917] 1965. *The State and Revolution*. Peking: Foreign Language Press.

Lenski, Gerhard. 1966. *Power and Privilege*. New York: McGraw-Hill.

Lewin, Leif, Bo Jansson, and Dag Sörbom. 1972. *The Swedish Electorate 1887–1968*. Stockholm: Almqvist and Wilksell.

Light, Paul. 1985. *Artful Work: The Politics of Social Security Reform*. New York: Random House.

Lipset, Seymour Martin. 1959. *Political Man: The Social Basis of Politics*. Garden City, NY: Doubleday.

Lloyd, T. O. 1970. *Empire to Welfare State: English History 1906–1967*. London: Oxford University Press.

Longman, Phillip. 1987. *Born to Pay: The New Politics of Aging in America*. Boston: Houghton Mifflin.

Love, Joseph L. 1970. "Political Participation in Brazil, 1881–1969." *Luso-Brazilian Review* 7 (December):3–24.

————. 1971. *Rio Grande do Sul and Brazilian Regionalism, 1882–1930*. Stanford: Stanford University Press.

Lubeck, Paul M. 1986. *Islam and Urban Labor in Northern Nigeria*. London: Cambridge University Press.

Lubove, Roy. 1968. *The Struggle for Social Security: 1900–1935*. Cambridge: Harvard University Press.

Ludwig, Armin K. 1985. *Brazil: A Handbook of Historical Statistics*. Boston: G. K. Hall.

Mahadevan, K. 1986. "A System of Policy for Welfare of the Elderly Citizens." *Indian Journal of Social Work* 46:497–505.

Mallet, Alfredo. 1980. "Social Protection of the Rural Population." *International Social Security Review* 33:359–393.

Malloy, James M. 1976. "Social Insurance Policy in Brazil: A Study in the Politics of Inequality." *Inter-American Economic Affairs* 30 (Winter):41–67.

————. 1977. *Authoritarianism and Corporatism in Latin America*. Pittsburgh: University of Pittsburgh Press.

————. 1979. *The Politics of Social Security in Brazil*. Pittsburgh: University of Pittsburgh Press.

————. 1991. "Statecraft, Social Policy, and Governance in Latin America." Working Paper #151 (February). Notre Dame, IN: Kellog Institute for International Studies, University of Notre Dame.

Mamoria, C. B. and Satish Mamoria. 1983. *Labour Welfare, Social Security and Industrial Peace in India*. Allahabad, India: Kitab Mahal.

Mann, Golo. 1968. *The History of Germany Since 1789*. London: Chatto and Windus.

Manoilesco, Mihail. 1934. *Le Siecle du Corporatisme*. Paris: Felix Alcan.

Markovitz, Andrei S. 1986. *The Politics of the West German Trade Unions*. Cambridge: Cambridge University Press.

Marmor, Theodore R. 1973. *The Politics of Medicare*. Chicago: Aldine.

————. 1981. "Enacting Medicare." Pp. 105–134 in *The Aging in Politics*, edited by Robert Hudson. Springfield, IL: Charles C. Thomas.

Marsh, Robert M. 1988. "Sociological Explanations of Economic Growth." *Studies in Comparative International Development* 23:41–76.

Marshall, Ray. 1978. "The Old South and the New." Pp. 3–17 in *Employment of Blacks in the South*, edited by Ray Marshall and Virgil Christian. Austin: University of Texas Press.

Martin, Linda G. 1988. "The Aging in Asia." *Journals of Gerontology* 43:S99–S113.

Marx, Karl. [1867] 1967. *Capital*, vol.1 New York: International Publishers.

———. [1853] 1979. "The Future of British Rule in India." Pp. 217–222 in *Collected Works*, vol. 12. London: Lawrence and Wishart.

Marx, Karl and Frederick Engels. [1848] 1976. "Manifesto of the Communist Party." Pp. 477–519 in *Collected Works*, vol. 6. London: Lawrence and Wishart.

Mesa-Lago, Carmelo. 1978. *Social Security in Latin America*. Pittsburgh: University of Pittsburgh Press.

———. 1983. "Social Security and Extreme Poverty in Latin America." *Journal of Development Economics* 12:83–110.

———. 1986. "Comparative Study of the Development of Social Security in Latin America." *International Social Security Review* 39:127–152.

Metcalf, Michael. 1987. *The Riksdag: A History of the Swedish Parliament*. New York: St. Martin's Press.

Meyer, Charles W. 1987. "Social Security: Past, Present, and Future." Pp. 1–34 in *Social Security*, edited by Charles W. Meyer. Lexington, MA: Lexington Books.

Michaneck, Ernst. 1964. *For and Against the Welfare State: The Swedish Experience*. Stockholm: The Swedish Institute.

Miliband, Ralph. 1969. *The State in Capitalist Society*. London: Weidenfeld and Nicolson.

Milner, Henry. 1989. *Sweden: Social Democracy in Practice*. New York: Oxford University Press.

Ministry of Welfare Services, Malaysia. 1982. "The Situation of the Elderly in Malaysia." Pp. 289–292 in *The Elderly of Asia*. Asian Regional Conference on Active Aging, Manila, 24–28 January 1982. Manila: Social Research Center, University of Santo Tomas.

Mink, Gwendolyn. 1986. *Old Labor and New Immigrants in American Political Development*. Ithaca, NY: Cornell University Press.

Minkler, Meredith. 1986. "Generational Equity and the New Victim Blaming: An Emerging Public Policy Issue." *International Journal of Health Services* 16:539–551.

Mishra, Ramesh. 1977. *Society and Social Policy: Theoretical Perspectives on Welfare*. London: Macmillan.

———. 1984. *The Welfare State in Crisis: Social Thought and Social Change*. New York: St. Martin's Press.

———. 1985. "Rethinking the Welfare State: After the New Right." Paper presented at the Annual Meeting of the American Sociological Association, Washington, D.C.

Montas, Hemando P. 1982. "Problems and Perspectives in the Financing of Social Security in Latin America." Paper presented at the Second American Regional Conference of the International Social Security Association, Caracas, Venezuela.

Montgomery, G. A. 1939. *The Rise of Modern Industry in Sweden*. London: P. S. King and Son.

Moorhouse, Geoffrey. 1983. *India Britannica*. New York: Harper and Row.

Moreau, Pierre. 1974. *Social Protection of the Agricultural Population by Mutual Benefit Societies*. Report IV, of the XVIIIth General Assembly of the ISSA. Abidjan, October–November 1973. Geneva: General Secretariat of the ISSA.

Moreland, W. H., and Atul Chandra Chatterjee. 1957. *A Short History of India*. Fourth Edition. London: Longmas, Green and Company.

Morris, Nicholas. 1988. "Competition, Regulation, and Deregulation in Pension Fund Portfolio Management: The Case of the United Kingdom." Pp. 69–94 in *Pension Asset Management*, edited by Leslie Hannah. Homewood, IL: Irwin.

Mouton, Pierre. 1975. *Social Security in Africa: Trends. Problems and Prospects*. Geneva: International Labour Office.

Mouton, Pierre and Jean-Victor Gruat. 1988. "The Extension of Social Security to Self-Employed Persons in Africa." *International Social Security Review* 1/88:40–54.

Moynihan, Daniel P. 1990. "Surplus Value." *The New Republic*, June 4, pp. 13–16.

Mueller, Dennis C. 1979. *Public Choice*. Cambridge: Cambridge University Press.

Muller, Edward N. 1988. "Democracy, Economic Development, and Income Inequality." *American Sociological Review* 53:50–68.

Mulozi, Sam L. 1982. "Social Security Development in Africa: Trends Since 1970." Pp. 83–99 in *The ILO/Norway African Regional Training Course*. Geneva: International Labour Office.

Munnell, Alicia H. 1977. *The Future of Social Security*. Washington, D.C.: Brookings Institution.

———. 1988. "Social Security and National Saving." Pp. 63–88 in *Social Security and Economic Well-Being across Generations*, edited by John R. Gist. Washington, D.C.: American Association of Retired Persons.

Murat, Auguste. 1944. *Le Corporatisme*. Paris: Les Publications Techniques.

Musiga, Luke O. 1982. "Principles and Specific Problems of Management and Administration of Social Security in African Countries." Pp. 319–333 in *The ILO/Norway African Regional Training Course*. Geneva: International Labour Office.

Myers, Robert J. 1981. *Social Security*. Revised Edition. Homewood, IL: Irwin.

———. 1989. "Modifying Our Present Course." Pp. 13–18 in *Social Security Trust Funds: Issues for the 1990s and Beyond*. Washington, D.C.: American Association of Retired Persons.

Myles, John. 1984. *Old Age in the Welfare State: The Political Economy of Public Pensions*. Boston: Little, Brown.

———. 1988. "Postwar Capitalism and the Extension of Social Security into a Retirement Wage." Pp. 265–284 in *The Politics of Social Policy in the United States*, edited by Margaret Weir, Ann Shola Orloff, and Theda Skocpol. Princeton: Princeton University Press.

Nair, C. R. 1979. "Evolution and Development of National Social Security Policy in India with Special Reference to the Contributions of Trade Unions." Pp. 251–272 in *Role of Trade Unions in Social Security in Asia and the Pacific: Report of a Regional Seminar*. New Delhi: International Labour Office.

Nair, Sobha B. 1990. *Social Security and the Weaker Sections*. Delhi: Renaissance Publishing House.

Nayar, Baldev Raj. 1983. *India's Quest for Technological Independence*, vol. 1. New Delhi: Lancers.

Nelson, Harold D., ed. 1982. *Nigeria: A Country Study*. Washington, D.C.: U.S. Government Printing Office.

Neugarten, Bernice L. 1974. "Age Groups in American Society and the Rise of the Young-Old." *Annals of the American Academy of Political and Social Science* 415:187–198.

Neysmith, Sheila M. and Joey Edwardh. 1984. "Economic Dependency in the 1980s: Its Impact on Third World Elderly." *Ageing and Society* 4:21–44.

Nisbet, Robert A. 1953. *Community and Power*. New York: Oxford University Press.

Niskanen, William A. 1971. *Bureaucracy and Representative Government*. Chicago: Aldine.

Nolan, Patrick D. 1983. "Status in the World System, Income Inequality, and Economic Growth." *American Journal of Sociology* 89:410–419.

Normano, J. F. 1935. *Brazil: A Study of Economic Types*. Chapel Hill: University of North Carolina Press.

Nyrop, Richard F. 1985. *India: A Country Study*. Washington, D.C.: U.S. Government Printing Office

O'Connor, James. 1973. *The Fiscal Crisis of the State*. New York: St. Martin's Press.

Odetola, Theophilus Olatunde. 1978. *Military Politics in Nigeria*. New Brunswick, N.J.: Transaction.

Offe, Claus. 1972. "Advanced Capitalism in the Welfare State." *Politics and Society* 7:479–488.

———. 1984. *Contradictions of the Welfare State*. Cambridge: MIT Press.

O'Grady-LeShane, Regina and John B. Williamson. 1992. "Family Provision in Old-Age Pensions: Twenty Industrial Nations." Pp. 64-77 in *Families and Retirement*, edited by Maximiliane Szinovacz, David J. Ekerdt, and Barbara H. Vinick. Newbury Park, CA: Sage.

Ogunshola, A. O. 1979. "Social Security and Private Pension Practice in Nigeria." *Benefits International* 9 (2):5–12.

Ogus, A. I. 1982. "Great Britain." Pp. 150–264 in *The Evolution of Social Insurance*. 1881–1981, edited by Peter A. Kohler, Hans F. Zachner, and Martin Partington. New York: St. Martin's Press.

O'Higgins, Michael. 1989. "Social Welfare and Privatization: The British Experience." Pp. 157–177 in *Privatization and the Welfare State*, edited by Sheila B. Kamerman and Alfred J. Kahn. Princeton: Princeton University Press.

Okoli, Ekwueme F. 1980. *Institutional Structure and Conflict in Nigeria*. Washington, D.C.: University Press of America.

Oliver, John W. 1917. *History of the Civil War Military Pensions*. 1861–1885. Bulletin of the University of Wisconsin, No. 844. Madison: University of Wisconsin Press.

Olson, Laura Katz. 1982. *The Political Economy of Aging*. New York: Columbia University Press.

Olson, Mancur. 1965. *The Logic of Collective Action: Public Goods and the Theory of Groups*. Cambridge: Harvard University Press.

———. 1982. *The Rise and Decline of Nations: Economic Growth, Stagflation, and Social Rigidities*. New Haven. Yale University Press.

Olsson, Sven E. 1988a. "Sweden." Pp. 1–116 in *Growth to Limits: The Western European Welfare States Since World War II*, vol. 1, *Sweden. Norway. Finland, Denmark*, edited by Peter Flora. New York: Walter de Gruyter.

———. 1990. *Social Policy and Welfare State in Sweden*. Lund. Sweden: Arkiv.

O'Reilly, Mark. 1982. "More Winds of Change Needed." *Benefits International* 11 (July): 2–6.

Organization for Economic Co-operation and Development OECD. 1988a. *Reforming Public Pensions*. Paris: OECD.

———. 1988b. *The Future of Social Protection*. Paris: OECD.

———. 1988c. *Ageing Populations*. Paris: OECD.

Orloff, Ann S. 1991. "Cross Class Alliance, State Building and Social Policy: Canadian Policy Making for Old Age Protection in Comparative Perspective." *Research in Political Sociology* 5:235–275.

Orloff, Ann S. and Theda Skocpol. 1984. "Why Not Equal Protection? Explaining the Politics of Public Social Spending in Britain, 1900–1911, and the United States, 1880s–1920s." *American Sociological Review* 49 (December): 726–750.

Otobo, Dafe. 1986. "The New Trade Union Structure in Nigeria: Some Comments." *Nigerian Journal of Economic and Social Studies* 28:335–356.

Oyefeso, O. A. 1988. "Retirement Benefits in Nigeria: New Developments." *AREA Newsletter*, July, no. 3, pp. 1–2. Brussels: AREA Benefits Network.

Oyeneye, Olatunji Y. 1990. "Old Age in Nigeria: Yesterday, Today and Tomorrow." Unpublished inaugural lecture. Ago-Iwoye, Nigeria: Ogun State University.

Oyovbaire, Sam E. 1981. "The Nigerian Political System and Political Science." *Nigerian Journal of Economics and Social Studies* 23 355–377.

———. 1984. *Federalism in Nigeria*. New York: St. Martin's Press.

Ozawa, Martha N. 1976. "Income Redistribution and Social Security." *Social Service Review* 50:216–217.

Pachter, Henry M. 1978. *Modern Germany: A Social, Cultural and Political History*. Boulder, CO: Westview Press.

Paine, Thomas. [1797] 1945. "Agrarian Justice." Pp. 605–623 in *The Complete Writings of Thomas Paine*, edited by Philip S. Foner. New York: Citadel.

Palme, Joakim. 1990a. "Models of Old-age Pensions." Pp. 104–125 in *Needs and Welfare*, edited by Alan Ware and Robert E. Goodin. London: Sage.

———. 1990b. *Pension Rights in Welfare Capitalism: The Development of Old-Age Pensions in 18 OECD Countries, 1930 to 1985*. Stockholm: Institute for Social Research, University of Stockholm.

Pampel, Fred C. and John B. Williamson. 1985. "Age Structure, Politics and Cross-National Patterns of Public Pension Expenditures." *American Sociological Review* 50:787–798.

———. 1988. "Welfare Spending in Advanced Industrial Democracies, 1950–1980." *American Journal of Sociology* 93:1424–1456.

———. 1989. *Age, Class, Politics and the Welfare State: A Comparative Analysis*. Cambridge: Cambridge University Press.

Pampel, Fred C., John B. Williamson, and Robin Stryker. 1990. "Class Context and Pension Response to Demographic Structure in Advanced Industrial Democracies." *Social Problems* 37:535–550.

Panitch, Leo. 1976. *Social Democracy and Industrial Militancy*. Cambridge: Cambridge University Press.

———. 1980. "Recent Theorizing of Corporatism: Reflections on a Growth Industry." *British Journal of Sociology* 31:159–187.

Panter-Brick, S. K. 1970. *Nigerian Politics and Military Rule: Prelude to the Civil War*. London: Athlone Press.

Parkin, Frank. 1967. "Working-Class Conservatives: A Theory of Political Deviance." *British Journal of Sociology* 18:278–290.

Parrott, Alec L. 1985. *The Iron Road to Social Security*. Sussex, England: Book Guild Limited.

Parry, Richard. 1988. "United Kingdom." Pp. 155–240 in *Growth to Limits*, edited by Peter Flora. New York: Walter de Gruyter.

Passant, E. J. 1959. *A Short History of Germany 1815–1945*. Cambridge: Cambridge University Press.

Peil, Margaret. 1991. "Family Support for the Nigerian Elderly." *Journal of Comparative Family Studies* 22:85–100.

Peil, Margaret, Anne Bamisaiye, and Stephen Ekpenyong. 1989. "Health and Physical Support for the Elderly in Nigeria." *Journal of Cross-Cultural Gerontology* 4: 89–106.

Pelling, Henry. 1968. *Popular Politics and Society in Late Victorian Britain*. London: Macmillan.

Pension System in Chile. 1990. Santiago: Asociación de Administradoras de Fondos de Pensiones A. G.

Pensions Commission. 1991. *The Swedish National Pension System, Principal Report of the Pensions Commission, Summary*. Stockholm: Swedish Ministry of Health and Social Affairs.

Petras, James. 1969. *Politics and Social Forces in Chilean Development*. Berkeley: University of California Press.

Petri, Peter A. 1982. "Income, Employment, and Retirement Policies." Pp. 75–125 in

International Perspectives on Aging: Population and Policy Challenges, edited by Robert H. Binstock, Wing-Sun Chow, and James H. Schulz. New York: United Nations Fund for Population Activities.

Piven, Frances Fox and Richard Cloward. 1971. *Regulating the Poor*. New York: Pantheon.

———. 1982. *The New Class War*. New York: Pantheon Books.

Post, Kenneth and Michael Vickers. 1973. *Structure and Conflict in Nigeria 1960–1966*. Madison: University of Wisconsin Press.

Poulantzas, Nicos. 1973. *Political Power and Social Classes*, translated by Timothy O'Hagan. London: NLB.

———. 1978. *State, Power, Socialism*, translated by Patrick Camiller. London: NLB.

Powell-Price, J. C. 1955. *A History of India*. London: Thomas Nelson and Sons.

Pratt, Henry J. 1976. *The Gray Lobby*. Chicago: University of Chicago Press.

———. Forthcoming. *Gray Agendas: Interest Groups and State Pensions in Canada, Britain and the United States*. Ann Arbor: University of Michigan Press.

Pryor, Frederic. 1968. *Public Expenditures in Communist and Capitalist Nations*. Homewood, IL: Irwin.

Przeworski, Adam. 1985. *Capitalism and Social Democracy*. Cambridge: Cambridge University Press.

Quadagno, Jill S. 1984. "Welfare Capitalism and the Social Security Act of 1935." *American Sociological Review* 49:632–647.

———. 1988a. *The Transformation of Old Age Security: Class and Politics in the American Welfare State*. Chicago: University of Chicago Press.

———. 1988b. From Old-Age Assistance to Supplemental Security Income: The Political Economy of Relief in the South, 1935–1972." Pp. 235–263 in *The Politics of Social Policy in the United States,* edited by Margaret Weir, Ann Shola Orloff, and Theda Skocpol. Princeton: Princeton University Press.

Ragin, Charles C. 1987. *The Comparative Method: Moving Beyond Qualitative and Quantitative Strategies*. Berkeley: University of California Press.

Raj, B. and B. G. Prasad. 1971. "A Study of Rural Aged Persons in Social Profile." *Indian Journal of Social Work* 32:155–162.

Ramm, Agatha. 1967. *Germany 1789–1919: A Political History*. London: Methuen.

Read, Donald. 1982. *Edwardian England, 1901–1915*. New Brunswick, NJ: Rutgers University Press.

Rein, Martin and Lee Rainwater. 1986. "The Institutions of Social Protection." Pp. 25–56 in *Public/Private Interplay in Social Protection: A Comparative Study*, edited by Martin Rein and Lee Rainwater. London: M. E. Sharpe.

Richter, Frank J. and Charles J. Parrish. 1983. "An Analysis of the Variation in Social Security Expenditure Patterns among Nations." Paper presented at the annual meeting of the Gerontological Society of America, San Francisco.

Riesman, David. 1950. *The Lonely Crowd*. New Haven: Yale University Press.

Rimlinger, Gaston V. 1971. *Welfare Policy and Industrialization in Europe, America and Russia*. New York: Wiley.

Rivlin, Alice M., Ralph C. Bryant, Charles L. Schultze, Joseph White, and Aaron Wildavsky. 1990. "Four Reasons Not to Cut Social Security Taxes." *Brookings Review* 8 (Spring):3–8.

Robock, Stefan H. 1975. *Brazil: A Study in Development Progress*. Lexington, MA: Lexington Books.

Roett, Riordan. 1984. *Brazil: Politics in a Patrimonial Society*. Third Edition. New York: Praeger.

Roland, Peter. 1989. "Worker Participation, Pensions and Rehabilitation." Pp. 1–4 in *Social Report* (10/11-89 e) Bonn: Inter Nationes.

Rothermund, Dietmar. 1988. *An Economic History of India*. London: Croom Helm.

Rothman, David J. 1971. *The Discovery of the Asylum*. Boston: Little, Brown.

Rothstein, Bo. 1985. "Managing the Welfare State: Lessons from Gustav Möller." *Scandinavian Political Studies* 8:151–170.

Rubinow, I. M. 1913. *Social Insurance, with Special Reference to American Conditions*. New York: Henry Holt.

Rudolph, Lloyd I. and Susanne H. Ruldolph. 1987. *In Pursuit of Lakshmi: The Political Economy of the Indian State*. Chicago: University of Chicago Press.

Russell, A. K. 1973. *Liberal Landslide*. Hamden, CT: Archon Books.

Samarasinghe, S. W. R. de A. 1982. "Aging and the Aged in Sri Lanka: A Socio-Economic Perspective." Pp. 145–180 in *The Elderly of Asia*. Asian Regional Conference on Active Aging. Manila, 24–28 January 1982. Manila: Social Research Center, University of Santo Tomas.

Sanda, A. O. 1987. "Nigeria." Pp. 164–183 in *Social Welfare in Africa*, edited by John Dixon. London: Croom Helm.

Sarma, A. M. 1981. *Aspects of Labour Welfare and Social Security*. Bombay: Himalaya Publishing House.

Scarpaci, Joseph L. and Ernesto Miranda-Radic. 1991. "Chile." Pp. 25–42 in *International Handbook on Old-Age Insurance*, edited by Martin B. Tracy and Fred C. Pampel. New York: Greenwood Press.

Scase, Richard. 1977. *Social Democracy in Capitalist Society: Working-Class Politics in Britain and Sweden*. London: Croom Helm.

Schlabach, Theron F. 1969. *Edwin E. Witte: Cautious Reformer*. Madison: Wisconsin State Historical Society.

Schlesinger, Joseph A. 1984. "On the Theory of Party Organization." *Journal of Politics* 46:369–400.

Schmidt, Manfred G. 1982. "The Role of Parties in Shaping Macroeconomic Policy." Pp. 97–116 in *The Impact of Parties: Politics and Policies in Democratic Capitalist States*, edited by Francis G. Castles. Beverly Hills: Sage.

———. 1989. "Learning from Catastrophes: West Germany's Public Policy." Pp. 56–99 in *The Comparative History of Public Policy*, edited by Francis G. Castles. New York: Oxford.

Schmitter, Philippe C. 1971. *Interest Conflict and Political Change in Brazil*. Stanford: Stanford University Press.

———. 1972. "Paths to Political Development in Latin America." Pp. 83–105 in *Changing Latin America: New Interpretations of its Politics and Society*, edited by Douglas A. Chalmers. New York: Academy of Political Science.

———. 1974. "Still the Century of Corporatism?" *Review of Politics* 36:85–131.

———. 1981. "Interest Intermediation and Regime Governability in Contemporary Western Europe and North America." Pp. 287–330 in *Organizing Interests in Western Europe: Pluralism, Corporatism, and the Transformation of Politics*, edited by Suzanne Berger. Cambridge: Cambridge University Press.

———. 1985. "Neo-corporatism and the State." Pp. 32–62 in *The Political Economy of Corporatism*, edited by Wyn Grant. London: Macmillan.

Schneider, Margaret G. 1937. *More Security for Old Age*. New York: Twentieth Century Fund.

Schulz, James H. 1988. *The Economics of Aging*. Fourth Edition. Dover, MA: Auburn House.

Schulz, James H., Allan Borowski, and William H. Crown. 1991. *Economics of Population Aging: The "Graying" of Australia, Japan, and the United States*. New York: Auburn House.

Schulz, James H., Guy Carrin, Hans Krupp, Manfred Peschke, Elliot Sclar, and J Van Steenberge. 1974. *Providing Adequate Retirement Income: Pension Reform in the United States and Abroad*. Hanover, NH: University Press of New England.

Schwartz, Stuart B. 1986. *Sugar Plantations in the Formation of Brazilian Society: Bahia, 1550–1835*. New York: Cambridge University Press.

Scott, Franklin D. 1977. *Sweden: The Nation's History*. Minneapolis: University of Minnesota Press.

Seager, Henry Rogers. 1910. *Social Insurance: A Program of Reform*. New York: Macmillan.

Shalev, Michael. 1983. "The Social Democratic Model and Beyond: Two Generations of Comparative Research on the Welfare State." *Comparative Social Research* 6:315 352.

Shragge, Eric. 1984. *Pension Policy in Britain*. London: Routledge and Kegan Paul.

Simey, T. S. and M. B. Simey. 1960. *Charles Booth, Social Scientist*. London: Oxford University Press.

Simone, Vincent J. 1983. "Latin America: The Effect of Social, Economic and Political Trends on Benefit Planning." *Pension World* (April):6, 54.

Singh, Patwant. 1966. *India and the Future of Asia*. New York: Knopf.

Singhal, D. P. 1983. *A History of the Indian People*. London: Methuen.

Sinha, Pramod K. 1980. *Social Security Measures in India*. New Delhi: Classical Publications.

Sklar, Richard L. 1963. *Nigerian Political Parties*. Princeton: Princeton University Press.

Skocpol, Theda. 1979. *States and Social Revolutions*. Cambridge: Harvard University Press.

———. 1984. "Emerging Agendas and Recurrent Strategies in Historical Sociology." Pp. 356–391 in *Vision and Method in Historical Sociology*, edited by Theda Skocpol. Cambridge: Cambridge University Press.

———. 1985. "Bringing the State Back In: Strategies of Analysis in Current Research." Pp. 3–37 in *Bringing the State Back In*, edited by Peter B. Evans, Dietrich Rueschemeyer, and Theda Skocpol. Cambridge: Cambridge University Press.

Skocpol, Theda and Edwin Amenta. 1985. "Did Capitalists Shape Social Security?" *American Sociological Review* 50:572-575.

———. 1986. "States and Social Policies." *Annual Review of Sociology* 12:131–157.

Skocpol, Theda and John Ikenberry. 1983. "The Political Formation of the American Welfare State in Historical and Comparative Perspective." *Comparative Social Research* 6:87–148.

Sloan, John W. 1984. *Public Policy in Latin America*. Pittsburgh: University of Pittsburgh Press.

Smeeding, Timothy S. 1990. "Social Thought and Poor Children." Focus 12(Spring):11-14.

Snell, John L. and Hans A. Schmitt. 1976. *The Democratic Movement in Germany, 1789–1914*. Chapel Hill: University of North Carolina Press.

Social Security Bulletin. 1981. Annual Statistical Supplement, 1979. Washington, D.C.: Social Security Administration.

Social Security in Africa. 1983. Lome, Togo: Regional Economic Research and Documentation Center.

Spate, O. H. K. 1957. *India and Pakistan*. London: Methuen and Company.

Spear, Percival. 1965. *A History of India*, vol. 2. Baltimore: Penguin.

Statistisches Bundesamt. 1986. *Statistisches Jahrbuch für die Bundesrepublik Deutschland*. Stuttgart-Mainz: Kohlhammer.

Stein, Bruno. 1980. *Social Security and Pensions in Transition*. New York: Free Press.

Steinmetz, George. 1988. "Explaining Historical Changes in Social Policy: The Case of

Imperial Germany, 1871–1914." Paper presented at the annual meeting of the American Sociological Association, Atlanta, Georgia.

——. 1990. "The Myth and the Reality of the Autonomous State: Industrialists, Junkers, and Social Policy in Imperial Germany." *Comparative Social Research* 12:239–293.

Steinmeyer, Heinz-Dietrich. 1991. "Federal Republic of Germany." Pp. 75–95 in *International Handbook of Old-Age Insurance*, edited by Martin B. Tracy and Fred C. Pampel. New York: Greenwood Press.

Stepan, Alfred. 1978. *The State and Society*. Princeton: Princeton University Press.

Stephens, John D. 1979. *The Transition from Capitalism to Socialism*. London: Macmillan.

Stimson, James. 1985. "Regression in Space and Time: A Statistical Essay." *American Journal of Political Science* 29:914–947.

Stinchcombe, Arthur. 1978. *Theoretical Methods in Social History*. New York: Academic Press.

Szymanski, Albert. 1978. *The Capitalist State and the Politics and Class*. Cambridge, MA: Winthrop.

Tampke, Jürgen. 1981. "Bismarck's Social Legislation: A Genuine Breakthrough?" Pp. 71–83 in *The Emergence of the Welfare State in Britain and Germany*, edited by W. J. Mommsen. London: Croom Helm.

Thane, Pat. 1978. "Non-Contributory Versus Insurance Pensions, 1878–1908." Pp. 84–106 in *The Origins of British Social Policy*, edited by Pat Thane. London: Croom Helm.

——. 1984. "The Working Class and State 'Welfare' in Britain, 1880–1914." *The Historical Journal* 27: 877-900.

——. 1985. "The Labour Party and State." Pp. 183–216 in *The First Labour Party 1906–1914*, edited by Kenneth D. Brown. London: Croom Helm.

Therborn, Goran. 1989. "'Pillarization' and 'Popular Movements': Two Variants of Welfare State Capitalism: The Netherlands and Sweden." Pp. 192–241 in *The Comparative History of Public Policy*, edited by Francis G. Castles. New York: Oxford University Press.

Thompson, Carol L., Mary M. Anderberg, and Joan B. Antell. 1982. *The Current History Encyclopedia of Developing Nations*. New York: McGraw-Hill.

Thompson, K. 1979. "Trends and Problems of Social Security in Developing Countries in Asia." Pp. 109–144 in *Role of Trade Unions in Social Security in Asia and the Pacific: Report of a Regional Seminar*. New Delhi: International Labour Office.

Thompson, Lawrence H. 1990. "The Financing Debate: A Scorecard." *Social Insurance Update*, newsletter of the National Academy of Social Insurance, No. 12, March.

Tilly, Charles. 1984. *Big Structures, Large Processes, Huge Comparisons*. New York: Russell Sage.

Tilton, Timothy A. 1974. "The Social Origins of Liberal Democracy: The Swedish Case." *American Political Science Review* 68:561–571.

Tishler, Hace S. 1971. *Self-Reliance and Social Security, 1870–1917*. Port Washington, N.Y.: Kennikat Press.

Tocqueville, Alexis de. [1840] 1976. *Democracy in America*, vol. 2, translated by Henry Reeves. New York: Knopf.

Tokunboh, M. A. 1985. *Labour Movement in Nigeria: Past and Present*. Ikeja, Nigeria: Lantern Books.

Tomasson, Richard F. 1970. *Sweden: Prototype of Modern Society*. New York: Random House.

——. 1983. "Old-Age Pensions Under Social Security: Past and Future." *American Behavioral Scientist* 26: 699–723.

————. 1984. "Government Old Age Pensions Under Affluence and Austerity: West Germany, Sweden, The Netherlands, and the United States." *Research in Social Problems and Public Policy*, 3:217–272.

Tomlins, Christopher. 1985. *The State and the Unions: Labor Relations, Law. and the Organized Labor Movement in America, 1880–1960*. Cambridge: Cambridge University Press.

Topik, Steven. 1987. *The Political Economy of the Brazilian State, 1989–1930*. Austin: University of Texas Press.

Tordoff, William. 1984. *Government and Politics in Africa*. Bloomington, IN: Indiana University Press.

Trachtenberg, Alan. 1982. *The Incorporation of America: Culture and Society in the Gilded Age*. New York: Hill and Wang.

Tracy, Martin B. 1979. *Retirement Age Practices in Ten Industrial Societies, 1960–1976*. Geneva: International Social Security Association.

————. 1991. *Social Policies for the Elderly in the Third World*. New York: Greenwood Press.

Trattner, Walter I. 1974. *From Poor Law to Welfare State*. New York: Free Press.

Treble, James H. 1970. "The Attitudes of the Friendly Societies towards the Movement in Great Britain for State Pensions, 1878–1908." *International Review of Social History* 15:266–299.

Tufte, Edward R. 1978. *Political Control of the Economy*. Princeton: Princeton University Press.

Turner, Frederick Jackson. 1920. *The Frontier in American History*. New York: Henry Holt.

U.S. Bureau of the Census. 1987. "An Aging World." *International Population Reports Series P-95*, no. 78. Washington, D.C.: U. S. Government Printing Office.

U.S. Bureau of Pensions. 1925. *Laws of the United States Governing the Granting of Army and Navy Pensions*. Washington, D.C.: U.S. Government Printing Office.

U.S. Congress, House of Representatives Committee on Ways and Means. 1935. *Hearings on the Economic Security Act*. Washington, D.C.: U.S. Government Printing Office.

U.S. Congress, Senate Committee on Finances. 1935. *Hearings on the Economic Security Act*. Washington, D.C.: U. S. Government Printing Office.

U.S. Department of State. 1983. "Social Security: Nigeria's National Provident Fund." Memorandum to the Secretary of State from the American Embassy in Lagos dated 6/17/83. Archives of the Social Security Administration, Office of International Policy, Washington, D.C.

————. 1987. "Foreign Labor Trends Nigeria 1986." Memorandum to the Department of State from the American Embassy in Lagos dated 4/8/87. Archives of the Social Security Administration, Office of International Policy, Washington, D.C.

U.S. Senate, Special Committee on Aging. 1981. *Social Security in Europe: The Impact of An Aging Population*. Washington, D.C.: U.S. Government Printing Office.

U.S. Social Security Administration. 1981. "Chile Reforms Social Security." Archives of the Social Security Administration, Office of International Policy, Washington, D.C.

————. 1990. *Social Security Programs Throughout the World, 1989*. Washington, D.C.: U.S. Government Printing Office.

Ullmann, Hans-Peter. 1981. "German Industry and Bismarck's Social Security System." Pp. 133–149 in *The Emergence of the Welfare State in Britain and Germany*, edited by W. J. Mommsen. London: Croom Helm.

United Nations. 1970. *Social Change and Social Development Policy in Latin America*. New York: United Nations.

Uricoechea, Fernando. 1980. *The Patrimonial Foundations of the Brazilian Bureaucratic State.* Berkeley: University of California Press.

Varma, Ranbir. 1964. "Industrial Labour as a Factor of Economic Growth in India." Pp. 144–158 in *Contemporary India,* edited by Baidya Nath Varma. New York: Asia Publishing House.

Wagner, Adolf. [1883] 1983. "The Nature of the Fiscal Economy." Pp. 1–8 in *Classics in the Theory of Public Finance,* edited by Richard A. Musgrave and Alan R. Peacock. London: Macmillan.

Wald, Kenneth D. 1983. *Crosses on the Ballot: Patterns of British Voter Alignment Since 1885.* Princeton: Princeton University Press.

Wallace, Steven P., John B. Williamson, Rita G. Lung, and Lawrence A. Powell. 1991. "A Lamb in Wolf's Clothing? The Reality of Senior Power and Social Policy." Pp. 95–114 in *Critical Perspectives on Aging,* edited by Meredith Minkler and Carroll L. Estes. Amityville, NY: Baywood.

Wallerstein, Immanuel. 1980. *The Modern World-System II: Mercentilism and Consolidation of the European World-Economy, 1600–1750.* New York: Academic Press.

Warren, Bill. 1980. *Imperialism: Pioneer of Capitalism.* London: New Left Books.

Weaver, Carolyn. 1982. *The Crisis in Social Security: Economic and Political Origins.* Durham, NC: Duke Press Policy Studies.

Webb, Sidney and Beatrice Webb. 1920. *The History of Trade Unionism.* New York: Longmans, Green.

Weiner, Myron. 1964. "Interest Groups in Indian Politics." Pp. 77–109 in *Contemporary India,* edited by Baidya Nath Varma. New York: Asia Publishing House.

———. 1967. *Party Building in a New Nation.* Chicago: University of Chicago Press.

Weir, Margaret, Ann Shola Orloff, and Theda Skocpol. 1988. "Understanding American Social Politics." Pp. 3–27 in *The Politics of Social Policy in the United States,* edited by Margaret Weir, Ann Shola Orloff, and Theda Skocpol. Princeton: Princeton University Press.

Weise, Robert. 1970. "Social Security for Rural Workers in Brazil." *Social Security Bulletin* 33 (6):18–20.

Western, Bruce. 1991. "A Comparative Study of Corporatist Development." *American Sociological Review* 56:283–294.

Wilensky, Harold L. 1975. *The Welfare State and Equality: Structural and Ideological Roots of Public Expenditures.* Berkeley: University of California Press.

———. 1976. *The 'New Corporatism,' Centralization, and the Welfare State.* Beverly Hills: Sage Publications.

———. 1981. "Leftism, Catholicism, and Democratic Corporatism: The Role of Political Parties in Recent Welfare State Development." Pp. 345–382 in *The Development of Welfare States in Europe and America,* edited by Peter Flora and Arnold J. Heidenheimer. New Brunswick, NJ: Transaction.

Wilensky, Harold L. and Charles N. Lebeaux. 1965. *Industrial Society and Social Welfare.* Glencoe, IL: Free Press.

Wilensky, Harold L., Gregory M. Luebbert, Susan R. Hahn, and Adrienne M. Jamieson. 1985. *Comparative Social Policy: Theories, Methods, Findings.* Berkeley: Institute of International Studies, University of California.

Wilensky, Harold L. and Lowell Turner. 1987. *Democratic Corporatism and Policy Linkages.* Berkeley: Institute of International Studies, University of California.

Williamson, John B. 1984. "Old Age Relief Policy Prior to 1900: The Trend toward Restrictiveness." *American Journal of Economics and Sociology* 43:369–384.

————. 1987. "Social Security and Physical Quality of Life in Developing Nations: A Cross-National Analysis." *Social Indicators Research* 19:205–227.

Williamson, John B., Linda Evans, and Lawrence A. Powell. 1982. *The Politics of Aging.* Springfield, IL: Charles C. Thomas.

Williamson, John B. and Jeanne J. Fleming. 1977. "Convergence Theory and the Social Welfare Sector: A Cross-National Analysis." *International Journal of Comparative Sociology* 18:242–253.

Williamson, John B. and Fred C. Pampel. 1986. "Politics, Class, and Growth in Social Security Effort: A Cross-National Analysis." *International Journal of Comparative Sociology* 27:15–30.

————. 1991. "Ethnic Politics, Colonial Legacy, and Old Age Security Policy: The Nigerian Case in Historical and Comparative Perspective." *Journal of Aging Studies* 5:19–44.

————. Forthcoming. "Paying for the Baby Boom Generation's Social Security Pensions: United States, United Kingdom, Germany, and Sweden." *Journal of Aging Studies.*

Williamson, John B., Judith A. Shindul, and Linda Evans. 1985. *Aging and Public Policy: Social Control or Social Justice?* Springfield, IL: Charles C. Thomas.

Williamson, John B. and Joseph W. Weiss. 1979. "Egalitarian Political Movements, Social Welfare Effort and Convergence Theory: A Cross-National Analysis." *Comparative Social Research* 2:289–302.

Williamson, Peter J. 1989. *Corporatism in Perspective.* London: Sage.

Wilson, Dorothy. 1979. *The Welfare State in Sweden.* London: Heinemann.

————. 1991. "United Kingdom." Pp. 199–215 in *International Handbook on Old-Age Insurance,* edited by Martin B. Tracy and Fred C. Pampel. New York: Greenwood Press.

Witte, Edwin E. 1963. *The Development of the Social Security Act.* Madison: University of Wisconsin Press.

Wolpe, Howard. 1974. *Urban Politics in Nigeria.* Berkeley: University of California Press.

Wolpert, Stanley. 1977. *A New History of India.* New York: Oxford University Press.

Woodsworth, David E. 1977, *Social Security and National Policy.* Montreal: McGill-Queens's University Press.

World Bank. 1983a. *World Tables.* vol. 1, *Economic Data.* Third Edition. Baltimore: Johns Hopkins University Press.

————. 1983b. *World Tables.* vol. 2, *Social Data.* Third Edition. Baltimore: Johns Hopkins University Press.

————. 1984. *World Development Report 1984.* New York: Oxford University Press.

————. 1991. *World Development Report 1991.* New York: Oxford University Press.

Yesufu, T. M. 1982. *The Dynamics of Industrial Relations: The Nigerian Experience.* Ibadan, Nigeria: University Press Limited.

Young, Crawford. 1988. "The African Colonial State and Its Political Legacy." Pp. 25–66 in *The Precarious Balance,* edited by Donald Rothchild and Naomi Chazan. London: Westview Press.

Zeiter, Ilene R. 1983. "Social Security Trends and Developments in Industrial Countries." *Social Security Bulletin* 46 (March): 52–62.

Zöllner, Detlev. 1982. "Germany." Pp. 1–92 in *The Evolution of Social Insurance, 1881–1981,* edited by Peter A. Kohler, Hans F. Zacher, and Martin Partington. New York: St. Martin's Press.

Name Index

Subject Index

AFL-CIO, 99. *See also* American Federation of Labor; Congress of Industrial Organizations

Age structure: graying of, 217; in Brazil, 138; in Germany, 38; in India, 157–58; in Sweden, 81; in the United Kingdom, 59; in the United States, 107–8; impact on policy, 42, 107, 116, 210, 220; quantitative analysis, 189, 191. *See also* Elderly, influence on policy

American Association for Labor Legislation (AALL), 95

American Association of Retired Persons (AARP), 112, 221

American exceptionalism, 113, 115

American Federation of Labor (AFL), 90, 92, 108, 112, 114, 210; opposition to public pensions, 90

Beveridge Report, 52

Brazil: associated dependent development, 130; bureaucratic authoritarian state, 119; *Caixa de Aposentadoria e Pensões* (CAP), 122, 136; clientelistic political system, 128; Constitution of 1988, 132; *coronelismo*, 120; delayed dependent capitalist development, 121; economic growth, 121, 130; *Estado Novo*, 124; Goulart administration, 128; Iberian Catholic cultural heritage, 125; *Instituto de Aposentadoria e Pensões* (IAP), 126–29, 131, 136; ISSB plan, 126–28, 131, 221; *Lei Eloy Chaves*, 122; *Lei Organica*, 128; military, influence of, 119; military rule, 129–33; mutual-aid societies, 122; National Institute for Social Security (INPS), 131–32; National System of Social Security and Social Assistance (SINPAS), 131; new union movement, 130; patrimonial state, 119; populist era, 127–29; *previdência social*, 125–26; Pró-Rural, 131; "Revolution of 1930," 123; "Revolution of 1964," 129; rural oligarchy, 120; *sindicato* system, 125; Vargas era, 123–29

California State Pension movement, 112

Charity Organization Society, 48, 57, 62–63, 70*n*23, 210, 219, 223

Chile: coverage of rural population, 134; government subsidized minimum pension, 135; interest in Chilean model by other countries, 136; mandatory individual private insurance, 135; privatization of the public pension system, 135; provident fund administered by private institutions, 135

Civil service, 66, 105, 118–19, 165, 174; impact on policy: in Brazil, 126, 129, 137, 221; in Germany, 23–24, 34, 37, 40*n*66, 41, 223; in India, 149, 152–53, 158, 160–62, 222; in Nigeria, 179–80, 223; in Sweden, 71, 83–84, 223; in the United Kingdom, 45, 50, 52, 61, 185; in the United States, 98–100, 114. *See also* Corruption

Class theory, 3–4, 7–12, 59, 164, 182, 184, 186, 207–15; class based interest groups, 38, 162. *See also* Colonial legacy; Economic dependency theory; Neo-Marxist perspective; Social democratic perspective

Colonial legacy, 164–65, 169; British versus French colonial policy, 165, 181; impact on policy, 213–14: in Brazil, 118–20; in India, 142, 154, 161–63; in Nigeria, 179, 181; impact on well-being of elderly, 167; neocolonialism, 11

Colonialism. *See* Colonial legacy

Committee on Economic Security (CES), 95–96

Communist party, 68, 121, 128. *See also* Neo-Marxist perspective; Socialism

Congress of Industrial Organizations (CIO), 90, 99, 112

Contextual analysis, 3–5, 208, 227; applied: to Brazil, 117, 139–40; to Germany, 41–42; to India, 142; to Nigeria, 165; to Sweden, 41–42, 86; to the United Kingdom, 57, 61–64; to the United States, 92–93, 109–11, 116; quantita-